# Controlling
# Stress and Tension

# Controlling Stress and Tension

## A Holistic Approach

Daniel E. Girdano, *Ph.D.*

George S. Everly, Jr., *Ph.D.*

Dorothy E. Dusek, *Ph.D.*

PRENTICE HALL, Englewood Cliffs, New Jersey 07632

*Library of Congress Cataloging-in-Publication Data*

GIRDANO, DANIEL A.
 Controlling stress and tension : a holistic approach / Daniel A.
Girdano, George S. Everly, Jr., Dorothy E. Dusek.—4th ed.
  p.   cm.
 Includes bibliographical references and index.
 ISBN 0-13-175506-4
 1. Stress management.  2. Stress (Psychology)  I. Everly, George
S. (date).  II. Dusek, Dorothy.  III. Title.
RA785.G37  1993
155.9'042—dc20

92-37794
CIP

Acquisitions editor: Ted Bolen
Editorial production supervision: F. Hubert
Prepress buyer: Herb Klein
Manufacturing buyer: Bob Anderson
Cover design: Karen Salzbach

Printed in the United States of America
10  9  8  7  6  5  4  3  2  1

ISBN 0-13-175506-4

PRENTICE-HALL INTERNATIONAL (UK) LIMITED, *London*
PRENTICE-HALL OF AUSTRALIA PTY. LIMITED, *Sydney*
PRENTICE-HALL CANADA INC., *Toronto*
PRENTICE-HALL HISPANOAMERICANA, S.A., *Mexico*
PRENTICE-HALL OF INDIA PRIVATE LIMITED, *New Delhi*
PRENTICE-HALL OF JAPAN, INC., *Tokyo*
SIMON & SCHUSTER ASIA PTE. LTD., *Singapore*
EDITORA PRENTICE-HALL DO BRASIL, LTDA., *Rio de Janeiro*

# Contents

CHAPTER THREE

The Body's Response to Stress    *37*

## PART II
## WHAT CAUSES STRESS,
## AND WHAT IS YOUR STRESS PROFILE?

CHAPTER FOUR

Stressful Emotions, Thoughts, and Beliefs    *60*

CHAPTER FIVE

Psychosocial Causes of Stress    *74*

**PART III**
**HOW TO PREVENT AND REDUCE STRESS:**
**INTERVENTION AND MANAGEMENT TECHNIQUES**

# Controlling
# Stress and Tension

# CHAPTER ONE

# Stress and Health

To be optimally healthy, we must be able to cope with life's trials and tribulations while minimizing the detrimental effects of excess stress. Coping is any attempt to neutralize stress arousal. Coping systems include behaviors, physiological reactions, cognitions, perceptions, and motor acts. Coping can be healthy and growth-producing (competent) or unhealthy (incompetent), causing additional problems that persist long after stress arousal has diminished. *Competent coping* results in retaining optimal health and being in control while meeting the demands of life. *Incompetent coping* results in sacrificing health and control and being unable to meet demands.

People characterized by incompetent coping need unhealthy physical or psychological help to cope. In psychophysiological terms this is referred to as *recruitment*. There are numerous examples of recruitment. Bradshaw (1990) gives examples of some common ego defenses people use when reality becomes intolerable: conversion ("I eat, drink alcohol, or take drugs when I can't cope with reality"), denial ("It didn't happen," or "It's not really happening to me"), dissociation ("I can't remember what happened"), minimizing ("Oh, it wasn't really that bad"), projection ("It's your reaction, not mine"), repression ("It didn't happen"), and withdrawal from the world. These are all examples of incompetent coping.

**HEALTH**

Wanting to stay healthy is a basic motivator for avoiding stress. Health, like love, is a little difficult to define, because it is a state of being rather than a self-contained thing. Health is sometimes called *wellness* or *well-being*, and its definition usually includes the balanced integration of body, mind, and spirit. Good health assumes that an individual is free from conditions and symptoms that prevent one from moving about without pain. A person in good health can relate openly and honestly with others, enjoy a high self-concept, and participate in other aspects of life that make one feel good. Some would translate good health as happiness. Others would say good health is good stress management.

The modern practice of medicine puts major emphasis on treating disease. The holistic approach we use in this book, though, is directed toward preventing disease in the first place. The overriding message of the holistic approach to controlling stress and tension is this: As we move toward optimal health, we can prevent excess stress, and as a result there will be no need for treatment. Because stress is at the root of most illness, our goal in this book is therefore to help you identify your stressors and combat them before they turn into disease and dysfunction.

To identify which parts of life may undermine wellness, consider the six basic components of health:

1. physical capability        4. social interaction
2. emotional status          5. economic status
3. intellectual functioning   6. spiritual development

There may be overlap among these components, which proves only that health consists of several interdependent dimensions. Each component is described in terms of high to low levels of health, happiness, or wellness. Read each description, and find the point at which you feel your stress level begins. That point is usually identified with something you wish to do, but cannot or do not do now.

**Physical Capability**

Physical health can be easily identified. It is acceptable to be "under the weather" at one time or another, and indeed the Western medical system thrives on physical illness. Pharmacologic advertising perpetuates the need for medicines to control the symptoms of such illness. When people lose the freedom to move about without pain or other limitation, their physical health is clearly compromised. It is no wonder that most people who are asked, "How healthy are you?" respond in terms of their physical health.

There is a universal sensibility or energy that resides in all of us—we're born with it and we work throughout life to keep it balanced. Early physiologists spoke of *homeostasis*—the maintenance of the body in a balanced (healthy) state. The continuum of physical capability, then, ranges from a high end that is balanced, healthy, strong, and energetic to a low end characterized by immobility, physical passivity, and perhaps premature death due to organic malfunction. Between these two ends of the continuum are the varying degrees of physical fitness. High-level physical wellness connotes a strong, healthy body, one that is fed nourishing foods, is allowed sufficient rest, has competent modes of releasing stress, and strives to maintain the healthy functioning of all its systems.

Physical functioning is the most obvious sign of all the components of health. Physical characteristics can therefore be used to study the complete stress picture of our life. Our physical systems perform such vital activities as breathing, pumping blood, and manufacturing hormones such as insulin and adrenalin. To insure uninterrupted attention to these functions, we are born with very little cerebral control over them. Thus, how our body looks and performs provides a fairly unadulterated picture of our overall health and how well we manage stress in our life.

**Emotional Status**

According to Tomkins (1962), all human beings are born with nine innate emotions programmed into their facial tissues: six primary motivators (interest, enjoyment, surprise, distress, fear, and anger); one auxiliary emotion (shame); and two defensive responses (disgust and dissmell). The purpose of these basic emotions is to protect and motivate. As with all purposeful physiological behavior, each emotion triggers a pure stimulus–response reaction until a response is conditioned to a new stimulus. This happens especially at the emotional level as children learn myriad ways of frightening themselves, learn to use anger as a threat, and become distressed at perceived rather than "real" dangers. Many continue to react with their childhood perceptions and emotional responses, making their emotional status unstable.

All events and thought processes register almost immediately at the emotional level and are evaluated consciously or subconsciously before the individual reacts. This conscious or subconscious appraisal is based on experiences. It thus includes a filtering of personal emotional perceptions, and the body reacts to the filtered thoughts. Emotional health, though, is based on realistic responses to actual situations rather than filtered responses (left over from the past) to imagined or perceived situations.

In the etiology of stress-related diseases, the emotional level connects the mental and physical planes. The relatively new science of psychoneuroimmunology (PNI) explains how emotional status is connected with physical health or illness. Imbalances at the emotional level manifest themselves as heightened sensitivity to feelings of vulnerability, separateness, and inferiority and to poor self-concept—feelings that make up the low end of the emotional health continuum. At the high end of the continuum we find the positive emotions of interest, joy, delight, peace, and love—emotions routinely experienced by emotionally healthy people. In addition, individuals who are emotionally healthy have learned how to examine their feelings and, through the skills of competent coping, to release negative feelings. Behavior is directly related to emotional responses to stressful situations. A person who is emotionally overactive almost certainly has related illnesses.

## Intellectual Functioning

The mental plane is often regarded as the highest plane of existence because it is the mind that governs the whole body. The mental plane gives expression to emotions and controls behavior through body movements. The mental plane is where we decide (consciously or unconsciously) to be angry, loving, defensive, or attacking. The body then carries out this decision. This is not to say that the mind and body are two separate entities, with one more important than the other. It is to say that the main computer probably resides in the skull.

The high end of this scale is *mastery* of the intellectual process. This includes being able to define relationships between things and to relate the known to the unknown. The intellectual process also includes the ability to combine things into new forms, to diagnose, to analyze, and to reason. Mastery of the intellectual process relieves us from the need to think or worry about performance, and thus from the anxiety of failure. It allows us to be relaxed, comfortable, and self-assured. Another aspect of intellectual functioning is inspiration, the fuel on which our creative energy runs. Inspiration produces the smile, the glow, and other nonverbal cues that indicate mental alertness.

The low end of the intellectual functioning scale is mental incompetence—the inability to think, reason, or show rationality. This may have a physical cause, as in the case of a stroke or mental retardation. Or it may result from temporary or chronic psychosis or neurosis.

Therapeutic techniques such as Rational Emotive Therapy and Reality Therapy are based on the knowledge that thought processes can govern emotions, and subsequently physiological functioning. The technique of creative visualization has given structure to the natural human ability to form mental pictures of desired goals and the means to obtain them. This sets in motion the thought patterns needed to do what is necessary to obtain the goals. Many of the stress-management techniques discussed in Chapter 10 involve using the intellect to gain mastery over the stressors in our lives.

**Social Interaction**

This category includes participation in formal and informal activities with others, such as family, work, and intimate emotional relationships. At the low end of the scale is social alienation—withdrawal from interaction with others. Complete love and acceptance of others are at the top of the scale.

The world is designed as a mutual support system in which all things relate to one another. Thus, the need for satisfying relationships is universal. Social isolation is known to create social and emotional pathology. When we ignore the inter-relatedness of ourselves with others, we suppress the motivation for much of our behavior. Whether we realize it or not, much of our behavior is influenced by our need to be accepted by others. Feeling loved and accepted by others is a critical level in Maslow's hierarchy of needs for achieving a high quality of life. Those who do not feel loved and accepted express this lack through negative social behaviors and/or behaviors detrimental to health such as chemical or food addictions.

The number-one stress producer in the workplace is interpersonal conflict: One worker in four has a stress-related problem, and interpersonal conflict accounts for more than 80 percent of our bad moods. Most of our stressors are people, not things. People may be our best support system, but they are also our worst stressors.

**Economic Status**

Economic status involves the ability to maintain a healthy standard of living, and is dependent on such issues as income, insurance eligibility, employment discrimination, and premature retirement that may be precipitated by illness. The low end of this scale is reflected in poverty; the top end might be defined as "doing what you love to do" and living in abundance.

Each human has a talent. Those who have discovered what their talent is and how to use and be paid for it tend to be more satisfied in life. All too often people cannot see the practical application of their talent in existing occupations and so they fit themselves into jobs not suited to them. Some people discover their talent later in life and make occupational changes; others do not. The ones who do find or make occupations to fit their talent experience more fulfillment. Suppressing natural talents and not doing what one really loves to do often lead to a subsconscious resentment of the world, and to anger, hostility, and a self-punishing emotional state that is harmful to physical health.

Economic status is determined in part by belief (an aspect of mental health). Some believe in the principle of abundance, others in the principle of scarcity. Some individuals have ample money, but because they believe there will never be enough to go around, they live a poor lifestyle, saving all they earn for retirement. Thus, they experience poor economic health.

While a comfortable standard of living is necessary for a high quality of life, the top of the scale does not necessarily involve the accumulation of money. It involves doing what you love to do and feeling economically successful.

## Spiritual Development

The spiritual aspects of human existence can be seen at the physical and emotional planes, but they reach their highest level on the mental plane. Although there is a universal oneness that is experienced as a feeling, it is on the mental plane where humans can attain a higher consciousness.

Perhaps because of a potential territorial conflict with religion or an inability to understand anything that cannot be scientifically measured, emphasis on the spiritual domain has been largely ignored in Western society. Changes are occurring today in health and stress management that involve the spirit of being healthy— totally healthy rather than healthy in a segmental manner. In this brief discussion we understand *spirit* not as religion but rather as the energy that connects all things, an energy that is more than just the molecules of medicines and organs. The new physicists tell us that the only difference between things is the speed at which their energy travels (in the decreasingly minute form of molecules, atoms, electrons, and quarks). Spirit, in this sense of pervasive energy, is something we might borrow to rediscover the spirit of health.

Energy occurs in two forms—materialized (what we see, feel, and hear, such as cars and houses, wind and light) and unmaterialized (everything else in the universe). Even "solid" objects are revealed as molecules in motion when viewed under very high-powered microscopes. Energy flows through the universe, through the earth, through our bodies. It is materialized by our thoughts. The majority of our thoughts are in the form of beliefs. These are our programs, our roles, our scripts, and our values—preconceived ways we view the world around us that determine how we are going to behave. Our beliefs are responsible for the quality of our lives. As we change our beliefs, we can change the quality of our lives, including our health. As there are no limits to our thoughts, there are no limits to how healthy or unhealthy we can become.

At the high end of the scale of spiritual development we find those who feel connected—with other people, societies, and countries, and indeed with all living things, including the earth. At the low end of the scale we might find those without hope for themselves, others, the world, and the universe.

**STRESS**

*Stress* is the body reacting. It is psychophysiological (mind-and-body) arousal that can fatigue body systems to the point of malfunction and disease. A *stressor* is any condition or event that causes a stress response. Stressors may belong to any of the quality-of-life components just discussed—physical, emotional, intellectual, social, economic, or spiritual. *Stress management* is the ability to reduce stress arousal or to cope in a competent manner with stressors.

Prolonged stress can fatigue or damage the body to the point of malfunction and disease. Stress may therefore be thought of as a response that links a stressor stimulus to any stress-related disease, symptom, or dysfunction (see Figure 1.1).

Stress is negative when it exceeds our ability to cope, fatigues our body systems, and causes behavioral or physical problems. Stress is positive when it forces us to adapt, and thus to increase the strength of our adaptation mechanisms. Stress is also positive when it warns us that we are not coping well and that a lifestyle change is warranted if we are to maintain optimal health.

In physical terms, stress means strain, pressure, or force on a system. In the context of the human organism, it is the body reacting to the environment through the buildup of internal pressure and the strain of muscles tensing for action. It is this physical pressure and strain that, if prolonged, can fatigue or damage the body. Walter B. Cannon defined stress as the "fight or flight syndrome": When one becomes stressed, the proper use of that stress is either to fight off the threat or to run from it. To do either, the body prepares itself through the physiological mechanisms of coping—the cognition and the motor act, or behavior, that alleviate the stressor. Stress is a natural defense mechanism that has allowed our species to survive. It is a physical response designed to protect our physical lives. We need stress and would not want to eradicate our capacity for stress response even if this were possible. The goal is to manage our stress by diminishing the excess stress in our lives—the stress that is inappropriate for accomplishing our objectives.

The stress response of modern man and woman is often in-

**FIGURE 1.1**

Stress and Disease

Stressor ──────► Stress Response ──────► Stress-Related Dysfunction
Disease

(stimulus)                (response)                (target organ effect)

appropriate to the situation and inappropriate in its level of intensity. Physical stressors still exist; most of the stressors of modern society are primarily social or ego-related. When a stressor is ego-related or is a response to a social situation, it cannot be solved by a physical response. In addition, it may not be alleviated for a long period. If the threat is in our imagination and the stress response is stimulated, we cannot physically run from it. Pressure builds up, and part of us wants to strike out while the other part strains to hold back. Externally, nothing happens. Internally, the body is a raging inferno of stress and tension.

Stressors occur daily; they are part of life. When the body tolerates stress and performance is good, the stress is positive, healthy, and challenging. Hans Selye, one of the pioneers of the modern study of stress, termed this *eustress*. This action-enhancing stress is what gives the athlete the competitive edge and the public speaker the enthusiasm to project optimally. Eustress helps us overcome lethargy. Selye termed negative, debilitating, or harmful stress *distress*. Distress produces overreaction, confusion, poor concentration, and performance anxiety, and usually results in subpar performance. An individual in distress cannot cope competently. Prolonged distress moves the organism into the health danger zone. Somewhere between eustress and distress is a level of *optimal stress*. Figure 1.2 illustrates this concept.

The best way to find and use our optimal stress level is to develop the ability to recognize the signs and symptoms of distress. That sounds simple enough, but in actuality it isn't. This is because the body's sensitivity to the awareness of stress arousal may be-

FIGURE 1.2

Point of Optimal
Stress

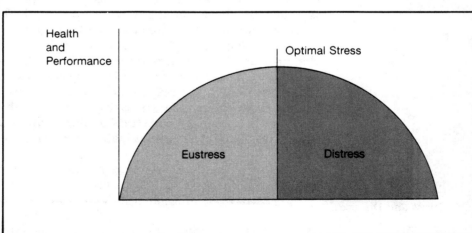

come dulled. The human organism characteristically becomes accustomed to its level of arousal, which often becomes the body's normal state. In other words, people become conditioned to their level of stress arousal if it lasts for a few weeks.

Researchers in the field of psychophysiology have identified hundreds of physiological and behavioral effects of excessive stress arousal, and the ones you experience represent your unique pattern of response. Some people always respond with the same system, such as the muscle system. Every time they become stressed, they develop the same tension headache or a spasm in the same muscle. For reasons not well understood at this time, their muscle system has become sensitized into a storage depot for excess nervous impulses. Individuals who respond to stress with the same kind of stress response in one or two systems of their body are described as *rigid responders*. Those who do not respond in such a predictable pattern are referred to as *random responders*. It is thought that a rigid response leads to organ system fatigue, malfunction, and eventually a variety of diseases.

## STRESS AND DISEASE

All too often our interest in health begins when our health deteriorates and pain and dysfunction begin to dictate a lifestyle of diminished capacity. Virtually everyone knows disease. It is a condition of the body that presents symptoms peculiar to it. Disease or the fear of diminished capacity has prompted the study of stress, now a well-documented precursor of illness. The primary vehicle and unifying thread in this research is the psychosomatic concept. This concept of illness explains how our environment and social interactions, our perception of our environment, and our personality and emotional states produce a physical stress response. It also explains how stress arousal can eventually lead to illness. It reveals a map of the interrelations among our mind, body, and social environment.

## Psychosomatic Disease

The term *psychosomatic* was first used in 1927 by Felix Deutsch to describe the mind–body interactions in illness. The first major publications on this topic were written in 1935 by Helen Dunbar. *Psychosomatic disease* refers to any condition thought to be the result of excess emotional arousal, maladaptive coping, and chronic distress. The basis for the concept of psychosomatic disease is that the mind plays an important role in many diseases. All psychosomatic diseases affect the structure and function of the human body. Emotional disturbances such as anxiety, anger, fear, and frustration can increase the body's susceptibility to organic diseases. In 1965, Rene Dubos noted that even infectious organic diseases do not commonly occur simply from some pathogenic (disease-causing) microbes entering the body.

Dubos has studied the role of what we are calling the psychosomatic phenomenon. The sciences concerned with microbial diseases, he explains, have developed almost exclusively from the study of acute or semiacute infections caused by virulent microorganisms acquired through exposure to an (external) source of infection. In contrast, the microbial diseases most common in our communities today arise from microorganisms that are (always present) in the environment. These organisms remain in the body and under normal conditions do not cause obvious harm; they have pathological effects only when the person is under conditions of stress. In this type of microbial disease, the event of infection is less important than the hidden manifestation of the smoldering infectious process. The stressful disturbance that converts latent infection into overt pathology is all-important.

Thus, stress may act as a catalyst for an organic disease already present, either (1) allowing the disease to establish a "foothold" in the body from which to spread destruction or (2) accelerating the spread of the disease throughout the body. In short, almost any organic disease may have a psychosomatic component, depending, of course, on the psychological makeup of the individual.

The psychosomatic phenomenon appears to lower the body's resistance or immunity to disease. In psychosomatic illness, Dubos points out, being infected or having some organ system begin to degenerate is not the critical factor in the course of the illness. The critical factor is the body's ability to defend itself against these common infectious and degenerative processes, which are part of everyday life. We now know that distress impedes the body's ability to defend itself against all diseases.

## DISORDERS OF AROUSAL

Research has substantially increased our understanding of how stress arousal can be precipitated by a wide variety of environmental stimuli. In addition, stress arousal can result in an equally wide variety of disorders whose only common characteristic is that they occur in response to the arousal. Therefore, diseases caused or characterized by excessive stress arousal are commonly called *disorders of arousal.* They can be psychological disorders, such as those caused by anxiety, or very definable stress-related syndromes, such as cardiovascular or gastrointestinal diseases.

Research on the physiology of arousal is centered in the subcortical centers of the brain within the limbic, hypothalamic, and reticular activation centers. Over the last fifty years these centers of the brain have continued to be the focal point of research into

emotional arousal. These structures are involved in sensory stimulation and emotional expression. They are also responsible for
integration of the nerve stimuli sent from the brain to the body
and thus have a profound impact on physical and mental health.

These brain structures allow specific and nonspecific activation
and seem to be responsible for hyperalertness, hypersensitivity,
and nervous system hyperactivity in association with worry,
threat, and the avoidance behavior of flight. Limbic system arousal
and sensitization have been implicated in a variety of anxiety disorders, personality disorders, post-traumatic reactions, addictive
disorders, and withdrawal syndromes (Post, 1985).

Somatic disorders of arousal, including many stress-related
medical syndromes, likewise seem to be associated with limbic
system arousal. Reviews by Lown and colleagues (1976) and Verrier and Lown (1984) conclude that ventricular fibrillation in the
absence of coronary heart disease may be related to increased tone
of the sympathetic ("fight or flight") nervous system in these portions of the brain. Similarly, increased sympathetic activity may
be a factor in the development of essential hypertension (Eliot,
1977; Gellhorn, 1964; Suter, 1984). Increased sympathetic activity
has also been implicated in coronary artery disease (Corley, 1985);
sudden death (Corley, 1985); migraine headaches and Raynaud's
syndrome (Suter, 1984); muscle contraction syndromes and headaches (Gellhorn, 1967; Weil, 1974; Malmo, 1975); peptic ulcers
(Wolf, 1985); and irritable bowel syndrome (Latimer, 1985).

The theory that various disorders of limbic- or hypothalamic-
system arousal are involved in psychosomatic disease represents
one of the most substantial advances in the study of mind–body
interactions. This theory implicates stress in the etiology of diseases ranging from the common cold to cancer. The information
received from the environment, the way it is perceived and evaluated, and how this influences thought processes and muscle activity can contribute to disease. The pathway from the social
environment to ill health is a complex one involving the interaction
of mind and body, as diagramed in Figure 1.3. Even positive events
can produce stress when they demand change and adaptation, but
most stress begins with the negative, painful, and unpleasant
events of our lives. An inseparable aspect of environmental stress
is our varied and complex social interaction, which is fraught with
feelings, expectations, and often frustration.

The information from the environment is processed by different
pathways, two of which are represented in Figure 1.3. One pathway
is thought to be largely subconscious, and is thus named the subconscious appraisal pathway. If this pathway is stimulated, coping

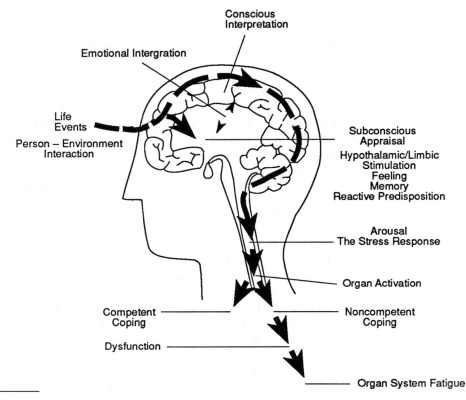

Conscious
Interpretation

Emotional Intergration

Life
Events

Person – Environment
Interaction

Subconscious
Appraisal

Hypothalamic/Limbic
Stimulation
Feeling
Memory
Reactive Predisposition

Arousal
The Stress Response

Organ Activation

Competent
Coping

Noncompetent
Coping

Dysfunction

Organ System Fatigue

FIGURE 1.3

The Psychosomatic
Concept

action may eventually be required, in which case the pathway's innate physical and emotional reflexes prepare the body for action. It is important to note that this system only prepares the body for action and that this preparation is independent of the final action. It is the second, or voluntary, pathway that determines whether this arousal is necessary and used.

The voluntary pathway controls perception, evaluation, and decision making and is responsible for voluntary action. How you perceive an event largely depends on your concept of self, ego strengths, value system, and even heredity. The emotions aroused are tempered by your psychological defenses, which are gained from experience, especially childhood responses. These lead to physical arousal, and you feel a need to act. Action itself is also complex; often, as a result of the consequences of a possible action, the reaction to a stressor is no action at all. (For example, you may hold back a harsh comment after you realize it may hurt someone's feelings.)

Background action is arousal that is not conscious or noticed by an individual. It supports any potential action that may follow. The idea of background action is intriguing because it probably developed from humans' superior intelligence and their capacity to perform several activities at the same time. Sport offers a good example. Novice basketball players must concentrate very intently in learning to dribble, just as novice ice skaters must work very hard to stay up on their skates. As people learn a sport they establish the neural pathways that allow the most efficient transmission of messages between the brain and the muscles. They develop the necessary muscles, and build the confidence to perform the activity. Day by day the activity becomes automatic, until the accomplished basketball player can dribble the length of the court while remembering the coach's selection of plays in any situation. Now apply this example to stress behaviors. If we live stressful lives, our body learns how to position itself for action very efficiently. Imagine a fighter having to think about tensing his muscles or concentrate on getting his heart to pump more blood to his muscles.

When we are frightened by a situation or hurt because of the way people talked or looked at us, our bodies are affected by stress responses that have become automatic. We can be (and usually are) stressed. We behave in a stressful or defensive manner without knowing it, because we have the stressful situation on that automatic or subconscious level that allows us to do two or more things at once. A person who has a low threshold for frustration and is quick to become defensive might have developed a predisposition to be reactive. This predisposition is referred to as *tone*. The person who is highly "toned" is conditioned to react in a stressful manner when any numbers of situational triggers are present. Often the triggers are unknown on a conscious level or are "forgotten" if a certain memory is too painful to think about. Victims of childhood physical, emotional, and/or sexual abuses often bury the memory of the actual abuse. However, the brain remembers the feeling and responds to triggers in a stressful manner even when no conscious appraisal is apparent. Thus our emotions exert an important measure of background control over our thoughts and behaviors.

To summarize, we become very efficient at being aroused, even when we are not conscious of the arousal or the triggering situation. We often feel stressed and do not know why. It is not until we consciously interpret the stress arousal that we can begin to deal with the stress, for at this point our emotions are integrated with our thoughts and we interpret the experience in view of our knowledge and the situation. If we appraise the threat and no solution is forthcoming, our stress arousal is compounded by stress arising from fear of failure or harm. If a solution is forthcoming and it involves an angry attack on the stressor, then the stress is likewise compounded. If a solution is planned and then inhibited, stress arousal is again compounded. If a solution is forthcoming, stress arousal can begin to dissipate; however, the physiological resolution may take as long as twenty-four hours.

As illustrated in Figure 1.3, both the subconscious and voluntary pathways can lead to physical arousal; arousal is not totally dependent upon voluntary action. If the body prepares for action (for example, by bracing itself in a defensive posture), but the action is then thwarted, the person is often left with chronic low-to-moderate tension. Prolonged physical arousal can go unheeded because the symptoms are not overt and do not produce noticeable pain or discomfort. However, if fatigue of an organ system ensues, or if the system malfunctions, noticeable symptoms will appear.

The signs and symptoms of stress arousal appear when a body system is excessively stimulated. The normal functioning of the system is altered, and persistence of the condition for an extended period may be damaging. Prolonged overactivation of an organ system can eventually fatigue that system and cause temporary or permanent pathological change or disease. Additionally, prolonged stimulation may alter our resistance to disease. It is like driving a car with underinflated tires. The tires wear unevenly and "fatigue" sooner than expected, perhaps even causing serious damage to the car and injury to the driver.

There is a general misconception that illness starts when symptoms first appear. In most illness the more observable symptoms are preceded by less observable and less disabling symptoms (arousal), which are unnoticed by the unaware. In the case of psychosomatic illnesses, response to a social or environmental situation is followed by prolonged physical and emotional arousal, which is followed in turn by neurological sensitivity to arousal, fatigue and then malfunctioning of an organ system, and finally observable symptoms. This process is outlined in Figure 1.4.

Emotional arousal, which usually precedes physical arousal, can be classified as a less observable symptom, even though we usually know when we are being aroused. Although we are aware of emotional arousal, most of us do not link it with physical illness, and we tend to tolerate it or deny its existence. Because our bodies and minds adapt, hyperarousal seems to be the normal state. How often have you experienced an extreme sense of relaxation or even a "letdown" after finishing a prolonged project or when just starting a vacation? It is then that you realize just how tense you were

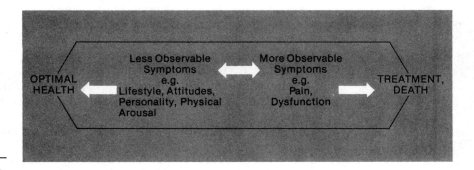

**FIGURE 1.4**

The Health–Illness Continuum

during the project, though at the time that tension was "normal" for you. Often there is an extreme difference between the relaxed state and our perceived "normal" state.

Less observable symptoms also include certain attitudes and personality traits. Research has firmly established that certain personality types are more prone than others to illness. This book contains several self-assessment tests for the personality traits and attitudes that are often linked to illness. Evidence clearly shows that some lifestyles promote the development of psychosomatic illness. Thus, where you live, how you live, and where and with whom you work and play can help determine the status of your health or illness.

The ability to recognize the less observable symptoms comes with training. One essential in the training process is knowledge. For many individuals, knowing what activities to do and why these activities help will increase their motivation to adopt a healthier lifestyle. The most significant contribution of the psychosomatic concept is that it demonstrates the possibility of altering, intervening, or preventing, through knowledge and training, the detrimental effects that our environment, our perceptions, and our imagination have on the arousal of the control systems of the body.

# REFERENCES

BRADSHAW, JOHN. (1990). *Homecoming.* New York: Bantam.

CANNON, W. B. (1939). *The wisdom of the body* (2nd ed.). New York: W. W. Norton & Co., Inc.

CORLEY, K. (1985). Pathopsychology of stress. In S. Burchfield (ed.), *Stress* (pp. 185–206). New York: Hemisphere.

DEUTSCH, F. (1959). *On the mysterious leap from the mind to the body.* New York: International Universities Press.

DUBOS, R. (1965). *Man adapting.* New Haven: Yale University Press.

DUNBAR, H. (1935). *Emotions and bodily changes.* New York: Columbia University Press.

ELIOT, R. (1977). Stress and cardiovascular disease. *European Journal of Cardiology, 5,* 97–104.

ENGEL, G. L. (1975). A unified concept of health and disease. In T. Millon (ed.), *Medical behavior science.* Philadelphia: Saunders.

GELLHORN, E. (1964). Motion and emotion. *Psychological Review, 71,* 457–75.

————. (1958). The physiological basis of neuromuscular relaxation. *Archives of Internal Medicine, 102,* 392–99.

————. (1967). *Principles of somatic-autonomic integration.* Minneapolis: University of Minnesota Press.

HINKLE, L. E. (1973). The concept of stress in the biological and social sciences. *Science, Medicine and Man, 1,* 43.

LATIMER, P. (1985). Irritable bowel syndrome. In W. Dorfman and L. Cristofar (eds.), *Psychosomatic illness review* (pp. 61–75). New York: Macmillan.

LEIGH, HOYLE. (1982). Evaluation and management of stress in general medicine: The psychosomatic approach. In L. Goldberger and S. Breznitz (eds.), *Handbook of stress.* New York: Free Press.

LOWN, B., et al. (1976). Basis for recurring ventricular fibrillation in the absence of coronary heart disease and its management. *New England Journal of Medicine, 294,* 623–29.

MACLEAN, P. (1949). Psychosomatic disease and the "visceral brain": Recent developments bearing on the Papez theory of emotion. *Psychosomatic Medicine, 11,* 338–53.

MALMO, R. (1975). *On emotions, needs and our archaic brain.* New York: Holt Rinehart & Winston.

NAUTA, W. (1979). Expanding borders of the limbic system concept. In T. Rasmussen and R. Marino (eds.), *Functional neurosurgery.* New York: Raven Press.

NAUTA, W., and V. DOMESICK (1982). Neural associations of the limbic system. In A. Beckman (ed.), *Neural substrates of behavior.* New York: Spectrum Publ.

PAPEZ, J. (1937). A proposed mechanism of emotion. *Archives of Neurological Psychiatry, 38,* 725–43.

POST, R. (1985). Stress sensitization, kindling and conditioning. *Behavior Brain Science, 8,* 372–73.

POST, R., and J. BALLENGER (1981). Kindling models for the progressive development of psychopathology. In H. Pragg (ed.), *Handbook of biological psychiatry.* New York: Marcel Dekker.

SELYE, HANS. (1956). *The stress of life.* New York: McGraw-Hill.

SOLOMON, G. (1985). The emerging field of psychoneuroimmunology with a special on AIDS. *Advances, 2* (winter), 6–19.

SUTER, S. (1984). *Health psychophysiology.* Hillsdale, N.J.: Erlbaum.

TOMKINS, S. (1962). *Affect, imagery, consciousness.* New York: Springer.

VAN DER KOLK, B., M. GREENBERG, H. BOYD, and J. KRYSTAL (1985). Inescapable shock, neurotransmitters, and addiction to trauma. *Biological Psychiatry, 20,* 314–25.

VERRIER, R., and LOWN, B. (1984). Behavioral stress and cardiac arrhythmias. *Annual review of physiology, 46,* 155–76.

WEIL, J. L. (1974). *A neurophysiological model of emotional and intentional behavior.* Springfield, Ill.: Chas. C Thomas.

WOLF, S. (1985). Peptic ulcer. In W. Dorfman and L. Cristofar (eds.), *Psychosomatic illness review* (pp. 52–60). New York: Macmillan.

# CHAPTER TWO

# Systems That Control Stress Arousal

**THE NERVOUS SYSTEM: AN OVERVIEW**

Every system of the body is involved at some time in the stress response, by means of nervous stimulation of an organ, nervous and hormonal stimulation of the endocrine system, and/or the action of the neuropeptide system. It appears, though, that the central nervous system (CNS), or brain, is always involved, and thus becomes the logical starting point in analyzing systems that control the stress response. Before venturing into neurophysiology, however, we would like to give a brief description of the evolution of the human brain so that we might acquire insight into its more scientific aspects. Figure 2.1 depicts what MacLean (1973) called the *triune brain*, with its communication links within and among the three levels.

The triune brain is three brains in one: (1) a brain that relates to the physical world, (2) a brain that relates to the inner world, and (3) a brain that relates to abstraction and creativity. The current human brain began as brain 1 in Figure 2.1, the reptilian (or

**FIGURE 2.1**

The Triune Brain and Its Intercommunication Links (adapted from Pearce, 1985)

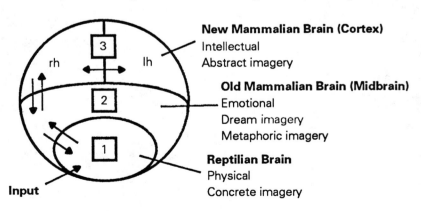

New Mammalian Brain (Cortex)
Intellectual
Abstract imagery

Old Mammalian Brain (Midbrain)
Emotional
Dream imagery
Metaphoric imagery

Reptilian Brain
Physical
Concrete imagery

rh     lh

Input

physical) brain that helped us survive for hundreds of millions of years by registering and responding to physical input. Following the adage "ontogeny recapitulates phylogeny" (meaning that as we develop, we repeat everything that has come before us), the reptilian brain continued to function as we added brain 2, the old mammalian (or emotional) brain. The emotional brain wrapped around the physical brain, and these two areas set up an intimate communication network. Now, in addition to responding to physical stimuli, humans began to place an emotional value on their relationship to the physical world and to each other. Finally, the evolution of the third brain (the cortex, or neocortex) enabled us to work with abstract imagery, think on an intellectual plane, and create thoughts and forms not necessarily based on physical input. This brain was called the new mammalian, or intellectual, brain.

The reptilian, or physical, brain is the part through which we sense our physical world and respond to it. It senses the warmth of sunlight and adjusts our body temperature quite automatically. And it judges the warmth as enjoyable or annoying, which is also the function of the next-higher portion of the brain, the midbrain.

The midbrain, also called the metaphoric brain, handles not only emotions but all internal images. It receives concrete, physical images from the lower brain and abstract images from the cortex, and its job is to make some kind of cohesive relationship out of those images. Pearce (1985) calls the midbrain the "heart" of the central nervous system, for it handles our loves, hates, fears, attractions, aversions, bonding, and all other relationships.

The new brain, or cortex, makes it possible for us to analyze, synthesize, create, compute, and otherwise play with the information furnished by the two lower brains. The two hemispheres of the cortex are not connected at birth, and therefore undergo concurrent development. At about age one, the corpus callosum begins to provide a communication link between the two hemispheres, and specialization begins to occur in each. Before the development of the corpus callosum is completed (somewhere around age four, according to Sperry, 1970), the two hemispheres communicate only with their respective parts of the lower brains. Once the corpus callosum is developed, the hemispheres can communicate freely without any input from the lower brains, making it possible for us to think and plan without emotional and physical interference. This ability has created the double-edged sword of being able to think and create on a very high plane, but without compassion for the physical body or for human relationships and ethics. This is an important aspect in the current study of psychosomatic disease, as we will discuss later.

As an example of the contribution of the three parts of the brain, imagine seeing the letters *D O G*. The physical brain registers the physical, concrete form of the letters. The midbrain translates the letters into abstract images for the new brain, which in turn creates a variety of meanings for those three concrete symbols.

Note in Figure 2.1 that the lines of communication between the two lower brains are bidirectional, showing the constant synchrony of these two areas. There is also strong bidirectional communication, though not as complete a synchrony, between the midbrain and the right hemisphere of the cortex. However, that same bidirectionality is not seen between the midbrain and the left hemisphere of the cortex; in fact, it appears that the two are only casually connected. Therefore, the lower-brain signals that reach the left hemisphere must travel through the right hemisphere and across the corpus callosum (Pearce, 1985). This has been described as the neurophysiological basis of being able to "do research in a vacuum," and has important undertones for psychosomatic disease.

By understanding the original nature and development of these three parts of the brain, which in current terminology are the *hypothalamus* (the physical brain), the *limbic system* (the emotional brain), and the *cortex* (the thinking brain), we are afforded insight into the process of psychosomatic disease. Pearce (1985) has likened the three parts of the brain to a light bulb with three filaments. When the old-brain filament is energized, all three areas respond. The same occurs when either of the other two parts of the brain is stimulated—it is automatically supported by the remaining two parts. Pearce explains,

> The wattage of each brain changes as we move up the evolutionary scale. The old brain is the most stable, but also the weakest. The midbrain is less stable but more powerful. The new brain is the least stable and most powerful of all. The old brain is not only amplified far beyond its original reptilian design by this integrated circuitry; it can be modified or distorted by its more sophisticated neighbors. And, logically, the actions of any of the three can be modified or distorted, as well as amplified and/or clarified, by the others.

As we proceed to discuss the neurophysiological basis of the stress response and how that response is translated into physical conditions and diseases, remember this ancient design of the central nervous system.

**THE BASIC SYSTEMS OF CONTROL**

Currently, scientific research supports the existence of four basic systems in the human body that are highly implicated in the control of the psychosomatic process. These are (1) the autonomic nervous system, (2) the endocrine system, (3) the immune system, and (4) the neuropeptide system. The first two are primarily in control of the stress response; the other two work with them in the psychosomatic disease process.

As parts of the greater whole, all four systems are, of course, interconnected. There is, however, a focus of control that takes us back to the previous discussion of the brain. The center of physical control is the hypothalamus, which receives constant emotional input from the limbic system. This concept of limbic-hypothalamic center is sometimes extended to include the pituitary gland, and may be referred to in the literature on psychosomatic disease— and in the more recent research on psychoneuroimmunology (PNI)—as the *limbic-hypothalamic-pituitary* axis. Figure 2.2 illustrates the portions of the central nervous system to be discussed in this section. Our intention in this discussion is to elaborate on the two systems primarily responsible for controlling the stress response.

**The Autonomic Nervous System (ANS)**

Actions of the central nervous system—the brain, brainstem, and spinal cord—can be classified as either *autonomic* or *voluntary*. Autonomic functioning is automatic, or reflexive: it regulates heart rate, body temperature, respiration, and other vital functions without our having to think about doing so. The voluntary system allows us to think before we act.

There are two main classifications within the autonomic nervous system: (1) the *sympathetic* nervous system, which sets off the alarm response that in turn energizes the body to respond to stress, and (2) the *parasympathetic* nervous system, which reverts the energized systems back to normal function. Some researchers (for

FIGURE 2.2

The Central Nervous System

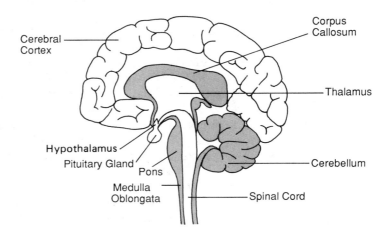

example, Bulloch, 1985) have included the entric system, which helps regulate the stomach and intestines, as a third part of the autonomic system, but our discussion here will be limited to the sympathetic and parasympathetic systems, for they are the parts of the ANS primarily involved in stress and psychosomatic health or disease.

The sympathetic system is best known for its lifesaving "fight or flight" capacities. When this system is stimulated, all its parts react with a mass discharge to accomplish a common purpose—enabling the body to act above and beyond its normal everyday function. For example, in a fight-or-flight situation the body needs more blood, more oxygen, and more energy. And so the heart beats faster and pumps more blood per beat. At the same time, the body makes more efficient use of the available blood supply by constricting blood vessels in these organs, such as the gastrointestinal tract, that are not essential to the stress response. This decreases the function of the unneeded organs and allows an increased flow of blood to essential organs such as the heart and skeletal muscles. In the lungs, the bronchials (which carry air) expand and breathing becomes deeper, faster, and generally more efficient. The pupils of the eyes enlarge, improving visual sensitivity, and salivary secretion increases. The adrenal glands secrete adrenalin, which reinforces and prolongs the sympathetic effect and stimulates the liver to release more glucose to fuel the action. Adrenalin also stimulates the adipose tissue to release fatty acids to fuel the muscles. (See Table 2.1 for a summary of the effects on the body of the fight-or-flight response.) Thus, stimulation of the sympathetic system increases the activity of the organs needed for the fight-or-flight response and inhibits the organs that are not essential. Prolonged stimulation or inhibition of organs can cause malfunction and in turn promote stress-related illness.

The fight-or-flight response, mediated by epinephrine, norepinephrine, and dopamine (hormones of the sympathetic and adrenal systems), demands an integrated adjustment of many processes, as shown in Table 2.1. This response is facilitated by other hormones of the endocrine system and central nervous system (adapted from Martin, Mayes, Rodwell, & Granner, 1985).

The parasympathetic system, in contrast with the sympathetic system, does not exhibit a mass reaction to stimulation. It acts on specific organs, increasing the action of some while inhibiting that of others. Parasympathetic stimulation of the organ systems given in Table 2.1 would have the following effects: The heart would slow down, most blood vessels would expand, and the functions of the gastrointestinal system would increase. The bronchials would con-

**TABLE 2.1   Physiological Changes in the Fight-or-Flight Response**

| ORGAN | CHANGE |
| --- | --- |
| Fat tissue | Increased breakdown of stored fat, more fatty acids and glycerol in the bloodstream |
| Brain | Increased blood flow, increased metabolism of glucose |
| Cardiovascular system | Increased heart rate and force of contraction, vasoconstriction of peripheral blood vessels |
| Lungs | Increased respiratory rate, dilation of bronchi, increased oxygen supply |
| Muscles | Increased breakdown of glycogen to glucose for immediate energy supply, increased contraction, decreased uptake of glucose, increased uptake of fatty acids for energy |
| Liver | Increased glucose production via gluconeogenesis |
| Skin | Decreased blood flow |
| Gastrointestinal tract | Decreased protein synthesis |
| Genitourinary tract | Decreased protein synthesis |
| Lymph tissue | Increased breakdown of protein |

Source: Adapted from Martin, Mayes, Rodwell, & Granner (1985).

strict, as would the pupils, and salivary secretion would increase. After the arousal response, the parasympathetic system works to normalize the function of all the organs involved.

Most organs in the body respond to both the sympathetic and parasympathetic systems. Some organs, however, are stimulated by only one. In this case, it is the controlling system that determines whether the organ is activated or inhibited.

### Structure and Function

The lower structures of the autonomic nervous system respond to the physical world and are basically reflexive. These structures include the spinal cord, the cerebellum (the center of muscle coordination), the medulla oblongata (which controls heart rate, circulation of blood, respiration, coughing, and sneezing), the pons (a network that sends nerve impulses to various parts of the brain), the thalamus (the switchboard that sends incoming signals to proper brain areas), and the hypothalamus. Throughout this area of the brain (see Figure 2.3) is a specialized system called the reticular formation, which we will discuss later.

If humans have any resemblance to other animal species, it is in the basic programs stored within these lower centers. The actions or behaviors governed by these centers are natural, direct, and open, without a great deal of learned inhibition. Activities centered in survival and reproduction (such as preparing a homesite, establishing and defending territory, hunting, homing, hoarding, mating, forming simple social groups, and doing routine daily activities) are instinctive and performed by lower animals as well as humans. But with their higher level of brain evolution, humans have shown the ability to override some of these basic responses for psychological and social survival.

**The Hypothalamus.** Located at the base of the forebrain, the hypothalamus is not so much a distinct, identifiable organ as a combination of tissues with a somewhat vague boundary. These tissues are made up of a number of nuclei, or nerve centers, that control the basic autonomic functions.

The hypothalamus is at the very center of the limbic system and has profuse communcation pathways with all levels of this system (Ganong, 1985). It sends signals in two major directions: (1) down through the brainstem, mainly to the reticular formation of the pons, medulla, and hypothalamus and thalamus; and (2) up to many areas of the cortex. The hypothalamus affects the cortex indirectly, but dramatically, through its control of the brainstem portion of the reticular activating system.

The hypothalamus is the major integrator of the body's regulatory systems (such as hunger, thirst, temperature, blood pressure, heart rate, and sex). Stimluation of appropriate areas of the hypothalamus can activate the sympathetic system strongly enough to increase arterial blood pressure by more than 100 percent. Other areas control temperature by allowing more or less blood to flow to the surface of the skin. Still others increase or decrease salivation, control sexual responses, and regulate the digestive process and other responses to physical threat.

In MacLean's triune brain, the hypothalamus is the physical

FIGURE 2.3

The Inner Brain

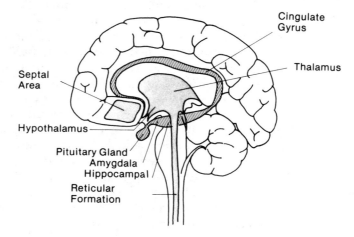

brain: it receives physical messages and responds on a basic, physical level. When it receives messages that are either threatening or new and unique, it responds with a sympathetically controlled alarm reaction. When the threat abates or the new message is somehow integrated, calming messages are sent through the parasympathetic system to the excited organs so that their function is normalized.

Consider, for example, the response to noise. A noise is first perceived by the lower centers before it is registered in the cortex. Once the hypothalamus is stimulated, it prepares for possible action by increasing the discharge of hormones, increasing the availability of energy, preparing the cardiovascular (heart and circulatory) system by shifting blood flow to essential organs, and at the same time tensing the muscles. The conscious cortex may ultimately prevent the action, but the body is prepared for any eventuality and is technically in a state of stress. It is the hypothalamus, with its intimate relationship to the pituitary gland, that provides the link between the nervous system and the endocrine system.

The hypothalamic-controlled ANS communicates through neurotransmitters, or neurohormones, with the parts of the body it affects. The sympathetic-system nerve endings secrete the neurotransmitter norepinephrine to activate receptors on the cells of the organs the nerve endings modulate, and parasympathetic-system nerve endings secrete acetylcholine. These neurotransmitters bind with receptors in the cell walls of the target organs, changing the permeability of the organ's cell wall and causing targeted internal events to occur. In addition to changing cell permeability, the neurohormones may activate an enzyme in the cell membrane of the target organ, thereby causing enzymatic events to initiate the autonomic response characteristic of that organ.

**The Limbic System.**    The limbic system offered its predecessor, the physical brain, a measure of freedom from stereotyped behavior. Primarily, this newer system added feeling and emotion, which further assured attendance to basic survival activities by making activities pleasurable or unpleasurable. Feelings such as fear, anger, and love became attached to certain situations, guiding behavior toward that which protected and away from that which threatened. Understandably, two of our major neural pathways (those governing eating and reproduction) have intricate connections to the pleasure and unpleasure centers of the limbic system (Ganong, 1985). The concepts of reward or pleasure and punishment or unpleasure are important to the concept of stress.

As we have seen, the brain continued to develop with the addition of the cerebral cortex, also called the neocortex or forebrain (Figure 2.4). The addition of a vast number of cortical cells allowed the development and storage of analytical skills, verbal communication, writing ability, fine motor control, additional emotion, memory, learning and rational thought, as well as more sophisticated problem-solving and survival abilities. New dimensions were added to oral and sexual behaviors, and vision replaced smell as the primary sense. Voluntary control of movement made reactions more than mere reflex responses. For better or worse, an individual's reality could be determined by his or her own perceptions. Behavior could be weighed against possible outcomes. Symbolism, goals, motivation, and anticipation became part of the functioning human being.

Even though the brain developed in three stages, its three areas do not function independently. Although the lower centers deal mainly with survival and the higher centers permit the existence of complex society, we cannot view the lower centers as primitive entities requiring control by the higher centers. We must understand the function of each of these specific nervous-system structures in order to understand stress and how to overcome it. At the same time, we cannot think of stress as anything but total brain integration.

As stress is an integrated response of the body, it must have an integrative conduit, and that area has been demonstrated to be the limbic system (MacLean, 1949). As we saw in our discussion of the triune brain, the limbic system is the hub of the central

**FIGURE 2.4**

The Cerebral Cortex

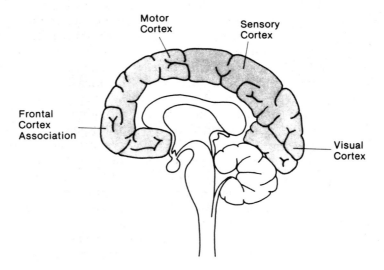

nervous system and the human stress response as well. This system (particularly the septal, hippocampal, and hypothalamic areas) integrates cognitive appraisals from the prefrontal cortex with the higher-order emotions arising in the cingulate and amygdaloid areas. The result of this input is neuromuscular articulation and stress-related symptoms and signs (MacLean, 1949; Doane & Livingston, 1986).

**The Reward System.** The reward system may help us to understand the drive to cope with our internal and external environments. Major reward areas are located at the limbic and hypothalamic levels, and are involved with tuning reactivity (how easily we are aroused), motivation, and emotional memory.

Coping with adversity is an attempt to move our emotional, physical, mental, or spiritual being away from pain or toward pleasure and reward. CNS reward systems have developed over time, presumably to reinforce useful behaviors and extinguish harmful ones. In addition, these reward systems regulate the basic drives related to pleasure, pain, emotional comfort, sexual satisfaction, hunger, satiety, and thirst. If we learn to throw our reward systems off balance, we subsequently strive to bring them back into balance—from a very deep subconscious level up to an intentional conscious level.

The middle limbic area of special interest in the reward pathway is the *nucleus accumbens*. This specialized area has been pinpointed as a site of intense reward, mediated by dopamine, the neurohormone that normally controls homeostasis through the process of negative feedback (the natural reward systems, such as food, sex, and water, have an upper boundary of satiety through this feedback system). The nucleus accumbens provides such intense reward that experimental animals allowed to stimulate this area with intravenous psychomotor stimulants will stimulate themselves to death if the response cost is low.

Although scientific controversy exists as to whether there is one main reward pathway or many redundant pathways, it is accepted that the experiencing of pleasure most likely includes dopamine effects in the brain. Neurons that produce dopamine make up much of the mesolimbic system, and dopamine is the mediating neurotransmitter in many mesolimbic receptor sites.

In recent years the costs of cocaine, crack, and other drug addictions (and the crime that accompanies them) have spurred research on the natural reward systems. It has been found that the body produces its own opiate-like substances to help alleviate pain and produce pleasure. Since then, receptors for nicotine, cocaine, and marijuana have also been discovered. The relationship between drugs and stress management is not subtle—human beings seek pleasure and avoid pain. This is a driving principle of human behavior.

**The Reticular Formation.**   The reticular formation is often referred to as the *reticular activating system* (RAS) or the *ascending reticular activating system* (ARAS). It is a network of nerve cells (or neurons) that extends from the spinal cord up through the thalamus. The RAS itself is neither sensory (connected to the sense organs) nor motor (connected to the muscles), but it links sensory and motor impulses. It is a two-way street, carrying impulses from brain to body and from body to brain.

The RAS was discovered by Moruzzi and Magoun (1949), who noted that its nerve connections projected to the limbic system, the hypothalamus, the thalamus, and throughout the cortex in order to stimulate or alert the brain. The RAS receives information from all of the body's incoming nerves, filters this input, and then forwards to the brain only that information that is new or persistent (Bloom, Lazerson & Hofstadter, 1985). When RAS centers in the pons area of the brainstem signal new stimuli, the message immediately heightens awareness both in the cortex and also in the limbic-hypothalamic center, which integrates memory and houses the reward or pleasure mechanism. A feeling tone is added to the stimuli, and we may consciously choose to either ignore or attend to the stimuli.

A unique feature of the messages that pass through the RAS is that they are general as well as specific. In hearing, for example, once a sound is perceived by the auditory mechanism it sends both specific and nonspecific impulses through the appropriate parts of the RAS. The specific arousal alerts the brain for increased attention to the sound, while the nonspecific impulses cause a general arousal of the cortex. Even before the cortex appraises the potential threat of the sound, this general arousal stimulates the limbic system and the hypothalamus, which in turn prepare the body for potential action. Muscle tension and hormonal and metabolic action increase before the cortex identifies the source of the stimulus. These increases are sensed by, and further alert and arouse, the RAS. If action occurs, the arousal was purposeful and the products of arousal were utilized. If the sound is never consciously appraised or if no action is pursued, the RAS became aroused (stressed) for no reason, and the products of arousal must circulate until they can be reabsorbed or otherwise used up. This process is illustrated in Figure 2.5.

Of great importance in the study of stress and psychosomatic disease is the capacity of the RAS for reverberation (prolonged

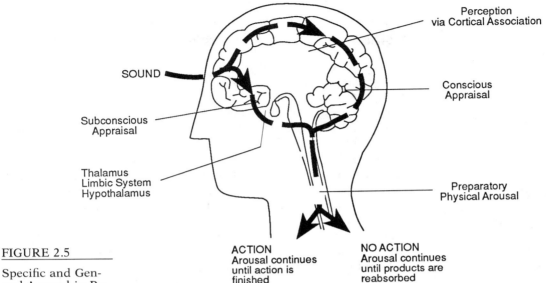

SOUND

Perception
via Cortical Association

Conscious
Appraisal

Subconscious
Appraisal

Thalamus
Limbic System
Hypothalamus

Preparatory
Physical Arousal

ACTION
Arousal continues
until action is
finished

NO ACTION
Arousal continues
until products are
reabsorbed

FIGURE 2.5

Specific and General Arousal in Response to Stress

vibration) of an impulse, which will prolong a response. This means that the RAS can maintain a resting level of activity reflecting the general state of the other brain structures. A high level of resting activity increases and prolongs arousal, whereas a lower level of resting activity inhibits and shortens potential arousal. If you live a stressful life and find you are stressed many times during the day, the parts of your brain that become aroused to deal with that stress also affect the RAS, which adapts to frequent arousal by staying aroused. It is as though the RAS were saying, "Well, if you are going to be aroused so often I might as well just stay aroused and save the time and energy of going up and down." The RAS also has the capacity to recruit impulses from other brain structures, and it will adapt to stimuli. It is partly because of this ability to adapt that repeated situations cause less conscious stress than do novel experiences. For example, the noise of a city is less stressful for the permanent resident than it is for the visitor from a quieter environment.

The RAS is an essential part of the integrated system called the limbic-hypothalamic-pituitary axis, which is responsible for an integrated physiological response to a life situation perceived to be threatening. This response allows the organism to cope with the situation in a way that ensures its survival. However, when the response is chronically elicited, changes occur in the normal physiological state of the individual. Under repeated stimulation (prolonged vibration) of the limbic-hypothalamic-pituitary axis, the transient elevations of activity become permanent. This phenomenon can be thought of as a hypersensitivity to stimulation, or a lowered threshold for activation of emotional arousal. Gellhorn (1970) calls it *tuning*. With chronic stimulation, the level of tuning increases in the part of the sympathetic nervous system that involves activity; the increased tuning is thus described as *work*. Gellhorn (1970) notes that this sympathetic tuning serves as a nervous predisposition to stress arousal, anxiety, and related psychosomatic disorders such as were mentioned in Chapter 1.

As we have seen, however, the activity of body organs is controlled by the relative level of activity of the sympathetic and parasympathetic nervous systems (as well as by endocrine activity). Tuning may be thought of as a balance between these two parts of the nervous system. According to Gellhorn, tuning dominated by sympathetic stimulation is *ergotropic tuning*. As ergotropic activity or tone increases, there is a reciprocal decrease in tone in the trophotropic system, and vice versa. Increasing ergotropic tone through constant stimulation, thus decreasing the tone in the opposing trophotropic system, augments dysfunction and pathology in the enervated organ systems. Increasing the activity in the trophotropic system through relaxation training reduces the tone in the opposing ergotropic system. Thus, any relaxation activity, especially those involving skeletal muscles, can charge the trophotropic system and discharge the ergotropic tuning, providing protection against chronic arousal and significantly reducing anxiety and other conditions related to arousal.

John Weil (1974), another pioneer in the study of the neurophysiology of stress, has elaborated on Gellhorn's tuning model by broadening the concept of sympathetic versus parasympathetic tuning. He believes that aspects of both systems work in concert with various hypothalamic-limbic structures on the basis not so much of anatomical structure as of physiological activity that results in either arousal or tranquility. Weil suggests that the arousal system can be "charged" by high-intensity stimulation or by an increased rate of repeated low-intensity stimulation.

Once charged, the limbic-hypothalamic-reticular hub is capable of sustaining a high level of arousal through the discharge of impulses, providing nonspecific tonic activation. Gellhorn and Keily (1972), Benson (1975), and Weil (1974) suggest that decreases in proprioceptive input to the RAS and the limbic-hypothalamic-pituitary axis may be the underlying mechanism in relaxation training that charges or tunes the trophotropic system.

Gellhorn (1968) and Weil (1974) formulated the theory of autonomic-nervous-system tuning, and Everly and Benson (1988) have augmented the concept of tuning by proposing that excessive chronic arousal or excessively high levels of arousal can cause an increase in the dendrites of limbic system neurons, thus increasing limbic stimulation. Furthermore, with excessive stimulation those neurons grow more excitatory postsynaptic receptors and experience a decrease in inhibitory presynaptic receptors. This may be the microanatomical basis for what Gellhorn refers to as tuning. Perhaps, then, the central purpose of meditation or mind quieting is to reverse the tuning that occurs with hyperarousal.

### Autonomic Control of the Stress Response

The autonomic nervous system is the system with ultimate control over how the body responds to new information. When the senses (sight, sound, touch, smell, and taste) bring new information into the brain, an immediate low-level physical arousal is orchestrated by the lower-brainstem areas. The conductor of this orchestration is the hypothalamus. It immediately prepares the body with the arousal response. Background theme is added by the limbic system, which lends a feeling of pleasure or unpleasure. The intensity of response depends on the "tone" that has been set by the firing of RAS neurons. The cortex then assesses the physical arousal and tone and either enhances or inhibits them with conscious thought, tapping both conscious and subconscious memories. If the new information triggers a feeling of threat or a need for increased sensitivity, the stress response is heightened; if it triggers a feeling of safety, the stress response is allowed to diminish.

The fight-or-flight response is by no means the only contributor to the stress response. Actually, there are many emotional situations that can alter the body's function, and different emotions bring about different physical states. When we feel anger, we become flushed, excited, and full of energy. Wolf and Wolff (1947) have reported that in anger situations, the mucous membranes of the nose and stomach redden, swell, and become congested to the point of hemorrhage. Often gastritis can be traced to this cause. When we are afraid, we tremble, our knees feel weak, and we often have difficulty speaking. Here, the mucous membranes of the nose and stomach become pale and shrunken.

It is difficult to generalize about how the nervous system affects stress-related disorders, for stimulation or inhibition of the organ systems involved in the stress response can both lead to body malfunction. Also, the nervous system both controls and is influenced by the other major system that controls the stress response of the body—the *endocrine* system. It is particularly harmful when these two systems get caught in a positive-feedback cycle, with each exciting the other and thereby increasing the stress response.

**The Endocrine
System**

The endocrine system consists of glands that secrete substances called *hormones* into the bloodstream. These various hormones influence virtually all bodily activities. The glands we are most concerned with in this section are the *pituitary gland* and the *adrenal glands,* although all the glands are involved to some extent in the stress response.

### The Pituitary: The Master Gland

The intimate relationship between the hypothalamus and the pituitary gland can be seen in Figure 2.2. As various areas of the hypothalamus are stimulated, it in turn stimulates corresponding areas in the pituitary. Thus, thoughts, anticipations, and nervous-system responses can and do become hormonal actions. Some portions of the hypothalamus stimulate the parasympathetic nervous system and inhibit the stress response. Other areas of the hypothalamus activate the sympathetic nervous system and increase the stress response.

Hormone-releasing factors are produced in the hypothalamus and released into a local bloodstream to the anterior pituitary, which releases pituitary hormones into the bloodstream and on to their target organs. This is an example of hormonal stimulation of the pituitary gland. The hypothalamus also executes nerve control over the pituitary through neurological connections between select nuclei in the hypothalamus and the posterior portion of the pituitary gland. The hypothalamic cells that produce hormone-releasing factors and the ones that stimulate neurological release of pituitary hormones are neurologically linked with the limbic system and the cortex. These links constitute a basic connection between our thoughts and emotions and psychosomatic disease (Rossi, 1986).

### The Adrenal Glands

Although all the endocrine glands may eventually become involved in the stress response, the adrenal glands are responsible for most of the physical manifestations of stress arousal, such as increased heart and respiration rates. There are two adrenal glands, one sitting over each kidney. The adrenal consists of two parts: an inner section called the *medulla* and an outer layer called the *cortex* (Figure 2.6).

The medulla responds to the hypothalamic messages that

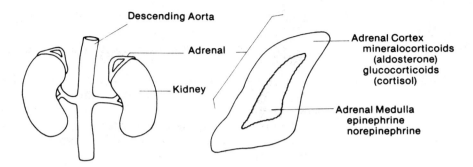

**Descending Aorta**

**Adrenal**

**Kidney**

**Adrenal Cortex**
mineralocorticoids
(aldosterone)
glucocorticoids
(cortisol)

**Adrenal Medulla**
epinephrine
norepinephrine

FIGURE 2.6

Adrenal Glands
and Hormones

travel along sympathetic nerves extending into the medulla. When the hypothalamus is alerted, an impulse is sent to the adrenal medulla, and this area immediately releases the hormone *epinephrine* (commonly called *adrenalin*), which primarily affects the cardiovascular system. With the effects of this hormone, along with its close kin, *norepinephrine (noradrenalin)*, and a third hormone, *dopamine*, the stress response is fully manifested throughout the body. As long as the control centers of the brain perceive the need for arousal, stimulation of the adrenal medulla continues. Prolonged stress can eventually fatigue the medulla.

The hypothalamus acts on the adrenal cortex not through nerve impulses but by means of a hormone secreted by the pituitary gland in response to a hypothalamic hormone-releasing factor. This hormone, ACTH (adrenocorticotrophic hormone), circulates through the bloodstream to the adrenal cortex. Once the adrenal cortex is stimulated, it in turn secretes hormones into the blood that manifest the stress response in a number of ways. The two primary secretions of the adrenal cortex are *glucocorticoids* (primarily *cortisol*) and *mineralocorticoids* (primarily *aldosterone*).

Cortisol affects metabolism (that is, the total body processes) by increasing the availability of energy (in the form of glucose, fatty acids, and amino acids), either for the stress response or for recovery from an extreme period of overactivity. It increases, as much as tenfold, a metabolic process of the liver called *gluconeogenesis*, through which the body forms glucose out of available glycogen and amino acids. This assures the body, especially the central nervous system, of an adequate supply of the most efficient energy source (blood glucose) for use during this period of heightened need. Furthermore, during gluconeogenesis, cortisol decreases the use of glucose by muscles and fatty tissue, probably by making the system insulin-resistant, thus producing a mild diabetic effect.

During the stress response, cortisol mobilizes both fatty acids and proteins in the blood. The mobilization of protein reduces the stores of protein in all body cells (except in the liver and in the gastrointestinal tract, which is where the mobilization takes place). Hence, if the stress response is maintained for a long period, the supply of protein available for the formation of mature white blood cells and antibodies diminishes to the point of disease susceptibility. In this way, prolonged stress can promote muscular wasting and impair the immune system.

When fatty acids are mobilized from adipose stores, they circulate through the bloodstream in order to be available as an energy source for muscle tissue. When fatty acids are actually used for physical resolution of the stress response, they present little health threat. However, high levels of fatty tissue in the blood appear to promote atherosclerosis (fatty plaquing of the arteries), especially when they are present over time. In this day of "pseudostressors" such as caffeine, nicotine, sedentary lifestyles, and nonassertive response to stress, the fatty acids called out during the stress response may circulate in the bloodstream for hours until they are taken up by the tissues and stored away for future use.

Aldosterone is the other major adrenal cortex hormone secreted in increased amounts during the stress response. The body reacts to aldosterone by preparing itself for increased muscular activity and better dissipation of heat and waste products. It does this by retaining extra sodium (salt), which results in increased water retention. This leads to increases in blood volume, blood pressure, and the amount of blood the heart pumps out with each beat. As with other body systems, prolonged manifestation of the stress response can endanger the cardiovascular system.

**SUMMARY: THE PURPOSE OF THE STRESS RESPONSE**

The body responds to new stimuli by preparing to take physical action in order to protect life. The reptilian part of the brain instantly alerts all other parts of the body. The higher brain centers add feeling and meaning to the new information, and action may or may not be taken. If there is a feeling or perception that the new information is a threat to *physical or psychological* survival, the stress response is continued through additional stimulation of both the autonomic nervous system and the endocrine system. If the response to stress is physical action, the stress products and reactions within the body are utilized and dissipated. If the stress is not resolved and the products of the alarm reaction are not used for their intended purpose (action), the body continues to be stimulated and over time it will adapt to the increased sympathetic tone and hormonal output of the stress response. It does so through what might be called "diseases of adaptation," such as high blood pressure, atherosclerosis, or ulcers. If the stressor is resolved, the body resumes its normal level of functioning. Those with good parasympathetic tone return to normal faster than those without it.

# REFERENCES

BENSON, H. (1975). *The relaxation response.* New York: Avon.

BLOOM, F., A. LAZERSON, and L. HOFSTADTER (1985). *Brain, mind, and behavior.* New York: W. H. Freeman & Company Publishers.

BULLOCH, K. (1985). Neuroanatomy of lymphoid tissue: A review. In R. Guillemin, M. Cohn, and T. Melnechuk (eds.), *Neural modulation of immunity* (pp. 111–41). New York: Raven Press.

DOANE, B., and K. LIVINGSTON (1986). *The limbic system.* New York: Raven Press.

EVERLY, G., and H. BENSON (1988). Disorders of arousal and the relaxation response. Paper presented to the Fourth International Conference on Psychophysiology, Prague, Czechoslovakia.

GANONG, W. (1985). *Review of medical physiology* (12th ed.). Los Altos, CA: Lange Medical Publications.

GELLHORN, E. (1968). CNS tuning and its implications for neuropsychiatry. *Journal of Nervous and Mental Diseases, 147,* 148–62.

———. (1970). The emotions and the ergotropic and trophotropic systems. *Psychologische Forschung, 34,* 48–94.

GELLHORN, E., and W. F. KEILY (1972). Mystical states of consciousness: Neurophysiological and clinical aspects. *Journal of Nervous and Mental Diseases, 154,* 399–405.

MACLEAN, P. D. (1949). Psychosomatic disease and the "visceral brain": Recent developments bearing on the Papez theory of emotion. *Psychosomatic Medicine, 11,* 338–53.

———. (1973). A triune concept of the brain and behavior. In D. Campbell and T. J. Boag (eds.), *The Clarence M. Hincks memorial lecture series.* Toronto: University of Toronto Press.

MARTIN, D. W., P. MAYES, V. W. RODWELL, and D. K. GRANNER (1985). *Harper's review of biochemistry* (20th ed.). Los Altos, CA: Lange Medical Publications.

MORUZZI, I., and H. MAGOUN (1949). Brain stem reticular formation. *Electroencephalography and Clinical Neurophysiology, 1,* 445–73.

PEARCE, J. B. (1985). *The magical child matures.* New York: Bantam.

ROSSI, E. L. (1986). *The psychobiology of mind–body healing.* New York: W. W. Norton & Co., Inc.

SPERRY, R. W. (1970). Conscious phenomena as direct emergent properties of the brain. *Psychological Review, 77* (6), 184.

WEIL, J. L. (1974). *A neurophysiological model of emotional and intentional behavior.* Springfield, IL: Chas. C. Thomas.

WOLF, S., and H. G. WOLFF (1947). *Human gastric function* (2nd ed.). New York: Oxford University Press.

# CHAPTER THREE

# The Body's Response to Stress

This chapter discusses how the major systems of the body respond to stress, thereby helping to explain how psychosomatic diseases and conditions of these systems may occur. Where necessary, we have given background information on the basic function of a system.

It is apparent that although the central mechanisms for arousal, as outlined in Chapter 2, are basically the same for all individuals, each person reacts to prolonged stress arousal in different ways. Why some individuals respond to their stressors by developing ulcers and others by becoming asthmatic or hypertensive has been questioned since the inception of the psychosomatic concept. Franz Alexander (1965), one of the pioneers in psychosomatic medicine, proposed that just as pathological microorganisms have a specific affinity for certain organs, so do certain emotional conflicts afflict certain internal organs. More recently, Bernie Siegel (1986) concluded that individuals suffering from psychosomatic diseases sensitize the target organs of the body in a form of negative feedback. Ernest Rossi and Milton Erickson (Rossi, 1986) propose that the person who experiences stress reacts appropriately to alleviate the original stressful situation but then becomes conditioned to that psychophysiological response, so that even when the original stress is over, the body continues to react in this newly learned way. Eventually, the organ or system responding to prolonged stress arousal breaks down due to exhaustion.

Regardless of whose theory of organ specificity is "right," the points that are important to any discussion of stress-related disease include at least the following:

- Stressful events, situations, or experiences elicit the generalized stress arousal discussed in Chapter 2 and summarized in Table 2.1.
- The stressor is appraised immediately at the hypothalamic level, and the arousal response begins.
- Simultaneously, the hypothalamus alerts the limbic system and the higher cortical levels.
- Feeling tone is added by the limbic system and fed back to the lower centers of the brain, and in this manner the stress response may be prolonged. The cortex adds perception and conscious thought, further stimulating arousal.
- Depending on the emotional value (positive or negative) along with the conscious appraisal of the stressor, the appropriate systems of the body are asked to help solve the stressful problem.
- Upon solution of the problem or disappearance of the stressor, the trophotropic system attempts to get the system(s) back to normal.
- RAS arousal may continue, increasing the reactivity tone of the central nervous system.
- If a person is often confronted with stressors causing central-nervous-system arousal, the system develops a higher resting nervous reactivity.
- Upon responding at a psychophysiological level to the initial stressor, the body learns a response that, though appropriate at the time, may continue to be elicited by prolonged arousal.

These points help us understand that it is not so much the one-shot, generalized alarm reaction that brings about psychosomatic illness; it is the prolonged state of arousal in response to which we somehow "choose" one or more systems to defend the body against stress. These systems become susceptible to all kinds of stressors and keep fighting until exhaustion. The resulting diseases and conditions might be called *diseases of prolonged arousal*.

Figure 3.1 illustrates the flow of stress arousal from the brain to the stress response. This process was explained in more detail in Chapter 2.

Harold G. Wolff, an early proponent of psychosomatics, considered stress to be an internal or resisting force that is usually stirred to action by external situations or pressures that appear as threats—but not so much physical as symbolic threats (that is, threats involving values and goals). However, mobilizing our physical defenses (which were originally designed for battling physical threats) in response to symbolic (social or psychological) sources of threat produces an inappropriate response because of its psychological overtones. To determine whether a response is appropriate, we have to consider the outcome. Physical arousal to physical threat is appropriate: it is usually shortlived and is usually dissipated with action. Physical arousal to symbolic threat is prob-

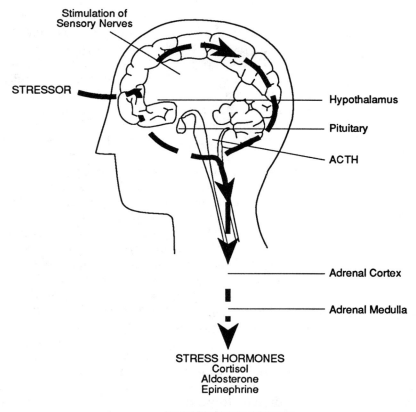

Stimulation of
Sensory Nerves

STRESSOR

Hypothalamus

Pituitary

ACTH

Adrenal Cortex

Adrenal Medulla

STRESS HORMONES
Cortisol
Aldosterone
Epinephrine

THE STRESS RESPONSE

Increased neural excitability
Increased cardiovascular activity
   Heart rate, stroke volume,
   cardiac output, blood pressure
Increased metabolic activity
   Gluconeogenesis
   Protein mobilization
      Decreased antibody production
      Muscle wasting
   Fat mobilization
Increased sodium retention
Increase in neurological sweating
Change in salivation
Change in GI system tonus and motility

FIGURE 3.1

The Stress-
Response Pathway

lematic in at least two ways: (1) in our modern society we can seldom resolve psychological threats to the ego with physical activity in order to resolve stress, and (2) symbolic threat tends to last longer because of emotional input and internal dialogue, and therefore is not as easily dissipated. When physical action is not warranted, it is not performed, and the reaction becomes detrimental to the body (Weiner, 1982; Zegans, 1982).

Hans Selye, perhaps the most noted stress researcher, contributed a concept that is fundamental to the understanding of stress-related disease. In 1926, as a second-year medical student, he first noted that patients suffering from a number of diverse diseases displayed a common set of symptoms. At the time, he called this the "syndrome of just being sick" (Selye, 1974).

Selye took his interest of the "sick syndrome" into the laboratory, where he injected impure and toxic gland-preparations into laboratory animals. Regardless of the gland tissue and hormones injected, the animals developed a stereotyped syndrome (a set of symptoms that occur at the same time). These symptoms included increased activity and enlargement of the adrenal cortex, atrophy of the thymus gland and lymph nodes, and development of ulcers in the gastrointestinal system. Selye soon found that this same syndrome occurred in response to other kinds of stress: heat, cold, trauma, infection, and many others. This syndrome identified by Selye became known as the *biological stress syndrome* or the *general adaptation syndrome* (GAS). The three stages of the GAS are alarm, resistance, and exhaustion (Selye, 1956). (See Figure 3.2.)

*Alarm* is the initial response to a stressor. In the alarm stage the body shows generalized stress arousal. This stage is characterized by widespread sympathetic discharge; increased ACTH secretion by the pituitary; and stimulation of the adrenal glands. Adrenal stimulation in turn assists in the full-blown fight-or-flight response. The body shows generalized stress arousal, but no one specific organ system is affected, although most and in some cases all of the body systems show measurable changes.

The *resistance* stage is marked by the channeling of the arousal into one or several organ systems. Decreases in ACTH occur, as does *specificity of adaptation*—the channeling of the stress response into the specific organ system or process most capable of dealing with it. However, it is this adaptation process that contributes to stress-related illness. The specific organ system becomes aroused, and with prolonged arousal and chronic resistance it may fatigue and begin to malfunction. As the system deteriorates, problems specific to the system begin. For example, stress arousal in some parts of the nervous or cardiovascular systems can produce life-threatening debilitation in a short time. The human body, which is programmed to survive, seems to channel the arousal into less sensitive systems such as the muscular system, thereby reducing the immediate danger to the body.

The resistance stage becomes particularly troublesome when

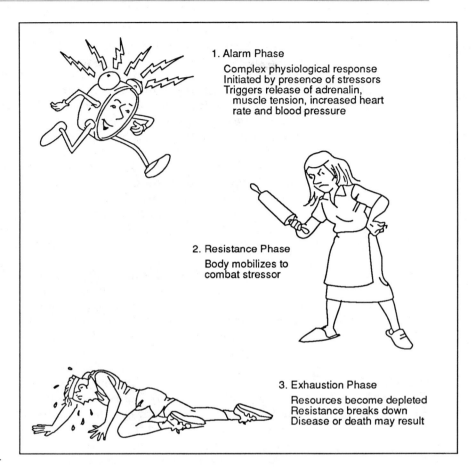

1. Alarm Phase

   Complex physiological response
   Initiated by presence of stressors
   Triggers release of adrenalin,
      muscle tension, increased heart
      rate and blood pressure

2. Resistance Phase

   Body mobilizes to
   combat stressor

3. Exhaustion Phase

   Resources become depleted
   Resistance breaks down
   Disease or death may result

**FIGURE 3.2**

General Adaptation
Syndrome

resistance goes beyond responding to the initial stressor. It is as though the body has learned a new mode of defensive adaptation and continues it until it becomes a disease or condition in itself. Rossi (1986) explains:

> The psychosomatic mode of adaptation was learned during a special (usually traumatic) state-dependent psychophysiological condition; it continues because it remains state-bound or locked into that special psychophysiological condition even after the patient apparently returns to his normal mode of functioning (p. 59).

*Exhaustion* occurs after prolonged stress because the organs and systems of resistance have been depleted of their energy to perform. During this final stage, the organ system or process involved in the repeated stress response breaks down. ACTH secretion increases, and the response takes on the generalized character of the alarm stage.

In the stage of exhaustion, disease or malfunction of the organ system or even death may occur. Sometimes exhaustion of one weakened system will shift the resistance to a stronger system, forcing that system into the adaptation process. To illustrate the damage that can be caused by adaptation, let's consider hypertension as a response to stress. The body can adapt to high blood pressure without constantly eliciting an alarm reaction, but the increased pressure promotes kidney and heart damage, which can eventually kill the individual if the situation is allowed to continue. Adaptation may be a lifesaving process, but it must also be recognized as a type of disease process. In fact, Selye often referred to stress-related diseases as "diseases of adaptation" (Shontz, 1982).

To Selye, stress was more than a response; it was a process that enabled the body to resist the stressor in the best possible way by enhancing the functioning of the organ system best able to respond to the stressor.

The following sections describe how the major systems of the body respond to stress.

**THE MUSCLES'
RESPONSE**

The muscles are our only means of expression. We cannot move toward pleasure or away from danger without muscle movements. Speech, facial expression, eye movements, indeed every mode of expression, feeling, and resolution of an emotion is achieved through muscle movement. Yet the muscles are under the command of the will, awaiting orders and obligingly obeying them. Oddly enough, many of the orders are given subconsciously, are counterproductive, and contribute significantly to stress and tension. This is because chronically tense muscles (1) complete a feedback loop and further stimulate the mind, resulting in greater stress states, and (2) result in numerous psychosomatic disorders, including headache, backache, spasms of the esophagus and colon (the latter resulting in either diarrhea or constipation), posture problems, asthma, tightness in the throat and chest cavity, some eye problems, lockjaw, muscle tears and pulls, and perhaps rheumatoid arthritis.

It is important here to reemphasize the word *chronic*. Stress disorders are caused by chronic, long-term overactivity. Acute, even violent, muscle contractions are not as harmful to the body as are slight or moderate contractions sustained over a long period.

Muscles have only two states, *contraction* and *relaxation*—although there are varying degrees of contraction, called *tension*. When relaxation occurs, there is an absence of muscle contraction or tension. In this sense, activities that we commonly term *relaxation* (as in the sentence "I am going to the movies to relax") are better termed *recreation*. Movies may be recreational, but seldom do they produce muscle relaxation.

A muscle is a mass of millions of cells that can shorten when stimulated by nerve impulses. This shortening moves bones, traction occurs, tension develops, but no work is done. It is this situation that is referred to as *muscle tension* and is linked with the psychosomatic disorders previously mentioned. Pain probably develops because a partially contracted muscle closes a blood vessel, causing an inadequate amount of blood to be delivered to the tissues. Pain can also develop when a chronically shortened muscle exerts an abnormal pulling pressure on a joint; when a chronically shortened muscle is overexerted and its fibers thereby torn; or when the proper function of an organ is disrupted, which is the case in smooth-muscle disorders such as diarrhea, constipation, and esophageal spasms.

It is possible to measure the strength of a muscle contraction, or muscle tension, by placing electrodes on the muscle before it is contracted. This is accomplished through the use of an instrument called an *electromyograph* (EMG). The electrical activity of the muscle is sensed, amplified (the electric potential of muscle fibers is measured in microvolts, or millionths of volts), integrated, and recorded. The signal can be converted to a light or a sound and then fed back to the subject, in which case the EMG becomes a biofeedback device. Any muscle in the body can be measured in this manner. Thus, keying into muscle tension is relatively simple: back muscles would be most indicative of backache, while certain head and neck muscles can indicate general muscle tension associated with mental work, stress, and frustration.

Even though muscles maintain their own resting level of contraction, purposeful movement is under the control of the central voluntary parts of the brain, primarily the cerebellum and motor cortex. The most specific and exacting control comes from the motor cortex, which contains specific areas corresponding to particular areas of the body, such as the finger area, leg area, and neck area. Stimulation of any of these areas of the brain results in the movement of muscles in the corresponding body area. When the brain finally decides on an action, impulses are directed from the motor cortex, and the muscle contracts.

Remember that muscles receive only two commands—contract or relax; this is the limit of their capabilities. A finely coordinated action involves an unbelievable number of contract and relax commands, the sequence of which must be learned, practiced, and stored in the memory. Even then a coordinated movement is impossible without constant feedback about the result of the contraction. This feedback allows you to instantly approve and refine the muscle action until your brain can accomplish the act without your conscious control; you only have to think "Pick up the pencil," not figure out how to accomplish the act.

Let's now consider this in relation to stressful muscle tension. Imagine a potentially threatening situation in which you are contemplating some defensive action. You think defensively, you prepare to move, and you automatically assume a defensive posture. Whether you are correct in interpreting the situation as a threat is not important. What is important is that you have engrams (learned patterns) for this type of reaction, and they can be assumed without your consciously thinking about it. The muscle action for bracing, defensive posturing, or preparing for action can be completed even though your mind is not consciously considering such action. So you can see how hidden fears or anger can result in chronic stressful muscle tension.

Although anticipation is necessary for preparation, it has been found that muscle tension develops and remains until the task is completed or the mind is diverted to a new thought process. Interestingly enough, successful completion of a task results in more rapid resolution of muscle tension than does failure to complete the task. Also, if you imagine a muscle movement or an action (for example, a defensive posture), you will experience the same preparatory muscle tension that occurs when you are actually engaging in the activity. This may explain why highly anxious people who are often in a high state of expectation often prove to have a great amount of muscle tension.

The muscle tension and movements described in the last few paragraphs are controlled by the motor cortex of the brain. Impulses from the motor cortex are normally carried to the muscles by the spinal cord and a cable of neurons called the *pyramidal tract*. In addition, a pathway called the *extrapyramidal motor system* sends signals from the hypothalamus and upper limbic area to the muscles. Stimulation through this pathway causes a variety of unconscious postures and rhythmic movements. Like the reticular formation, discussed in Chapter 2, this system seems to be both specific and nonspecific. Nonspecific activation may result in *nonspecific tonus*, or increased general tension throughout the system. This hidden state of tension may last over time and can augment a "voluntary" bracing action or cause a muscular overreaction.

Either stimulation results in chronic muscle tension, which can lead to illness. Of course, relaxation can replace tension if the inherent rhythm is dominated by a low-arousal, tranquil rhythm. Such is the purpose of the relaxation exercises and techniques given in Chapters 11–17.

**THE GASTRO-INTESTINAL RESPONSE**

When Hans Selye conducted his classic experiments on stressed laboratory animals, he found ulcerations of the stomach lining to be one of the responses. But why would the gastrointestinal (GI) system be involved? It serves no function in the fight-or-flight response and logically should not be controlled by the parts of the brain that anticipate or interpret possible threats. Yet, GI disorders are responsible for filling more hospital beds in the country than are any others, and science has clearly established that many GI disorders have psychological roots.

The gastrointestinal system (Figure 3.3) is responsible for accepting food, mechanically breaking it down by churning it in the

FIGURE 3.3

The Gastrointestinal System

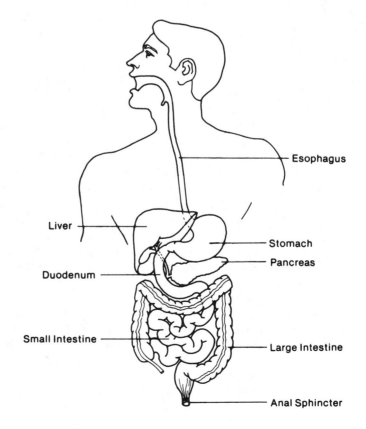

Esophagus

Liver

Stomach

Pancreas

Duodenum

Small Intestine

Large Intestine

Anal Sphincter

stomach, moving it through the intestines and supplying enzymes that will finally convert small food particles into the blood sugar, simple fatty acids, or amino acids the body uses for energy or for building tissue. The GI system has an inherent rhythm and is governed by numerous automatic reflexes that control its movements, its emptying, and its secretion of enzymes. The GI system is also associated with the motivation system, in that hunger must lead to food-gathering behavior. The centers that control hunger and appetite are located in the hypothalamus and are closely related to pleasure and unpleasure (see the discussion of the limbic system in Chapter 2). Hunger and satiety are definitely emotional states, so perhaps the newer limbic pleasure centers have opened a Pandora's box and allowed other emotions to likewise affect the functioning of the GI system.

The GI system responds to emotional situations in a more complex manner than the typical sympathetic versus parasympathetic process described in the preceding chapter. Also, an understanding of the GI system dispels the stereotype that the sympathetic system arouses and the parasympathetic relaxes, for overstimulation of either of those two divisions of the autonomic nervous system can result in disease.

Response to stress arousal can be measured in every structure along the alimentary canal, starting with the mouth. Since Pavlov's classic studies, it has been clearly demonstrated that emotional states influence the flow of saliva. You may have had the experience of getting up before an audience to deliver a speech and finding your mouth dry. This occurrence has long been used as a measure of fear: in ancient China suspected criminals were made to chew rice, and the lack of a mucous wad was taken as an indication of guilt. Yet, seeing the dentist preparing to drill a tooth often turns on saliva to the point that the dentist must continuously vacuum it away.

The emotions can also induce spastic contraction of the muscles in the esophagus, which leads to the stomach. This disrupts peristalsis (the rhythmic movement that carries food through the digestive system) and makes swallowing difficult and in some situations impossible.

The stomach, too, has been recognized as part of the emotional response system. Most anxiety tests take into consideration the state of the stomach. Statements such as "I have no appetite," "I have a gnawing feeling in the pit of my stomach," and "I feel nauseated" are the most often described physical symptoms of anxiety and emotional arousal.

Doctors have been able to observe the activity in the stomach lining. They have noted that in situations producing anger, resentment, or aggression, the lining increases its secretions of hydrochloric acid and various enzymes and becomes engorged with blood. The membrane eventually becomes so frail that eruptions occur spontaneously and ulcerations develop. Situations producing fright, depression, listlessness, and withdrawal produce the opposite reaction—the stomach lining functions below its normal level. But even that situation is not without problems: Decreasing the blood flow to the secreting glands lessens the natural protection of the area against certain harsh substances such as hydrochloric acid, which helps break down food in the stomach.

In the intestines, similar patterns have been observed. Stress arousal has been shown to alter peristaltic rhythm. This alteration in normal peristalsis in both the small and large intestines is responsible for two of the most classic stress responses: diarrhea, if movements are too fast and normal drying through water absorption does not take place; and constipation, if movement through the intestines is very slow and there is excessive drying. Chronic constipation can lead to more severe intestinal blockage. Blockage of the bile and pancreatic ducts as well as inflammation of the pancreas (pancreatitis) have been linked with stress arousal, although little research has been conducted in this area.

## THE BRAIN'S RESPONSE

Even though we discussed the brain as part of the control system (see Chapter 2), we can also view it as a response system, because its electrical activity can be analyzed. First, we should understand how its nerve cells function. These neurons constantly exchange ions (atoms that carry tiny electrical charges) across their cell membranes. This activity forms wave patterns, which can be followed through the use of an *electroencephalograph* (EEG). This instrument measures the frequency or rate of the wave pattern in cycles per second, or hertz (Hz). Unlike the muscles, which remain electrically inactive until they are stimulated to action, the cells of the brain emit a constant electrical rhythm.

The dominant, quiet rhythm of the brain has been designated by the Greek letter alpha. It is characterized by a wave pattern that fluctuates at the rate of 8 to 13 cycles per second, and it emits energy that typically varies from 25 to 100 microvolts. An increase in the activity of the brain changes this basic alpha rhythm, producing a wave pattern that is higher in frequency (13 to 50 cycles per second) but emits less energy. This faster wave of lesser voltage has been designated as beta. Another common wave pattern, called theta, fluctuates between 4 and 7 cycles per second, and an even slower wave pattern, delta, fluctuates at less than 4 cycles per second and usually occurs only during sleep.

Analysis of complex brain-wave patterns has been used to diagnose abnormal brain states. More recently, the practice of referring to wave patterns to describe various activation states has become popular. The alpha wave has been associated with the absence of meaningful cause-and-effect thinking; this is a quiet state of mind in which stress arousal is at a minimum. The beta pattern is characterized by a focusing of attention, problem solving, and relating the self to the external world. While this is not necessarily a stressful state, stress arousal is more possible in the beta state. Less is known about the mental state associated with the theta pattern, although researchers report that the thought patterns are directed internally and are less related to specific external events. Daydreams, fantasies, and what some researchers term "creative images" are more likely to occur during the theta state. More information on the brain wave and its associated mental states is presented in the chapters on biofeedback and meditation.

Apart from the more measurable physical responses of the brain to stress, there are psychological or mood responses as well. During rest and relaxation, the brain is said to be in *homeostasis*, meaning that the subjective moods of the individual are in harmony, promoting a healthful relationship between mind and body. During stress, the psychological mechanisms of the mind are thrown into turmoil. A "mood disturbance" is one common characteristic of the stress reaction. Stress commonly elicits confusion, fear, extreme emotional sensitivity, and feeling of ego-threat. Many researchers feel that schizophrenia, a severe state of being out of touch with reality, is a way of compensating for the excessive trauma of life. Schizophrenics simply become unable to cope with the stresses of reality through traditional coping mechanisms, and unconsciously decide to remove themselves from reality to escape those stresses. In support of this theory, there has been some success in returning schizophrenics to reality by providing warm and supportive environments.

**THE CARDIO-VASCULAR RESPONSE**

Not all diseases are psychosomatic, and not all of the psychosomatic diseases can be considered psychogenic (see the description of psychosomatic diseases in Chapter 1). However, in the case of cardiovascular disease, it is almost impossible to completely rule out the role of stress. The question is exactly how much of a contributor stress is in relation to the other risk factors. The answer is obscured by the indirect nature of stress and the long-term development of this chronic disease.

Diseases of the cardiovascular system (Figure 3.4) include problems related to the heart itself (its basic structure and rhythm), to systemic blood flow and blood pressure, to the structure of the blood vessels, and to the constituency of the blood. It is obvious that each aspect cannot be considered separately from the others; they are all intricately related, and malfunction of one affects the others.

The heart's job is to pump blood to the cells of the body. The

**FIGURE 3.4**

The Cardiovascular System

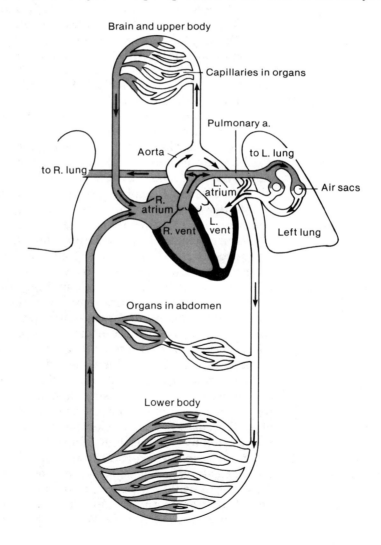

blood contains oxygen and energy-producing substances, which are the basic necessities for the life of the cell. To pump blood, the heart, a cavity surrounded by muscle, must contract. As the muscle contracts, the cavity becomes smaller. This increases the pressure of the blood within the chamber. When the pressure in the cavity is greater than that outside it, the blood is ejected into the miles of blood vessels, arteries, and veins that travel to every part of the body. Each blood vessel contracts in a similar manner, thus helping to maintain the pressure and aid the movement of the blood traveling through the system. Once ejected, the blood is pushed along under pressure, which in the average adult male is about 120 mmHg (slightly less for females). When the heart completes its contraction phase, it relaxes and the pressure in the system drops to about 80 mmHg in the average male (again, slightly less for females). These pressure indications (120/80) are used to express blood pressure, which is easily measured by a cufflike instrument called a *sphygmomanometer.*

It should be obvious that the fewer times a heart must contract or beat to accomplish the necessary supply functions, the more rest it will get. The heart has an inherent rhythm that is determined by the membrane potential of a special area in the right atrium called the *pacemaker*. Even when the heart is denied nervous stimulation, it is capable of independent action; however, the heart is constantly receiving impulses from the brain, and its inherent rhythm is continually influenced by the central nervous system. The heart receives impulses from both the sympathetic and parasympathetic nervous systems (see Chapter 2). Thus, it is under moment-to-moment control by various centers of the brain that are in touch with the metabolic and physiological demands of the body. In addition to neural regulation, the heart can also be influenced by the hormone epinephrine, which can increase the contractibility of the heart muscle (the *myocardium*), increasing the speed and strength of the contraction.

A significant survival mechanism of the cardiovascular system is that the heart is capable of anticipating physiological and metabolic demands by increasing its action before it actually has to. As we have seen, however, the anticipation of such demands very often increases the activity of the system, but then the final action is thwarted by the conscious cortex. In this case, the cardiovascular response is to no avail. Similarly, many psychological states increase cardiovascular activity when no action is actually required. A new or unusual experience frequently elevates the heart rate, as does fear, anger, anxiety, and most situations that threaten the ego. You will recall Harold Wolff's definition of stress as a physical response to a psychological or symbolic threat that is inappropriate in kind and intensity in our complex society; stressors are usually symbolic, requiring no physical action. But our response is nevertheless physical. Thus, a chronically stressed person often has a chronically overworked heart.

Another cardiovascular problem related to stress is chronically elevated blood pressure, or *hypertension.* It has been estimated that perhaps 15 to 20 percent of the adult population suffers from hypertension, usually considered to be a pressure above 160/95. Approximately 90 percent of the cases are called *essential hypertension,* meaning the origin is unknown. Since the primary work of the heart is to overcome the pressure in the arteries to which the blood must flow, high blood pressure greatly increases the work of the heart and contributes to cardiovascular problems.

Like the heart, the blood vessels have an inherent tone that can be altered moment to moment by both parts of the autonomic nervous system and by hormones (epinephrine and norepinephrine) to reflect the physiological demands placed on the system. Anticipation and psychological states such as fear, anger, and anxiety will alter the diameter of blood vessels, producing a physical response to symbolic or imagined threats.

A third problem concerning the cardiovascular system is *atherosclerosis,* the destruction of the vessels by the infusion of fatty plaques, which contain cholestrol, triglycerides, and other fatty elements. The relationship between stress and vascular problems appears to be that during stress arousal, the hormones epinephrine and cortisol mobilize fats and cholesterol for use by the muscles, and the fats and cholesterol circulate in the bloodstream until they are used or reabsorbed. (The process was described in Chapter 2.) Although there are many factors in the development of atherosclerosis, constantly saturating the system with unneeded fats through the stress mechanism can only exacerbate the problem.

An artery infused with such plaques will eventually lose elasticity and harden, producing *arteriosclerosis* (an advanced form of atherosclerosis). This disease is directly responsible for over half a million deaths annually in the United States.

When an artery in an advanced state of disease loses its elasticity, it elevates the blood pressure, thus contributing to hypertension and disease of the heart itself. In addition, atherosclerotic plaques, by narrowing the diameter of the blood vessels, diminish oxygen delivery and may bring on a *myocardial infarction,* or heart attack, if the coronary arteries are affected.

Many factors contribute to the development of atherosclerosis and hypertension, including a diet high in cholesterol and saturated fats (which add to the amount of potential fatty deposits in the blood vessels), lack of exercise (which decreases the utilization of these nutrients), smoking (which mimics sympathetic nervous system stimulation, narrowing the blood vessels and increasing the heartbeat), obesity, sex (males are more at risk), age, heredity, and, of course, stress, which underlies many of the others.

Another vascular problem associated with stress is the *vascular headache*, also known as the *migraine headache*. Migraines are thought to be caused by an exaggerated constriction of blood vessels in and around the brain followed by a reflex dilation or enlarging of those vessels, which causes the release of toxic chemicals that irritate local nerve endings and add to the pain. The root of this type of attack is complex and appears to involve, in a headache-prone individual, a psychogenic trigger of the sympathetic nervous system, which then causes the initial constriction of the blood vessels. This phase, known as the *prodromal phase*, is characterized by nausea, increased irritability, and an unusual sensitivity to noise and light. Physiologically, this phase seems to deplete the level of the hormone *serotonin* in the system. It may be the loss of this hormone that causes the reflex dilation of the vessels and the accompanying intense pain.

Little is known of the underlying cause of migraine. The migraine-prone individual may have abnormal metabolism of serotonin, or may be deficient in an enzyme that oxidizes this hormone. Recent clinical investigations have shown that certain types of migraine headaches can be alleviated by controlling the central nervous system through elaborate relaxation training. This points not to the alleviation of any chemical imbalance, but to control over the initial psychogenic trigger.

**THE SKIN'S RESPONSE**

It is sometimes difficult to think of the skin as a separate system capable of responding to stress arousal, but its complex function and intricate nervous control make it a sensitive response system and its accessibility makes it a convenient window into the body. When you observe the stress response of any body system, you are looking through that system into the mental activity responsible for the response.

The skin has two basic response patterns that show the world what is going on in the body and in the mind. One is often referred to as *electrical language*, because it seems to speak if you have the proper listening device. Each of the millions of cells that make up the skin system contains chemicals that have an electrical nature. As the body expresses itself, the chemical activity of the skin cells changes, producing different patterns of electrical activity. This electrical activity can be measured on the skin surface. The constant but ever-changing activity of the skin appears as "chatter," and although complex and sometimes difficult to interpret, it is used by police authorities in most lie-detector systems and by health professionals to help understand an individual's emotions, motivations, and problem-solving techniques.

The second basic response system of the skin is its temperature. There are small blood vessels under the skin that change in response to emotion. During tense, anxious periods they shut down and allow less blood to pass, causing the skin to appear pale and the skin temperature to decrease. At other times, the blood vessels open and allow the skin to flush with blood, thus increasing the skin temperature.

With this type of response pattern, it is not hard to visualize how prolonged emotional responses could change the activity of the skin long enough to result in malfunction and disease. Certain skin conditions or illnesses have been found to have roots in our psychological response patterns. For example, eczema, a skin lesion characterized by redness, swelling, itching, and fluid discharge, has been associated with emotional stimulation. The reddening and itching are indicative of abnormal blood flow to the area, while the fluid discharge is indicative of an increased rate of fluid production by the skin cells. Laboratory studies have established that in eczema-prone individuals, emotional arousal increases the amount of fluid exuded by the skin cells, while relaxation diminishes it. Eczema patients have been classified as being restless, impatient, and unduly irritable, but the relationship of these characteristics to the skin condition has not been clearly established.

Similar preliminary work has been done with patients suffering from urticaria (hives), psoriasis, and acne, but these investigations are still in their infancy.

## THE IMMUNE SYSTEM'S RESPONSE

### Structure and Function of the Immune System

The immune system (see Figure 3.5) provides natural and acquired defense against foreign elements that enter the body through the air we breathe, the food we eat, or in other ways. The immunity we are born with, *innate immunity*, is provided by the skin, the acidic secretions of the stomach, mobile white blood cells, and other natural body structures and biochemicals that defend against all invaders in a nonspecific manner. Also, we develop what is called *acquired immunity*. This is a process whereby the body recognizes foreign agents called *antigens* (bacteria, toxins, and viruses) and responds to each by producing antibodies specific to it. There are two lines of acquired immunity defense, *humoral* and *cellular*,

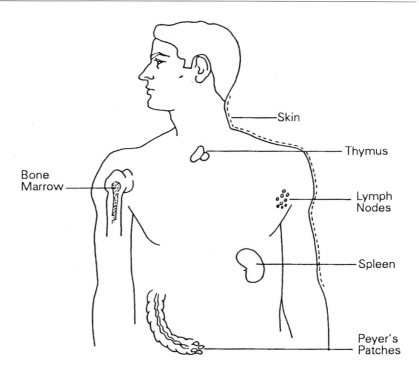

**FIGURE 3.5**

Major Centers of
Immune System
Tissue

which are very important to our discussion of stress and psychosomatic disease. Both originate in the bone marrow, where undif-
ferentiated stem cells are produced.

In humoral immunity, the stem cells migrate from the bone
marrow to the various lymphatic tissues throughout the body (see
Figure 3.5), where they mature into white blood cells called *beta-
cell lymphocytes* (B-cells). When an antigen enters the body and is
taken up by the bloodstream, it is detected by the B-cells as the
blood is filtered through the lymph nodes, spleen, and so on. The
antigen serves to stimulate the B-cells to evolve into plasma cells
that then synthesize specific antibodies that attack the invading
antigen. Figure 3.6 depicts this process.

The development of cellular immunity is similar to that of
humoral immunity, except that the stem cells of the bone marrow
travel to the thymus gland, where they mature into *T-cell lymphocytes* (T-cells) that attack invading antigens directly. Some of these
T-cells travel to the skin to make the entire surface of the body
part of the immune system (Edelson & Fink, 1985). It is important
to the discussion of stress and psychosomatic disease to note that
T-cells and B-cells have receptor sites that respond to neurotrans-

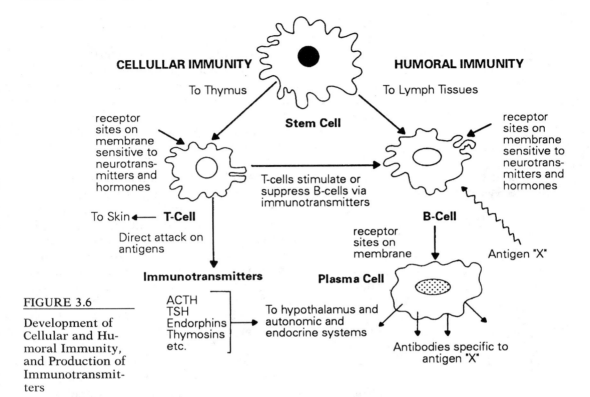

**FIGURE 3.6**

Development of Cellular and Humoral Immunity, and Production of Immunotransmitters

mitter substances of the autonomic nervous system and to hormones of the endocrine system. This means that immunity can be influenced by the control systems discussed in Chapter 2.

In the 1960s immunology came of age as a science, and it is now one of the most exciting branches of research into illness and disease, especially with the AIDS threat. For years, immunologists were so busy discovering the complexity of the immune system itself that they paid little attention to its communication with the other systems of the body. More recently, however, research in a new branch of immunology, *psychoneuroimmunology* (PNI), has begun uncovering the physiological mechanisms that control the intimate communication among the nervous, endocrine, and immune systems. It is this research that gives us the missing link between how our thoughts and emotions influence our health or disease states.

Immunological research has found that neurotransmitters (such as epinephrine and norepinephrine) can attach to immune cells and change their ability to multiply and destroy invading agents. Furthermore, research has identified the "hard-wiring" system of nerve fibers that transmit messages between the brain and lymphocytes that fight infection and cancer in the body (Ghanta, Hiramoto, Solvason & Spector, 1985; Solomon, 1985).

In addition to immune-cell response to neurotransmitters and hormones of the endocrine system, it is apparent that the immune system talks back to the other control systems through immuno-transmitters such as ACTH, thyroid-stimulating hormones, and other polypeptides such as the endorphins and thymosins. T-cells also have the ability to stimulate or suppress B-cells.

**Stress and the Immune System**

Our current knowledge of the coherent mechanisms of communication among the nervous, immune, and endocrine systems is altering the old medical belief that thoughts and emotions had nothing to do with disease. The medical findings of world-renowned physicians and researchers such as O. Carl Simonton, Stephanie Matthews-Simonton, Bernie S. Siegel, Joan Borysenko, and Jean Achterberg, to name a few, has led to widespread recognition that thoughts, emotions, attitudes, and beliefs have a great bearing on health, disease, and the ability to rebound from illness.

There are basically three ways that the immune system may become dysfunctional and lead to stress-related illnesses: (1) underactivity, (2) hyperactivity, and (3) misguided activity (Bowers & Kelly, 1979). Characteristic diseases caused by these three types of dysfunction are, respectively, cancer, asthma, and rheumatoid arthritis. Underactivity or depression of the immune system occurs in response to stress-induced release of adrenal cortex hormones. Various researchers (Shavit, Termin, Martin, Lewis, Liebeskind & Gale, 1985; Stein, Keller & Schleifer, 1985) have found that even slight depression of the immune system greatly increases susceptibility to pathogens. The hyperactive immune response seen in asthma involves a highly irritable mucosal lining of the lungs. When the lining is irritated, the resulting hyperimmune response can cause symptoms ranging from mild discomfort to respiratory failure. Autoimmune diseases are examples of a misguided immune system that attacks its own tissues as well as those of invading antigens. Autoimmune disorders are often associated with immune-deficiency syndromes, injuries, aging, and malignancies (Rossi, 1986). Breakdown in communication within the nervous, endocrine, and immune systems through neurotransmitters, endocrine hormones, and immunotransmitters is basic to all immune dysfunctions (Achterberg & Lawlis, 1984).

If stress arousal is prolonged, any or all of the biochemicals, organs, and systems involved will be affected until fatigue occurs. At that point, infections, common colds, and slight skin conditions appear. As the fatigue continues, the conditions worsen and more serious illnesses develop. When the immune response to disease elements is diminished by 50 to 60 percent, the body may respond with persistent and repeated infections requiring antibiotics, with summer colds, with serious skin-disease inflammation, and with chronic respiratory conditions such as bronchitis, asthma, or tuberculosis (Muramoto, 1988). Immune-system fatigue diminishes the body's ability to resist all invading viruses, bacteria, and toxins.

**THE PREVENTION AND TREATMENT OF PSYCHOSOMATIC DISEASES OF AROUSAL**

The allopathic or traditional medical establishment continues to be perplexed by psychosomatic diseases of adaptation. Selye (1974) suggested that medication could be given to counteract stress hormones that ravage the system, or that the adrenal glands could be removed surgically. He also noted that if a nonspecific shock could cause these conditions (which he characterized as "getting stuck in a groove"), perhaps various forms of nonspecific shock therapy could counteract the conditions. Since there is such clear evidence of a mind–body connection in the genesis of disease, there is growing acceptance in the medical community of the addition of more holistic practices in the fight against psychosomatic disease.

One of the most highly researched psychosomatic diseases is cancer, which will serve here as an example of how holistic modalities based on psychosomatic theory may facilitate healing. A major line of evidence of the mind–body connection in cancer centers in studies of life-change stress (Dohrenwend & Dohrenwend, 1974). It appears that any form of trauma involving a significant life-change can activate the cortical-hypothalamic-pituitary-adrenal response, producing the adrenal cortical hormones that suppress the immune cells that continually search out and destroy cancer cells in the system. In addition, a negative self-concept, depression, and anxiety are all associated with immune-system suppression or underactivity. Coping ability is also a significant factor in whether stress will have an immunodepressant effect or not (Locke, Kraus, Leserman, Hurst, Heisel & Williams, 1984).

To address the psychosomatic component of this disease directly, prevention of prolonged stress arousal is the first line of defense. Prevention can take the form of:

- learning to avoid stressful situations;
- cognitively restructuring or reframing events previously thought of as stressful (through assertiveness training, realistic setting and attaining of interpersonal and professional goals, and so on);
- learning to reduce the arousal tone of the central nervous system through meditation or other quieting activities.

If disease has become apparent, these preventive measures are also used in treatment (Siegel, 1986). In addition, active intervention in the form of imagery has been found helpful in some cases of cancer. The reasoning behind the use of imagery in fighting disease is that mind modulation of body processes is considered to be a psychoneurophysiological fact; if the mind can contribute to the sickness, it can also contribute to getting well. Matthews-Simonton, Simonton, and Creighton (1978) have successfully used imagery and the technique of cognitive reframing to treat cancer, and Hall (1982–83) has found that their methods seem to enhance cellular immunity. While such therapists and researchers as Hall and Matthews-Simonton, Simonton, and Creighton have found the use of active imagery to be successful, others such as Meares (1982–83) and Benson (1975) have approached prevention and treatment through quieting the mind. Herbert Benson's "relaxation response" was designed to bring about an inner stillness of central origin. Meares developed a form of intensive meditation (which he called "mental ataraxis") that was also designed to quiet the arousal of the cortical-limbic-hypothalamic hub and to create a mind state devoid of striving and protecting the ego. The combination of imagery and some form of meditation is used by most current practitioners of psychosomatic medicine (Rossi, 1986).

## REFERENCES

ACHTERBERG, J. (1985). *Imagery and healing*. Boston: Shambala.

ACHTERBERG, J., and G. LAWLIS (1984). *Imagery and disease*. Champaign, IL: Institute for Personality and Ability Testing.

ALEXANDER, F. (1965). *Psychosomatic medicine*. New York: W. W. Norton & Co., Inc.

BENSON, H. (1975). *The relaxation response*. New York: Avon.

BORYSENKO, JOAN. (1987). *Minding the body, mending the mind*. Reading, MA: Addison-Wesley.

BOWERS, K., and P. KELLY. Stress, disease, psychotherapy, and hypnosis. *Journal of Abnormal Psychology, 88*(5), 490–505.

DOHRENWEND, B., and B. DOHRENWEND (eds.) (1974). *Stressful life events: Their nature and effects*. New York: John Wiley.

EDELSON, R., and J. FINK (1985). The immunological function of the skin. *Scientific American*, June, 46–53.

GHANTA, V., R. HIRAMOTO, H. SOLVASON, and N. SPECTOR (1985). Neural and environmental influences on neoplasia and conditioning of NK activity. *Journal of Immunology, 135*(2), 848s–52s.

HALL, H. (1982–83). Hypnosis and the immune system: A review with implications for cancer and the psychology of healing. *American Journal of Clinical Hypnosis, 25*(2–3), 92–103.

Locke, S., L. Kraus, J. Leserman, M. Hurst, S. Heisel, and R. Williams (1984). Life change stress, psychiatric symptoms, and natural killer-cell activity. *Psychosomatic Medicine, 46,* 441–53.

Matthews-Simonton, S., C. O. Simonton, and J. L. Creighton. (1978). *Getting well again.* New York: Bantam.

Meares, A. (1982–83). A form of intensive meditation associated with the regression of cancer. *American Journal of Clincal Hypnosis, 25*(2–3), 114–21.

Muramoto, N. (1988). Natural immunity insights on diet and AIDS. *East/West Journal,* September, 50.

Rossi, E. (1986). *The psychobiology of mind–body healing.* New York: W. W. Norton & Co., Inc.

Selye, H. (1956). *The stress of life.* New York: McGraw-Hill.

———. (1974). *Stress without distress.* New York: Signet.

Shavit, Y., G. Termin, F. Martin, J. Lewis, J. Liebeskind, and R. Gale (1985). Stress, opiod peptides, the immune system, and cancer. *Journal of Immunology, 135*(2), 834s–37s.

Shontz, F. (1982). Adaptation to chronic illness and disability. In T. Millon, C. Green, and R. Meagher (eds.), *Handbook of clinical health psychology.* New York: Plenum.

Siegel, B. S. (1986). *Love, medicine and miracles: Lessons learned about self-healing from a surgeon's experience with exceptional patients.* New York: Harper & Row, Pub.

Solomon, G. (1985). The emerging field of psychoneuroimmunology with a special note on AIDS. *Advances, 2* (winter), 6–19.

Stein, M., S. Keller, and S. Schleifer (1985). Stress and immuno-modulation: The role of depression and neuroendocrine function. *Journal of Immunology, 135*(2), 827s–33s.

Wechsler, R. (1987). The new prescription: Mind over malady. *Discover,* February, 51–61.

Weiner, H. (1982). Psychosomatogenesis. In T. Millon, C. Green, and R. Meagher (eds.), *Handbook of clinical health psychology.* New York: Plenum.

Zegans, L. (1982). Stress and the development of somatic disorders. In L. Goldberger and S. Breznitz (eds.), *Handbook of stress.* New York: Free Press.

# CHAPTER FOUR

# Stressful Emotions, Thoughts, and Beliefs

**EMOTIONS**
An emotion is an energy complex made up of ideas, beliefs, attitudes, and opinions, as well as past experiences, postures, and actions. An emotion is not a single isolated thought, but a process involving energy and arousal combined with specific thoughts and physical reactions that are intended to give direction to the alleviation of a stressor. Richard Lazarus (1991) describes emotions as relational: they are always about person–environment relationships. Emotions have *valance*—a plus or minus, or "hot" or "cold"; they are never neutral. Emotions are basic to the way we think, act, and decide, and to what we believe to be true. Our emotions are basic motivators, they guard our basic needs, and they enrich and intensify our lives. We safeguard our lives not only by knowing not to eat something that doesn't smell or taste good, but also by recognizing when someone else is showing the emotions that may be important to our physical, mental, and emotional health. When these emotions are elicited in early childhood they are "anchored" as an energy form in our brain; the best theory at this time is that these memory experiences are formed as holograms in the mind.

According to Tomkins (1962), all babies are born with nine emotions programmed into their facial muscles (see box). These may be better understood as innate programs, or templates, that are precursors of our fully developed emotional processes. The emotional responses we learn early in life are reactions to our basic needs and to external stimuli. As we grow older we also create emotional patterns from our thoughts, based on our appraised significance of life events. We develop and practice these emotional patterns until they are fairly habitual reactions. Because we are taught directly or indirectly not to show our emotions, we develop negative self-talk that also becomes part of our emotional patterns. If we do not like the way an emotion feels or aren't allowed to have it, we may "block" it out of our consciousness altogether. This does not inhibit the emotional response, just our realization of its presence.

---

**Nine Innate Emotions**

*Primary Motivators:* Interest, Enjoyment, Surprise, Distress, Fear, Anger

*Auxiliary Emotion:* Shame

*Innate Defensive Responses:* Disgust, Dissmell

---

During the first year of life we develop and use primarily the old reptilian brain to sense and respond to the physical world. At about age two the midbrain begins to develop. The old brain still brings in all the outside messages, and the midbrain now begins coloring the information with "like" and "dislike." With the development of the midbrain, the child becomes not only a physical self, but also an emotional self, relating outside events with joy and laughter, fear and crying, love and happiness. These actions take on a stimulus–response form as memory patterns develop. For example, a child may form a negative emotional memory pattern from being left with a sitter when the parents go out. After the first traumatic time, the child may begin to cry whenever either parent merely prepares to leave. In fact, the child's reaction to early separations from the parents becomes the basis for his or her reaction to all separations and losses later on in life.

As growth and development continue, the functions of the neocortex are added to the functions of the midbrain and old brain. This makes it possible for the mere thought of the parents leaving to elicit in the child the emotional habit form of fear, anger, or even rage. Nothing external or physical has actually happened, such as the parents preparing to leave, calling a sitter, or telling the child that they plan to go out. But because the child can now think in "what if" terms, he or she can retrieve any emotional pattern having an experiential base. Accompanying this pattern may be subconscious beliefs such as "They must not love me or they wouldn't go away without me" and an even more basic belief,

"I must be an unlovable person" or "I must be a bad person." Left unchanged, these beliefs are carried into adulthood and used as a basis for other negative emotional experiences.

Most of us have blocked emotional memories of traumatic experiences in childhood, and according to Jackins (1978), when emotional energy is blocked, the mind loses its capacity to analyze, evaluate, and synthesize situations and experiences. When negative emotions from an experience are blocked, the mind cannot integrate the experience. What's more, the blocked emotional energy continues to build with new experiences that are like the original traumatic experience. This buildup further diminishes the ability of the mind to function clearly, and behavioral responses to the new stimulus become less logical because they are based on an experience that probably happened when we were not old enough, powerful enough, or skilled enough to do anything about it.

Because the emotional patterns we learn in response to actual, physical input are stored in our mind and body, we can subsequently stimulate them merely by thinking about them or by having a certain part of our body (where we hold the stress) stimulated. Through our ability to relive stressful situations, we learn how to scare ourselves to death, worry ourselves until we are distraught, and build the most harmless situation into a catastrophe. By the same token, however, we can retrieve pleasure, joy, laughter, and happiness by thinking about times when we felt those emotions.

## Emotional Energy

Emotion is an energy complex involving nerves, muscles, and glands. This energy is a neurophysiological pattern that readies the body for confrontation, retreat, expression, or no expression. Emotions are instantaneous forms of experience and reaction. When we are being emotional, we are expressing immediate physical reality, and this expression takes place before we can even be consciously aware of it. Our emotions are forms of immediate experience. When we are experiencing our emotions, we are in direct contact with our physical reality. Because the purpose of an emotion is to produce action, it is difficult to imagine an emotion without concurrent physical arousal specific to that action.

Emotional energy carries messages that we have named fear, anger, and so forth, on the basis of experience. Lazarus (1991) observes that whether or not there is a label or a universally correct word for an emotion, all of us have had the following emotional experiences:

1. anger—being slighted or demeaned
2. anxiety—facing existential threats

3. sadness—experiencing irrevocable loss
4. guilt—transgressing a moral imperative
5. shame—failing to live up to an ego ideal
6. envy—wanting something another has
7. jealousy—resenting a third person for having, seeming to have, or threatening what one wants
8. disgust—taking in or standing too close to (metaphorically speaking) an indigestible object or idea
9. hope—fearing the worst, yet yearning for better
10. happiness—making acceptable progress toward a goal
11. pride—experiencing enhancement of one's self, or one's social worth, by being credited for a highly valued object or accomplishment
12. gratitude—crediting another with an altruistic gift
13. love—desiring reciprocated affection from another valued person
14. compassion—being moved by another's suffering

These experiences are stored in the brain in the form of memory patterns, and when the body is triggered it responds with a pattern. To illustrate, take a moment to gasp as though you are surprised or frightened. Your body will instantly brace itself. The muscles contract, the lungs and heart modify their action, and, if this "as if" situation is taken to great extent, all systems involved in this emotion may alter their functions. Through nerve stimulation, the muscles tense, the heart beats faster and/or harder, respiration quickens and/or deepens, the pupils dilate, and glands are stimulated to either reduce or increase their secretions, depending on the function of the gland. The adrenals are stimulated and begin dumping out hormones to help answer the emergency signals that have been given at the brain level. The emergency signals reflect the perception of a situation that demands attention. The situation may be one of perceived joy or humor, or of perceived danger. Also, it may have its roots in the external world or within a thought pattern that has little external base. The response to the emergency signal is the emotional reaction pattern, or, as we first identfed it in this book, the stress response.

Emotions such as anger, happiness, and jealousy display motion more than fear, guilt, and contentment; yet all of them have a psychoneuroimmunological response pattern. Some PNI experts (for example, Wechsler, 1987) expect that we will eventually have a neurological-hormonal profile for each of the emotions, or perhaps we will be able to categorize emotional response patterns as either healthy or unhealthy by their impact on the immune system. Furthermore, the learning experience and cognitive control of each individual may help to place all of his or her emotions in the healthy category through recognition, restructuring the meaning of the emotion, and letting go of an "unhealthy" emotion once the associated emotional experience is over.

If an emotion you experience is positive, tension builds and then is released, perhaps as a shout or laughter. There is a sense of pleasure with the release of emotional tension. When the emotion is negative, tension builds up and tends to be stored. Usually, during this time negative self-talk increases the tension. King (1985) believes that all pain is caused by extreme and unrelieved tension. Emotional messages do not dissipate until they are delivered, and delivery means that the message is recognized and allowed to play itself out. When blocked-up emotion energy is released, certain body aches and pains may also go away.

## Stressful Emotional Patterns

Children learn very early that very few emotions are acceptable. At first, laughter and giggling are usually highly prized by adults, but as children grow into adolescents they quickly learn that loud laughter and silly giggling are not acceptable in public; they are rewarded for not crying, reprimanded harshly for displaying anger, and chided for being fearful. They are asked to not show that they have been emotionally hurt, to be selective about whom they should love, and to contain their exuberance. As a result, most adults engage in negative mind-talk when they get angry, when they are hurt or fearful, or even when they want to shriek with happiness and joy.

Because of the years of negative mind-talk that accompanies emotions, everyone denies emotions to some degree or another. When a person gets angry and says, "It's really silly to get mad," the emotion is not honored. But it happens anyway. And it is stored in a favorite place (or places) in the body along with all the other anger that has been denied and not released, there to become part of the phase of resistance described in Selye's GAS model. Release of an emotion is necessary before the body can go back to a relaxed healthy state, or back into balance. Most of us know the effectiveness of a good laugh or a good cry as a release to make us feel better.

Bradshaw (1990) points out that dysfunctional families deny their children the right to feel or to talk about feelings. This keeps the children from being in touch with what they are feeling, because they are first of all shamed out of expressing any feelings and moreover aren't allowed to talk about them. In some families, children are allowed to express only certain emotions, such as guilt.

By studying your emotions along with the physical symptoms

of illness you usually exhibit, you may be able to identify which emotion(s) may be the primary stress responder(s) in your life. In order to target those emotion(s) for resolution, complete the following exercise. Count how many times fear, anger, hurt, or other negative emotions are mentioned. If a certain emotional response predominates, there is a message there for you.

### *Exercise*

1. Think of a recent experience that stirred up negative emotions in you (these are usually stressful situations). Now close your eyes and take yourself back into that situation. See in your mind's eye where it occurred and who was there; get a very clear picture of the situation; listen to what everyone was saying, including what you were saying to yourself; allow yourself to experience the feelings you felt then and immediately afterwards. Also remember what you were saying to yourself after the experience.

2. Now identify all of your feelings during and after the situation by putting a check *in front of* any of the following emotions that apply:

"The situation I am remembering made me feel . . ."

| | |
|---|---|
| anxious | |
| lonely | |
| submissive | |
| confused | |
| inadequate | |
| irritated | |
| miserable | |
| critical | |
| discouraged | |
| foolish | |
| depressed | |
| enraged | |
| helpless | |
| guilty | |
| furious | |
| hostile | |
| bewildered | |
| embarrassed | |
| insecure | |
| bored | |
| jealous | |
| ashamed | |
| hateful | |
| insignificant | |
| rejected | |
| stupid | |
| inferior | |
| weak | |
| frustrated | |

3. The two major negative emotions are *anger* and *fear*. On the line after each feeling you have checked, write the one that better fits your feelings at the time. For example:

_____√_____ Rejected *Anger*        _____√_____ Insecure *Fear*

4. Count your responses in the list of feelings, and determine which of the two basic emotions (anger or fear) you identified with more often.

5. Write down some of the phrases you were saying to yourself *during* the situation:

6. Write down some of the phrases you were saying to yourself *after* the situation:

**THOUGHTS AND BELIEFS**

Once we have recognized an emotional pattern (whether it is "stuffed" or not), it tells us about our basic attitudes and opinions. There is always a belief, attitude, or opinion that coincides with our emotional response to a situation. Most of the time, we are not aware of the thought pattern because the reaction is a habit, not a well thought out response. To change a negative emotional reaction, we must perform five basic operations:

1. Recognize and honor the emotion rather than deny, repress, rationalize, or otherwise not honor it.
2. Break the habitual loop that the emotion triggers.
3. Identify the negative thought complex behind the negative emotion.
4. Replace the negative thought complex with a new, positive thought complex.
5. Respond to situations from the new belief complex.

At the core of our being is the basic belief structure that has guided our thoughts and actions throughout our lives. Positive changes must be made at this level so that they reflect a change in our perceptions, and in turn in the way our bodies react to mental and emotional input.

Our state of health, physical development, coping behaviors, moods, feelings, emotional response, and level of stress are all expressions of ideas, and are all subject to alteration by a change in thoughts (King, 1985). Our thinking or belief system is the ultimate control system in our lives. The conscious mind attempts to control our stress by controlling our actions and behaviors. Control is the way we function to meet our needs. When our mind focuses on some goal, our thoughts can control and manipulate our world until we achieve the goal.

If we don't wish to display our emotions, we can suppress them with our mind. If we can't control our physiology by covering up symptoms (such as by using a deodorant or taking drugs), our mind can choose to ignore the symptoms up to the point of endangering our health. On the positive side, our thought system can change stressful situations into controlled ones. If we are depressed or unhappy, we can choose to do activities we did when we felt good, and these are likely to make us feel better (Glasser, 1984).

We choose various behaviors to control overload in our life. If life's events are overloading our system we sometimes choose to gain control by withdrawing and doing nothing. Sometimes such behavior may be maladaptive, as in the case of illness, misery, or depression, indicating that we have outrun our positive coping ability. Illness, misery, or depression may eventually cause another stressful situation in the long run, but at least for the moment the stress is being controlled. Glasser felt that people sometimes choose the stress of misery or depression as a mechanism to control their anger, as an attempt to get others to help when they are afraid to ask, as an excuse for their unwillingness to do something more effective, or simply to manipulate others into doing what they themselves want. Illness, alcohol abuse, and drug abuse are other common ways of attempting to gain control.

Control may be thought of as the use of thoughts and behavior in an attempt to reduce conflict. One of the most basic conflicts is between what is real and what is ideal. Anthropologists long ago determined that discrepancies between the real and the ideal cause value crises for individuals and societies. Children are usually taught through socialization to desire very high ideals, which are often impractical as behaviors for adults. For example, achievement and/or success is a taught value, but its cost to health, happiness, and integrity is not usually discussed. The core of a stress response may be a constant striving for the unattainable, carrying with it the negative thoughts and self-talk that accompany failure to reach goals in our society.

Thus far we have noted that the physical body is aroused by

emotions. Emotions may be thought of as the intermediary between the body and the thinking brain. In the final analysis, most stress stems from the thought process. Patent (1984) pointed out that we have 50,000 or more thoughts a day (most of them identical to ones we had the day before) and that the majority of our thoughts are beliefs from which we interpret the world around us.

**Thoughts**

*Thought* refers to all complex interactions and transformations performed on the information taken in from the environment. Thought requires a store of information on the self, the environment, and the interaction between the two. The thought process can be found in both the conscious-awareness mode and the nonconscious, nonawareness mode. An example of how our thought processes are involved in the stress reaction can be seen in perhaps the most typical stressful situation—psychological stress, or "thought overload." As unlimited as the mind may seem, it does appear to have a limited capacity for attention—perhaps nature's way of limiting the potential confusion of thought overload. When overloaded, the mind reverts to habitual responses rather than thinking things through logically. We take short cuts and often eliminate the important step needed to properly utilize our capacity to make good choices. Just as the short cuts people take from sidewalk to sidewalk wear paths in the grass, so our "thinking short cuts" become well-used thought patterns or habits. It is these short cuts that become our patterned responses to stressful situations. The quick response of paranoia to a threat often replaces rational thought and can become a patterned, maladaptive thought process.

In addition, when our body function is disrupted and we are stressed, we are burdened with another potential overloading factor. Our survival program dictates that the brain attend to important messages from the body even though they consume thought capacity. If one of these messages concerns a nagging physical symptom and another an overwhelming stressful emotion, these will have a significant impact on the ability of the system to function properly. As we have seen, the autonomic nervous system supports the thinking process. It provides background action necessary for vigilance or potential action. Under optimal conditions it is silent. When it becomes hyperaroused its input is no longer supportive; rather, it takes the leading role. Primary thought processes are sidetracked or slowed by the disruption, and in this way thought efficiency decreases. Anxiety and anxious reactivity are examples of this phenomenon.

People become aware of stress arousal or emotions when their normal actions are disrupted. We have seen that the adaptive function of the stress response is to bring into conscious awareness a potentially life-threatening problem. When emotional and physical arousal fight for attention the autonomic system begins to receive an error message, which must be attended to before additional processing can be resumed. However, the human organism has the capacity to override error messages. This capacity is a survival adaptation that allows us to function (albeit at a diminished capacity) even when malfunction messages are received. As we have seen, Hans Selye referred to diseases that result from this process as "diseases of adaptation." For example, the body can "turn off" the stress alarm in the face of chronic hypertension and physically appear to adapt; however a stroke may eventually result from the chronically elevated blood pressure. The psychological-adaptation process of denial allows one to ignore a problem until finally an excessive buildup of anger erupts in skin problems, ulcers, or excessively violent behavior.

We do not think as clearly during stress as when we are relaxed. This often leads to coping techniques that are not useful, and if these tactics are used too often they become negative habits. Anger, for example, is often used to get others to stop pushing us. During overload it may become our habitual way of controlling stress. Anger used consistently is maladaptive and usually causes additional stress.

Thoughts allow us to anticipate a situation, assume a defensive posture, and increase background arousal if necessary. In a situation of prolonged stress arousal, thinking efficiency may be decreased due to overload. What we believe dictates how we will react to a stressor and what we will experience from the situation. We maintain control by taking small steps that do not exceed our ability to cope.

Small steps may require new behaviors that we can manage. This is called *competent coping*. Large steps, in the form of behaviors that challenge deep beliefs, usually force us beyond our normal ability to cope, and recruitment occurs. *Recruitment* is the use of maladaptive behaviors—for example, ego defense, rationalization, withdrawal, and illness. Attempts to control stress in times of overload usually result in *maladaptive coping*. A feeling of being out of control is usually the result of too much input demanding too many responses.

## Beliefs

Beliefs are enduring patterns of thought. Most beliefs are learned early in life from parents, relatives, peers, and authority figures. The beliefs we accept from others or form on our own become the programs that determine behavior on mental, physical, and spiritual levels. A true belief is a nonconflicted, solid idea that governs our day-to-day thoughts and actions. The beliefs we hold about ourselves and about life in general are the foundations for all our behavior. Beliefs provide a framework through which we measure, analyze, and evaluate experience, a framework that determines our response to experience. As such, beliefs provide a sense of security, even when an experience is negative. To be able to function in this world, we must have beliefs.

If information about reality is not consciously rejected by our mind, or if it doesn't directly conflict with our existing beliefs, then we accept it as true. Once incorporated as a belief, the information is generally forgotten, even though it continues to operate. This does not mean that beliefs are lost to conscious awareness, only that the mind no longer pays attention to them. It is something like having money in the bank. Even though we may not be using it right now, it influences how we live and affects many of our decisions. In the case of beliefs, they become such a familiar way of interpreting the world that we take them completely for granted.

Self-image is an example of a belief, a base, or a foundation upon which an individual's entire personality and behavior (and, eventually, reaction to stressors) are built. For example, if the self-image is strong and positive, day-to-day experiences will seem to verify that, and thereby strengthen self-image, and a beneficent cycle is set up. If the self-image is weak or negative, day-to-day experiences will likewise seem to verify that, and thereby weaken self-image.

Beliefs act as guidance systems for the flow of life. Where there is conflict, the flow is distorted, and this distortion may lead to acute or chronic tension, often expressed on the muscular, organ, or cellular level. Such tension can lead to pain and illness, and this is the basis for the psychosomatic concept. Some experts in the field of behavioral psychology believe that all illness is grounded in conflicting personal beliefs, ideas, and actions.

## SUMMARY

Before we look closer at the events and situations that cause stress, let's summarize how emotions, thoughts, and beliefs influence stress arousal and subsequent illness.

By definition, stress is an arousal reaction to some stimulus, event, object, or person. This reaction is characterized by heightened arousal of physiological and psychological processes. The stimulus for this arousal reaction is the stressor.

*Stressor:* an event or condition that may be purely physical, social, or psychological—including anticipation and imagination—and that triggers a stress reaction.

Stress is the body's reaction to a stressor. Emotion is physical arousal with the addition of specific thoughts intended to direct action toward alleviation of the stressor. Thoughts allow us to anticipate a situation, assume a defensive posture, and increase background arousal if necessary. In a situation of prolonged arousal, thinking efficiency may decrease due to overload. What we believe dictates how we will react to a stressor and what we will experience from the situation. We maintain control by taking small steps that do not exceed our ability to cope. Small steps require a stretch into an area we can manage, and this is called *competent coping.* Large steps that challenge our beliefs will go beyond our ability to cope, and recruitment will occur. Recruitment consists of usually negative maladaptive behaviors, such as ego defense, rationalization, withdrawal, and illness. Attempts to control stress in these times of overload usually result in *maladaptive coping.* When stressed, we usually feel we are out of control—the result of too many inputs demanding too many responses. In these situations our interpretation of the world is negative and our perceived ability to function is low. The natural response is an attempt to diminish stress at either the input or the response level. At one end we try to manipulate input into something predictable, or decrease our awareness of potential inputs. At the response level we may attempt to respond the same way to each occurrence; this response is seldom appropriate. Depression, a common form of psychological withdrawal, and excessive use of depressant drugs and alcohol are "maladaptive" attempts at control. They can limit the input or response and reduce stress, but are maladaptive in that they cause additional stress problems in the future. The decision to use a controlling behavior may not be a conscious decision. People rarely stop and say, "Things are out of control so I think I will drink too much or get depressed." Instead the situation goes through a series of body and mind filters, and if these systems cannot cope with the situation, the attempt to control is maladaptive.

Stressors may be divided into three general classes: For examples of each class, see Table 4.1.

**TABLE 4.1   The Major Causes of Stress**

| PSYCHOSOCIAL LIFESTYLE | BIOECOLOGICAL | PERSONALITY |
|---|---|---|
| Adaptation | Biorhythms | Self-perception |
| Overload | Noise | Anxious reactivity |
| Frustration | Nutrition | Time urgency |
| Deprivation | Heat, cold | Control |
|  |  | Anger, hostility |

1. *Psychosocial.* These are person–environment stressors that are a function of the interaction between social behaviors and the way our senses and our minds interpret those behaviors. In other words, much of our societal stress is determined by the meanings we assign to the events in our lives. Different individuals are likely to interpret events differently or to assign different meanings to the same situation. This explains why each person's pattern of societal stress is unique.

2. *Bioecological.* These stressors are biological and arise out of our relationship with our environment. They are only minimally subject to differing interpretations.

3. *Personality.* These stressors reflect the dynamics of an individual's self-perception and characteristic beliefs, attitudes, and behaviors that may somehow contribute to excessive stress.

Between the stressor and the stress reaction lies a multitude of factors that can change the stress reaction. One person's reaction to a given stressor may differ from another person's. The factors that make the stress reaction unique to the individual may be thought of as filters through which the stressful situation dissipates some of its potentially harmful energy. Experience is one such filter. It is known that novelty heightens the response to stress, whereas past experience with a similar situation diminishes the response. Another filter is one's emotional reactivity (how ergotrophically tuned a person may be). Still another potential filter is one's thought process, or the ability to think the situation through logically and rationally. Perhaps the most important filter is the basic belief a person has formed about his or her life in relation to such factors as security, vulnerability, and purpose.

The pathway of the stress reaction starts with the stressor, which is usually an external situation or event, but can also be our imagination. The situation alerts the body through the limbic-hypothalamic-RAS arousal mechanism, which quickly alerts the corresponding areas of the cortex. The alerting impulse triggers an emotional pattern that starts to direct the type of response. We then evaluate and reevaluate the potential response plans we are formulating to alleviate the stressor. Understanding how emotions, thoughts, and beliefs interact with a stressor to influence the stress response is essential to understanding the stressors discussed in Chapters 5–8 and the stress management techniques presented in the remaining chapters.

## REFERENCES

BRADSHAW, J. *Homecoming.* New York: Bantam.

DUSEK, D., and DANIEL A. GIRDANO (1992). *The body as teacher: Symptom metaphors for health.* Winter Park, CO: Paradox Publishing.

JACKINS, H. (1978). *The human side of human beings.* Seattle: Rational Island Publishers.

GLASSER, W. (1984). *Taking effective control of your life.* New York: Harper & Row, Pub.

KING, S. (1985). *Kahuna healing.* Wheaton, IL: Theosophical Publishing House.

LAZARUS, R. (1991). Progress on a cognitive-motivational-relational theory of emotion. *American Psychologist*, August, 819–34.

PATENT, A. (1985). *You can have it all.* Piermont, NY: Money Mastery Publishing.

TOMKINS, S. (1962). *Affect, imagery, consciousness.* New York: Springer Publishing Co.

WECHSLER, R. (1987). A new prescription: Mind over malady. *Discover*, February, 51–61.

# CHAPTER FIVE

# Psychosocial Causes of Stress

This chapter examines the basic psychosocial origins of the stress reaction. Psychosocial stressors originate in the complex interaction between socialization and perception. That is, they are sociological events we may perceive as undesirable on the basis of our experiences or other learning processes.

Four psychosocial processes appear to have the strongest connections with stress: (1) adaptation, (2) frustration, (3) overload, and (4) deprivation. We will examine these potential sources of distress and look at examples of how each touches our daily lives. Before you read each section, be sure to complete the self-assessment exercise that precedes it. These exercises help clarify the material that follows.

**ADAPTATION**

We are simultaneously experiencing a youth revolution, a racial revolution, a sexual revolution, a colonial revolution, an economic revolution, and the most rapid and deep-going technological revolution in history.

This description of the massive process of change was true in 1970 and is even more in evidence today. "Era of change" could be the single most descriptive phrase for the twentieth century.

Most of us have been reared with the feeling that change is good and desirable, as it usually denotes an easier and more productive life. However, in his book *Future Shock*, Alvin Toffler suggested that even though change is a necessary element in societal behavior, if it is too intense or too massive, the participants may cease reaping its rewards and begin realizing how devastating it can be. Though Toffler spoke somewhat as a philosopher and social critic, the scientific literature strongly supports his contentions.

Your health and even your very survival are based largely on your body's ability to maintain a healthy balance of mental and physical processes. This equilibrium is called *homeostasis*. It has been suggested that excessive change is harmful to health because it tends to destroy homeostasis and thereby force the body to restore homeostasis through adaptation.

---

*Homeostasis:* equilibrium in the internal functions of the body.
*Adaptation:* the tendency of the body to fight to restore homeostasis in the face of forces that upset this natural bodily balance.

---

In the early 1960s, Thomas H. Holmes and Richard H. Rahe attempted to discover whether change did have major effects on human health. *Generic change*—that is, change having either positive or negative consequences—was the focus of their research. Based on earlier work by Adolph Meyer with "life charts" (paper-and-pencil tools for creating a medical biography), Holmes and Rahe compiled a list of positive and negative life events that seemed to contribute to the stress reaction. From these efforts emerged the Social Readjustment Rating Scale (SRRS), first published by Holmes and Rahe in 1967. This scale originally listed forty-three life events, and each carried a weighting indicating the amount of stress to be attributed to it. The weightings were determined by the sample populations being tested, and the weighting units were called *life change units* (LCUs). The most highly weighted life event was the death of a spouse (100 LCUs) and the lowest-weighted event was minor violations of the law (11 LCUs). Interestingly enough, outstanding personal achievement was weighted with 28 LCU, only one point less than trouble with in-laws! This points to one of the more important aspects of this study of life events: it concentrated on generic change, a force that causes stress through the destruction of homeostasis.

Remember, it is change, or the disruption of homeostasis, that produces stress and adaptation, whether the event is desirable or undesirable. Negative or distressful events are usually the most harmful, for they are more disruptive for a longer period. They have a secondary effect in that they stimulate fear, self-doubt, catastrophic imaginings, and other negative thoughts that linger in

## SELF–ASSESSMENT EXERCISE 1
## QUESTIONNAIRE A

A list of events follows. Check each event that has happened to you during the *last twelve months.*

| Life Event | Point Value |
|---|---|
| _____Death of spouse | 100 |
| _____Divorce | 73 |
| _____Marital separation | 65 |
| _____Jail term | 63 |
| _____Death of a close family member | 63 |
| _____Personal injury or illness | 53 |
| _____Marriage | 50 |
| _____Fired from work | 47 |
| _____Marital reconciliation | 45 |
| _____Retirement | 45 |
| _____Change in family member's health | 44 |
| _____Pregnancy | 40 |
| _____Sex difficulties | 39 |
| _____Addition to family | 39 |
| _____Business readjustment | 39 |
| _____Change in financial status | 38 |
| _____Death of a close friend | 37 |
| _____Change to different line of work | 36 |
| _____Change in number of marital arguments | 35 |
| _____Mortgage or loan over $10,000[a] | 31 |
| _____Foreclosure of mortgage or loan | 30 |

If you are a college graduate or over twenty-five, use questionnaire A. If you are a full-time student or under twenty-five, use questionnaire B. If you are between these two life phases, complete both questionnaires and use the higher score.

[a]An updated version might be "Mortgage or loan payment more than 25 percent of salary."

the mind. However, positive events can likewise be stressful in that they also initiate change that necessitates adaptation. Usually, though, positive change does not produce the secondary effect of the negative event, and thus is given fewer points in the weighting of life events.

One question that always arises in weighting life events is: "Doesn't a specific event exert differing amounts of stress on different individuals?" Technically, the answer is yes, because everyone's perception of the events in their lives differs. How you perceive an event in your life is tempered by your past experiences. For example, knowing what to expect is a great help in overcoming stress. Someone who has not lived through an event will anticipate the event as being more stressful than someone who has already experienced it. Novelty is always stress-arousing, but that new

## SELF–ASSESSMENT EXERCISE 1
## QUESTIONNAIRE A (CONTINUED)

| Life Event | Point Value |
|---|---|
| _____Change in work responsibilities | 29 |
| _____Son or daughter leaving home | 29 |
| _____Trouble with in-laws | 29 |
| _____Outstanding personal achievement | 28 |
| _____Spouse begins or stops work | 26 |
| _____Starting or finishing school | 26 |
| _____Change in living conditions | 25 |
| _____Revision of personal habits | 24 |
| _____Trouble with boss | 23 |
| _____Change in work hours, conditions | 20 |
| _____Change in residence | 20 |
| _____Change in schools | 20 |
| _____Change in recreational habits | 19 |
| _____Change in church activities | 19 |
| _____Change in social activities | 18 |
| _____Mortgage or loan under $10,000 | 17 |
| _____Change in sleeping habits | 16 |
| _____Change in number of family gatherings | 15 |
| _____Change in eating habits | 15 |
| _____Vacation | 13 |
| _____Christmas season | 12 |
| _____Minor violations of the law | 11 |
| | Score: _____ |

Add up the point values for all of the items you checked. Then read the section "Adaptation" to interpret your score.

Source: Holmes and Rahe, 1968.

situation becomes tempered through subsequent experiences. Nevertheless, some events are stressful no matter how many times you experience them, and as such they are only minimally less stressful through experience.

Take moving, for example. The first move is the most difficult, and you become more efficient with experience, but each move still requires much adaptation. If you own a house, the process of finding a realtor, negotiating prices, being displaced during showings, trying to live in a perpetually clean house for weeks or months, finding a new residence, securing new loans, and countless other details is a source of constant stress. Packing, accumulating records, taking care of making the move itself, and finding a new physician and dentist and new stores, schools, and friends are additional stressors. Thus, even if the move is to a better job in a

## SELF-ASSESSMENT EXERCISE 1
## QUESTIONNAIRE B

The following are events that occur in the life of a college student. Check each event that has happened to you during the *last twelve months.*

| *Life Event* | *Point Value* |
|---|---|
| _____Death of a close family member | 100 |
| _____Jail term | 80 |
| _____Final year or first year in college | 63 |
| _____Pregnancy (to you or caused by you) | 60 |
| _____Severe personal illness or injury | 53 |
| _____Marriage | 50 |
| _____Any interpersonal problems | 45 |
| _____Financial difficulties | 40 |
| _____Death of a close friend | 40 |
| _____Arguments with your roommate (more than every other day) | 40 |
| _____Major disagreements with your family | 40 |
| _____Major change in personal habits | 30 |
| _____Change in living environment | 30 |
| _____Beginning or ending a job | 30 |
| _____Problems with your boss or professor | 25 |
| _____Outstanding personal achievement | 25 |
| _____Failure in a course | 25 |
| _____Final exams | 20 |
| _____Increased or decreased dating | 20 |
| _____Change in working conditions | 20 |
| _____Change in your major | 20 |
| _____Change in your sleeping habits | 18 |
| _____Several-day vacation | 15 |
| _____Change in eating habits | 15 |
| _____Family reunion | 15 |
| _____Change in recreational activities | 15 |
| _____Minor illness or injury | 15 |
| _____Minor violations of the law | 11 |
| | Score: _____ |

Add up the point values for all of the items you checked. Then read the section on "Adaptation" to interpret your score.

nicer place, and even if moves have been made before, there is still much change and much adaptation. Moving is therefore considered a stressful event.

With this concept of generic change as a stressor in mind, Rahe and Holmes amassed data from their Social Readjustment Rating Scale. The SRRS is administered by asking respondents to indicate how many of the forty-three items they have experienced over the past twelve months. A total LCU score is then obtained by adding up the LCUs for all of the items that have been checked. This scale has proved to be a remarkable predictor of physical and mental illness for a two-year period after the accumulation of the stressors.

The original SRRS, provided at the beginning of this section, has undergone several revisions. Two of the later versions, the Life Events Inventory and the Life Change Events Scale, are among the most popular instruments used today. These scales were made to be used with adults and do not include events that are known stressors for other populations. For this reason, numerous other life-event inventories have been created. The life-event concept has been validated with military personnel (Rahe, 1967), teenagers (Marx, Garrity & Bowers, 1975), and children (Coddington, 1972), and across cultures (Rahe, 1969).

Despite the impressive amount of data accumulated in support of the relationship between life events and illness, subsequent researchers have sought to improve the life-event scaling process initiated by Rahe and Holmes. From these efforts, two major criticisms of the major life-event scales have emerged:

1. Scales such as the SRRS fail to consider the notion that the perceived desirability of a given life event may affect its ultimate stressfulness. Indeed, studies have indicated that if a life event is perceived as negative or undesirable, it is more likely to result in illness than if it is perceived as neutral or positive. (Mueller, Edwards & Yarvis, 1977; Sarason, Johnson & Siegel, 1978)
2. Minor, daily-life "hassles" may be a far more important predictor of illness than the major life events. (Zarski, 1984; Kanner, Coyne, Schaefer & Lazarus, 1981)

The result of such criticism has been the creation of the Life Experiences Survey (LES) by Sarason and his colleagues and the "hassles scale" by Kanner and his colleagues.

As new classifications of stressors are identified for particular populations, new event scales will be developed to increase the accuracy of prediction. Although the scales and populations change, the basic approach of Rahe and Holmes remains the same—compiling a list of stressful events unique to a certain population, having that group determine the stressfulness of the items, and conducting arduous studies on correlations between the cluster of events and subsequent illness. The items in the student questionnaire at the beginning of this section were formulated for college students, so the weighting of the events was established by that group. It is still too early to present any definitive statistics regarding that test, since it is a relatively new one, but it is expected that the correlations between life change and subsequent illness will be similar to those of the other tests.

It is important to remember that no one event has ever been related to illness. Rather it is the accumulated effects of numerous events occurring in a concentrated period that is predictive of illness. Thus, in scales such as the SRRS, it is the cluster of stressful events, and their total score, that becomes the focus for analysis. Those individuals who accumulate higher scores seem most susceptible. In most of the published scales, "high" susceptibility equals 300 or more points, "low" equals 150 or fewer, and "moderate" is in between.

An important word here is *susceptibility*. A high score does not mean that the individual will *definitely* become ill. It means that the individual is more susceptible to illness than those with lower scores. There are many intervening variables, the most important of which might be the stress intervention techniques currently practiced by the individual.

If you have not yet done so, go back and add up your score on self-assessment exercise 1. If your total score for the year was under 150 points, your level of stress, based on life change, is low. If your total was between 150 and 300, your stress level is borderline; you should minimize other changes in your life at this time. If your total was more than 300, your life-change level of stress is high; you should minimize any other changes in your life and work more vigorously at instituting some of the stress intervention techniques presented in Chapters 9–18 of this book.

Now that you have determined your life-change score, let us see how life change may lead to illness. Remember that change, whether favorable or unfavorable, requires adaptation. Change disturbs the equilibrium, inducing a temporary destruction of homeostasis. Such disequilibrium is met by the body with attempts to restore homeostasis. Selye (1976) pointed out that adaptation stresses the body by requiring a concerted effort on its part to restore balance. This effort to restore homeostasis requires *adaptive energy*, and unfortunately, adaptive energy will eventually diminish if the disequilibrium becomes highly intense or chronic. When the person's adaptive energy is drained, dysfunction can occur on a localized, or specific, level. When the body is totally depleted of adaptive energy, general bodily exhaustion may result in death.

That excessively intense disequilibrium (change) can result in death is supported by the studies of George Engel (1977), who found that over 250 cases of sudden death usually occurred within minutes or hours of a major event in the person's life. Of added interest is the fact that most of these people were in good or fair health before they died.

Engel looked for patterns to the sudden-death phenomenon, and his investigations supported Holmes and Rahe's contention that favorable as well as unfavorable change can be stressful. While the leading category of sudden deaths was those deaths preceded by some "traumatic disruption of a close human relationship," another major category consisted of people who died suddenly during moments of great triumph or personal satisfaction. Engel noted the example of a fifty-five-year-old man who died during a joyous reunion with his eighty-eight-year-old father after a twenty-year separation. The father then died as well.

In his 1966 work *Psychological Stress and Coping Processes,* Richard Lazarus proposed that stress usually depends less on life events than on the cognitive processes involved in the individual's perception of those events. He noted that although life events can indeed predict illness, some individuals with high life-change scores simply do not get ill. Conversely, many individuals have low life-change scores but do get ill. These noteworthy observations led Richard Rahe to suggest that future research focus on moderating variables such as factors that allow people to tolerate high levels of change without suffering illness. Rahe (1979, p. 3) stated that the

> qualities of life change events are qualities of the individual rather than aspects of the environment. It should be clear to investigators that when they gather sentiments of upsettingness, desirability . . . and what have you, they are measuring a variety of subjective responses to the environment which confound objective estimates of life change.

What are some of the factors that seem to moderate the process whereby life events lead to illness?

**Control.** Albert Bandura (1982) has argued that "it is mainly perceived inefficacy in coping with potentially aversive events that makes them fearsome. To the extent that one can prevent, terminate, or lessen the severity of aversive events, there is little reason to fear them." In other words, situations in which we perceive ourselves as being helpless or trapped or feeling out of control will be far more stressful than situations over which we believe we have some control.

**Challenge.** Suzanne Kobasa (1979) has identified the personality factor of "change as perceived challenge," meaning that one tends to believe that change is a normal process of living and can be an incentive for personal growth.

## SELF–ASSESSMENT EXERCISE 2

Choose the most appropriate answer for each of the following ten statements and write the letter of your response in the space to the left of the question.

*How often do you . . .*

_____    1. Feel stifled or held back in your personal or professional life?
      (a) almost always
      (b) often
      (c) seldom
      (d) almost never

_____    2. Feel a need for greater accomplishment?
      (a) almost always
      (b) often
      (c) seldom
      (d) almost never

_____    3. Feel as though your life needs guidance or direction?
      (a) almost always
      (b) often
      (c) seldom
      (d) almost never

_____    4. Notice yourself growing impatient?
      (a) almost always
      (b) often
      (c) seldom
      (d) almost never

_____    5. Find yourself feeling you are in a "rut"?
      (a) almost always
      (b) often
      (c) seldom
      (d) almost never

**Commitment.** Kobasa (1979) has also identified the personality factor of commitment, or the tendency to involve oneself in life experiences, rather than to be alienated or threatened by them or to passively observe them.

Kobasa and her colleagues have called these three moderating factors *hardiness.* Hardiness seems to be a powerful force that protects us from the potentially harmful effects of high life-change.

In summary, change can be a positive force for growth or a negative force that may lead to mental and/or physical deterio-

## SELF–ASSESSMENT EXERCISE 2 (CONTINUED)

_____ 6. Find yourself disillusioned?
   (a) almost always
   (b) often
   (c) seldom
   (d) almost never

_____ 7. Find yourself frustrated?
   (a) almost always
   (b) often
   (c) seldom
   (d) almost never

_____ 8. Find yourself disappointed?
   (a) almost always
   (b) often
   (c) seldom
   (d) almost never

_____ 9. Find yourself feeling inferior?
   (a) almost always
   (b) often
   (c) seldom
   (d) almost never

_____ 10. Find yourself upset because things haven't gone according to plan?
   (a) almost always
   (b) often
   (c) seldom
   (d) almost never

_____ Total Score

Calculate your total score as follows:

(a) = 4 points    (c) = 2 points
(b) = 3 points    (d) = 1 point

Write your total score in the space provided and read the section on "Frustration."

ration. The key lies not so much in whether the change is positive or negative, a major life event or a minor hassle, but rather in how intense and chronic its impact is. And in the final analysis, the impact of life changes will be as intense and chronic as you _perceive_ it and _allow_ it to be.

**FRUSTRATION**     Have you ever gotten uptight because the car in front of you was going too slowly? Have you ever stood in a long line and become anxious because it didn't move fast enough? If you've experienced these or similar situations, then you know what it is like to be frustrated.

*Frustration:* the thwarting or inhibiting of natural or desired behaviors and goals.

Frustration occurs when we're blocked from doing something we want to do, whether that something is a behavior we wish to perform or a goal we wish to attain. Emotionally, we respond to frustration with feelings of anger and aggression, and with the nervous and hormonal responses that accompany them. Frustration, then, causes the stress response, and in a highly technological, urban society this source of stress should be recognized so that it may be dealt with. Four major sources of everyday frustration in urban and suburban America are overcrowding, discrimination, socioeconomic factors, and bureaucracy. All are examples of psychosocial causes of stress.

**Overcrowding**

Perhaps the major psychosocial factor in frustration is overcrowding. As our cities slowly grow into mass urban corridors, or *megalopolises*, social scientists wonder about the effects of such increasing human density on the overall quality of life. Unfortunately, reports on the impact of crowding on health and happiness are conflicting or at least inconclusive.

The essence of the confusion seems to lie in the definition of *crowding*. According to Freedman (1975), crowding is the *space* allotted per organism, or the *sensation* or *perception* of being crowded. The latter part of the definition makes the way we perceive a situation the determinant of whether crowding exists. Crowding, then, becomes a function not solely of space and people, but also of an individual's perception or feeling of being crowded. Such a perception is highly relative. Three could be a crowd in one situation, and thirty-three might not be a crowd in a different situation. If you perceive yourself as being crowded (inhibited in your behavior or goal attainment by the presence of others), then overcrowding exists, and it is a psychosocial stressor for you.

A review of experiments with animals has shown that crowding produces excessive stress-hormone secretion, excessive adrenalin secretion, atrophy of the thymus gland (which involves the immune system) and of secondary sexual characteristics, and elevated blood pressure. Researchers at the National Institute of Mental Health (1969, p. 167) have concluded that "there is abundant evidence that among animals, at least, crowded living conditions and their immediate consequences . . . impose a stress that can lead to abnormal behavior, reproductive failure, sickness, and even death."

This research on animals seems conclusive, but there is still doubt whether these findings apply to humans. The problem in research on humans is that a feeling of crowding depends on our perception, which is a function of complex sensory and thought processes in addition to the more basic lower-brain processes that we share with the so-called lower animals. In addition, this complex integration of perceptual processes may be different for different types of people. However, in general, research supports the theory that when individuals feel inhibited or frustrated due to overcrowding, the stress response results.

For instance, Tanner (1976) studied train commuters in Stockholm and found that the first passengers on a commuter train experienced less stress than those who boarded the train after the halfway point. This was true even though the earlier boarders had to tolerate the crowding for twice as long. He concluded that the resultant stress was not a function of crowding alone, but came more from the later arrivals' being inhibited from gaining a seat and from stowing their coats and briefcases. Singer (1975) studied New York City commuters and came to similar conclusions. He found that the commuters boarding after the halfway point had higher secretions of stress-related hormones than those who boarded earlier.

Finally, studies of crowding in penal institutions have found that inmates confined to cells with many other prisoners exhibit higher blood pressure than those in less crowded cells. Highly crowded cells create an atmosphere of insecurity and depersonalization that was more frustrating and inhibitive than the atmosphere in less crowded cells.

**Discrimination**      Discrimination may be the most widely destructive form of frustration-caused stress. *Discrimination* refers to unfavorable actions taken against others because of religion, race, social status, gender, physical characteristics, national origin, or even general lifestyle. Although it is widely denounced as un-American and inhumane, discrimination appears to be ingrained in much of our social fiber and has been the basis of many social and occupational attitudes and practices.

Prejudice and discrimination can stifle anything from simple day-to-day activities to long-range goals and dreams. The 1969 National Institute of Mental Health report suggested that the effects of prejudice and discrimination, particularly on children, were the retardation of intellectual functioning and a decreased probability of healthy personality development. The report indicted prejudice as a potential cause of increased violent tendencies and a general distrust of democratic institutions and systems. Finally, it concluded that prejudice harmed the development of self-concept in children.

So-called reverse discrimination has appeared in the United States as a means of compensating for the injustices of the past. All the same, it too is discrimination and involves essentially the same stress reactions for those discriminated against. Therefore, reverse discrimination is just as harmful to health as the discriminatory practices it was designed to correct.

**Socioeconomic Factors**

Stress may also be caused by frustrating socioeconomic conditions. Inflation, unemployment, excessive taxation, and general economic recession or depression can create stress on massive social scales, as was apparent in the Great Depression of the 1930s. During periods of economic turmoil, ambitions may be shattered. Maintaining financial security may become a day-to-day endeavor. Sending one's children to college, retiring early, owning a house—all of these aspirations may be frustrated by financial insecurity. The stress of such realities can be as detrimental to the health of the frustrated individual as it is to his or her finances. It has been shown that mental disorders, suicide, crime, and disease increase significantly during socioeconomic hardship, and family and marital relationships seem to be strained as well.

The effects of poverty on those at the lowest socioeconomic levels may lead to personal insecurity. Many of those living at the poverty level have a sense of powerlessness and hopelessness, and many suffer from a general personality disorientation in which they believe their role in life is meaningless. Such conditions are clearly harmful to the health of these people and of society in general.

**Bureaucracy**

If you feel trapped in a job that is unrewarding or without a future, one possible explanation may be that you are caught in the tentacles of a massive bureaucracy. Large bureaucracies seem to promote stress from frustration. They are almost inherently frustrating because of their complexities, "red tape," and impersonal nature. They often dampen individual initiative and motivation, and decrease job satisfaction. There is an increasing demand for job satisfaction among today's workers, and jobs that offer self-esteem and education as part of the work functions are in high demand. It is clear that money is no longer the sole determinant of job satisfaction. The bureaucracy cannot seem to meet the job-satisfaction demands of the new, enlightened worker of today.

Those served by bureaucracies are also victims of stress when they are frustrated by bureaucratic inefficiencies. The growth of

**TABLE 5.1   The Stages of Burnout**

STAGE 1: STRESS AROUSAL (includes any two of the following symptoms)

1. Persistent irritability
2. Persistent anxiety
3. Periods of high blood pressure
4. Bruxism (grinding your teeth at night)
5. Insomnia
6. Forgetfulness
7. Heart palpitations
8. Unusual heart rhythms (skipped beats)
9. Inability to concentrate
10. Headaches

STAGE 2: ENERGY CONSERVATION (includes any two of the following)

1. Lateness for work
2. Procrastination
3. Needed three-day weekends
4. Decreased sexual desire
5. Persistent tiredness in the mornings
6. Turning work in late
7. Social withdrawal (from friends and/or family)
8. Cynical attitudes
9. Resentfulness
10. Increased alcohol consumption
11. Increased coffee, tea, or cola consumption
12. An "I don't care" attitude

STAGE 3: EXHAUSTION (includes any two of the following)

1. Chronic sadness or depression
2. Chronic stomach or bowel problems
3. Chronic mental fatigue
4. Chronic physical fatigue
5. Chronic headaches
6. The desire to "drop out" of society
7. The desire to move away from friends, work, and perhaps even family
8. Perhaps the desire to commit suicide

*Note:* These stages usually occur sequentially, from stage 1 to stage 3, although the process can be stopped at any point.

## SELF–ASSESSMENT EXERCISE 3

Choose the most appropriate answer for each of the following ten statements and write the letter of your response in the space to the left of the question.

*How often do you . . .*

_____ 1. Find yourself with insufficient time to do things you really enjoy?
   (a) almost always
   (b) often
   (c) seldom
   (d) almost never

_____ 2. Wish you had more support/assistance?
   (a) almost always
   (b) often
   (c) seldom
   (d) almost never

_____ 3. Lack sufficient time to complete your work most effectively?
   (a) almost always
   (b) often
   (c) seldom
   (d) almost never

_____ 4. Have difficulty falling asleep because you have too much on your mind?
   (a) almost always
   (b) often
   (c) seldom
   (d) almost never

_____ 5. Feel people simply expect too much from you?
   (a) almost always
   (b) often
   (c) seldom
   (d) almost never

the consumer movement may reflect, to some degree, the frustration and anger of those who feel at the mercy of corporate policies they neither understand nor agree with.

**Summary**

Overcrowding, prejudice and discrimination, socioeconomic conditions, and large bureaucratic structures are four major sources of frustration, or the inhibition of human behavior, in modern urban society. Such inhibition can produce psychophysiological

## SELF–ASSESSMENT EXERCISE 3 (CONTINUED)

_____ 6. Feel "overwhelmed"?
  (a) almost always
  (b) often
  (c) seldom
  (d) almost never

_____ 7. Find yourself becoming forgetful or indecisive because you have too much on your mind?
  (a) almost always
  (b) often
  (c) seldom
  (d) almost never

_____ 8. Consider yourself to be in a high-pressure situation?
  (a) almost always
  (b) often
  (c) seldom
  (d) almost never

_____ 9. Feel you have too much responsibility for one person?
  (a) almost always
  (b) often
  (c) seldom
  (d) almost never

_____ 10. Feel exhausted at the end of the day?
  (a) almost always
  (b) often
  (c) seldom
  (d) almost never

_____ Total Score

Calculate your total score as follows:

  (a) = 4 points   (c) = 2 points
  (b) = 3 points   (d) = 1 point

Place your total score in the space provided and read the section on "Overload."

stress reactions that are expressed in anger, aggression, increased sympathetic nervous activity, and increased mental trauma.

Now that you have reviewed some of the causes of frustrational stress, return to self-assessment exercise 2. The highest score possible is 40 and the lowest is 10. The higher your score, the greater your perception of frustration and the more stressful frustration would appear to be for you. General guidelines are: 25 to 40 =

high frustration/high stress; 20 to 24 = moderate frustration/moderate stress; 10 to 19 = low frustration/low stress.

Since frustration is characteristically inhibitive or thwarting, it appears to be one of the major factors in a condition known as *burnout*. The other major factor is overload, to be discussed in the next section.

---

*Burnout:* a state of mental and/or physical exhaustion caused by excessive stress.

---

Burnout is caused by excessively prolonged or excessively intense stress arousal. George Everly (1984, 1985) notes that two of the major causes of burnout are bureaucratic atmospheres and overwork. Everly's description of the three stages of burnout is illustrated in Table 5.1.

Fortunately, burnout is not permanent—it is reversible. Furthermore, it is preventable. Relaxation, proper diet, and physical exercise not only help you recover from burnout, but can prevent this problem from occurring in the first place. These topics are discussed in depth later in this book.

**OVERLOAD**

Have you ever felt that the pressures of life were building up so that you could no longer meet their demands? Perhaps you felt as though there simply wasn't enough time in the day for you to accomplish all the things that needed to be done. During this time you may have noticed a decline in your social life and more of a "self-centeredness." Perhaps you lost sleep, and so became tired and irritable. You may even have become more susceptible to colds and flu. If any of these things sounds familiar, chances are you were a victim of *overload*.

*Overload*, which means the same as *overstimulation*, refers to the state in which the demands around you exceed your capacity to meet them. Some aspect or aspects of your life are placing *excessive* demands on you. When these demands exceed your ability to comply with them, you experience distress. Overload is perhaps better explained by the analogy of a receptionist deluged with ten clients all at once, each of whom must be spoken to individually. Like that receptionist, the brain can process only a limited number of incoming stimuli. Forcing the brain to exceed its natural processing capabilities, as during a period of overstimulation, will lead to a breakdown of the system, just as the receptionist will break down from exhaustion if pushed too far beyond his or her limitation.

---

*Overload:* a level of stimulation or demand that exceeds the capacity to process or comply with that input; overstimulation.

---

The four major factors in overload are: (1) time pressures, (2) excessive responsibility or accountability, (3) lack of support, and (4) excessive expectations from yourself and those around you. Any one or a combination of these factors can result in stress from overload.

Overload is perhaps the most pervasive of the psychosocial stressors in our country. It encompasses the city, the occupational environment, the school, and even the home.

**Urban Overload**   Visitors to large cities often comment on the unfriendly or impersonal ways of urban life in contrast with the more personal suburban or rural lifestyles. Many scientists are at a loss to explain an event such as the rape of a female in a large city, witnessed by over a dozen people who made no attempts to help her. Such shocking lack of concern for the welfare of others and the blatant egocentric attitudes that seem to fester in many large cities are of concern to us all. Social psychologist Stanley Milgram (1970) developed the concept of overload to explain the impersonal attitude of many urban dwellers. He viewed the large urban center as a vast collection of potential stressors—mass media, mass transportation, vast technological innovations, intense interpersonal stimulation, a deadline-oriented society, and excessive and diverse responsibilities. Milgram suggested that lack of interpersonal concern is a defense mechanism by which urbanites cope with this bombardment of social stimuli. Impersonality protects urbanites' psychological well-being by shielding them from all but the most necessary environmental demands.

**Occupational Overload**   Within the work environment such things as deadlines (time pressure), excessive responsibility and accountability, lack of managerial or subordinate support, and excessive role expectations from self, supervisor, or subordinates can all create overload. Task overload occurs when the work environment places demands that are beyond a person's resources. In our time- and money-oriented society, it is not surprising that many jobs are deemed more stressful than is healthy for the employee. This is especially true in this age of increased organizational accountability. Think of the tasks that are creating (or have created) overload for you. Make a list of them for further reference as you read the intervention techniques in Chapter 10.

To demonstrate the effects of time pressure on workers, Friedman, Rosenman, and Carroll (1958) studied tax accountants at the peak season (just prior to April 15). Analysis of blood samples revealed significant increases in serum cholesterol and blood-coagulation times. Both of these signs indicate excessive stress, which may eventually contribute to the development of heart disease.

Perhaps the best example of occupational task overload is seen in air-traffic controllers. ATCs are faced with a combination of excessive time pressures, life-and-death responsibility, often insufficient support (either managerial or technical), and a virtually damning expectation for perfection from themselves and others. Research on these workers clearly demonstrates the stressful outcome of task overload. For example, at Chicago's O'Hare Field researchers found that ATCs were under greater stress than pilots having to fly ten-hour flights in simulators. This conclusion was reached by measuring secretions of the adrenal medullae and the adrenal cortex (the main stress hormones). Compared with telegraphists, ATCs showed considerably stronger stress reactions on the job, based on analysis of their blood. Research has revealed that ATCs are occupationally predisposed to certain stress-related diseases, the most significant of which is hypertension, followed by peptic ulcers, and finally diabetes. The highly stressful jobs of ATCs must certainly help explain why 32.5 percent of those examined in one study suffered from either gastric or duodenal ulcers (Grayson, 1972).

These studies demonstrate the devastating effects of task overload as a stressor. The important point here is not that work is stressful, but rather that certain intrinsic elements of a job task may be highly stressful if the occupational demands are hyperstimulating and exceed the individual's resources.

**Academic Overload**

Overload doesn't stop in the urban milieu or on the job; it reaches into the classroom as well. Teachers are experiencing increased demands for accountability, and are expected not only to contribute to the search for knowledge (research) and serve the community in a professional manner, but also to excel in teaching skills. These demands are often coupled with such sidelights as advising, collecting milk money, and parent-student counseling—tasks upon which salary increase, promotion, and/or tenure often depend.

The academic environment is also becoming increasingly stressful for students. This society's demand for higher education has created a highly competitive academic environment reaching back even to the primary grades. Children are pressured to do well academically to ensure college admission. Once in college, the student is exposed to the possibility of graduate or professional schooling, but many graduate and professional schools demand "honors status" for a student to even be considered for admission. Added to the grade battle are admissions tests, which are stressors in themselves. Little wonder that test anxiety is becoming a major problem in the academic world. Test anxiety may lead to inaccurately low evaluations of a student's scholastic achievement or potential.

For many students the academic grind has led to dropping out of school, poor self-concept, and more severe mental disturbances (the most severe of which has been suicide). In response to the growing pressures of education, many schools have increased their funding for counseling and mental health services; this is especially true in higher education. Schools have initiated programs to help students learn to study, reduce test anxiety, and generally improve coping skills.

## Domestic Overload

The home has always been a potential source of overload stress. The small, comparatively low-cost "first home" of many couples with children is easily outgrown, and space is at a premium. In addition to perceived crowding, there is now a multiplicity of electronic gadgets around the home—televisions, radios, CD players, and VCRs—that contribute to overload stress. Never-ending home repair, yard work, and everyday household chores round out a picture of the home as an overload stressor.

Unfortunately, it seems that no matter where you go or what you do, you become a prime candidate for this society's far-reaching stressor: overload.

Self-assessment exercise 3 was designed to assess your level of stress due to overload. Total your points and see how stressed you are by overload. Roughly speaking, a total of 25 to 40 indicates a high stress level, one that could be psychologically and physiolog-

## SELF-ASSESSMENT EXERCISE 4

Choose the most appropriate answer for each of the following ten statements and write the letter of your response in the space to the left of the question.

*How often do you:*

_____  1. Feel that your work is not stimulating enough?
        (a) almost always
        (b) often
        (c) seldom
        (d) almost never

_____  2. Lose interest in your daily activities?
        (a) almost always
        (b) often
        (c) seldom
        (d) almost never

_____  3. Find yourself becoming restless during your daily routine?
        (a) almost always
        (b) often
        (c) seldom
        (d) almost never

_____  4. Feel "insulted" by the simplicity of your work?
        (a) almost always
        (b) often
        (c) seldom
        (d) almost never

_____  5. Wish your life were more exciting?
        (a) almost always
        (b) often
        (c) seldom
        (d) almost never

ically debilitating. As mentioned in the last section, overload is one of two major factors in burnout.

**DEPRIVATIONAL STRESS: THE EFFECTS OF BOREDOM AND LONELINESS**

The idea that overstimulation of your mental and emotional processes can result in stress and ill health probably did not surprise you. But now consider the notion that understimulation of these very same processes can result in the same stress response and the same deterioration of your health. We call this state *deprivational stress.*

## SELF-ASSESSMENT EXERCISE 4 (CONTINUED)

_____    6. Find yourself becoming anxious from a lack of stimulation?
(a) almost always
(b) often
(c) seldom
(d) almost never

_____    7. Find yourself becoming bored?
(a) almost always
(b) often
(c) seldom
(d) almost never

_____    8. Feel that your usual activities aren't challenging enough?
(a) almost always
(b) often
(c) seldom
(d) almost never

_____    9. Find yourself daydreaming during your work?
(a) almost always
(b) often
(c) seldom
(d) almost never

_____   10. Feel lonely?
(a) almost always
(b) often
(c) seldom
(d) almost never


_____      Total Score

Calculate your total score as follows:

(a) = 4 points    (c) = 2 points
(b) = 3 points    (d) = 1 point

Place your total score in the space provided and read the section on "Deprivational Stress."

---

_Deprivational Stress:_ the psychophysiological stress response caused by states of boredom and/or loneliness.

---

Deprivational stress has been defined as "the internal bodily reaction to cognitive understimulation"—that is, our body's response to boredom (monotonous, unchallenging tasks) and lone-liness (emotional deprivation) (Galdston, 1954, p. 45).

In affluent societies, advanced technology relieves humans of many tasks, but the human time and interest in those tasks are often replaced with the boredom of watching a machine do the work. Highly repetitive or insufficiently challenging tasks can re-sult in distress.

Boredom appears to prey quite heavily on American adoles-cents. Some psychologists suggest that as many as 20 percent of American adolescents are psychologically handicapped by bore-dom and depression. Such a handicap may lead to loss of self-esteem and eventually to self-destructive behaviors such as drug abuse and even suicide. That suicide has become one of the leading causes of adolescent death appears to support this contention. As a result, billions of dollars are spent each year on entertainment and diversions for adolescents. All of these signs appear to indicate that massive technological advances are serving to bore many Americans to death!

Loneliness can also be a devastating stressor. Children who are not given adequate, caring attention are known to suffer from stim-ulus deprivation. Such emotionally deprived children may suffer a decreased production of growth hormones, and subsequent re-tardation of growth and development. But when these children are placed in an emotionally supportive environment, their growth returns to normal. Nevertheless, psychological scars may persist for a lifetime.

James Lynch (1977) has demonstrated how stressful loneliness can be. Lynch noted that for the major causes of death in this country (heart disease, cancer, and automobile accidents), mor-tality was higher among single, widowed, and divorced individuals of all races and both sexes than among married individuals. Sim-ilarly, in the United States unmarried men between forty-five and fifty-four have a 123 percent greater death rate than married men. Lynch (1977, p. 187) concluded that "in a number of cases of premature coronary disease and premature death, interpersonal unhappiness, the lack of love, and human loneliness seem to appear as the root of the physical problems." These suggestions are un-derscored by the fact that the health of married people seems to be improving, while the health of unmarried individuals is not.

How well do you tolerate deprivational stress? Self-assessment exercise 4 was designed to help you find out. If your score is 25 to 40, you are vulnerable to deprivational stress; you seem to need stimulation to avoid stress. If your score is 20 to 24, you are average. If your score is 10 to 19, you have a high tolerance for low stimulation.

**POST-TRAUMATIC STRESS**

> *Post-traumatic stress:* the stress response engendered by some traumatic stressor event, typically defined as an intensely aversive physical and/or psychological experience outside the usual realm of human experience.

**Historical Background**

*Post-traumatic stress* is the term used for a stress response engendered by some traumatic event. A traumatic event is typically defined as an intensely aversive physical and/or psychological experience outside the usual realm of human experience. A traumatic event may be thought of as something that overwhelms our normal defenses and coping mechanisms. It has been noted that about 25 percent of individuals who are exposed to a traumatic event will suffer some form of post-traumatic stress reaction. Overall, it has been estimated that 9 percent of the young adults in the U.S. have experienced some form of post-traumatic stress (Davidson, 1991). A partial list of potential traumatic stressors is provided in Table 5.2.

**TABLE 5.2   Traumatic Events**

| PERSONAL TRAUMATA | COMMUNITY TRAUMATA |
|---|---|
| robbery | flood |
| physical assault | earthquake |
| rape | fire |
| automobile accident | building collapse |
| a "life or death" struggle | airplane crash |
| physical abuse | multiple-injury accident |
| psychological abuse | terrorism |
| sexual abuse | injury or death of a child |
| a perceived serious threat to one's well-being | |
| a perceived serious threat to a family member or close friend | |
| observing any of the personal or community traumata listed here | |

History, clinical observations, and recent research all tell us that excessive stress resulting from a traumatic event takes on a unique form and pattern (American Psychiatric Association, 1987). In 1865, no less an observer than Charles Dickens wrote of a railway accident in which he was involved (Trimble, 1981). Dickens's diary contained numerous accounts of the accident, and he subsequently described his reactions to the disaster in the following way: "I am curiously weak—weak as if I were recovering from a long illness." That description is intriguing in that Dickens himself was not physically injured, but was only an observer to several hours of "horrifying" sights and sounds.

Similar accounts of extreme stress reactions, including phobic reactions, nightmares, flashbacks, and a host of stress-related physical illnesses, have been recorded as early as 1666, the year of the Great Fire of London (Trimble, 1981).

Civilian accounts of extreme stress and psychopathological reactions to trauma are well known, but it is the effects of combat that have prompted the psychiatric community to focus upon posttraumatic stress. Army surgeons have used terms such as "shell shock," "soldier's heart," and "post-traumatic neurosis" to describe the effects of wartime traumatic stress on soldiers. These accounts date as far back as the American Civil War and extend through World War I, World War II, and the Korean War, and they received a great deal of press coverage after the war in Vietnam.

In 1980, the American Psychiatric Association officially described a mental disorder that can develop in response to trauma. That disorder is now known as post-traumatic stress disorder (PTSD). In 1987, the diagnostic criteria for PTSD were slightly altered, but the core concepts remained the same. PTSD is listed in the APA's *Diagnostic and Statistical Manual of Mental Disorders* (3rd ed., rev.) under the overall heading of *anxiety disorders*. The official diagnostic criteria are as follows (APA, 1987, p. 238):

A. The person has experienced an event that is outside the range of usual human experience and that would be markedly distressing to almost anyone—for example, serious threat to one's life or physical integrity; serious threat or harm to one's children, spouse, or other close relatives or friends; sudden destruction of one's home or community; or seeing another person who has recently been, or is being, seriously injured or killed as the result of an accident or physical violence.

B. The traumatic event is persistently reexperienced in at least one of the following ways:
   1. recurrent distressing recollections of the event (in young children, repetitive play in which themes or aspects of the trauma are expressed)

2. recurrent distressing dreams of the event
3. suddenly acting or feeling as if the traumatic event were recurring (includes a sense of reliving the experience, illusions,
hallucinations, and dissociative flashback, even upon awakening or when intoxicated)
4. intense psychological distress at exposure to events that symbolize or resemble an aspect of the traumatic event, including
anniversaries of the trauma

C. Persistent avoidance of stimuli associated with the trauma or
numbing of general responsiveness (not present before the
trauma), as indicated by at least three of the following:
1. efforts to avoid thoughts or feelings associated with the trauma
2. efforts to avoid activities or situations that arouse recollections
of the trauma
3. inability to recall an important aspect of the trauma (psychogenic amnesia)
4. markedly diminished interest in significant activities (in young
children, loss of recently acquired developmental skills such
as toilet training or language skills)
5. feeling of detachment or estrangement from others
6. restricted range of affect, such as being unable to have loving
feelings
7. sense of a foreshortened future—for example, not expecting to
have a career, marriage, children, or a long life

D. Persistent symptoms of increased arousal (not present before the
trauma), as indicated by at least two of the following:
1. difficulty falling or staying asleep
2. irritability or outbursts of anger
3. difficulty concentrating
4. hypervigilance
5. exaggerated startle response
6. physiologic reactivity upon exposure to events that symbolize
or resemble an aspect of the traumatic event (for example, a
woman raped in an elevator subsequently breaking out in a
sweat whenever she enters an elevator)

## The Nature of Post-Traumatic Stress

The symptoms just listed provide a working definition of a complex
psychological condition. As we can see in criteria B, C, and D of
the preceding list, PTSD exhibits three specific symptom clusters
that reveal the pathological nature of the disorder:

1. recollective ideation: reexperiencing the traumatic event
2. numbing and withdrawal symptoms: persistent avoidance of people, places, and things associated with the trauma, and/or a psychological numbing in which the victim seems to withdraw into
a "shell"
3. persistent increased stress arousal

PTSD may also be seen as a combination of recalled images
and excessive arousal, especially of the sympathetic nervous sys-

tem (Everly, 1991). The numbing and withdrawal is then understood as a secondary reaction to the intrusive recollections and increased arousal. Figure 5.1 depicts the postulated relationships.

It may be that this latter formulation will better help us understand PTSD and other traumatic stress syndromes. For example, PTSD may represent an extreme variation of a survival mechanism. Remember that PTSD arises out of exposure to some event that is life-threatening or otherwise capable of overwhelming normal coping mechanisms. It may be that the mind's survival response is to deeply ingrain that event in the memory so that similar situations may be avoided in the future (or so that the person will be better prepared to cope with them). The body's survival response may be to create a chronic state of arousal that keeps one prepared for fight or flight at the slightest provocation or threat. Finally, it may be that the numbing, and especially the withdrawal symptoms, represent an energy-conservation mechanism designed to allow recovery of strength after a traumatic event (Everly, 1991).

Figure 5.1 also indicates that chronic acute traumatic syndrome has three potential outcomes:

1. stress-related physical disease,
2. psychiatric syndromes such as depression or chronic PTSD itself
3. post-traumatic personality disorders such as borderline personality disorder

An analysis of PTSD reveals two underlying factors: a neurological hypersensitivity and a psychological hypersensitivity (Ev-

**FIGURE 5.1**

A Process Model of PTSD (adapted from Everly, 1991)

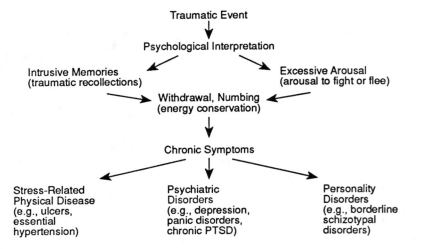

erly, 1991). Thus, PTSD is referred to as a *neurocognitive* formulation. In neurological terms, exposure to a traumatizing event may result in a hypersensitivity within the neural networks of the limbic system. Functionally, this hypersensitivity represents a lowering of the threshold for excessive arousal or excitation. Thus, the slightest irritation or provocation will result in rage, panic, withdrawal, impulsive actions, or other forms of extreme stress. Psychologically, it may be that exposure to a traumatizing event creates a hypersensitivity within important mechanisms used by all individuals to maintain psychological homeostasis. More specifically, trauma shatters some important assumptions about the nature of our world. It was Abraham Maslow who noted that a basic human need, second only to the need for food and shelter, is the need for safety.

To make the unknown aspects of the world somewhat safe, we all create assumptions about life in general. For example, one assumption many people hold is that life is always "fair." Another is that you get what you deserve and you deserve what you get; it is a "just" world. Another assumption might be that "good" always conquers "evil." Traumatic events by their very nature violate, challenge, and sometimes destroy these presuppositions about life and the world around us. In so doing, they create a psychological void. This void represents a "psychic puzzle" that yields a hypersensitivity to perceptions of threat, demoralization, and panic.

PTSD is not the only form that post-traumatic stress can take, however; it is simply the most severe. In addition to physical illnesses and personality dysfunctions, a post-traumatic reaction may manifest itself in the following ways (Horowitz, 1986):

- fear of a reoccurrence of the trauma
- shame over being a victim
- rage over being a victim
- rage toward the person or thing that caused the trauma
- guilt
- fear of a loss of control
- depression
- mourning
- phobic reactions

**Coping with Traumatic Stress**

A number of strategies that consider both neurological and psychological hypersensitivity have been used to cope with traumatic events. Neurological hypersensitivity manifests itself in the form of excessive arousal. This arousal is based upon either a biological propensity for arousal or a failure of the brain to dampen arousal.

Relaxation training is usually the best generic approach to lower the level of arousal. No one technique appears to be superior to others. One should practice the relaxation technique that seems easiest and most convenient to utilize. However, some individuals will find that during relaxation they tend to recall the traumatic experience. Such recollection can be stressful and therefore counterproductive. It is sometimes recommended that a more active relaxation technique be employed to reduce the intrusive ideation. Biofeedback is one such technology. In some instances, psychotropic medications are used to dampen the excessive arousal that is a natural constituent of PTSD.

Psychological hypersensitivity arises from a violated world view, or assumption about the world. The strategies often employed to reduce the disequilibrium associated with a violated world view include: (1) reinterpreting the traumatic event, (2) reinterpreting the role that one played in the event, (3) active behavior oriented toward increasing one's sense of control over similar events, (4) behaviors designed to increase one's general sense of control, (5) utilization of social support, and (6) changing one's world view so as to assimilate the trauma and thus reduce the anxiety associated with disconfirmation. Let us take a closer look at each of these.

One of the most common coping mechanisms for reducing stress and a sense of chaos is to reinterpret the traumatic event, perhaps by trying to find some positive aspect to it. For example, one might say that the trauma allowed one to finally "grow up" and face problems like an adult. Or one might say that the trauma revealed a previously unknown inner strength. In general these strategies allow the person to find "meaning" in an otherwise meaningless catastrophe. Although they may seem like a pedestrian effort to find the "silver lining" in a cloud of trauma, reinterpretation can prove quite useful as long as it doesn't stifle further growth and development or create new problems of its own.

Another strategy is to reinterpret the role one played in the trauma itself. Survivors of disasters sometimes cope by considering themselves fortunate even to have survived. A similar strategy might be to compare oneself with victims who were more adversely affected. Often, victims of physical harm cope by focusing not on the event but upon recovering from it beyond anyone's expectations. Where one tends to blame oneself for the traumatic event, it is sometimes helpful to search for other reasonable explanations for the event. If one is truly responsible, however, he or she should try to accept responsibility and then consider how to assist the recovery process and/or reduce the chances of similar events occurring. Also, viewing oneself as partially responsible for the traumatic event, one quickly discovers a reason for it. This coping strategy of self-blame is commonly used by victims, even when their role in the trauma was minimal, as a means of restoring order and predictability to the world.

The third common coping mechanism is engaging in some action that reduces the likelihood of a similar event, actively pursuing rehabilitation, or even pursuing punitive action through proper authorities. For example, a burglary victim may place locks on windows and dead-bolt doors, or even install an electronic alarm system. These strategies are likely to reduce the probability of a repeat trauma. The victim of an automobile accident may install an air bag in the car. Often, traumatized persons who are physically injured will not only pursue rehabilitation, but will use the opportunity to become more health-conscious. Finally, the victim of a crime or of human negligence may pursue punitive action through the court system. Such action may not only reduce the likelihood of further crimes or negligence, but it often results in a feeling of empowerment for the victim.

A fourth strategy to reduce psychological hypersensitivity after trauma is to engage in any activity that creates a sense of empowerment and control. It is well known that victims of trauma commonly suffer feelings of self-doubt, helplessness, and a general lack of control. Any activity that helps develop a sense of self-control tends to restore order to a world view whose assumptions have been violated. The activities do not have to be related to the trauma; rather, any activity that increases self-esteem will prove valuable.

Trauma often leaves the victim believing that the world is a malevolent place. This is in direct contradiction to the more deeply ingrained assumptions that the world is safe and secure. A strategy that helps refute the malevolent-world perspective is social support. We all need some form of social support; humans are social animals. Trauma increases our inherent need for social support. Yet trauma victims often hesitate to seek social support out of a dislike to show "weakness," a concern over being taken advantage of, and even a reluctance to have others feel sorry for them. Nevertheless, trauma actually increases the need for social support, and thus appropriate social support can have powerful healing effects. Sometimes that support must be obtained from a trained mental health professional such as a psychologist. Failure to obtain social support can needlessly protract psychological suffering. Pennebaker (1988) argues that simply discussing traumatization is inherently therapeutic. On the other hand, "holding it all inside" can be destructive to mental and physical health in the long run.

In some cases, finally, the trauma may be so overwhelming,

the victim's ability to cope may be so meager, or one's previously held assumptions about the world may have been so ineffective (or blatantly inappropriate) that the only reasonable coping strategy is to change one's world view, rather than try to salvage it.

A brief summary of the various coping strategies follows:

1. Dampen the tendency for overexcitation, overreaction, and excessive arousal.
2. Reinterpret the traumatic event.
3. Reinterpret your role in the trauma.
4. Increase your control over the traumatic situation.
5. Increase your personal sense of control.
6. Obtain social support (perhaps professional support).
7. Change your assumptions about the world.

The earlier one recognizes the symptoms of psychological trauma and seeks help, the more rapid the recovery is likely to be. The victim of psychological trauma usually requires assistance to recover. Professional help should always be sought in fully developed cases of PTSD. This information is offered *not* as a way of treating trauma, but rather as a way of familiarizing you with this extreme stress response so that formal treatment can be sought more readily when and if trauma strikes.

## REFERENCES

AMERICAN PSYCHIATRIC ASSOCIATION (1987). Diagnostic and statistical manual of mental disorders (3rd ed., rev.). Washington, DC: APA.

BANDURA, A. (1981). Self-efficacy mechanism in human agency. *American Psychologist, 37,* 122–47.

CODDINGTON, R. D. (1972). The significance of life events as etiologic factors in the diseases of children. *Journal of Psychosomatic Research, 16,* 205–14.

DAVIDSON, J. (1991). Clinical efficacy shown in pharmacologic treatment of post-traumatic stress disorder. *Psychiatric Times,* September, 62–63.

ENGEL, G. (1977). Emotional stress and sudden death. *Psychology Today, 1,* 114–18, 153–54.

EVERLY, G. (1984, November). A cognitive physiological therapy for the treatment of anxiety and panic attacks. Paper presented at the American Academy of Psychosomatic Medicine's annual conference, Philadelphia.

——— (1985). Occupational stress management. In G. Everly and R. Feldman (eds.), *Occupational health promotion* (p. 186). New York: John Wiley.

———— (1989). *A clinical guide to the treatment of the human stress response.* New York: Plenum.

———— (1991). Neurophysiological considerations in the treatment of PTSD: A neurocognitive perspective. In J. Wilson and B. Raphael (eds.), *International handbook for traumatic stress syndrome* (p. 356). New York: Plenum.

FREEDMAN, J. L. (1975). *Crowding and behavior.* San Francisco: W. H. Freeman Company Publishers.

FRIEDMAN, M., R. ROSENMAN, and V. CARROLL (1958). Changes in the serum cholesterol and blood clotting time in men subjected to cyclic variation of occupational stress. *Circulation, 18,* 852–61.

GALDSTON, I. (1954). *Beyond the germ theory.* New York: Health Educational Council.

GRAYSON, R. (1972). Air controllers syndrome: Peptic ulcer in the air traffic controller. *Illinois Medical Journal, 142,* 111–15.

HOLMES, T. H., and R. H. RAHE (1968). The Social Readjustment Rating Scale. *Journal of Psychosomatic Research, 11,* 213–18.

HOROWITZ, M. J. (1986). *Stress response syndrome.* London: Aronson.

KANNER, A., J. COYNE, C. SCHAEFER and R. LAZARUS. (1981). Comparison of two modes of stress measurement. *Journal of Behavioral Medicine, 4,* 1–39.

KOBASA, S. C. (1979). Stressful life events, personality, and health. *Journal of Personality and Social Psychology, 37,* 1–11.

LAZARUS, R. S. (1966). *Psychological stress and coping processes.* New York: McGraw-Hill.

LYNCH, J. J. (1977). *The broken heart: The medical consequences of loneliness.* New York: Basic Books.

MARX, M. B., T. F. GARRITY, and F. R. BOWERS. (1975). The influence of recent life experiences on the health of college freshmen. *Journal of Psychosomatic Research, 19,* 87–98.

MILGRAM, S. (1970). The experience of living in cities. *Science, 165,* 1461–68.

MUELLER, D., D. EDWARDS, and H. YARVIS. (1977). Stressful life events and psychiatric symptomology. *Journal of Health and Social Behavior, 18,* 307–17.

NATIONAL INSTITUTE OF MENTAL HEALTH (1969). *The mental health of urban America.* Washington, DC: U.S. Government Printing Office.

PENNEBAKER, J. W. (1988). Confiding traumatic experiences and health. In S. Fisher and J. Reasons (eds.), *Handbook of life stress, cognition, and health.* New York: John Wiley.

RAHE, R. H. (1979). Life change events and mental illness: An overview. *Journal of Human Stress, 5,* 2–10.

———— (1967, February). *Life crisis and health change* (Report Number 67–4). U.S. Navy Bureau of Medicine and Surgery.

SARASON, I., J. JOHNSON, and J. SIEGEL (1978). Assessing the impact of life changes. *Journal of Consulting and Clinical Psychology, 46,* 932–46.

SELYE, H. (1976). *The stress of life.* New York: McGraw-Hill.

SINGER, J. (1975). Commuter stress. *Science Digest,* August, 18–19.

TANNER, O. (1976). *Stress.* New York: Time-Life Books.

TOFFLER, A. (1970). *Future shock.* New York: Random House.

TRIMBLE, M. R. *Post-traumatic neurosis.* Chichester, England: Wiley.

ZARSKI, A. (1984). Hassles and health. *Health Psychology, 3,* 243–51.

# CHAPTER SIX

# Bioecological Causes of Stress

A *bioecological stressor* is a stimulus, arising out of our relationship with our environment, that produces a stress response in most of us through an innate biological mechanism. This type of stressor is only minimally colored by our higher perception and thought processes, and this is what separates it from the other two major categories of stress (psychosocial and personality).

Five classes of biologically relevant stimuli that may play a role in distress are (1) biological rhythms, (2) eating and drinking habits, (3) drugs, including alcohol and nicotine, (4) noise pollution, and (5) changes in climate and altitude. We will discuss each of these in this chapter.

**BIOLOGICAL RHYTHMS**

Time has always been recognized as a major stressor. Most people think of deadlines as the only cause of time-related stress. There are, however, other stressful aspects of time. The natural world also runs on time; solar or light time, lunar time, and seasonal time are but a few examples. The human body also runs on time—temperature time, metabolic time, energy time, and hormonal time, to mention a few. As social, cultural, technological beings, we have arrogantly ignored our biological time or rhythm for the sake of convenience and conformity. We try to synchronize work and recreation schedules with what is socially and economically efficient. We utilize artificial light, and we speed through time zones. All of these things and more affect the body's natural tempo and rhythm. Undue irritability, emotional instability, and increased susceptibility to illness may result from being out of phase with the body.

Some day, internal rhythm or body time may dictate work and

social schedules, but for the time being, increasing your personal knowledge of your own body rhythm will at least allow you to better understand, expect, and even predict fluctuations in moods, feelings, and sensitivities. It may save you the anguish of trying to find flaws or triggers in your social interactions and how you motivate yourself. Stress arousal can be diminished by your understanding and expectations of fluctuation in body weight, muscle tone, energy, strength, hunger, sleep, excretion demands, motivation, attention, and productivity.

*Biological rhythms* are naturally recurring cycles of activities governed by the nervous and hormonal systems. Some of these activities are completely internal, stubbornly resisting change; others are greatly influenced by external stimulation, such as exposure to light. Still others, such as eating, adapt themselves to clock time and social activities. Biological rhythms recur in periods of minutes, hours, days, or years. Each completes a cycle that appears graphically as a sine wave, as shown in Figure 6.1. Each cycle has a beginning and an end. Each has a *zenith*, or peak, and a *nadir*, or low point. A *cycle* is one complete revolution around a given point. The *amplitude* is the amount of deviance from baseline, and the *frequency* is the number of cycles in a given period.

## Circadian Rhythms

The most researched cycle is the twenty-four-hour cycle, called the *circadian* (Latin: "about a day") *rhythm*. Some of the body processes that fluctuate in a circadian rhythm are body temperature, blood pressure, respiration rate, blood sugar, hemoglobin level, adrenal-hormone level, amino-acid levels, and urine production. As these fluctuate, so do energy level, attention span, and motivation. As strength changes, so do vulnerabilities. The same dose of a drug may have a mild effect at one time of the day, a more profound effect later in the day.

Body temperature fluctuations seem to reflect psychophysiological changes occurring during the circadian period: the highest temperature, which coincides with one's most productive hours of the day, is usually in the early afternoon, and the nadir is usually

**FIGURE 6.1**

Sine Wave Cycle

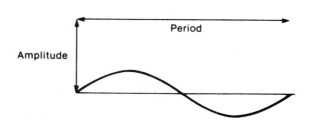

in the early hours of the morning. Many illnesses become terminal at two or three o'clock in the morning, when vitality is at its lowest, and more children are born in the morning, when the strength to resist labor contractions diminishes. The zenith of the temperature rhythm is often associated with increased attention and muscle coordination. This is perhaps the best time to take both psychological and physiological tests.

Just as temperature fluctuates rhythmically throughout the day, so does metabolism. Proteins are utilized differently, and calorie counters may find that calories taken in the morning are burned up more quickly than those taken later in the day. The list seems endless. Hormone secretion by the adrenal glands peaks just before morning rising time and falls to its nadir at night. The male hormone testosterone is at its zenith around eight or nine o'clock in the morning. Liver enzymes, which are responsible for the breakdown of the basic unit of body energy adenosine triphosphate (ATP), fluctuate throughout the day, increasing during more active periods.

Our ability to perform is certainly different at different times during the day. Biologically and behaviorally, we are different people between ten and twelve in the morning and ten and twelve at night.

## Ultradian Rhythms

The term *ultradian rhythm* has been given to cyclical rhythms that occur in periods shorter than a day. Most current research is centered in the 90-to-100-minute rest–activity cycle. It has long been known that sleep is characterized by rhythmical patterns of dream or REM (rapid eye movement) sleep occurring every 90 minutes. More recently it has been found that while we are awake, our attention appears to wax and wane in 90-to-100-minute cycles also. Increased vigilance gives way to altered states of consciousness and daydreaming. We have all had the experience, while reading or studying, of suddenly realizing that nothing on the last three pages was at all familiar. There you sat, reading the words, turning the pages while your mind was in another world. The next time that happens, jot down the time and see if the sequence is rhythmical.

Another situation that spontaneously occurs is that all of a sudden we find ourselves standing in front of the open refrigerator door. It is not lunch time and we did not consciously plan to be eating at this time, but here we are! We find this especially true on days when our activity is lowest, and we repeat this food-finding behavior about every 90 minutes. It seems that about every 90 minutes we experience stomach contractions and exhibit more intense oral activity. As mentioned earlier, these basic biological rhythms stubbornly resist change, although it has been found that extreme boredom and/or stress shorten the 90-minute oral cycle to 60 minutes or less. This may be the causal link between stress arousal and weight-control problems.

Thus, the basic 90-minute ultradian rhythm during sleep and during consciousness may explain fluctuations in drive, motivation, and attention. These changes, if expected, can be planned for and adjusted to rather than fought.

In identifying any pattern of behavior, record keeping is a necessity, so take some time now to fill out the form that follows. This form can be photocopied for subsequent record keeping, or you can record your answers on a blank sheet of paper. Observing your own biological and psychological patterns may help you understand some of your behaviors and reactions to stress. Pay particular attention to sleep patterns—not only quality of sleep, but the time it takes to fall asleep once you go to bed: both are good indicators of tension. Whether you need an alarm to wake up is a good indication of whether your sleep cycle is synchronized with social demands. The same goes for hunger and eating patterns. You may find that you are forcing your body to perform at times when your energy levels are down. You may find the same is true of your enthusiasm and/or intellectual functioning levels. Most important, you may find your patterns of behavior are a reflection of the natural cycles of your body, and not responses to social and environmental circumstances.

### Biological Rhythms Form:
### Circadian and Ultradian Rhythms

Choose four different times of the day, at least two hours apart, starting on awakening (exclude times that fall within one hour after physical activity), and answer the following questions at each of these times. Repeat daily, using the same periods each day.

1. Heart rate: _____ beats per minute

2. Body temperature: _____ degrees

3. Body weight: _____ pounds

Circle one of the following numbers according to how you feel now:

| | | | | | | | | | |
|---|---|---|---|---|---|---|---|---|---|
| 4. | Alert | 7 | 6 | 5 | 4 | 3 | 2 | 1 | Dull |
| 5. | Energetic | 7 | 6 | 5 | 4 | 3 | 2 | 1 | Sluggish |
| 6. | Happy | 7 | 6 | 5 | 4 | 3 | 2 | 1 | Sad |
| 7. | Self-assured | 7 | 6 | 5 | 4 | 3 | 2 | 1 | Doubtful |

|   |   |   |   |   |   |   |   |   |   |
|---|---|---|---|---|---|---|---|---|---|
| 8. | Tranquil | 7 | 6 | 5 | 4 | 3 | 2 | 1 | Anxious, tense, rushed |
| 9. | Outgoing | 7 | 6 | 5 | 4 | 3 | 2 | 1 | Withdrawn |
| 10. | Exhilarated | 7 | 6 | 5 | 4 | 3 | 2 | 1 | Depressed |
| 11. | Hungry | 7 | 6 | 5 | 4 | 3 | 2 | 1 | Sated |
| 12. | Weather good | 7 | 6 | 5 | 4 | 3 | 2 | 1 | Weather poor |
| 13. | Sexual feeling heightened | 7 | 6 | 5 | 4 | 3 | 2 | 1 | Sexual feeling depressed |
| 14. | Concentration good | 7 | 6 | 5 | 4 | 3 | 2 | 1 | Concentration poor, daydreaming a lot |

Presence of specific pain or illness symptoms, such as headache, diarrhea:

15. _____ present

16. _____ present

17. _____ present

At the end of the day record the clock times for:

18. Meals, including snacks _____ _____ _____ _____

19. Urination _____ _____ _____ _____ _____

20. Bowel movements _____ _____ _____ _____ _____

_____

21. Drug intake, including coffee, tea, cigarettes _____ _____

_____ _____

22. Awakening _____

23. Going to sleep for the night _____

24. Naps _____ _____

25. Was sleep good or poor? _____

26. Most productive time of day: _____

Least productive: _____

27. Overall, today was good _____ average _____ poor _____

**Infradian Rhythms**

Another cyclic variation that has received much attention in recent years is the *infradian rhythm*. Longer than the circadian rhythm, this cycle may last for days, weeks, or even months. The most familar of all infradian cycles is the female menstrual cycle, which consists of hormonal, structural, and functional changes that occur in a stubbornly systematic manner, month after month. Because it could have a practical application as a birth-control device, it has been thoroughly researched and written about, and is now common knowledge to most adults. More recently, this cycle has been used to describe ebbs and flows in emotional responses and moods, and has been related to fluctuations in motivation, hunger, and performance.

Less practical and thus less researched infradian rhythms include hypothesized four-to-six-week fluctuations in the emotion, moods, motivation, and thus productivity of men. Another example is *arctic-winter madness*, a short period of dramatic, often psychosis-like change in emotionality in people living at polar latitudes. This condition may be related to endocrine fluctuations resulting from a lack of sunlight-formed vitamin D. There may be countless other undetected infradian cycles that could account for the periodic fluctuations in weight, appetite, stability of sleep, alertness, work output, creativity, irritability, and emotionality that we all experience.

Biological processes, especially hormonal secretions, do fluctuate rhythmically, and since hormone stability influences most of the aforementioned psychophysiological processes, we are fairly safe in assuming the existence of inherent rhythms. However, research on infradian rhythms is a most difficult undertaking, and scientific verification will be slow in coming. But if you are sufficiently motivated and persevere, you can conduct some personal research by religiously charting your own responses on the Biological Rhythms Form over an extended period.

**What Determines Biological Rhythms?**

Biological rhythms can be viewed as natural fluctuations in body processes that promote survival by automatically dictating that periods of high energy be interspersed with periods of rest. Generally speaking, biological rhythms are fixed by generations of genetic programming, but they have a built-in flexibility that allows maximum adaptation, thus increasing survival chances. As the seasons change, so does the amount of heat and light imposed on the body, and so metabolic and hormonal adaptation is required. The biological rhythm that controls these processes has the ability to change—probably in response to changing light, although the exact mechanism is not known for certain.

It would be beyond the scope of this book to cite all the physiological processes that are influenced by light, but most if not all biological rhythms can be slightly changed by changing light.

## SELF–ASSESSMENT EXERCISE 5

Choose the most appropriate answer for each of the following ten statements and place the letter of your response in the space to the left of the question.

_____ 1. How many cups of caffeinated coffee do you drink in an average day?
(a) 0 or 1
(b) 2 or 3
(c) 4 or 5
(d) more than 5

_____ 2. How many cigarettes do you smoke in an average day?
(a) 0 to 10
(b) 11 to 20
(c) 21 to 40
(d) more than 40

_____ 3. Do you add salt to your food?
(a) Yes
(b) No

_____ 4. How many cups of caffeinated tea do you drink in an average day?
(a) 0 or 1
(b) 1 or 2
(c) 3 or 4
(d) more than 4.

_____ 5. How many soft drinks do you consume during an average day?
(1) 0 or 1
(b) 1 or 2
(c) 3 or 4
(d) more than 4

_____ 6. How much alcohol (liquor, wine, or beer) do you consume during an average week?
(a) 0 to 7 drinks
(b) 8 to 15 drinks
(c) 15 to 21 drinks
(d) more than 21 drinks

While this basic fact is known, the exact mechanism is still theoretical. Most of the research on this question centers in the *pineal gland*, a tiny structure buried deep in the brain between the two cerebral hemispheres. The pineal gland has been recognized for thousands of years as a controller of activity and appears by this or other names in most of the yoga and meditation literature. It was thought by Indian mystics to be a vestigial third eye. The pineal gland has an indirect connection with the outside world through nerve tracts that, by a very indirect route, are connected to the optic tract. Like the hypothalamus, the pineal gland receives

## SELF–ASSESSMENT EXERCISE 5 (CONTINUED)

_____   7. Do you eat a nutritionally balanced diet?
   (a) No
   (b) Yes

_____   8. All together, how many pastries, pieces of pie, pieces of cake, donuts, or candy bars
   do you eat in any average day?
   (a) 0
   (b) 1 or 2
   (c) 3 or 4
   (d) more than 4

_____   9. Do you eat a well-balanced breakfast most mornings?
   (a) No
   (b) Yes

_____  10. How many slices of white bread do you eat during an average day?
   (a) 0
   (b) 1 or 2
   (c) 3 or 4
   (d) more than 4

_____   Total Score

Calculate your total score as follows:

   For questions 7 and 9
   (a) = 4 points
   (b) = 0 points

   For all other questions:
   (a) = 1 point   (c) = 3 points
   (b) = 2 points  (d) = 4 points

Place your total score in the space provided and then read the sections on "Eating and Drinking Habits" and "Drugs."

neural impulses and gives off hormonal responses. The pineal gland is also controlled by the sympathetic nervous system hormone norepinephrine and by a complex interaction of the hormones serotonin and melatonin.

Through the pineal gland the body does have a system of adapting to various environmental lighting situations. This is important not only for adapting to the changing seasons, but for adapting to socially imposed environmental changes such as lighting, travel, and shift work. The industrial revolution, maximal production, efficiency, war, and around-the-clock police, fire, and medical attention have all prompted the shift- or night-work concept. The few studies conducted on shift workers have shown an increase in accidents between two and four in the morning, accompanied by a decrease in work performance. Police officers are more apt to sleep on duty during these hours. Airline pilots exhibit their quickest reaction time and best psychomotor coordination between two and four in the afternoon and their poorest performance between two and four in the morning. Radar operators are more likely to make errors and have a harder time staying awake during the hours they would normally be asleep. (Have you ever wondered why the airlines offer reduced rates for overnight flights?)

It is not that the body cannot adjust to changes in lighting or time zones; rather, it cannot make the necessary adjustment in the short time usually allowed. For example, a night worker's body temperature cycle would be expected to be opposite that of a day worker's; yet it usually is not unless the night-shift schedule is maintained for several weeks—long enough for the body to adapt to a new schedule. In many companies a worker may rotate shifts each week, one week working nights and the next week working days. Such rotation allows the worker inadequate time to adapt.

The recent interest in jet lag has spurred several studies that have found a syndrome of symptoms: headache, gastrointestinal problems including loss of appetite, increased sweating, blurred vision, and alteration of sleep patterns (nightmares, insomnia), with the addition of menstrual difficulties for female flight attendants. This seems to be the price one must pay for making several phase shifts in a short period. These studies have shown that adaptation differs with each biological rhythm. For example, it takes five days for urinary electrolytes to adjust to a new schedule, eight days for heart rate, ten days for urinary steroids, and six days for temperature.

Concerned and forward-looking companies have increased layover time for airline crews and business travelers, correctly reasoning that the extra cost of room and board is a good investment when weighed against the potential costliness of accidents, poor business decisions, or illness.

In summary, we now have enough information on the health aspects of biological rhythms to realize that these cycles may explain certain mood and behavior fluctuations; changes in immunity; incidences of illness; variances in toxicity of drugs; changes in body weight, appetite, motivation, and activity levels; changes in sexual interest and performance; sensitivity to stress; and, in general, the development of psychosomatic disease. Knowledge of biorhythms may eliminate the tension of uncertainty by explaining and perhaps allowing us to predict fluctuations, thus reducing the frustration and self-doubt that often accompany normal fluctuations in mood and performance.

## EATING AND DRINKING HABITS

Everyone knows that good nutrition contributes to healthful living, but few realize the extent to which our eating and drinking habits contribute to our daily stress levels. The consumption or lack of consumption of certain foods and the consumption of some kinds of beverages can add to the stress of everyday life by stimulating the sympathetic stress response directly or by contributing to its stimulation through creating a state of fatigue and increased nervous irritability (Heimbach & Levy, 1986). Either condition lowers your tolerance to the common stresses of day-to-day living. There are several eating and drinking habits that may be involved in stress. Some of the more common ones are examined in this section.

## Sympatho-mimetic Agents

Sympathomimetic agents are chemical substances that mimic the sympathetic stress response. Many foods naturally contain these substances. When consumed, they trigger a stress response in the body, the severity of which will depend on how much of the chemical was consumed.

The most common of these sympathomimetic stressors in the American diet is *caffeine*, a chemical that belongs to the xanthine group of drugs. Xanthines are powerful amphetaminelike stimulants that increase metabolism and create a highly awake and active state. They also trigger release of the stress hormones that, among other actions, are capable of increasing heart rate, blood pressure, and oxygen demands on the heart. Extreme, prolonged stress-hormone secretion can even initiate myocardial necrosis— that is, destruction of the heart tissue.

Coffee (*Coffea arabica*) is the most frequently consumed source of caffeine in the American diet. Americans over the age of fourteen consume an average of three cups of coffee a day! The average brewed six-ounce cup of coffee contains about 108 milligrams of caffeine. Caffeine consumption of more than 250 milligrams per day is considered excessive and will have an adverse effect on the human body. A lethal dose of caffeine could be consumed in the form of twenty cups of coffee, if drunk all at once! Frequent side effects of excessive coffee drinking are anxiety, irritability, diarrhea, arrhythmia (irregular heartbeat), and inability to concentrate, in addition to a host of symptoms characteristic of the stress response. Coffee may also stimulate the secretion of the digestive enzyme pepsin in the stomach. In an empty stomach, this enzyme combined with the natural oils in coffee can irritate the stomach lining. All in all, not a very good way to start the day.

Additional sources of xanthine stimulants are tea (*Camelia theca*), cola beverages, chocolate, and cocoa. A six-ounce cup of tea contains about 90 milligrams of caffeine, as well as the other xanthines theobromine and theophylline. Yet tea does not contain the irritating oils found in coffee. Various cola beverages and other sodas (for example, Dr. Pepper) contain 50 to 60 milligrams of caffeine per twelve-ounce can or bottle. Finally, a one-ounce chocolate bar contains about 20 milligrams of caffeine.

Because colas, cocoa, and chocolate are favored by children, parents should seriously consider making them unavailable in the home, especially since a child's body is far less tolerant of chemical agents than an adult's body. It has been clearly shown that such foods in excess can harm the child by increasing anxiety and decreasing learning effectiveness—a fact many teachers are aware of.

Six to eight ounces of coffee can have a hypermetabolic effect on children—that is, excessively stimulate their metabolic system—and anything in excess of three cups of coffee in one hour for adults will adversely affect their behavior, as well as increase the possibility of stomach upset or irritation. For the child, more than two or three cola beverages may be excessive; for the adult, anything over four or five would be excessive during an average day. Chocolate has less caffeine, but other drawbacks (for example, its high calorie content and lack of nutritional value) make it undesirable; therefore, more than two average servings of chocolate a day would be excessive for a child, as would more than four or five for an adult. These general limits are computed by considering the effects of other food intake as well. Check your responses to items 1, 4, and 5 on self-assessment exercise 5 to determine your level of caffeine intake.

For alternatives to coffee or tea, many people have found herbal beverages such as winterberry or mint tea enjoyable. Unless they are mixed with common tea, their caffeine content is zero. Herbal teas do not irritate the stomach lining as does coffee, and some herbs (such as camomile) actually have a calming effect, as opposed to the stimulation caused by regular tea. To find out about herbal teas, browse through the tea section of your local natural-food store or supermarket.

## Vitamin and Mineral Deficiencies

Vitamin and mineral deficiencies may be due to poor diet but are exacerbated by chronic stress. The body must respond to stress with greater-than-normal levels of hormones, neurotransmitters, enzymes, and other biochemical substances necessary for arousal and adaptation responses. During stressful times, high levels of certain vitamins (such as vitamin C and B vitamins) are needed to maintain proper function of the nervous and endocrine systems. They are also called on to help carry out carbohydrate metabolism and gluconeogenesis (the process whereby the body forms glucose for more energy). Vitamin C and choline are necessary elements in the production of adrenal hormones, which are secreted during the stress response. Deficiencies of these vitamins lower tolerance to and ability to cope with stressors. In turn, excessive stress over prolonged periods may deplete the body of these vitamins, making an individual more prone to vitamin deficiency.

One common dietary component implicated in depletion of the B-complex vitamins is refined white sugar. Another is refined white flour. Sugar—and therefore sugar products such as cakes, pies, cookies, and candy (see Table 6.1)—is a good source of energy, but has no other redeeming feature. For sugar to be utilized for energy, however, the body must have B-complex vitamins. Natural foods that need these vitamins for their metabolism contain the necessary vitamins, but since sugar contains none of them, it must borrow them from other food sources. This may create a B-complex debt in the body. If this borrowing occurs frequently or if the body does not have sufficient sources of B vitamins from nutritious foods or supplements, the result may be a B-vitamin deficiency and symptoms such as anxiety, irritability, and general nervousness. This vitamin depletion may be exacerbated by stress because of

**TABLE 6.1   Hidden Sugar in Common Foods**

| FOOD | PORTION | TSP. SUGAR[a] |
|---|---|---|
| Chocolate bar | 1 average size | 7 |
| Chocolate fudge | 1½ square | 4 |
| Marshmallow | 1 average | 1½ |
| Chocolate cake | 1/12 cake (2-layer, icing) | 15 |
| Angelfood cake | 1/12 cake | 6 |
| Doughnut, plain | 3" diameter | 4 |
| Brownie | 2" × 2" × ¾" | 3 |
| Ice cream | ½ cup | 5–6 |
| Sherbet | ½ cup | 6–8 |
| Apple pie | 1/6 medium pie | 12 |
| Cherry pie | 1/6 medium pie | 14 |
| Pumpkin pie | 1/6 medium pie | 10 |
| Sweet carbonated beverage | 12 oz. | 9 |
| Ginger ale | 12 oz. | 7 |

[a]100 grams sugar = 20 teaspoons = ½ cup = 3½ ounces = 400 calories

the increased utilization of these vitamins in the stress response.

One way to ensure that you get enough of the essential vitamins and minerals is to eat balanced meals that include a high intake of natural (rather than highly processed) foods. The Senate Select Committee on Nutrition and Human Needs (1977) outlined seven dietary goals for the United States that serve as the basis for a good diet. By adhering to these guidelines (outlined in the following list), you can assure yourself of the elements necessary for demands on your body.

1.  Eat a variety of foods from each of the basic four food groups: fruits and vegetables; whole-grain products; dairy products; and meat, fish, and poultry. An example of such a diet (the Modified Basic Four Food Groups Plan) is given in Table 6.2.

2.  Maintain an acceptable body weight by consuming only as much energy (calories) as expended. If overweight, decrease energy intake and increase energy output. In addition to following these basic guidelines, eating to maintain acceptable weight may also include eating more slowly, preparing smaller portions, and not taking second portions.

3.  Reduce saturated fat consumption to 10 percent of total energy intake; balance that with 10 percent monounsaturated and 10 percent polyunsaturated fat intake. To do this, choose lean meat, fish, poultry, dry beans, and peas as protein sources and limit intake of butter, cream, shortenings, coconut and palm oil, hydrogenated margarines, and all food products containing these fats and oils. Overall fat consumption should be less than 30 percent of total caloric intake per day.

4.  Reduce cholesterol consumption to 300 or fewer milligrams per day. This calls for moderation in use of eggs and organ meats, and also requires that consumers carefully read food labels to determine the cholesterol content of packaged foods.

5.  Reduce consumption of refined and processed sugars by 45 percent so that they account for only 10 percent of total energy intake. Increase consumption of complex carbohydrates and naturally occurring sugars so that they total about 50 percent of daily caloric intake. To accomplish this, cut back on the consumption of all sugars (white, brown, raw, honey, and syrups) and products containing these sugars. Fresh fruits or fruits canned without sugar may be substituted. Again, reading food labels will help you identify the sugar content of products—but remember that the labels may not always say "sugar." Sugar content may be labeled as glucose, sucrose, maltose, dextrose, lactose, fructose, corn sweetener, and so on. A discussion on sugar's harmful effects on maintenance of blood glucose-levels appears later in this chapter.

6.  Limit intake of sodium by reducing consumption of salt to about 5 grams a day. This generally calls for learning to enjoy the unsalted flavor of foods; cooking with very small amounts of added salt; not putting more salt on food at the table; limiting intake of

salty products such as popcorn, chips, and pretzels; and reading product labels (even antacids) to determine how much sodium is in the product.

7. If you drink alcohol, do so in moderation (two drinks per day or less).

A diet that can be recommended for required intake of all vitamins, minerals, protein, and other essential elements is the Modified Basic Four Food Groups Plan suggested by the Center for Science in the Public Interest (1981). This eating plan is an improvement over the old Basic Four Food Group Plan because it recommends which foods in each group can be eaten anytime, and which should be eaten only now and then. It also recommends the number of servings for children and adults. An example of these dietary guidelines is given in Table 6.2.

Those who do not eat properly in order to get the essential amounts of vitamins, minerals, and protein may resort to vitamin supplements. Many excellent multivitamins can be found over the counter, and many are reasonably priced, so there is no need to invest in exotic vitamin regimens. It has been suggested that American urine is the most expensive in the world because of its high concentration of excess vitamins. Also, it is important to realize that excessive consumption of some vitamins—specifically the fat-soluble vitamins A, D, E, and K—can be toxic. However, if you feel that your diet lacks sufficient vitamins or that you are under extreme stress, vitamin supplements may be a consideration. Some companies have even marketed a "stress vitamin" capsule that is high in the vitamins depleted by the stress reaction. It is always a good idea, however, to consult a knowledgeable nutritionist before taking any dietary supplement or drastically altering your diet.

Table 6.3 lists the adult Recommended Daily Allowances (RDA) that act as basic guidelines for food intake, and Table 6.4 lists the usual supplementary ranges for selected nutrients.

**Hypoglycemic Stress**

The third way in which diet may predispose an individual to distress is through *hypoglycemia*, or low blood sugar. Symptoms may include anxiety, headache, dizziness, trembling, and increased cardiac activity. These symptoms may cause normal stimuli to become severely acute stressors by making the individual highly irritable and impatient. In effect, they lower the individual's stress tolerance. This is routinely seen in people who get "crabby" when they are hungry.

Although there are numerous causes for hypoglycemia, we are most interested in the two directly related to dietary behaviors.

**TABLE 6.2    Examples from the Modified Basic Four Food Groups Plan**

FRUITS AND VEGETABLES

Servings: Four or more per day
To be eaten anytime:
  All fruits and vegetables except those on the moderation list
  Unsweetened applesauce
  Unsalted vegetable juices
  White or sweet potatoes
To be eaten in moderation:
  Avocados, cole slaw, dried fruit, french fries, fruits canned in syrup, potatoes au
  gratin, sweetened fruit juices, vegetables canned with salt
To be eaten only now and then:
  Coconut
  Pickles

MILK PRODUCTS

Servings: Three to four per day for children, two per day for adults
To be eaten anytime:
  Buttermilk (from skim milk)
  Low-fat (1%) milk products
  Nonfat dry milk
  Skim milk and skim-milk products
To be eaten in moderation:
  Cocoa with skim milk
  Regular cottage cheese
  Ice milk
  2% milk, 2% yogurt
  Part-skim-milk mozzarella
To be eaten only now and then:
  Cheesecake
  Eggnog
  Hard cheeses
  Ice cream
  Whole milk, whole-milk yogurt

BEANS, GRAINS, AND NUTS

Servings: Four or more per day
To be eaten anytime:
  Whole-grain bread, rolls, cereal, matzo
  Sprouts
  Brown rice
  Oatmeal
  Dried beans and peas
  Lentils
To be eaten in moderation:
  Cornbread
  Granola
  Flour tortillas
  Macaroni and cheese
  Nuts, nut butters

**TABLE 6.2   Examples from the Modified Basic Four Food Groups Plan (continued)**

Tofu, soybean products
Waffles, pancakes with syrup
White rice, breads, rolls
To be eaten only now and then:
   Doughnuts, sticky buns, rolls
   Croissants
   Presweetened cereals

POULTRY, FISH, MEAT, AND EGGS

Servings: Two per day
To be eaten anytime:
   Cod, flounder, haddock, halibut, perch, pollock, sole
   Tuna packed in water
   Shellfish, except shrimp
   Egg whites
   Baked, roasted, or boiled skinless chicken or turkey
To be eaten in moderation:
   Fried fish
   Herring, canned mackerel or salmon, sardines, shrimp
   Oil-packed tuna
   Fried chicken
   Chicken liver
   Chicken or turkey with skin
   Flank steak
   Leg of lamb
   Lean pork loin or shoulder
   Round steak
   Ground round
   Rump roast
   Lean sirloin steak
   Veal
To be eaten only now and then:
   Bacon
   Commercial fried chicken
   Whole egg or yolk
   Fried beef liver
   Bologna, corned beef, salami, sausage, liverwurst, hot dogs
   Regular ground beef
   Trimmed ham
   Spareribs
   Untrimmed red meats

The complete dietary plan is available from the Center for Science in the Public Interest, 1501 16th Street N.W., Washington, DC 20036. © 1981

*Reactive hypoglycemia* is caused by high intake of sugars within a limited amount of time. Eating a meal high in sugars or even snacking on foods high in sugars may cause a hypoglycemic reaction in individuals prone to this disorder. *Functional hypogly-*

**TABLE 6.3** Recommended Daily Allowances (designed for the maintenance of good nutrition for practically all healthy persons in the United States)

| | AGE Years From | To | WEIGHT Kilograms | Pounds | HEIGHT Centimeters | Inches | FOOD ENERGY Calories | PROTEIN Grams | MINERALS CALCIUM Milligrams | PHOSPHORUS Milligrams | IRON Milligrams | VITAMINS VITAMIN A International units | THIAMIN Milligrams | RIBOFLAVIN Milligrams | NIACIN Milligrams | ASCORBIC ACID Milligrams |
|---|---|---|---|---|---|---|---|---|---|---|---|---|---|---|---|---|
| Infants . . . . | 0 | 0.5 | 6 | 14 | 60 | 24 | kg x 117 lb x 53.2 | kg x 2.2 lb x 1.0 | 360 | 240 | 10 | 1400 | 0.3 | 0.4 | 5 | 35 |
| | 0.5 | 1 | 9 | 20 | 71 | 28 | kg x 108 lb x 49.1 | kg x 2.0 lb x 0.9 | 540 | 400 | 15 | 2000 | .5 | .6 | 6 | 35 |
| Children . . . . | 1 | 3 | 13 | 28 | 86 | 34 | 1300 | 23 | 800 | 800 | 15 | 2000 | .7 | .8 | 9 | 45 |
| | 4 | 6 | 20 | 44 | 110 | 44 | 1800 | 30 | 800 | 800 | 10 | 2500 | .9 | 1.1 | 12 | 45 |
| | 7 | 10 | 30 | 66 | 135 | 54 | 2400 | 36 | 800 | 800 | 10 | 3300 | 1.2 | 1.2 | 16 | 45 |
| Males . . . . | 11 | 14 | 44 | 97 | 158 | 63 | 2800 | 44 | 1200 | 1200 | 18 | 5000 | 1.4 | 1.5 | 18 | 50 |
| | 15 | 18 | 61 | 134 | 172 | 69 | 3000 | 54 | 1200 | 1200 | 18 | 5000 | 1.5 | 1.8 | 20 | 60 |
| | 19 | 22 | 67 | 147 | 172 | 69 | 3000 | 54 | 800 | 800 | 10 | 5000 | 1.5 | 1.8 | 20 | 60 |
| | 23 | 50 | 70 | 154 | 172 | 69 | 2700 | 56 | 800 | 800 | 10 | 5000 | 1.4 | 1.6 | 18 | 60 |
| | 51 + | | 70 | 154 | 172 | 69 | 2400 | 56 | 800 | 800 | 10 | 5000 | 1.2 | 1.5 | 16 | 60 |
| Females . . . . | 11 | 14 | 44 | 97 | 155 | 62 | 2400 | 44 | 1200 | 1200 | 18 | 4000 | 1.2 | 1.3 | 16 | 50 |
| | 15 | 18 | 54 | 119 | 162 | 65 | 2100 | 48 | 1200 | 1200 | 18 | 4000 | 1.1 | 1.4 | 14 | 60 |
| | 19 | 22 | 58 | 128 | 162 | 65 | 2100 | 46 | 800 | 800 | 18 | 4000 | 1.1 | 1.4 | 14 | 60 |
| | 23 | 50 | 58 | 128 | 162 | 65 | 2000 | 46 | 800 | 800 | 18 | 4000 | 1.0 | 1.2 | 13 | 60 |
| | 51 + | | 58 | 128 | 162 | 65 | 1800 | 46 | 800 | 800 | 10 | 4000 | | 1.2 | 12 | 60 |
| Pregnant | | | | | | | +300 | +30 | 1200 | 1200 | +18 | 5000 | + .3 | + .3 | +2 | +20 |
| Lactating | | | | | | | +500 | +20 | 1200 | 1200 | 18 | 6000 | + .3 | + .5 | +4 | +40 |

*Source:* U.S. Drug Administration, (1980).

**TABLE 6.4    Daily Supplementary Ranges for Stress-Related Vitamins (in milligrams)**

| | |
|---|---|
| Thiamine | 2–10 |
| Riboflavin | 2–10 |
| Niacin | 50–5000 |
| Pantothenic acid | 20–100 |
| Pyridoxine HCl | 4–50 |
| Choline | 100–1000 |
| Vitamin C | 250–5000[a] |

[a]Intake above 5000 mg a day may have undesirable effects.

cemia occurs when meals are missed, and it may be exacerbated by sugar intake that results over time in a lower overnight (or fasting) blood-sugar level than would be considered normal.

The process by which such dietary behaviors lead to hypoglycemia is somewhat paradoxical, because hypoglycemia is preceded by a state of high blood sugar (hyperglycemia). What happens is that the high intake of sugar first raises the sugar level in the blood. This high blood-sugar level stimulates the release of insulin (within one or two minutes), which allows the excess sugar to enter all the tissues of the body. Therefore, it is not selectively saved for the central nervous system, whose function and vitality depend on blood sugar. Generally, if blood-sugar levels drop below 60 milligrams of glucose per 100 milliliters of blood, symptoms such as irritability, anxiety, and fatigue occur.

In extreme cases of high sugar intake, the symptoms of hypoglycemia may occur within a short period and may be so severe as to cause nausea, staggering, slurred and mixed speech, and fainting. Extreme hypoglycemic shock can result in coma and death, but in this situation there is generally some underlying cause, such as a pancreatic tumor or insulin shock, as seen in diabetics.

Whether due to perpetual high sugar intake or other physiological conditions, a low blood-sugar level due to hypoglycemia may be responsible for "midmorning slump" and continual hunger that seems to be sated only with sugar products such as cookies, crackers, candy bars, or soft drinks. As many Americans eat only a jelly roll, doughnut, or bowl of highly sweetened cereal for breakfast, it is to be expected that low midmorning blood sugar will bring about increased response to stress situations and diminished ability to perform. The same situation may occur in midafternoon or at any other time of day after high sugar intake—or merely from not eating.

The best way to avoid the stresses of hypoglycemia and its glucocorticoid stress response is to eat well-balanced meals (the size of which should be determined by the energy demands for the next few hours) containing a minimum of sugar and processed foods.

**Sodium Intake and Fluid Retention**

Salt (sodium chloride) is the mineral most responsible for regulating the body's water balance. The sodium ion in salt causes retention of water within the body; therefore, high levels of table salt or of foods naturally high in sodium may result in excessive fluid retention. Excessive fluid retention has the effect of increasing nervous tension (through edema, an abnormal accumulation of fluid) in the general nervous tissue and cerebral tissue.

Excess fluid retention can also lead to high blood pressure. In many people, increased blood pressure is the most common manifestation of the stress reaction. However, if a person's blood pressure is already high due to excessive fluid retention, the pressure elevation during distress may reach a danger point. It may become high enough to increase the risk of stroke or heart attack, or perhaps become chronically elevated.

The body has the ability to store salt, so daily survival needs are relatively low (less than 1 gram). However, the average American consumes 4 to 8 grams per day (an average shake of salt from the salt shaker is 100 milligrams). A good, nutritious diet provides the necessary daily intake of sodium.

Table 6.5 lists foods high in sodium, and Table 6.6 lists seasonings low in sodium that may be used as substitutes for table salt. Also, many salt substitutes are becoming popular, the most frequently used one being potassium chloride. You can switch to one of the commercial substitutes and derive some of the same taste benefit without risking stress.

The conscious manipulation of eating behavior to provide the nutrients essential for fighting stress is called *nutritional engineering,* and it can be a powerful addition to the holistic pattern for stress control. Use the suggestions in this section and expand on them to create your own program for controlling stress through diet.

**DRUGS**

Although people take drugs (including alcohol) for various reasons, a common motive is to get "high" or experience an altered state of consciousness, often in an attempt to reduce stress. An altered state can be defined as a deviation from the "normal" state of consciousness, in which most of us communicate, are goal-directed, and use rational, cause-and-effect thinking. Figure 6.2 shows some ways states of consciousness may be altered.

**TABLE 6.5    Foods High in Sodium**

| MOST CANNED FOODS | PORK PRODUCTS | SNACK FOODS |
|---|---|---|
| meats | ham | pretzels |
| soups | bacon | popcorn |
| stews | sausage | potato chips |
| sauerkraut | hot dogs | |

| CHEESES | SEASONINGS | BAKING SODA |
|---|---|---|
| processed cheese | prepared mustard | (sodium bicarbonate |
| cheese dips | catsup | contains about 1000 mg |
| snacking cheese spreads | Worcestershire | of sodium per level |
| | sauce | teaspoon) |
| | soy sauce | |
| MOST QUICK-ORDER | pickles | |
| FOODS AT DRIVE–IN | relishes | |
| RESTAURANTS | meat tenderizers | |
| | peanut butter (most | |
| | brands are heavy in | |
| | sodium additives) | |

As a rule, processed foods contain more sodium than fresh foods.

**TABLE 6.6    Seasonings That May Be Used in Low-Sodium Diets**

| | | |
|---|---|---|
| almond extract | ginger | paprika |
| bay leaf | lemon | parsley |
| caraway seed | lime | pepper |
| chili powder | maple extract | pimento |
| chives | mint | sage |
| cinnamon | mustard (dry) | sesame seeds |
| cloves | nutmeg | thyme |
| coconut | orange extract | vanilla extract |
| curry | oregano | vinegar |

To alter the normal ego-consciousness, one must move from the planning–doing state to a feeling–experiencing state, sometimes termed the *egoless state*. In the egoless state of consciousness the environment is perceived as nonthreatening; clothes, cars, colleges, and vacation spots are not important. Impressions do not have to be made, images protected, or feelings guarded. One does not think in terms of cause and effect; thus, the significance of subjective experiences or ideas is also changed. In many altered states one loses the feeling of needing to control the environment. In fact, there may be a diminished sense of where the self ends and the environment begins. Self-centered daydreams diminish, a sense

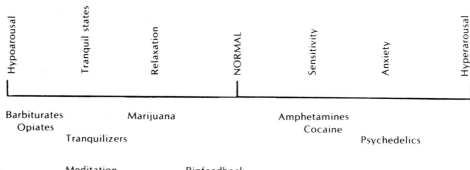

**FIGURE 6.2**

**Drugs and Non-drug Activities That Alter States of Consciousness**

of depersonalization occurs, and inhibitions are diminished. The sense of time changes with the reduction of attention to time-dictated events. The perception of body, self, and reality often changes, and many times visual imagery is experienced.

Altered states of consciousness provide glimpses of ego- or self-transcendence and enlightenment. Self-transcendence is egoless-ness and freedom from anxiety and defenses; it allows for expansion of experiences and feelings, and for increased knowledge of self. Ego, time, and space are transcended, giving rise to peace and tranquility.

Being in an altered state of consciousness means that one has shifted from the normal, taking-care-of-business state to some other level of consciousness. This other level may be as basic as daydreaming or as spiritual as cosmic consciousness, but be assured that we all wander in and out of normal consciousness many times throughout the day and night. The frequency of these occurrences depends a great deal on our external and internal environment—especially the level of stimulation around us—but the frequency can also be planned or allowed by one's own mind.

A drug-induced state of consciousness is often a pleasant experience. The intensity or quality of the experience depends on such factors as when and even where one takes the drug. The quantity and quality of the drug are important, as are one's mood when taking the drug, one's motivation for taking the drug, one's general state of health (especially emotional well-being), one's knowledge about drugs, and one's personality and expectations. Frustration and disappointment may develop when expectations are not met; fear, apprehension, and injury can result if the drug is too strong or is dangerously adulterated. Either way, one is not really in control of the experience and is in a sense imprisoned in an altered state of consciousness until the drug has been metabolized. More important, drugs change but do not stop the flood of sporadic thoughts that bombard the consciousness; thus, the goal of quieting the mind is not usually realized.

The sense of unreality and lack of ego that result from some forms of drug use may be calming in the sense that the drug temporarily blocks one from actively thinking about a problem. Unfortunately, the problem still exists. It is stored in parts of the brain and is producing feelings and other body alterations even though one is not actively aware of them. The psychoactive drugs, both legal and illegal, typically consumed to promote relaxation do not change body physiology. Problems are still present and continue to stress the system. The only difference is that the flow of active, here-and-now thoughts has been temporarily blocked.

The feelings of ego-transcendence vanish once the drugs wear off and can only be regained by repeated use of the drug. There is little positive carryover, little is learned in the drug state, and few people experience long-term positive change from the drug experience. Their world, their problems, and their coping mechanisms are the same as before. Drugs have fulfilled a limited goal, an altered state of consciousness, but they have not fulfilled the dream—that the experience would somehow grant the user greater insights and the ability to naturally transcend the ego and live a calmer, more relaxed and enlightened life.

The passivity of the drug experience is in itself a drawback. Experiences in which the individual just rides along, seeing, feeling, and experiencing, are somehow not as satisfying as those in which the individual is the active, creative center of the experience. Creative activities increase one's self-esteem, and in a circular pattern increase motivation and readiness for future unknown ventures.

An altered state can also be induced through such activities as meditation and daydreaming, or by hypoarousal or hyperarousal of the central nervous system. It is healthier to induce these states by mind direction than by using drugs. There are many popular techniques for inducing a self-transcendent, altered state of consciousness through mind direction or control. Yoga, meditation, muscle relaxation, autogenic training, and biofeedback are but a few examples. These constitute a more positive approach than drugs, not only because they are less dangerous, more socially acceptable, and more controllable, but also because they are active and creative, requiring and promoting self-control and self-discipline. They are learning exercises that result in temporary feelings of self-transcendence, thus providing the foundation and motivation to reeducate one's thoughts and coping processes. If mastered, they lead to an even higher state—that of conscious self-transcendence, an egoless or ego-expanded state in which ego boundaries are infinitely extended. This is a higher state because it is integrated with ongoing life and provides benefits to the individual, society, and humankind in general.

The final consideration in this section is the use of tobacco products. The harmful effects of smoking and chewing tobacco are well known. It is not our purpose to dissuade you from using tobacco; we merely inform you of how the drug *nicotine* contributes to distress. Nicotine stimulates the adrenals, which release hormones that elicit the stress response—increased heart rate, force of cardiac contraction, blood pressure, and respiration rate and release of fatty acids and glucose into the blood, among other body reactions.

Tobacco contains nicotine. Like caffeine, nicotine is a sympathomimetic chemical, and as such it is capable of stimulating all the adverse effects of the arousal response noted earlier. It causes a stress response each time it is taken into the body, whether by smoking a cigarette, inhaling the smoke of others, or chewing tobacco. The smoker and the person facing any one of the numerous psychosocial stressors discussed in the preceding chapter exhibit the same physiological state. One difference is that the chronic smoker's physiological functioning is continually elevated to the point where this arousal state becomes the "normal" state. Being without the stimulating effect of nicotine creates a mild depression and a generally uneasy feeling that lead to the desire for additional nicotine for a pickup.

As the chronic smoking habit develops, the stress tolerance to nicotine is increased and the adverse stress-related effects become somewhat reduced, but the constituents of the smoke continue to affect the respiratory system of the smoker. They also affect the nonsmoker. Because the nonsmoker has developed little if any tolerance to nicotine, the smoke can cause decreases in work performance. A smoky working area can irritate the eyes and nose of the nonsmoker, impeding detail work, concentration, and tolerance for more difficult work tasks. Smoky conditions can even result in increased absenteeism for the nonsmoker (see Oster, Golditz & Kelly, 1984; Whelan, 1984; Girdano, Everly & Dusek, 1985; Althoff, Svoboda & Girdano, 1988). Smoking also calls for greater intake of vitamins E and C for the smoker and perhaps also for the person

**TABLE 6.7    Comparison of Death Rate for Smokers and Nonsmokers**

| DISEASE | SMOKER–TO–NONSMOKER RATIO |
|---|---|
| Heart disease | 2 to 1 |
| Lung cancer | 11 to 1 |
| Stroke | 3 to 1 |
| Oral cancer | 4 to 1 |
| Bronchitis and other pulmonary diseases | 12 to 1 |
| Ulcers | 3 to 1 |

*Source:* Whelan, 1984; U.S. Surgeon General, 1986.

who is exposed to a good deal of smoke daily. Table 6.7 summarizes the risks of death for smokers versus nonsmokers.

Research in the last several years has offered strong evidence that two common "oral" habits, cigarette smoking and caffeine consumption, may be highly deleterious to health, either singly or when combined (see Krantz, Baum & Singer, 1983; Oster, Golditz & Kelly, 1984; Whelan, 1984; National Institutes of Health, 1986; U.S. Surgeon General, 1986), and that much of this effect is attributable to excessive stress. Now go back to self-assessment exercise 5 and examine items 1, 2, 4, and 5 (if the soft drinks contain caffeine). If you responded with *c*'s or *d*'s for those items, your diet could be hurting your health, regardless of your total score on the exercise.

**NOISE POLLUTION**

The study of noise as a stressor is somewhat complex, because noise, more than the other bioecological stressors examined in this chapter, has a strong psychosocial component. Noise can produce a stress response in one or more of the following ways:

1. by stimulating the sympathetic nervous system
2. by being annoying and subjectively displeasing
3. by disrupting activities

Noise also has a psychological aspect: It may be perceived as unwanted or somehow inappropriate. This reaction—and the accompanying stress response—can occur at any frequency level. For example, a conversation at a distance of three feet generates only about 60 decibels, far below the pain threshold; yet if you are trying to figure out your income tax or study for a final exam, this conversation could be highly stressful because it disrupts your activity. Similarly, what may be music to you may be noise to someone else. Thus, the music you play every day and find relaxing might be very annoying, and thus stressful, to another.

Whether noise has a predominantly physical or psychological effect, it is clearly capable of producing the stress response. Research has demonstrated that noise can produce cardiovascular changes. Studies on the effects of noise on blood circulation found that acute exposure to moderately high noise frequencies was capable of decreasing circulation to the arms, legs, hands, and feet. A more recent study discovered that repeated exposure to noise may result in a permanent rise in blood pressure due to structural adaptation of the heart and blood vessels. Finally, studies in an industrial environment demonstrated that workers exposed to moderate and high levels of noise had higher blood levels of the stress hormones.

Such findings prompted the National Institute for Occupational Safety and Health to go on record stating that noise is capable of stimulating changes in essential physiological functioning suggestive of a general stress reaction.

Noise seems not only to affect physiological functioning but also to produce evidence of stress in our behavior as well. This case is perhaps most strongly supported by the studies of Glass and Singer (1972). While researching the effects of noise on work, they discovered that workers under noisy conditions tended to suffer from shorter concentration spans and a lower frustration threshold.

Recognizing the stressful effects of noise on human behavior, the U.S. Department of Labor has stated that government employees should not be exposed to steady noise levels in excess of 90 decibels per eight-hour day. Table 6.8 gives the noise level of various activities.

Finally, we should consider adaptation to noise. In a review of the effects of noise on humans, Kryter (1970) cited studies clearly demonstrating that human beings are capable of adapting to excessive noise stress. These studies have mistakenly been interpreted as minimizing the harmful effects of noise. On the contrary, adaptation requires energy and therefore can deplete the body of biological and psychological stamina. Selye (1976) noted that while humans can adapt to stressors, they ultimately pay the price in biological depletion and, should the exposure become chronic, in eventual breakdown. The scientist-philosopher Rene Dubos (1968) noted that adaptation could have "indirect, deleterious" psychological costs to the individual.

It appears quite clear, then, that prolonged exposure to noise

TABLE 6.8    Noise Level (in Decibels) of Various Activities

| SOUND | DECIBEL LEVEL |
|---|---|
| Jet takeoff from 200' | 140dB |
| | 120 (painful to humans) |
| Rock music | 110 |
| Automobile horn from 3' | 110 (extremely loud) |
| Motorcycle | 100 |
| Garbage truck | 100 |
| Pneumatic drill | 90 |
| Lawn mower | 90 |
| Heavy traffic | 80 |
| Alarm clock | 80 |
| Shouting, arguing | 80 (very loud) |
| Vacuum cleaner | 75 (loud) |
| Freight train from 50' | 70 |
| Freeway traffic | 65 |
| Normal conversation | 60 |
| Light automobile traffic | 50 (moderate) |
| Library | 40 |
| Soft whisper | 30 (faint) |

can have physiologically and psychologically damaging effects on the human organism.

**CHANGES IN CLIMATE AND ALTITUDE**

When the body is exposed to changes in temperature, humidity, and altitude, it responds with stress arousal and then goes into the resistance phase, which readies it for prolonged exposure to the stressor. Carrying the concept of the general adaptation syndrome to completion, if the exposure to the stressor is too extreme or continues too long, the body can no longer protect itself, and the individual perishes. Every winter in the mountains, hunters, snowmobilers, skiers, and others become lost, disabled, or caught in an avalanche and suffer from frostbite or hypothermia as a result of the low temperatures, the altitude, or both. Likewise, fall football practice may take its toll in heat prostration or heat stroke.

Chapter 10 discusses techniques for reducing these bioecological stressors and offers precautions for those traveling to colder, hotter, or more humid climates, or to higher elevations.

**SUMMARY**

This chapter has examined biological rhythms, eating and drinking habits, drug use, noise, and changes in climate and altitude as bioecological stimuli capable of contributing to the distress that a person experiences in day-to-day existence.

The study of biological rhythms points out that human behavior should be synchronized whenever possible with the naturally occurring rhythms that surround us and are within us. In this chapter you were given a method for determining possible innate rhythms so that you might better synchronize your behavior with them.

Eating and drinking habits may contribute to stress. Sympathomimetic agents, depletion or deficiency of vitamins and minerals, hypoglycemia, and sodium may all affect the stress response.

Drugs may exacerbate levels of stress by providing a pseudoescape from problems that do not disappear even with the drug experience. Some drugs, such as nicotine, amphetamines, and cocaine, directly stimulate the stress response throughout the body, and the tobacco user's smoke has the same effect on nonsmokers as well.

Noise pollution is both a biological and psychosocial stressor. Regardless of certain human adaptive characteristics, noise in excessive quantity or quality is distressful.

Climate and altitude may also be considered bioecological stressors. Extreme cold, heat, humidity, or altitude increase stress on the body. Every precaution must be taken to protect the body in these conditions.

# REFERENCES

ALTHOFF, A., M. SVOBODA, and D. GIRDANO (1988). *Choices.* Scottsdale, AZ: Gorsuch & Scarisbrick.

CENTER FOR SCIENCE IN THE PUBLIC INTEREST (1981). *The new American eating guide.* Washington, DC: Center for Science in the Public Interest.

DUBOS, R. (1968). Environmental determinants of human life. In D. C. Glass (ed.), *Biology and behavior: Environmental influences.* New York: The Rockefeller University Press and Russell Sage Foundation.

GIRDANO, D., G. EVERLY, and D. DUSEK (1985). *Experiencing health.* Englewood Cliffs, NJ: Prentice-Hall.

GLASS, D. C., and J. SINGER (1972). *Urban stress.* New York: Academic Press.

HEIMBACH, J., and A. S. LEVY (1986, October 30–31). Changing public beliefs about diet and health. Paper presented to the Journalists Conference: Food Safety and Nutrition. FDA. New York.

KRANTZ, D., A. BAUM, and J. SINGER (eds.) (1983). *Handbook of psychology and health* (Vol. 1). Hillsdale, NJ: Erlbaum.

KRYTER, K. (1970). *The effects of noise on man.* New York: Academic Press.

NATIONAL INSTITUTES OF HEALTH. (1986). *Health implications of smokeless tobacco.* Consensus Development Conference Statement.

OSTER, G., G. GOLDITZ, and N. KELLY (1984). *The economic costs of smoking and benefits of quitting.* Lexington, MA: Lexington Books.

ROSENBERG, H. (1975). *The book of vitamin therapy.* New York: Berkley Windhover Books.

SELYE, H. (1976). *The stress of life.* New York: McGraw-Hill.

SENATE SELECT COMMITTEE ON NUTRITION AND HUMAN NEEDS (1977). Washington, DC: U.S. Government Printing Office.

U.S. DRUG ADMINISTRATION (1980). *Nutritive value of foods.* Washington, DC: U.S. Government Printing Office.

U.S. SURGEON GENERAL (1986). *Surgeon General's report on smokeless tobacco.* Washington, DC: U.S. Government Printing Office.

WHELAN, E. (1984). *A smoking gun.* Philadelphia: Spiegler.

# CHAPTER SEVEN

# Personality Causes of Stress

> *Personality:* the sum of the characteristics, attitudes, values, and behavioral patterns that individuals manifest in interactions with their environment.

No discussion of stress, much less any aspect of human behavior, would be complete without some mention of the elusive and complex construct of *personality*. What we think of ourselves and how we behave and react are elements of our personality and important determinants of stress.

For people the world over, it appears that personality traits fall into five basic categories (Harary, 1991):

- expressive style
- work style
- intellectual style
- interpersonal style
- emotional intensity

Discomfort in any of these areas may indicate that one lacks skills in that area.

In this chapter we first consider how self-concept can affect stress and disease. Next we look at the role that consistent patterns of behaving play in the onset of stress and the development of disease. We then examine the anxious-reactive personality as a way of illustrating how the manner in which a person responds to a threatening situation may affect the stress response and the eventual development of psychosomatic disease. Finally, we examine how a sense of control affects stress and how coping may affect stress as well. Once again, each section is preceded by a self-assessment exercise; complete each one before reading about the topic relating to it.

**SELF–PERCEPTION**

The origin of much personal stress may lie within the individual's concept of self. Psychologists have been pointing to self-concept as perhaps the single most influential factor in behavior. It would follow that self-perception plays an important role in stress and stress management also.

Your self-perception, or self-concept, is simply the image you hold of yourself. You form this image by evaluating your power and self-worth, based on input from your family, friends, and other people who hold significant places in your life. At a very early age (perhaps even before you begin to speak) you begin to accumulate information about yourself from these sources, and slowly but surely you form your self-concept. This formation may stop as early as the age of five or six or may continue until death.

What is your image of yourself? Self-assessment exercise 6 was designed to provide some insight into your self-concept. If you scored from 10 to 19 points, you have a high self-concept. A score of 20 to 24 indicates an average self-concept. If you scored between 25 and 40, your self-concept appears to be in need of bolstering.

**Components**

High self-concept is basic to all personal interactions. A healthy concept of self assures confidence, worth, security, spontaneity, and other descriptors of the actualized person. Some use the terms *self-concept* and *self-esteem* interchangeably, but it would seem that total self-concept consists of many different components (including self-esteem), each necessary to complete the ideal self (Girdano & Dusek, 1988). Six major components of self-concept—self-awareness, self-worth, self-love, self-esteem, self-confidence, and self-respect—will be discussed here.

### Self-Awareness

Being self-aware is realizing that you have an impact in this world, that your presence and actions can and do influence others and vice versa. This does not mean that you are *responsible* for the reactions of others; they may choose to feel enhanced or hurt by your presence, and this is their choice. Whether the smiles and intimacy, anger and criticism of others is intentional or not, every person has an impact on others.

## SELF—ASSESSMENT EXERCISE 6

Choose the alternative that best summarizes how you generally behave and place your answer in the space provided.

_____ 1. When I face a difficult task, I try my best and will usually succeed.
(a) almost always
(b) often
(c) seldom
(d) almost never

_____ 2. I am at ease around members of the opposite sex.
(a) almost always
(b) often
(c) seldom
(d) almost never

_____ 3. I feel that I have a lot going for me.
(a) almost always
(b) often
(c) seldom
(d) almost never

_____ 4. I have a very high degree of confidence in my own abilities.
(a) almost always
(b) often
(c) seldom
(d) almost never

_____ 5. I prefer to be in control of my own life as opposed to having someone else make decisions for me.
(a) almost always
(b) often
(c) seldom
(d) almost never

What is the purpose of being self-aware? To see the interrelationship of all people and the part that you play in your own growth and development, and also in others'.

### Self-Worth

Some parts of the self-concept are inborn, and self-worth is one of them. A basic tenet of the founders of the United States was that we are all created equal: No one person is worth more or less than any other human on this earth, and we all have the basic rights to

## SELF–ASSESSMENT EXERCISE 6 (CONTINUED)

_____   6.   I am comfortable and at ease around my superiors.
(a) almost always
(b) often
(c) seldom
(d) almost never

_____   7.   I am often overly self-conscious or shy when among strangers.
(a) almost always
(b) often
(c) seldom
(d) almost never

_____   8.   Whenever something goes wrong, I tend to blame myself.
(a) almost always
(b) often
(c) seldom
(d) almost never

_____   9.   When I don't succeed, I tend to let it depress me more than it should.
(a) almost always
(b) often
(c) seldom
(d) almost never

_____   10.  I often feel that I am beyond help.
(a) almost always
(b) often
(c) seldom
(d) almost never

_____   Total Score

Scoring:

Items 1 to 6:  a = 1, b = 2, c = 3, d = 4
Items 7 to 10:  a = 4, b = 3, c = 2, d = 1

Place your total score in the space provided and read the section on "Self-Perception."

life, liberty, and the pursuit of happiness. This is an instance in which the written laws of the land parallel spiritual doctrine. We come into this world and travel through it with a worth that is equal to that of all others. Nothing can be added to make one person worth more than another. Conversely, no horrible deed can reduce the basic human worth of a person. The only thing that reduces worth is when the individual assumes from life experiences that he or she has less than the 100 percent worth inherited at birth.

The gravest mistake one can make with self-worth is trying to earn it. No one can get more than 100 percent, and everyone already has that. It can be unearthed or realized by the individual, but it cannot be earned from someone else.

### Self-Love

Just as with self-worth, there is an inborn capacity for self-love; it is not something one earns from others over a lifetime of struggle. Unfortunately, many believe that they have to earn self-love through sacrifice and punishment of self, and through pleasing others. Those lacking in self-love must relearn compassion for themselves in all situations, through all emotions, and in all actions. This is done by letting go of judgments from outside the self—judgments learned from parents, friends, teachers, and society.

Part of relearning self-love is learning self-forgiveness, which revolves around the basic belief that we all do the best we can with the skills we have at the time. This is not to say that we cannot learn more effective ways to behave; rather it means accepting that "this is who I am and this is the way I behaved in that situation. I'm leaning to do it differently, but no matter how I do it and how it turns out, I love myself."

### Self-Esteem

This is probably the most familiar component of self-concept, and many people use the two terms interchangeably. However, self-esteem is a compassion for self that is earned through one's actions (unlike self-worth and self-love, which are inherent). Because self-esteem is earned, it comes from success. Many earn self-esteem through their academic accomplishments, sports, or doing their job well. Self-esteem that is rewarded internally is lasting, and it enhances the other self-concept components. However, self-esteem earned from the outside can be taken away at any time, which can be devastating. If the individual has earned esteem from the outside, the need for rewards and attention from others can become insatiable, and if that reward is removed or reversed (which happens from time to time within all relationships), feelings of powerlessness and anger from being powerless result. It follows that internal resources are truer and more helpful for enhancement of self-concept than are pats on the back from others.

Self-esteem is itself built on some basic components: honesty, especially with oneself; responsibility for one's perception of what is real; trust; listening to intuitions and acting on them; and positive intent toward others.

### Self-Confidence

Self-confidence is the earned or learned ability to cope with perceptions of the world (an individual's reality). Each person sets up his or her perception of the world and then handles those perceptions in a confident or not-so-confident manner. Success in this component comes from seeing planned outcomes develop into real outcomes by using past resources, trust, hope, and courage.

### Self-Respect

Self-respect is the ability to honor, or appreciate, one's emotional nature: to express fear, happiness, anger, love, and joy appropriately when they are felt. This does not mean "dumping" these emotions on someone else, but expressing them when the need is felt. Holding back from expressing an emotion not only blocks its energy, but also shows lack of self-respect. When a person respects who he or she is, expression of emotions is natural and appropriate.

**Effects on Behavior**

Researchers and clinicians have known for years that if in a given situation a person devalues himself and perceives himself as helpless and certain of failure, this perception will virtually ensure failure in that situation. This concept has been referred to as the *self-fulfilling prophecy:* the likelihood of failure at some task will be greatly increased if you imagine yourself failing even before the task in question has begun. The converse of this relationship is true as well: if you imagine yourself succeeding at your task, your probability of success will be greatly enhanced.

In his text *Self-Fulfilling Prophecies,* Russell Jones (1977) exhaustively reviewed self-expectations (for example, the self-fulfilling prophecy) in terms of social, psychological, and even physiological outcomes. He concluded that interpersonal social success, such psychological states as depression and anxiety, and even physiological arousal (for example, stress) can all be dramatically affected by self-expectancies. In accordance with Jones, Seligman (1975) writes in his classic text on helplessness:

> I am no longer convinced that special intensive training will raise a child's IQ by twenty points or allow him to talk three months early. . . . On the other hand, I *am* convinced that certain . . . environmental contingencies will produce a child who believes he is helpless—that he cannot succeed. If a child believes he is helpless he will perform stupidly, regardless of his IQ. On the other hand, if a child believes that he has control and mastery, he may outperform more talented peers who lack such a belief.

Finally, Murray (1983) examined the effects of self-perception on hostility. He found that low-self-esteem subjects were more

## SELF—ASSESSMENT EXERCISE 7

Place your answer to each of the following questions in the space provided before each number.

_____ 1. I have no patience with tardiness.
  (a) almost always
  (b) often
  (c) seldom
  (d) almost never

_____ 2. I hate to wait in lines.
  (a) almost always
  (b) often
  (c) seldom
  (d) almost never

_____ 3. People tell me that I tend to get irritated too easily.
  (a) almost always
  (b) often
  (c) seldom
  (d) almost never

_____ 4. Whenever possible, I try to make my activities competitive.
  (a) almost always
  (b) often
  (c) seldom
  (d) almost never

_____ 5. I feel guilty for taking time off from work that needs to be done.
  (a) almost always
  (b) often
  (c) seldom
  (d) almost never

vulnerable to interpersonal insult than high-self-esteem subjects. Furthermore, low-self-esteem subjects became angrier than high-self-esteem subjects when trying to be assertive toward their insult but failing to elicit an apology.

**Effects on Disease**

Not only are self-esteem and self-perception important both in the outcome of behavioral performance and in the severity of the stress experienced, but self-perception (especially the devalued, helpless, and hopeless image of self) may play a significant role in the even-

## SELF–ASSESSMENT EXERCISE 7 (CONTINUED)

_____   6. People tell me I'm a poor loser.
  (a) almost always
  (b) often
  (c) seldom
  (d) almost never

_____   7. I tend to lose my temper or get irritable when I'm under a lot of pressure.
  (a) almost always
  (b) often
  (c) seldom
  (d) almost never

_____   8. I tend to race against the clock.
  (a) almost always
  (b) often
  (c) seldom
  (d) almost never

_____   9. I hate to wait or depend on others in order to do what I want to do.
  (a) almost always
  (b) often
  (c) seldom
  (d) almost never

_____   10. I catch myself rushing when there is no real need to do so.
  (a) almost always
  (b) often
  (c) seldom
  (d) almost never

_____   Total Score

To obtain your total score, score each question as follows:

(a) = 4 points     (c) = 2 points
(b) = 3 points     (d) = 1 point

Place your total score in the space provided and read the section on "Patterns of Behavior."

tual onset of disease. One of the more intriguing aspects of the role of a devalued self-image in disease emerges from the study of cancer.

The bulk of personality research done with cancer patients concluded that there may, indeed, be such a thing as a "carcinogenic personality." This personality is characterized by gross self-devaluation, helplessness, and feelings of hopelessness. In effect, this personality sees itself in a totally passive and dependent role within its environment.

According to W. W. Meissner (1977) of the Harvard Medical School, cancer patients are relatively "selfless" individuals. They often display signs of great sacrifice and self-effacement. Finally, most exhibit feelings of "hopelessness" and "helplessness," feelings that are also typical of these people even before the onset of cancer. These individuals tend to see themselves as stupid, clumsy, weak, and inept even though their achievements are often enviable (Siegal, 1986). The cancer-prone personality is as good a description of low self-concept as one is likely to find.

As early as 1955, clinical observations led Lawrence LeShan to conclude that one of the major personality correlates of cancer was severely poor self-expectation coupled with self-dislike. Similar research by Simonton and Simonton verified LeShan's conclusions. The Simontons observed that a very pessimistic outlook on life characterized many cancer patients. More important, those with the lowest self-perceptions eventually succumbed to the disease, whereas patients who maintained optimism and the conviction that they could win over cancer survived.

Once these researchers began to realize the significance of the cancer patient's self-perception, they designed counseling methods to help improve patient self-perception and used them as an adjunct to more traditional cancer treatment. Reports by Simonton and Simonton (1975) and LeShan (1977) showed that progress was made through such an approach.

In summary, it should be emphasized, first, that perceptions of helplessness and self-devaluation can lead to increased stress. Second, a poor self-concept may also play a significant role in the onset of various diseases, the most dramatic of which may be cancer. It may be that a poor self-concept generally increases one's susceptibility to many disease forms. Third, by improving your perception of control and self-worth, you may begin to reduce and eliminate stress. You may find that as an added benefit you begin to see your "luck" in all endeavors change as well. Specific strategies for improving self-perception will be discussed in Chapter 10. Finally, it is important to note that self-assessment exercise 6 was *not* designed to give predictive insight into cancer; it merely gives you some feedback concerning your self-perception.

## PATTERNS OF BEHAVIOR

We have known for years that specific patterns of behavior can adversely affect your health. The prime example is the well known list of cardiovascular risk factors, which include smoking, lack of exercise, obesity, and high-fat diets. It has been clearly demonstrated that the consistent practice of one or more of these behaviors will increase susceptibility to premature heart disease.

It is possible that far more general behavioral traits could affect your health. Could it be that the way in which you *generally* interact with your environment may predispose you to stress and related disease? The answer is a definite yes! Evidence strongly suggests that the manner in which you choose to interact with your surroundings can play a major role in determining whether you develop premature heart disease.

Two cardiologists, Meyer Friedman and Ray Rosenman, in the normal course of treating their patients, noticed some recurring behaviors among them, especially in relation to how they dealt with time. They noticed the extreme anxiousness of their patients in the waiting room, and the constant focus of their conversations on time, work, and achievement.

From their contact with coronary patients, Friedman and Rosenman in the late 1950s formulated a construct of action–emotion behavior patterns that seemed to embody the coronary-prone individual. They referred to this construct as the *Type A personality*, and included in it the following characteristics:

1.  An intense sense of time urgency; a tendency to race against the clock; the need to do more and obtain more in the shortest possible time.
2.  An aggressive personality that at times evolves into hostility; high motivation, yet very easy loss of temper; a high sense of competitiveness, often with the desire to make a contest out of everything; the inability to "play for fun."
3.  An intense achievement motive, yet too often this "go for it" attitude lacks properly defined goals.
4.  Polyphasic behavior—that is, the involvement in several different tasks at the same time.

During a series of impressive research studies known as the Western Collaborative Studies, the Type A behavior pattern was shown to precede the development of coronary heart disease in 72 to 85 percent of the 3411 men tested. These results strongly suggest that a Type A personality may be predictive of the eventual onset of premature heart disease.

Since the pioneering studies of Friedman and Rosenman, a wealth of research data on the Type A behavior pattern has emerged. Physiologically oriented research has found Type A's to be more reactive in their sympathetic-nervous-system response when challenged or confronted by their environment, compared with individuals who possess none of the Type A characteristics (Dembroski, MacDougall, Herd & Shields, 1978; Diamond, Schneiderman, Schwartz, Smith, Vorp & Pasin, 1984). This sympathetic

## SELF–ASSESSMENT EXERCISE 8

Choose the response that best summarizes how you usually react during anxious moments and place the letter of that response in the space provided.

When I'm anxious I . . .

_____  1. Tend to imagine all of the worst possible things happening to me as a result of whatever "crisis" made me anxious to begin with.
(a) almost always
(b) often
(c) seldom
(d) almost never

_____  2. Do everything I can to resolve the problem immediately; if I don't I'll go crazy worrying about it later.
(a) almost always
(b) often
(c) seldom
(d) almost never

_____  3. Will relive the crisis over and over again in my mind, even though it may be over and resolved.
(a) almost always
(b) often
(c) seldom
(d) almost never

_____  4. Will be able to clearly picture the crisis in my mind hours or even days after it's over.
(a) almost always
(b) often
(c) seldom
(d) almost never

_____  5. Get the feeling that I'm losing control.
(a) almost always
(b) often
(c) seldom
(d) almost never

overresponsiveness has been suggested as the key pathogenic process leading to increased cardiovascular risk. Byproducts of chronic sympathetic activation include elevated serum-cholesterol levels, decreased vascular flexibility, increased blood pressure, and increased cardiac output—all of which, when chronic, can contribute to cardiovascular disease.

Research by numerous authors aimed at refining the Type A pattern and defining its specific pathogenic components has led us to believe that the anger/hostility component may be the most

## SELF—ASSESSMENT EXERCISE 8 (CONTINUED)

_____ 6. Feel my stomach sinking, my mouth getting dry, or my heart pounding.
   (a) almost always
   (b) often
   (c) seldom
   (d) almost never

_____ 7. Tend to make "mountains out of molehills."
   (a) almost always
   (b) often
   (c) seldom
   (d) almost never

_____ 8. Have trouble falling asleep at night.
   (a) almost always
   (b) often
   (c) seldom
   (d) almost never

_____ 9. Have difficulty in speaking or notice my hands and fingers trembling.
   (a) almost always
   (b) often
   (c) seldom
   (d) almost never

_____ 10. Notice my thoughts "racing."
   (a) almost always
   (b) often
   (c) seldom
   (d) almost never

_____ Total Score

Scoring:   (a) = 4 points    (c) = 2 points
           (b) = 3 points    (d) = 1 point

Total your score and read the section on "The Anxious-Reactive Personality."

significant disease-causing constituent (Diamond et al., 1984). Another interpretation of the results of this research is that those individuals who are chronically and globally cynical may be those Type A's who are at highest risk for cardiovascular disease. There is also some evidence that the time-urgent characteristic may be pathogenic as well (Dembroski, MacDougall, Herd & Shields, 1978), but the hostility trait seems to be the most pathogenic because of its high association with secretion of testosterone. Testosterone release is associated with atherosclerosis.

Thus, we have come far since the initial discovery in the late 1950s of the Type A pattern. Instead of Friedman and Rosenman's four-component construct, we now believe anger/hostility/cynicism and perhaps time-urgency are the major pathogenic factors of the pattern. Also, whereas we once believed that Type A was pathogenic for men only, we now believe it can be pathogenic for women as well. Finally, we can see that the Type A pattern includes not only adults, but adolescents and preschoolers as well (see Dembroski, MacDougall & Musante, 1979, and Weiss, 1981, for reviews).

What makes the Type A behave in such a manner? Studies on both male and female twins suggest that there may be some genetic involvement, but other research (Dembroski, 1978; Weiss, Herd & Fox, 1981; Margolis, McLeroy, Runyan, and Kaplan, 1983) points us more toward sociocultural origins. Parental expectations and high standards with frequent urging and criticism of actions, as well as an intensely competitive atmosphere, may all be involved.

Cultural influences in general must be considered important contributors, especially our culture's work ethic, which motivates individuals toward hard work and achievement and rewards them for it. However, one can be a hard worker without being hard-driving and competitive. So it is not only the underlying values of the culture, but also how the members of that culture perceive the methods for achieving what they value, that are important.

This idea points to an interesting phenomenon about the Type A behavior pattern: Those who exhibit it feel comfortable with it, value it, and reinforce it. They describe themselves as challenged and eager to meet the competition. They are happy with their work and wish they had more time to do more work. Type A personalities are confident and do not fear losing the struggle with life and work tasks. They are aggressive, ambitious, and competitive, are not fearful or anxious, and do not as a rule suffer neurotic states. On the contrary, they usually strive to control their environment and exert power over other people. Generally, they view their behavior as positive, and they receive rewards through their behavior. Thus, not only does society condition the behavior pattern, but it reinforces it as well. The Type A behavior pattern can exist only in an environment that stimulates it and allows it to function. Our fast-moving, competitive society does not lack challenges for those who would seek them out.

Evidence points to the Type A behavior pattern as being a learned behavior. As such, it can be unlearned, or at least modified. Stress-reducing techniques, both specific to Type A behavior and general, are presented in a later chapter, but for now let us reconsider self-assessment exercise 7. This exercise is a broad-ranged attempt at sampling the Type A behavior pattern. We emphasized the dimensions of anger/hostility (items 3, 4, 6, and 7) and time-urgent (items 1, 2, 5, 8, 9, and 10). A total score in excess of 24 may indicate presence of the Type A pattern (although this assessment *does not* measure cardiovascular risk). You may wish to take a more careful look at the anger/hostility items, for characteristics similar to these may be at the core of the Type A pattern.

**THE ANXIOUS-REACTIVE PERSONALITY**

Anxiety is a basic component of stress. As we discuss it here, anxiety is not only a *symptom* or manifestation of stress, but also a *cause* of further stress. Based on the observations of people who suffer from chronic anxiety and seem to complain of stress-related disorders, we've identified another personality type that appears to create excessive, chronic stress. We call this personality type the *anxious-reactive* personality. If you are one of these people, you suffer from anxiety far more than most people, because your reaction to a stressor results in a form of anxiety that seems to perpetuate itself. Therefore, the characteristic that makes you different from other people lies in the feedback mechanisms involved in the anxiety reaction. Most people experience anxious moments that quickly end when the stressor is removed. The anxious-reactive individual experiences stress that seems to persist, or increase, even after the stressor is gone. Before we describe the specific mechanism involved in this anxious-reactive personality and its role in excessive stress and disease, a description of anxiety in general seems in order.

Anxiety may be thought of as fear, and in effect the two words may be used synonymously. The anxiety-reaction process begins when the individual perceives a stimulus (person, place, or thing) as challenging or threatening. This perception occurs in the higher (neocortical) regions of the brain and entails interpretation, or assignment of meaning to the stimulus, which makes the individual insecure or perhaps apprehensive. These feelings of insecurity are transformed into physiological arousal of the endocrines and sympathetic nervous system. So now not only are the thought processes aroused, but the bodily processes are also. Fortunately, this hyper-aroused condition usually subsides shortly after the stimulus has been removed.

Most of us suffer from this form of arousal. It is quite common in this society to be occasionally faced with things that make us insecure and result in generalized anxiety. Ordinarily, the anxiety reaction represents no major threat to mental or physical health.

Yet, the more severe reaction characteristic of the anxious-reactive personality does seem to represent a significant challenge to health and well-being.

This self-perpetuating anxiety reaction—which persists or increases even after the original stimulus has been removed—is important to our discussion of stressors, because people prone to this reaction can become mentally and physically incapacitated by exposure to the mildest of stressors. Furthermore, they are highly prone to the development of chronic psychosomatic disorders.

The anxious-reactive personality is hypersensitive to the feedback mechanisms at work during the stress reaction. This means that the anxious individual suffers from a feedback "loop" that perpetuates the anxiety reaction. The basis of this anxiety feedback loop is as follows: Any arousal response to some perceived stressor can eventually assume the role of a stressor itself and, in turn, cause further arousal.

The feedback messages that further increase arousal can take three forms: *cognitive, visceral* (smooth muscle), and *musculoskeletal* (striated muscle). The first and perhaps most volatile feedback during stress reaches the body in the form of thoughts (cognitions) concerning the nature of the stressor and the possible outcomes. Fear-laden thoughts that follow the stressor are capable of inducing visceral arousal by way of the autonomic nervous system, and further thoughts may increase the musculoskeletal reaction of a stress response. These cognitions are perhaps the most harmful of the three feedback forms. Many individuals engage in what may be called "catastrophizing"; that is, they always perceive the stressor event as far worse than it really is. The catastrophizer often views all psychosocial stress in terms of life-or-death urgency. This tendency to consistently overreact may result in severe mental and physical incapacitation and trauma during a stress reaction, and may help bring on psychosomatic disease at an early age. Items 1, 2, 5, and 7 in self-assessment exercise 8 concern catastrophizing tendencies. How did you score on them?

Another sufferer from cognitive feedback is the person who relives any and all crises over and over in his or her mind for days or weeks after the incident. This "reliver" suffers from distress every time he or she relives the incident. Do you tend to relive stressful events? Items 3, 4, 8, and 10 in self-assessment exercise 8 dealt with that aspect. The "catastrophizer" and the "reliver" are forms of the anxious-reactive personality characterized by prolonged feedback about the stressful event. This mechanism is depicted in Figure 7.1.

The second form of feedback involved in anxious behavior and

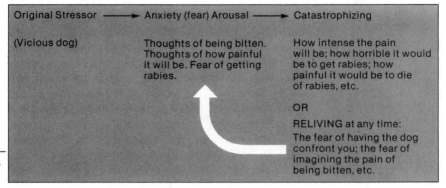

Original Stressor ⟶ Anxiety (fear) Arousal ⟶ Catastrophizing

(Vicious dog)

Thoughts of being bitten.
Thoughts of how painful
it will be. Fear of getting
rabies.

How intense the pain
will be; how horrible it would
be to get rabies; how
painful it would be to die
of rabies, etc.

OR

RELIVING at any time:
The fear of having the dog
confront you; the fear of
imagining the pain of
being bitten, etc.

**FIGURE 7.1**

Cognitive Activity
in the Anxiety
Feedback Loop

the stress reaction is visceral, or smooth-muscle, activity. This involves the heart, stomach, gastrointestinal tract, and so on. The awareness of smooth-muscle activity, such as heart pounding or stomach gurgling, can increase stressful cognitive processes. In this way, visceral awareness can perpetuate further visceral activity. How responsive are your visceral mechanisms? Item 6 in self-assessment exercise 8 concerns this issue.

Finally, anxiety feedback can occur in the musculoskeletal system. This involves overt movement of the striated muscles—those muscles attached to tendons and bones. In our own observations and research with public-speaking students, we have found that the awareness of trembling hands, awkward speech, or muscle tension can increase visceral activity, in the form of heart rate. Increased musculoskeletal activity has been found to lead to further increases in the same system. Item 9 in self-assessment exercise 8 deals with how reactive this system is during stress. Figure 7.2 is a diagram of the anxiety feedback loop at work in the visceral and musculoskeletal reactions.

In summary, the anxious-reactive personality is hypersensitive to stress reactions. These reactions may occur on cognitive, visceral, and/or musculoskeletal levels. Once these reactions have been perceived by the individual, they form an automatic feedback loop that perpetuates and in some cases worsens the severity of the stress reaction. Perhaps that most severe form of this anxiety feedback is found in the catastrophizing individual, who consistently perceives problems (stressors) in the worst possible context. For these people stress is a constant companion, affecting their daily behavior; catastrophizers are vulnerable to incapacitation from the slightest stressor and also to psychosomatic disease.

A total score of 25 to 40 in self-assessment exercise 8 would

**SELF—ASSESSMENT EXERCISE 9**

Answer each question and place the letter of your response in the space to the left.

_____ 1. How often do you find yourself feeling helpless or hopeless?
(a) almost never
(b) seldom
(c) often
(d) almost always

_____ 2. How often do you find yourself in a situation that seems out of your control?
(a) almost never
(b) seldom
(c) often
(d) almost always

_____ 3. How often do you find yourself needing to have your life well planned and organized?
(a) almost never
(b) seldom
(c) often
(d) almost always

_____ 4. How often do you find yourself feeling sad or depressed?
(a) almost never
(b) seldom
(c) often
(d) almost always

_____ 5. How often do you find yourself fearful of losing control over your life?
(a) almost never
(b) seldom
(c) often
(d) almost always

_____ 6. How often do you find yourself feeling insecure?
(a) almost never
(b) seldom
(c) often
(d) almost always

indicate a high degree of anxiety reactivity. A score of 20 to 24 is average, and a score below 20 indicates low reactivity.

**STRESS AND THE NEED FOR CONTROL**

In Chapter 5 we quoted noted psychologist Albert Bandura (1982) as stating that "it is mainly perceived inefficacy in coping with potentially aversive events that makes them fearsome. To the extent that one can prevent, terminate, or lessen the severity of aversive events, there is little reason to fear them." In other words, it

## SELF–ASSESSMENT EXERCISE 9 (CONTINUED)

_____ 7. How often do you find yourself needing to control the people around you?
   (a) almost never
   (b) seldom
   (c) often
   (d) almost always

_____ 8. How often do you find yourself needing to control your environment?
   (a) almost never
   (b) seldom
   (c) often
   (d) almost always

_____ 9. How often do you feel the need to have your daily activities highly structured?
   (a) almost never
   (b) seldom
   (c) often
   (d) almost always

_____ 10. How often do you feel secure?
   (a) almost never
   (b) seldom
   (c) often
   (d) almost always

_____ Total Score

Scoring:

Items 1 to 9

(a) = 1 point    (c) = 3 points
(b) = 2 points   (d) = 4 points

Item 10
(a) = 4 points    (c) = 2 points
(b) = 3 points    (d) = 1 point

After adding these items to obtain your total score, read the section on "Stress and the Need for Control."

can be argued that the most powerful stressor of all is real or imagined _loss of control_. Indeed, what may contribute to all of the psychosocial and personality stressors examined in this chapter is a real or imagined loss of control over one's life. Consider these stressors:

1. Lifestyle/environment change
2. Frustration

3. Overload
4. Underload
5. Low self-esteem
6. Type A personality (hostility/cynicism, time-urgency)
7. Anxious reactivity

Contributing to each is clearly a real or imagined loss of control.

Richard Lazarus, in his classic text *Psychological Stress and Coping Processes* (1966), theorized that the more we perceive ourselves in control of a situation, the less severe the stress reaction will be. This conclusion certainly suggests that feelings of hopelessness and helplessness may be the *fundamental cause* of excessive stress. This point was clearly demonstrated during World War II. Psychiatrists observed that soldiers who could return enemy fire suffered fewer mental disorders than those who could not return fire but simply had to take shelter and hope that they would not be harmed (Jones, 1977).

Similarly, it has been shown by Geer, Davison, and Gatchel (1970) that just the expectation of control over stressors can reduce stress. In their studies, one group of students was deceived into believing that their reaction times to shock could reduce the frequency of the shocks they would receive. The experimenters then reduced the number of shocks for all subjects, regardless of reaction time. The group that was told that they were, indeed, controlling the reduction experienced a decrease in their level of distress, measured by skin conductance. A group who received an equal number of shocks yet was told that they had no control over them experienced an increased stress response. Thus, anything that adds to the feeling of self-control is likely to reduce the severity of the stress reaction. This has been one of the more lauded advantages of biofeedback; that is, learning skills that allow a person to control the

**FIGURE 7.2**

Visceral and Musculoskeletal Activity in the Anxiety Feedback Loop

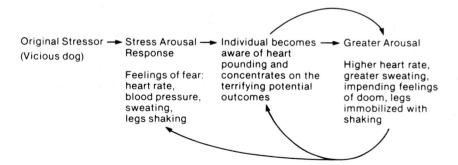

autonomic nervous system appear to greatly increase self-concept and a positive attitude (Green & Green, 1977).

David Glass (1977) has argued that the core of the Type A behavior pattern is the *need for control*. Type A individuals' manifest competitiveness, time-urgency, hostility, and low tolerance for frustration may all be seen as conscious expressions of a need to control themselves and their environment. In an attempt to test Glass's hypothesis, Dembroski, MacDougall, and Musante (1984) found that the need to control significantly correlated with the Type A pattern. Furthermore, they found evidence that autonomic-nervous-system arousal may create a psychological discomfort that could serve to increase the *need* to exert control.

On the positive side, such researchers as Lazarus (1966), Kobasa (1979), Bandura (1982), Matheny and Cupp (1983), and Fisher (1984) all offer considerable evidence that a real or imagined sense of control over self or environment is a powerful stress-reducing mechanism. Fisher (1984) has compiled perhaps the most impressive array of evidence that a sense of control may be the single most powerful stress-management tool. The classic studies of Weiss (1972) demonstrated that even animals (rats) given control over electric shock contingencies developed fewer ulcers than rats having no control over the shocks. George Everly (1984) developed a therapeutic intervention that has proved effective in the treatment of anxiety and panic attacks. This therapy, a neurocognitive intervention, is primarily designed to help patients develop a sense of control over anxiety and to teach them how to abort anxiety and panic attacks. In support of Everly's work, Holahan, Holahan, and Belk (1984) found an inverse relationship between self-efficacy and maladjustment with aging. Figure 7.3 depicts the self-efficacy and stress-control process.

Now go back and examine your responses to self-assessment exercise 9. Total scores in excess of 24 may indicate vulnerability to excessive stress due to feelings of impotency—for example, a sense of lack of control. Items 3, 5, 7, 8, and 9 indicate a *need to control;* items 1, 2, 4, 6, and 10 indicate feelings of *loss of control.*

## SUMMARY

This chapter isolated four aspects of personality—self-concept, consistent behavioral patterns (Type A), anxiety reactivity, and the need for control—and showed how they are implicated in stress and disease.

Self-concept is one of the most important determinants of stress and psychosomatic disease yet uncovered. Poor self-expectation will likely lead to failure at behavioral tasks. Hence, the desire to

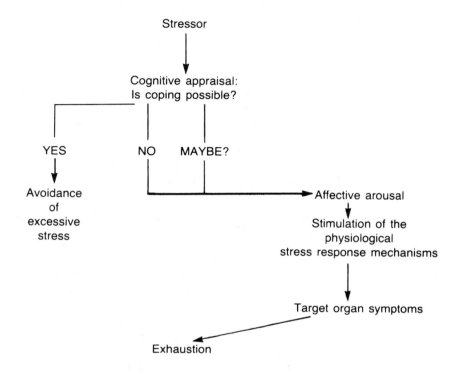

**FIGURE 7.3**

Control and Stress

"psyche up" athletes before contests, the need for an entertainer or a speaker to face the audience confidently, and the need for a student to face an exam with confidence. Self-devaluation in such situations usually results in the tendency to "freeze in the clutch"— more specifically, to play below one's potential in athletics, to suffer from stage fright, and to be incapacitated by test anxiety during an exam. Poor self-image has been more tragically linked with serious mental and physical diseases as well.

Behavior patterns are also highly implicated in the stress–disease continuum. The Type A, coronary-prone personality is a characteristic pattern of goal-oriented, ego-involved behavior highly correlated with coronary heart disease.

The anxiety reaction is part of a feedback loop, perpetuating and augmenting the stress response and lowering performance.

Finally, the need for control is a potential stressor, but the perception of control may be a stress reducer.

# REFERENCES

BANDURA, A. (1982). Self-efficacy mechanism in human agency. *American Psychologist, 165,* 122–47.

DEMBROSKI, T., J. MACDOUGALL, J. HERD, AND J. SHIELDS (1978). Effect of level of challenge on pressure and heart rate response in Type A and B subjects. *Journal of Applied Social Psychology, 9,* 209–38.

DEMBROSKI, T., J. MACDOUGALL, AND L. MUSANTE (1984). Desirability of control versus locus of control. *Health Psychology, 3,* 12–26.

DEMBROSKI, T., S. WEISS, J. SHIELDS, S. HAYNES, AND M. FEINLIEB (1978). *Coronary-prone behavior.* New York: Springer-Verlag.

DIAMOND, E., N. SCHNEIDERMAN, D. SCHWARTZ, J. SMITH, R. VORP, AND R. PASIN (1984). Harassment, hostility, and Type A as determinants of cardiovascular reactivity during competition. *Journal of Behavioral Medicine, 7,* 171–89.

EVERLY, G. (1984). Managing change. *Data Management, 22,* 21–25.

FISHER, S. (1984). *Stress and perception of control.* Hillsdale, NJ: Erlbaum.

FRIEDMAN, M., AND R. ROSENMAN (1974). *Type A behavior and your heart.* New York: Knopf.

GEER, J. H., G. DAVISON, AND R. GATCHEL (1970). Reduction of stress in humans through nonveridical perceived control of aversive stimulation. *Journal of Personality and Social Psychology, 16,* 731–38.

GIRDANO, D., AND D. DUSEK (1988). *Changing health behavior.* Scottsdale, AZ: Gorsuch & Scarisbrick.

GLASS, D. C. (1977). *Behavior patterns, stress, and coronary-prone behavior.* Hillsdale, NJ: Erlbaum.

GREEN, E., AND A. GREEN (1977). *Beyond feedback.* New York: Dell Pub. Co., Inc.

HARARY, K. (1991). The Omni-Berkeley personality profile. *Omni,* May, 48–59.

HINKLE, L. E. (1973). The concept of "stress" in the biological and social sciences. *Science, Medicine, and Man, 1* (43), 176–81.

HOLAHAN, C., C. HOLAHAN, AND S. BELK (1984). Adjustment in aging. *Health Psychology, 3,* 315–23.

JONES, R. (1977). *Self-fulfilling prophecies.* Hillsdale, NJ: Erlbaum.

KOBASA, S. C. (1979). Stressful life events, personality, and health. *Journal of Personality and Social Psychology, 37,* 1–11.

LAZARUS, R. S. (1966). *Psychological stress and coping processes.* New York: McGraw-Hill.

LESHAN, L. (1977). *You can fight for your life.* New York: Evans.

LIPPSITT, D., AND P. WHYBROW (eds.) (1977). *Psychosomatic medicine.* New York: Oxford University Press.

MCLEAN, A. (1974). *Occupational stress.* Springfield, IL: Chas. C. Thomas.

MARGOLIS, L., K. MCLEROY, C. RUNYAN, AND B. KAPLAN (1983). Type A behavior: An ecological approach. *Journal of Behavioral Medicine, 6,* 245–58.

MATHENY, K., AND P. CUPP (1983). Desirability and anticipation as moderating variables between life change and illness. *Journal of Human Stress, 9,* 14–23.

Meissner, W. W. (1977). Family process and psychosomatic disease. In Z. J. Lipowski, D. Lippsitt, and P. Whybrow (eds.), *Psychosomatic medicine*. New York: Oxford University Press.

Murray, E. (1983, February). Coping and anger. Paper presented at the Miami Symposium on Stress and Coping, Miami.

Rosenman, R. H., R. J. Brand, C. D. Jenkins, M. Friedman, R. Straus, and M. Wurm (1975). Coronary heart disease in the Western Collaborative Group Study: A final follow-up of 8½ years. *Journal of the American Medical Association, 233,* 872–77.

Seligman, M. (1975). *Helplessness.* San Francisco: W. H. Freeman & Company Publishers.

Siegel, B. S. (1986). *Love, medicine and miracles.* New York: Harper & Row, Pub.

Simonton, O. C., and S. Simonton (1975). Belief systems and management of the emotional aspects of malignancy. *Journal of Transpersonal Psychology, 7,* 29–47.

Weiss, J. (1972). Psychological factors in stress and disease. *Scientific American, 226,* 104–13.

Weiss, S. (1981). *Perspectives on behavioral medicine.* New York: Academic Press.

Zuckerman, M. (1974). The sensation seeking motive. In B. Maher (ed.), *Progress in experimental personality research* (Vol. 7, pp. 136–52). New York: Academic Press.

# CHAPTER EIGHT

# Occupational Stress and Stressors

As research on stress continues, more and more authorities are recognizing the costliness of excessive stress. Consider the following:

1. The National Council on Compensation Insurance has stated that stress now accounts for about 14 percent of all occupational-disease worker's compensation claims—up from 5 percent in 1980 (McCarthy, 1988).
2. The National Council on Compensation Insurance has noted that claim benefits paid for stress average $15,000, twice the amount paid for the average physical-injury claim (McCarthy, 1988).
3. Stress-related disorders have been estimated to cost business and industry in excess of $150 billion per year in the form of decreased productivity, absenteeism, and disability (Pelletier & Lutz, 1988).
4. Alcohol abuse (to which excessive stress may contribute) costs American industry about $44.2 billion per year (Pelletier, 1984).

Obviously, the indirect costs of excessive stress are difficult to estimate, but they are surely erosive to American industry. Just how many mistakes or just how much lost creativity is attributable to excessive stress may never be known.

This chapter provides information and insight about potential sources of harmful stress and inefficiency at work. Such knowledge can be valuable in developing a plan to manage that stress in a constructive way. This chapter consists of two sections: (1) a brief overview of occupational stress, focusing on evidence on how this kind of stress is manifested physiologically, and (2) specific occupational stressors.

## SELF–ASSESSMENT EXERCISE 10

Choose the response that best answers the question and place the corresponding letter in the space provided.

Questions 1–7: During the typical course of your job, how often do you . . .

_____ 1. face important time deadlines that you have difficulty meeting?
(a) once a day or more
(b) more than once a week but less than once a day
(c) once a week
(d) less than once a week

_____ 2. feel less competent than you think you should?
(a) once a day or more
(b) more than once a week but less than once a day
(c) once a week
(d) less than once a week

_____ 3. wish your work could be less complex?
(a) once a day or more
(b) more than once a week but less than once a day
(c) once a week
(d) less than once a week

_____ 4. feel overwhelmed by your job?
(a) once a day or more
(b) more than once a week but less than once a day
(c) once a week
(d) less than once a week

_____ 5. feel as though you're in the wrong job?
(a) once a day or more
(b) more than once a week but less than once a day
(c) once a week
(d) less than once a week

## OCCUPATIONAL STRESS

Swedish researchers have helped clarify some of the broadest conceptual aspects of work-related stress. Bertil Gardell (1976) was among the first to demonstrate that work environments that contribute to feelings of powerlessness and alienation are stressful for most workers. Marianne Frankenhaeuser (1986) focused on the variables of effort and distress. She defined *effort* as active coping and a striving to gain and maintain control, and *distress* as feelings of dissatisfaction, boredom, and unpredictability. In her model of job stress, high effort creates a condition of elevated catecholamines

## SELF—ASSESSMENT EXERCISE 10 (CONTINUED)

_____   6. feel frustrated by "red tape"?
   (a) once a day or more
   (b) more than once a week but less than once a day
   (c) once a week
   (d) less than once a week

_____   7. perceive yourself as lost in bureaucracy?
   (a) once a day or more
   (b) more than once a week but less than once a day
   (c) once a week
   (d) less than once a week

_____   8. I feel guilty for taking time off from work.
   (a) almost always true
   (b) usually true
   (c) seldom true
   (d) never true

_____   9. I have a tendency to rush into work that needs to be done before knowing the procedure I will use to complete the job.
   (a) almost always true
   (b) usually true
   (c) seldom true
   (d) never true

_____   10. Whenever possible, I will attempt to complete two or more tasks at once.
   (a) almost always true
   (b) usually true
   (c) seldom true
   (d) never true

_____   Total Score

Calculate your total score as follows:
   (a) = 4 points   (c) = 2 points
   (b) = 3 points   (d) = 1 point

Place your total score in the space provided and read the section on "Occupational Stressors."

(epinephrine and norepinephrine) in the body, while high distress is related to elevated levels of cortisol. (Conversely, low effort and low distress are related to lower levels of catecholamines and cortisol.) High levels of both effort and distress represent the most stressful environment, one in which the worker attempts to overcome boring, routinized, repetitive, or unpredictable constraints. Such environments give rise to extraordinary catecholamine and cortisol secretion, which contributes to cardiovascular disease (Henry & Stephens, 1977). Environmental conditions that engender feelings of loss of control, helplessness, and hopelessness are associated primarily with elevated levels of cortisol, depressive syndromes, and perhaps even neoplastic formation (Frankenhaeuser, 1986; Henry & Stephens, 1977). Workers who are motivated to work in a given environment and who see productive results enjoy a strong sense of personal control, accompanied by a sense of accomplishment and job commitment. Catecholamines increase moderately under these conditions, and cortisol seems to be suppressed. Lack of effort without distress is virtually unknown within the workplace.

Karasek and his colleagues (1981) constructed a model of job stress relating job demand with job control and/or flexibility. According to this model, the combination of excessive job demands and a lack of job flexibility and/or control creates a pathogenic work environment. Repeated empirical studies using several thousand employees showed that excessive work demand without perceived adequate control was associated with illness, especially coronary heart disease. Such work situations appeared to carry a risk of heart disease similar to the risk of smoking or of having an elevated cholesterol level.

**OCCUPATIONAL STRESSORS**

Research on causes of illness within the workplace indicates that there are four major work-related stressors:

1. overload
2. lack of control
3. being underqualified
4. job interference with interpersonal affairs.

These four stressors can affect illness indirectly, through their ability to cause emotional turmoil or distress (Smith & Everly, 1989). These findings support earlier research by Richard Lazarus (Lazarus & Folkman, 1984), which led to the conclusion that "stressors, like beauty, lie in the eyes of the beholder."

Stressors may be idiosyncratic, but they still exist on the job, and it is important to recognize that not all stress can be eliminated from work. Work almost always involves people interacting, and some stress is inherent in human interactions. Work also takes place very often in an impersonal and hurried environment with little social support. Some stress can be eliminated, however, and the first step is to uncover and eliminate or modify the stressors.

Following a model developed by Abelson (1986) in a study of organizational turnover, this section categorizes stressors as:

1. organizational
2. individual
3. environmental

**Organizational Stressors**

Organizational variables greatly influence employee job satisfaction. Very few employees report high job satisfaction in high-stress situations. Organizational factors tend to center in financial rewards and opportunities for individual growth.

### *Lack of Financial Rewards*

It has often been said that pay is only important on payday, when employees are reminded that they are more or less valued. Even so, substantial financial rewards are a constant reminder that the work is valued and the employee is probably hard to replace. On days when immediate rewards are absent, a high salary may help to bolster self-esteem and reduce frustration. Low pay may increase stress in exactly the opposite way, fueling the negative self-image and self-talk that destroy concentration and deflate the energy often necessary to fight simple depression and anxiety. Employees who are highly satisfied with most other aspects of their work will often overlook low pay, but low pay and lack of job satisfaction represent a deadly duo that greatly contribute to stress.

### *Lack of Career-Development Guidance*

Another potential source of stress from occupational frustration exists in the area of career development. A major study of job attitudes revealed that workers are demanding greater career-development opportunities (Colligan & Stockton, 1978). The following aspects of career development are considered important components of the working environment and are useful in contributing to job satisfaction and preventing occupational frustration:

1. the opportunity to fully use occupational skills
2. the opportunity to develop new, expanded skills
3. counseling to facilitate career decisions

Thus, it is important for managers to realize that workers on all levels are demanding intrinsic rewards from their jobs more than ever before. Many large corporations and even branches of the federal government (NASA, for example) have instituted formal career counseling and career-development programs. The results look highly promising.

### Overspecialization

In this era of highly specialized work, another source of occupational frustration is overspecialization. It has been accepted wisdom in industry that a high specialization—that is, having workers become expert in highly specific job areas—is a way of increasing the efficiency and quality of work. Conceptually, this is a sound procedure. However, because workers are searching for greater intrinsic rewards from their jobs, having them work in an overly fragmented or specialized job area may frustrate them. In our own consulting work with industry and business, we are impressed with the number of employees, on all levels and in all professions, who express a desire to "see the completed fruits of their labor." Workers do not want to perceive themselves as an insignificant cog in an immense wheel of industry; they want to identify with their companies and products. Far too often overspecialization robs the worker of this reward. This problem is a serious one on the assembly line, and it may even reach into the professions. In a local hospital famous for its emergency shock-trauma department, we were surprised to find nurses expressing desires to follow patients through recovery rather than seeing them only in the emergency room and never knowing how their treatment progressed.

### Work Overload

Job design and technology can contribute to occupational stress. Jobs without freedom produce more stress than autonomous and flexible ones. One of the most damaging situations involving a lack of freedom is excessive deadline pressure resulting in overload.

Sometimes there is simply too much work to do, or the work is too difficult. When these conditions result in mistakes on the job or contribute to ill health, work overload exists. Overload affects the individual by overstimulating psychological and physiological mechanisms. In effect, overload is a condition in which the individual is bombarded with excessive job demands—excessive in that they cause excessive stress when the worker attempts to meet all the demands.

There are three types of overload: (1) quantitative, (2) qualitative, and (3) a combination of both. Quantitative overload exists when too much work has to be done within a limited time. The individual is capable of completing all of the work, but the time restriction is what causes the reaction. This form of overload is most commonly found in the production industries and in clerical occupations.

Qualitative overload exists when the work to be completed exceeds the individual's technical or intellectual capabilities at that time. This form of overload is encountered most often in research and development organizations as well as in many of the so-called professions—health care, law, and so on.

Finally, the combination of quantitative and qualitative overload is commonly encountered in administrative/management positions in all industries, in all levels of the sales industry, and in entrepreneurial endeavors.

Let us examine the occupational conditions that seem to predispose one to overload. To do this, we have selected three specific stressors that may evolve into overload:

1. time pressures, which may develop into quantitative overload
2. job complexity, which may develop into qualitative overload
3. decision making, which may evolve into a combination of both forms of overload

### Time Urgency

Our society's race against the clock has been proven to be a major source of stress. Virtually every organization exerts some form of time pressure over its employees. It may be in the form of deadlines for work projects, deadlines for reports, sales deadlines, seasonal working limitations, or even unit production quotas, as in assembly-line or other factory environments. Time urgency is the most obvious condition that fosters the development of quantitative overload because time limitations serve to create restrictions on the quantity of work that can reasonably be completed. When the employee attempts to complete more work than is reasonable for the time restriction, a case of overarousal will exist—the heart will pump harder and faster as the individual attempts to work beyond his or her normal work rate. In addition, worry about what will happen if the work is not completed will cause the heart to work even harder. A vicious cycle is begun.

In some cases, deadlines will motivate you to achieve high levels of performance. However, when the time urgency causes mistakes or contributes to ill health, a condition of quantitative overload exists. At that point, time urgency becomes destructive. This condition has been referred to as the hurry sickness. You can perhaps recall instances when you were racing against the clock. How did you feel? Could you feel your temples pounding or your heart racing? Take a moment and try to remember the last time you were rushing against a deadline you couldn't meet.

Medical research on the effects of time urgency on health is most revealing. Research by cardiologists Meyer Friedman and Ray Rosenman (1974) led them to conclude that chronic time-urgency appears to harm the cardiovascular system. Typically, the results are premature heart attacks and/or high blood pressure.

Even the threat of impending quantitative overload has an adverse effect on workers. Many managers may recall the effects of time–motion analyses on workers: many employees tend to demonstrate contempt and suspicion for management. The workers resent management telling them how to do more work in less time. In some instances, such analyses have resulted in work slowdowns and sabotage if implemented from an authoritarian point of view.

Time urgency appears to be a way of organizational life. However, later in the book we shall introduce ways in which individuals may reduce the harmful effects on their minds and bodies of time urgency while still meeting most organizational demands.

### Job Complexity

Many people believe that life is growing more and more complex. The most common factor contributing to qualitative overload is job *complexity*, or the inherent difficulty of the work that must be done. The higher the complexity, the more stressful the job. The complexity of the work to be done can easily evolve into qualitative overload if the complexity exceeds your technical or intellectual capabilities at the time.

Job complexity is usually increased by the following factors:

1. increase in the amount of information to be used
2. increase in the sophistication of the information or in skills needed for the job
3. expansion or addition of job methods
4. introduction of a contingency plan

Although these four strategies will increase the probability of a better result, when excessive they will also increase the individual's stress-arousal level to where it actually inhibits his or her performance. Therefore, there is a point where increasing the complexity of the job no longer proves productive, but destructive. At this point the individual's abilities to problem-solve and reason have been surpassed, and mental fatigue and emotional and physical reactions ensue, all forms of the stress reponse. Medical research suggests that emotional and mental fatigue, headaches, and gastrointestinal disorders are common outcomes of chronic qualitative overload.

### Decision Making

Decision making pervades all aspects of life. Yet it has special applicability to the world of work. Decision making represents a unique combination of factors that may eventually lead to the development of quantitative and qualitative overload at the same time. Let us examine decision making as a potential source of occupational stress.

Decision making involves making a choice. Inherent in this process is evaluation—that is, determining the relative merits of one alternative versus another. The stressfulness of decision making is determined largely by:

1. the importance of the consequences of the decision
2. the complexity of the decision
3. the amount of information available
4. the locus of responsibility for the decision
5. the amount of time allotted for the decision-making process
6. the expectation of success

The importance of the consequences of any decision greatly contributes to the stressfulness of decision making. You know, for example, that deciding what kind of car to buy is more stressful than deciding where to eat lunch. There is simply more at risk, more to be lost should your decision be a poor one. The key to successful handling of a complex decision is being able to ascertain what is meaningful and what is superfluous information and being able to organize and synthesize that information.

While too much information can make decision making stressful, insufficient information can lead to even greater stress. If you have ever lacked sufficient information to make a decision, you know how frustrating this can be. We have chosen to discuss this topic in terms of overload because of the way most people react to such a condition. If you are faced with insufficient information for making a decision, your first reaction is usually to guess or to extrapolate the needed information. In most cases this guessing game results in a significant psychological strain as you attempt to foresee all of the possibilities. This strain is nothing other than overload.

Another factor that surely increases the stressfulness of decision making is the locus of responsibility—that is, who will be responsible for the decision. It is more stressful if one person alone has responsibility for a decision than if that responsibility can be shared. It is interesting to observe that many executives insist on single responsibility, for in many systems the individual will receive full recognition for a job well done. Such systems are also very quick to point out consistent incompetency. The fact remains, however, that single decision-making responsibility can be highly stressful and thus may stifle creativity in some individuals; upholding the status quo may be perceived as the safest decision.

Time is another factor in the stressfulness of decision making. With only a few exceptions, we can say that the shorter the amount of time allotted for decision making, the more stressful that decision process will be. One notable exception is the case in which far more time is allowed than is really required. Such conditions seem to breed worry and reconsideration; you might go back and change your mind, a habit that often leads to a less effective decision.

Finally, the expectation of success figures into the stressfulness of decision making. A comprehensive review of studies conducted by Jones (1977) suggests that if the decision maker fully expects to make a correct decision, his or her stress level will be lower than if there is doubt. Typically, the probability of making a correct decision will be enhanced as well. However, if the decision maker fully expects to fail, his or her stress level may be low also. Such a negative self-fulfilling prophecy may be used to cope with the stress involved in decision making, as there will be no disappointment when the individual does indeed fail—after all, it was expected. The only problem with this stress-reduction strategy is that it greatly increases the probability of failure and loss of self-esteem. Therefore, it is a destructive coping mechanism.

The amount of stress involved in decision making may be expressed as follows:

$$\text{Decision-Making Stress} = \text{Importance} + \text{Complexity} + \text{Lack of Information} + \text{Responsibility} + \text{Lack of Time} + \text{Lack of Confidence}$$

The multifaceted nature of the decision-making process explains why decision making can result in quantitative and/or qualitative overload. How many of these factors adversely affect your day-to-day decision making?

Organizational policies—not to be confused with human interactions and politics, which will be covered later—contribute to the stressful climate of the workplace. Policies that are rigid and insensitive to employee needs increase employee stress levels and can create an atmosphere in which decision making, the job of most employees and all managers, is fraught with stress.

## Individual Stressors

Individual stressors are perhaps the greatest contributors to occupational stress, because they include human interaction, the greatest source of stress in general. Another stressor of special is occupational frustration, which in turn is influenced by such stressors as job ambiguity and role conflict, stifled communication, discrimination, bureaucracy, inactivity, and boredom.

### Occupational Frustration

Have you ever thought that your job was holding you back? Have you ever considered yourself lost within the organization? Have you ever wished for more of a chance to use or develop your job skills? These are the types of thoughts that result from being frustrated on your job. Occupational stress from frustration exists when the job inhibits, stifles, or thwarts desired expectations and/ or goals. The body reacts adversely to the frustration of psychological desires, resulting in what we know to be the stress response. If we understand occupational frustration as this sense of being inhibited, then several major sources of occupational frustration immediately come to mind.

### Job Ambiguity and Role Conflict

Two of the major contributors to frustration on the job are job ambiguity and role conflict. Job ambiguity refers to the condition in which the job description or the level of job performance is confusing or virtually unknown to the employee. In a case like this, you might find yourself asking questions like "What should I do now?" or wondering "How did I do on the last assignment?" Job ambiguity may be caused by

1. unclear work objectives (goals)
2. confusion surrounding responsibility
3. unclear working procedures
4. confusion about what others expect of you
5. lack of feedback, or uncertainty surrounding your job performance

Consistently, such conditions result in job dissatisfaction and significant stress levels.

Role conflict exists when a job function contains roles, duties, or responsibilities that may conflict with one another. This is most commonly found among middle managers who find themselves caught between top-level management and lower-level management. Research has clearly demonstrated the middle-management position to be the most stressful of the three management levels.

Role conflict may also be caused by work roles that conflict with personal, familial, or immediate societal values. Individuals in the law-enforcement profession are those most frequently caught in this conflict. Once again, the result of such role conflict is job dissatisfaction and stress from frustration.

### Stifled Communication

The term *organizational communication* refers to the patterns and networks along which communications flow through an organization. Stifled organizational communication has been found to be the single most prevalent source of frustration in organizations today. Do you find yourself feeling isolated in your job or relying on information that comes too late or not at all? Have you ever had a conversation with someone and walked away asking yourself what that person had really said? These are common communication problems. Proper planning and organizing depend on effective communication. Ideally, communications flow up, from subordinates to superiors, and horizontally, from department to department, as well as in the traditional downward direction, from superiors to subordinates. In many cases, organizations frustrate employees by keeping open only the downward channels. Typically, the last channel to be maintained is the upward channel. This is not only frustrating, but a gross waste of human resources. Efficient organizational communication is perceived as so important that organizational communication is becoming a field in itself. University graduate programs are even offered in this area. Efficient communication can be a powerful source for stress reduction and increased performance on the job. Unfortunately, it is often overlooked or assumed to be working well.

### Discrimination

Hiring, pay, and promotional policies are discriminatory if they are based on non-work-related factors. Discrimination has long been known to be correlated with intense frustration and anger. The Colligan and Stockton study (1978) described earlier found occupational discrimination to be a major concern of the working middle class. This topic is of special interest in today's job market because the discrimination that plagued nonwhites and females in the work force is being replaced to some degree by so-called reverse discrimination, wherein nonwhites and females are being looked upon favorably for jobs and promotions. Discrimination of any type is harmful to the organization and the person because it leads to job dissatisfaction, anger, resentment, and a sense of hopelessness embodied in the "what's the use of trying to do a good job?" attitude.

### Bureaucracy

Another source of occupational frustration, and perhaps the most insidious source of this form of stress, is bureaucracy. Bureaucracy is a form of organizational planning. The man most responsible in the twentieth century for formalizing and advocating bureaucracy was Max Weber (1864–1920). Weber was concerned with designing an "ideal" organizational structure based on logic and rational thought. According to Weber, there are four major characteristics of a bureaucracy:

1. Specialization and division of labor.
2. A set of rules governing all aspects of organizational behavior: This is to ensure uniformity and organizational stability.
3. Emotionless management: Relationships within the organization should be typified by objectivity and a lack of enthusiasm, hatred, and so forth.
4. A hierarchy of positions: The entire organizational structure must follow the principle of centralized hierarchy—that is, offices built upon offices—so that there exists absolute control over subordinate functions. *Bureaucracy* literally means "rule by office."

It must be understood that Weber's design was to be an ideal one. No bureaucracy yet created has lived up to his expectations. The major reason for this failure is probably that the complexity of the human personality is simply not applicable to the bureaucratic structure. In theory, bureaucracy is the most logical and efficient organizational structure possible; in practice, it may be the most counterproductive form of organized work effort.

Reviewing bureaucracy as an organizational entity, Gouldner (1954) and Bennis (1966) have pointed out the most common criticisms of this form of organization as it exists today. Among them are

1. frustration of personal and professional development
2. the fostering of mediocrity on the job
3. the reinforcement of the establishment of complex rules (red tape)
4. stifled communication due in part to excessive paperwork (more red tape)
5. impersonality in supervisory practices
6. arbitrary rules virtually impossible to rescind
7. stifled creativity

### Inactivity and Boredom at Work

Have you ever noticed that some people become nervous when they don't have enough to do? Have you ever gone looking for something to work on when you didn't really have to? Inactivity and boredom on the job can cause a stress response. They may manifest themselves as nervousness, an inability to sit still, or a noticeable tenseness. Hans Selye categorizes this form of stress as *deprivational stress*.

If you suffer from deprivational stress on the job, then your job is failing to provide you with meaningful psychological stimulation. Two occupational settings are noted for this form of stress: the assembly line and the large bureaucracy.

Perhaps the best place to begin to look at boredom is on the assembly line. Here the employee is asked to perform some highly repetitive task. After a relatively short orientation period, he or she will be able to perform the required task with minimal challenge. Before long the task will become boring and stimulation of another kind will be sought—something to occupy the mind in a more meaningful manner. If such stimulation is found and does not distract from task performance, all will be fine. However, in some cases the thing that the employee chooses to occupy his or her mind detracts from job performance; there are more mistakes or a slower work rate. In other cases the employee may be unable to keep his or her mind occupied; job satisfaction then begins to decline.

The most notable of the reactions to boredom on the job is seen in the numerous cases of "assembly-line hysteria," which have been studied by the National Institution for Occupational Safety and Health (NIOSH). NIOSH was called in to invesigate mass outbreaks of illness in factories. The illness seemed to consist of nausea, muscle weakness, severe headaches, and blurred vision. In reviewing several outbreaks of this mass syndrome, the investigators could discover no organic reason for the illnesses. They then concluded that the illnesses were psychogenic. The majority of the cases seemed to occur under the following conditions: (1) job boredom, (2) repetitive tasks on the job, (3) no opportunity for workers to communicate, and (4) low job satisfaction (Colligan & Stockton, 1978).

The industrial literature is full of examples of worker reactions to job boredom. Cases of low production-efficiency, alcohol and drug abuse, and even assembly-line sabotage have been recorded, not to mention employee turnover.

Boredom and inactivity may affect white-collar workers as well. In our own consulting work with large bureaucracies, we have observed the results of the boredom that overspecialization and job redundancy create. A common complaint from white-collar workers in such organizations is that there is "not enough stimulating work to do." Many federal agencies appear to manifest this problem. To maintain sanity, people find ways of compensating for their low job satisfaction and stifled creativity. The most common compensation device we've seen is employees' working at minimally acceptable levels of job performance during the week and then expressing themselves on the weekend through their avocational pursuits. This "living for the weekend" attitude is obviously debilitating to the organization.

**Environmental Stressors**

Environmental stressors range from the physical environment of the work station and the organization's location in the community to the location of the community itself. More often the stress in this category is that of adapting to the environment and living with the changes that accompany most work situations. Obviously, unfavorable environments and changes result in more severe stress; however, even positive changes require adaptation and can be stressful. As with most issues there usually is a continuum. The competitive environment, for example, might range from boring and nonexistent to cutthroat.

### Occupational Change and Adaptation

Change within an organization is a necessary and vital component of growth and continued productivity; it can also be a source of stress for many employees. Change is stressful because it disrupts the psychological and physiological rhythms that accompany all human behavior. Change requires the expansion of psychological and physiological energies, whether the change is good or bad. Hans Selye summarizes this point by stating that the expenditure of adaptive energy is what makes change stressful. Change becomes harmful at the point where adaptive energy is depleted. The result is psychological or physiological breakdown—illness. Numerous research efforts have documented this phenomenon (see Gunderson & Rahe, 1974; Selye, 1976).

There are numerous sources of adaptive stress (stress due to change) within the organizational world. Some of the more common ones are as follows.

### Technological Change

Business and industry are ever more dependent on technology. Space-age technology has contributed to increased efficiency of all work functions, from production to clerical processes to high-level managerial decisions. Computers appear to be the key to a successful business enterprise. However, with this expanding role for technology in business and industry comes the impact that such technological change has on workers. Even though technology is a very positive force in the working world, it still requires role changes for those who are affected by it. Such changes require adaptation.

Can you think of one way in which technology has required adaptation for you or your company? It shouldn't be hard. How often does technology force a change followed by some necessary adaptation? Alvin Toffler, in his book *Future Shock*, concluded that change solely for the sake of change is harmful. Furthermore, when change is indicated, it must be integrated into the system so as to minimize the harmful impact on the people who must cope with the change.

### *Relocation*

Another common source of adaptive stress is relocation, both vocational and residential. When you are forced to relocate, a great deal of stress generally follows. Even if the relocation is in conjunction with a raise and promotion, you will still have to cope with a new environment. The following factors intensify stress from relocation:

1. the complexities of moving possessions from one location to another
2. the severing of interpersonal relationships
3. the formation of new interpersonal relationships
4. the necessity of adjusting to new cultural and/or socioeconomic conditions

All of these factors are compounded if you must relocate residence and work setting simultaneously.

For many individuals change is exhilarating. Even so, change, whether good or bad, requires the expenditure of adaptive energy and is therefore stressful. So even positive changes should be carefully considered during periods of high stress, unless of course the change removes you from the stressors.

### *Promotion*

The stressfulness of being promoted is considered by most to be a small price to pay for the rewards of the promotion. Take a moment and consider the impact of the following factors that generally accompany a promotion, in addition to the obvious rewards:

1. significant changes in job function
2. increased responsibility for people, production, and money

3. changes in social role (Have you ever noticed that with some promotions come certain social obligations that cause intense social and even financial stress?)

These factors involve considerable adaptation for most individuals. Even if they are all positive for you, they take some getting used to.

### Reorganization

Departmental or organizational restructuring often happens when a new administration takes over. Such major reorganization happens rarely, but it can be a major source of adaptive stress. Feelings of insecurity, anticipation, and apprehension usually dominate the minds of those affected by reorganization. If you are ever in such a reorganization, the first thing on your mind will probably be job security. Your next question will typically be, "How do I fit into this new arrangement?" During such uncertain periods your work will probably fall off, or you may stress yourself through overload in an attempt to demonstrate your worth to the new management. In either case it behooves you as well as the new management to quickly resolve questions of job security following reorganization.

### Time Change and Biorhythms

If you must rotate work shifts you don't need this book to tell you that this is stressful, requiring significant adaptation. Even changes in time zones during travel are stressful. To better understand the effects of changes in working times, we need to reconsider the concept of biorhythms, which we discussed in Chapter 6. Two common occupational examples of how stress affects the body when the natural biological rhythms have been disturbed are jet lag and shiftwork fatigue.

Jet lag commonly affects transcontinental and transoceanic travelers. This problem can prove costly for business executives who must conduct high-level business affairs. Jet lag has also been found to be a major problem for pilots and airline crews who make long flights frequently.

Workers who must alternate shifts report many of the same symptoms found in jet lag. The most severe symptoms occur when changing to or from the 11-at-night to the 7-in-the-morning shift. Workers who rotate shifts have been found to suffer from more illnesses; gastrointestinal illnesses and fatigue are the most common problems reported. Some workers can adapt to the time change in about a week; most workers require three weeks; some never properly adjust.

### Retirement

Retirement is stressful for many people who have spent most of their adult life working. The association between self-esteem and job is a significant one. People who say "I *am* an engineer" rather than "I am *employed* as an engineer" reflect the tendency of employees to identify themselves in terms not so much of broad personal characteristics as of job-related characteristics and roles. Thus, when workers retire, and particularly if they are forced to retire from a very rewarding job, they typically suffer some of the following symptoms:

1. depression
2. a sense of worthlessness and a loss of self-esteem
3. decreased appetite
4. lack of motivation in general
5. increased cardiovascular complaints
6. decreased sexual drive

More important, the U.S. Bureau of Labor Statistics reports data that suggest that workers who are forcibly retired will survive, on the average, only thirty to forty months after their retirement.

Other factors that increase the stressfulness of retirement are:

1. a great number of years at the same job
2. lack of interests outside the job, such as family, hobbies, and social involvement
3. a high affiliation with the job
4. lack of preparation for retirement—for example, retirement counseling or even informal mental preparation
5. lack of alternative sources of income
6. lack of alternative sources of ego gratification (self-esteem)
7. knowing others who have retired and encountered difficulties adjusting

### Physical Environment of Work

**Noise.**  Noise as a source of stress is a rather unique variable. It can prove stressful because of its psychological characteristics—that is, by being unwanted or distracting. It can also prove stressful simply because of its physical characteristics—that is, volume and/or frequency.

The physical characteristics of noise (intensity and frequency) are the points most often mentioned in discussions of noise as a stressor. Sound levels above 35 to 40 decibels will typically awaken a sleeping person, and sound levels in excess of 55 decibels are sufficient to make normal conversation difficult. Of greater biological significance are noise levels in excess of 65 to 70 decibels. Evidence suggests that at this level there is increased sympathetic-nervous-system arousal characteristic of a stress response. The major component of this response is increased adrenal functions. As decibel levels increase, the body reacts with greater cardiovascular responses characteristic of stress (Kryter, 1970). Such reactions as increased heart rate or increased blood pressure become evident.

As chronic noise levels approach 85 decibels, the potential for permanent hearing loss increases significantly. Perhaps the most insidious aspect of this process is that chronic noise exposure is typically selective in its attack on auditory acuity. The usual case of hearing loss occurs only on specific frequency levels, depending on the amount of the exposure. Therefore, it may be very difficult for a worker to notice a hearing loss until it becomes severe.

The federal government has mandated that workers exposed to an average eight-hour total of 90 decibels must wear protective ear equipment. In addition to the harmful effects caused by the intensity of noise, frequency can also be a factor. Frequencies in excess of 20,000 cycles per second are most often implicated in the harmful effects of noise. However, it has been shown that frequencies in the 15-to-20-cycles-per-second range appear especially stressful because of their extremely low vibration levels. Such levels appear to harm the internal organs of many humans. In some cases, frequencies between these levels may actually reduce the stressful effects of noise.

**Lighting.** Too little light or too much light can create a stress response (see Hopkinson & Collins, 1970). The luminance of a light source may be measured in nits (candles per square meter). Tasks that involve fine detail in workmanship (such as watchmaking) require a great deal of light. The recommended luminance for such tasks is around 800 to 1000 nits. General office work and general factory work require around 100 nits. Most stores require around 60 to 100 nits. Hallways usually require around 30 nits.

When lighting is below these recommended minimums, the eyes must strain to see the work. The most common form of stress eyestrain results in tension headaches caused by the muscular adjustments needed to maintain proper visual acuity.

The most common characteristic of too much light is glare. Glare results from having the light source so bright that it interferes with focusing on the object being viewed. In effect, the light source competes within the retina with the object you are interested in viewing. The result is excessive retinal stimulation. Glare appears also to cut down on the length of time that a worker can spend at a given task without developing headaches.

**Temperature.**  As most readers will confirm, working conditions that are too hot or too cold can be stressful. The ideal average temperature (at 50 percent relative humidity) for sedentary work ranges from 70 to 75 degrees Fahrenheit for someone wearing a suit and long-sleeved shirt. Light standing-work is done best at about 66 to 72 degrees. Manual labor appears to be done best at a few degrees lower (see McIntyre, 1973).

Ambient temperature in excess of 81 degrees Fahrenheit appears to erode productivity on tasks that consist of complex reasoning or minute detail and require intense concentration. This is especially true in temperatures in excess of 86 degrees Fahrenheit. This decline in productivity appears to be due to the psychophysiological arousal characteristic of the stress response. However, temperatures in the low 80s have little effect on light mental tasks such as basic arithmetic or typing, or on light manual tasks such as most production-line work.

High humidity can significantly increase the stress from heat. The reason is that the body cools itself by evaporation of perspiration. Evaporation is retarded by high humidity, and the result is greater retained heat in the body. Fresh circulating air tends to assist in the cooling process.

Although most stress caused by temperature is heat-related, cold can also affect industrial performance. As the work environment gets colder, blood flows out of the hands and feet to curb heat loss through radiation. When this happens, fine motor-control is gradually lost and manual performance is hindered. Such performance declines significantly when hand temperatures drop below 55 degrees Fahrenheit. In general, however, excessive heat appears to be a larger contributor to stress and decreased occupational performance.

**Physical Posture.**  Cramped muscles and inactivity seem to plague white-collar workers. Muscle tension in the head, neck, and shoulders is the most prevalent example of what can happen from laboring over piles of paper every day. Leg cramps and even some lower-back problems can result from chronic sitting. Typists know all too well the aching forearms, wrists, and fingers that can result from hours of typing. In addition to these specific problems are the effects of sedentary work on the cardiovascular system. Before long, exercise programs become a necessity for a healthy mind and body.

**SUMMARY**

Despite the difficulty of objectively measuring the costs of stress to business and industry, the occupational stress epidemic is perceived to be severe enough to have prompted the mobilization of a stress-management industry to combat the problem. It is important to recognize that all stress cannot be eliminated from work. Work is a place where people interact, and some stress is inherent in human interactions. Work is also very often done in an impersonal and hurried environment with little social support, since the purpose of work is productivity.

Reduction of debilitating stress is the primary objective of occupational-stress management. A secondary focus is aligning personality, skill level, and task to decrease stress and increase productivity. Turnover or functional transfers can reduce organizational strain caused by mismatches of skill and task. A more efficient approach would be to find and reduce the stress situations before inefficiency, decreased productivity, and ill health occur. If stress-management programs are effective, we may soon see corporate savings sufficient enough to be passed on to consumers, thereby creating a lever to be used in the marketplace by competition-minded corporations.

# REFERENCES

ABELSON, M. A. (1986). Strategic management of turnover: A model for the health service administrator. *Health Care Management, 11*(2), 61–71.

BENNIS, W. G. (1966). *Changing organizations.* New York: McGraw-Hill.

COLLIGAN, M. J., AND W. STOCKTON (1978). The mystery of assembly line hysteria. *Psychology Today*, June, 93–114.

FRANKENHAEUSER, M. (1986). A psychobiological framework for research on human stress and coping. In M. Appley and R. Trumbell (eds.), *Dynamics of stress* (pp. 101–16). New York: Plenum.

FRIEDMAN, M., AND R. ROSENMAN (1974). *Type A behavior and your heart.* New York: Knopf.

GARDELL, B. (1976). Reactions at work and their influence on nonwork activities. *Human Relations, 29*, 885–904.

GOULDNER, A. W. (1954). *Patterns of industrial bureaucracy.* Glencoe, IL: Free Press.

GUNDERSON, E. K. E., AND R. H. RAHE (1974). *Life stress and illness.* Springfield, IL: Chas. C Thomas.

HENRY, J., AND P. STEPHENS (1977). *Stress, health and the social environment.* New York: Springer-Verlag.

HOPKINSON, R. G., AND J. B. COLLINS (1970). *The ergonomics of lighting.* London: MacDonald

JONES, R. A. (1977). *Self-fulfilling prophecies.* Hillsdale, NJ: Erlbaum.

KARASEK, R., et al. (1981). Job decision, job demands, and cardiovascular disease. *American Journal of Public Health, 71,* 694–705.

KRYTER, K. (1970). *The effects of noise on man.* New York: Academic Press.

LAZARUS, R., AND S. FOLKMAN (1984). *Stress, appraisal, and coping.* New York: Springer.

MCCARTHY, M. (1988). Stressed employees look for relief in worker's compensation claims. *Wall Street Journal,* April 7, p. 34.

MCINTYRE, D. (1973). A guide to thermal comfort. *Applied Ergonomics, 4,* 66–72.

PELLETIER, K. (1984). *Healthy people in unhealthy places.* New York: Delta.

PELLETIER, K., AND R. LUTZ (1988). Healthy people, healthy business. *American Journal of Health Promotion, 2,* 5–12, 19.

SELYE, H. (1976). *The stress of life.* New York: McGraw-Hill.

SMITH, K., AND G. EVERLY (1989). The relationship between job stressors, cognitive-affective arousal and illness among AICPA members. Unpublished research report.

THOMPSON, V. (1961). *Modern organizations.* New York: Knopf.

**SUMMATION OF CHAPTERS 4–8**

In Chapters 4–8 we classified the numerous origins of the stress reaction into four meaningful groups. In Chapter 5 we examined how one's perception interacts with socialization to produce psychosocial stressors, and we looked at some of the most frequently encountered sources of psychosocial stress. In Chapter 6 we examined biological sources of stress, which are therefore less affected by subjective perceptions. In Chapter 7 we analyzed how personality characteristics and perception of self and others can play a significant role in the stress response. In Chapter 8 we examined the effect of occupational stressors.

At this point, you can get a total picture of your own stress vulnerability by transferring each of your scores from the ten self-assessment exercises to the Personal Stressor Profile Sheet on the following page. After you have filled in your scores on each of the scales, connect all of the points. You have now plotted a graph of your stressor profile. Although there is no linear relationship between the self-assessment exercises, the line will help you visually assimilate your total profile and will be most helpful when you compare results from retests at some later date. Knowing the source of your stress can be a valuable tool in managing that stress.

Now, armed with a summary of your sources of stress, you can go on to the remaining chapters, which deal with stress interventions. Using the information about yourself that you have gained from the previous chapters, you can formulate your own strategy for stress management, using the techniques you will be learning in the next chapters. Later you may want to come back and retake the self-assessment exercises, formulating a second, third, or fourth profile as a record of your progress.

*A final note:* You may be quite vulnerable to stress from a specific determinant even though your score was low on the assessment test in which it occurred. The reason for this is simply that several of the exercises consisted of two or three aspects under the same general heading. For example, you may be a "catastrophizer" of the greatest magnitude, and this may cause your life to be a very stressful one. However, it is possible that your score on the anxious-reactive scale was low because you didn't suffer from the other feedback mechanisms. Therefore, it is important that you carefully consider *each question* in which you score 3 or 4 points and determine how significantly this aspect of stress affects your life.

On the other hand, remember that while these ten scales are extremely useful tools for beginning to assess the sources of stress in your life, they are *not* clinically validated psychological tests and should not be treated as such.

**Personal Stressor Profile Summary Sheet**

| EXERCISE: | 1 | 2 | 3 | 4 | 5 | 6 | 7 | 8 | 9 | 10 |
|---|---|---|---|---|---|---|---|---|---|---|
| | Adaptation | Frustration | Overload | Depri-vation | Nutrition | Self-Perception | Type A Behavior | Anxious Reactivity | Control | Occupational Stressors |
| Scores Indicative of: | •400 | •40 | •40 | •40 | •40 | •40 | •40 | •40 | •40 | •40 |
| | •350 | •35 | •35 | •35 | •35 | •35 | •35 | •35 | •35 | •35 |
| High Vulnerability to Stressors | •300 | •30 | •30 | •30 | •30 | •30 | •30 | •30 | •30 | •30 |
| | •250 | •25 | •25 | •25 | •25 | •25 | •25 | •25 | •25 | •25 |
| Moderate Vulnerability to Stressors | •200 | •20 | •20 | •20 | •20 | •20 | •20 | •20 | •20 | •20 |
| Low Vulnerability to Stressors | •150 | •15 | •15 | •15 | •15 | •15 | •15 | •15 | •15 | •15 |
| | •100 | •10 | •10 | •10 | •10 | •10 | •10 | •10 | •10 | •10 |

This profile is an educational tool and was designed to promote basic health education. It is in no way designed to be a substitute for the diagnostic procedures used by physicians or psychologists. Any concerns about your physical or mental health should be directed to your family physician, your local medical society, or your local psychological society.

# CHAPTER NINE

# The Holistic Approach to Managing Stress

Beginning in this chapter, we will discuss the merits of a holistic stress-management program and introduce techniques for alleviating stress and tension. Some of the techniques are specific to the causes of stress described in Chapters 4–8; others are general techniques for reducing stress reactions. Detailed instructions are provided along with a discussion of the basic mechanisms underlying each technique. The desired outcome is for the individual to be able to create a total, personalized system of controlling stress and tension.

How a person manifests stress depends on the individual and his or her environment and social, cognitive, and emotional processes. The stress response itself represents an awesome array of neurological and endocrinological mechanisms. The symptoms of a prolonged stress response are numerous and diverse. Because stress can be caused by many different kinds of stressors, it cannot be lastingly managed, controlled, or even reduced by any one technique—there is no best stress-management technique.

---

*Holism: a concept of controlling stress and tension encompassing the complete lifestyle of the individual. Holistic stress management incorporates intervention at the physical, psychological, and social levels simultaneously.*

---

To be truly effective, holistic stress management must be:

1. individualized
2. based on personal preferences and practicalities
3. multidimensional
4. flexible

**Individualized.**    Stress-management techniques must be individualized, because stressors and stress are unique to the individual. What helps your friend or neighbor may not help you, and vice versa. Therefore, you may have to experiment with numerous stress-management techniques to find out which are best for you.

**Based on Preference.**    Stress-management techniques must be based on individual preferences and personal practicality. They should not be intrusions or burdens. If you are going to practice stress management, you must consider it beneficial.

**Multidimensional.**    Stress-management strategies must be multidimensional, for stress itself is multidimensional. Because there is no best stress-management technique, a stress-management program should be formulated. Such a plan would attack the stress response from several perspectives. It should take into consideration the stressors, the personality of the individual, the use of relaxation techniques, and how best to vent or express the stress response.

**Flexible.**    The stress-management plan should be flexible, not rigid. It should be dynamic, not static. A flexible, personal stress-management plan prepares you to confront and either constructively avoid or utilize the many facets of stress.

The following outline categorizes the different techniques by the type of response they produce. From this information you can start to build your own stress-management program by selecting techniques that will alleviate a specific type of stress or produce a specific type of response.

I.  Quieting the external environment so as to reduce stimulation of the individual.
   *A. Effects*
      1. produces a cognitive awareness of life events and lifestyle
      2. cognitively restructures environment, thought patterns, and behavior
   *B. Technique*
      1. Social engineering
II. Quieting the internal environment in order to reduce sensory stimulation of the central nervous system.
   *A. Effects*
      1. decreases proprioceptive stimulation
      2. produces a calming or relaxation response
      3. conditions the relaxation response

    **B. Techniques**
      **1.** breathing
      **2.** muscle relaxation
      **3.** biofeedback
      **4.** hatha yoga
      **5.** physical exercise
**III.** Conditioning the mind to reduce arousing thoughts and increase peaceful thoughts.
    **A. Effects**
      **1.** reduces "mind chatter," arousing memories, and anticipations
      **2.** directs thoughts so as to produce peace and tranquility
      **3.** gains philosophical awareness
    **B. Technique**
      **1.** Meditation
        **a.** concentrating (for example, through a mantra or visual imagery)
        **b.** free-floating mind-void
        **c.** contemplation of the spiritual (for example, some types of affirmations or prayer)

## INTERVENTION POINTS: COMPLETING THE PICTURE OF STRESS–DISEASE INTERVENTION

By now you should understand that many diseases are psychosomatic and that stress can cause disease. Once you have identified your individual stressors and stress response and have mastered specific techniques that can produce the desired effects, the next step in building your own stress-management program is to learn where the specific techniques can most effectively intervene in the psychosomatic disease process. There are several points at which intervention in the stress–disease cycle is possible (see Figure 9.1). Remember that stress operates in many dimensions and is not always predictable. How we react to our environment is determined to a large extent by our attitudes, values, personality, and emotional development, as well as by our ability to relax, our diet and physical activity patterns, the ability to modify our lifestyles, and other such factors. Since stress reactions occur in various ways and on various levels, stress management should be approached from varied perspectives incorporating mental, physical, spiritual, social, and environmental interactions.

## I. Techniques for Quieting the Internal Environment

### Social Engineering

Our environment is filled with stressors. The action or behavior of each individual or institution in the world becomes the input to other individuals. As we go about our daily activities, each individual with whom we interact, the people with whom we live,

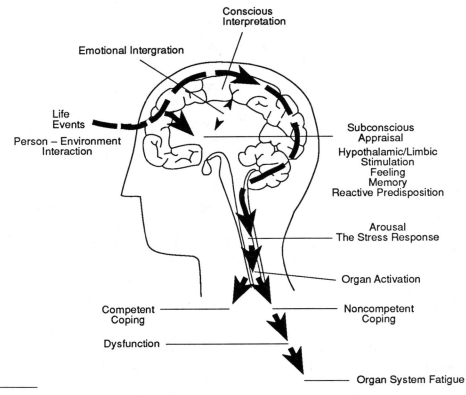

**FIGURE 9.1**

The Psychosomatic
Concept

those in the next car, the ones we pass on the street or sit with in meeting halls, and to some extent those we see on the television present some manner of stimulation. Obviously, the more people we see, the greater the opportunity for contact. The intimacy of that contact is also of prime importance. If we know others well enough, not only does their behavior become our stimulation, but so do their thoughts, dreams, and unspoken expectations.

All of life's pursuits create potential stressors—from noise and pollution to competition for a seat on the bus, a place on the highway, or a position with a company. Generally speaking, more people mean more complexity in social as well as in institutional organization.

One of the easiest and most effective techniques of stress management is to identify stress-promoting activities and develop a lifestyle that modifies or avoids these stressors. A change in lifestyle may be as simple as getting out of bed earlier or driving to work by a different route, or as complex as choosing a profession, a mate, or a life goal. Social engineering, shown at its intervention point in Figure 9.2, is the technique of taking command of and modifying one's life. In one sense, it is the most conscious point of intervention, but as stress management becomes a way of life, one begins unconsciously to modify one's position in relation to sources of stress by selecting a less stressful lifestyle.

Social engineering strategies may be simple or extremely complex (based on the nature of the stressor). But one thing is definite: There are virtually unlimited strategies available to the imaginative mind. In this book you will find many guidelines to make social engineering a valuable asset in the holistic approach to reducing stress.

One social engineering strategy involves the analysis of biological rhythms. We have to balance work and recreation schedules

**FIGURE 9.2**

Social Engineering as an Intervention Technique

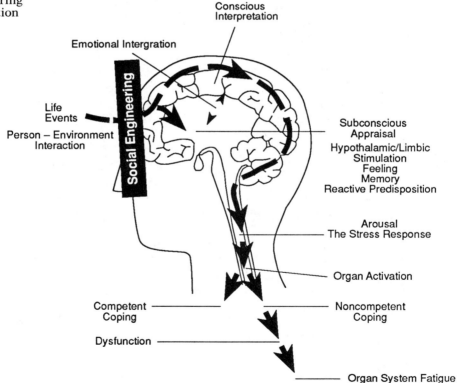

with what is socially and economically efficient, and the result is that we become out of sync with our natural biological rhythms. The consequences may be increased susceptibility to illness, increased irritability, and emotional instability. If you know more about your natural biological rhythms, you can plan your activities to more closely coincide with them.

Another social engineering strategy involves conscious concern about the foods you eat. Manipulation of diet as a strategy for reducing stress is called *nutritional engineering*. The food you eat can have an effect on your reaction to stressors, as certain foods can deplete the body's ability to respond to stressful situations. Some foods may increase lethargy and irritability, causing you to overreact to normally unstressful situations.

Analysis of biorhythms and nutritional engineering can help you modify or avoid the sources of stress that normally arise from the environment and from social interaction. These activities are designed to quiet the external environment in order to reduce the stressors in your life. They should prompt cognitive awareness of life events and then be utilized in restructuring your environment, thought patterns, and behavior.

### Cognitive Restructuring

To a large degree, the amount of stress caused by society and the environment depends on what information is taken in and what is blocked; how the information is perceived, evaluated, and given meaning; and what effect this whole process has on mental and physical activity.

Attitude, which is the meaning and value given to various events in life in combination with characteristic ways of behaving (behavioral patterns), can be referred to as an individual's personality. The personality has the awesome capacity of transforming a normally neutral aspect of life into a psychosocial stressor. Few events are innately stressful, but we make them stressful by the way in which we perceive them. A person may alter stress-causing attitudes by learning how these attitudes are formed and then working to change that process through cognitive restructuring. This strategy is shown at its intervention point in Figure 9.3. If cognitive restructuring is effective, the way in which you perceive a particular event will be changed to the point that there will be little or no physical arousal.

Here is a summary of cognitive restructuring techniques:

1. To alleviate poor self-esteem and depression:
   a. learn and practice assertiveness

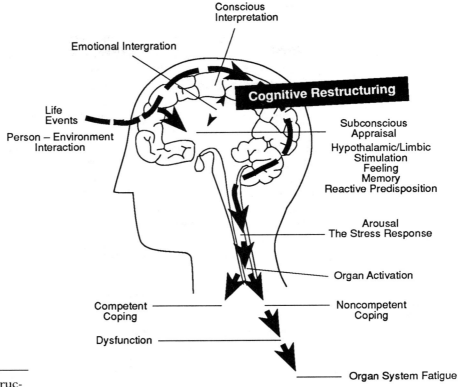

Conscious
Interpretation

Emotional Intergration

**Cognitive Restructuring**

Life
Events

Person – Environment
Interaction

Subconscious
Appraisal

Hypothalamic/Limbic
Stimulation
Feeling
Memory
Reactive Predisposition

Arousal
The Stress Response

Organ Activation

Competent
Coping

Noncompetent
Coping

Dysfunction

Organ System Fatigue

FIGURE 9.3

Cognitive Restruc-
turing as an Inter-
vention Technique

    **b.** verbalize your positive qualities
    **c.** accept compliments
    **d.** examine beliefs that block positive self-concept
    **e.** check reality
    **f.** let go of judgments

  **2.** To alleviate time urgency:
    **a.** use time management
    **b.** use alternative goals
    **c.** practice concentration
    **d.** practice thought stopping
    **e.** reduce negative self-talk

Reducing stress through cognitive restructuring is covered more
fully in Chapter 10.

## II. Techniques for Quieting the Internal Environment

Figure 9.4 illustrates that the information being received is alerting the central nervous system by two distinctly different pathways. One is the subconscious-appraisal pathway, governed by the autonomic nervous system, the system that prepares the body for any potential action that might be needed. However, action or responses themselves are conscious and occur only after the appropriate part of the brain—the other pathway—processes and evaluates the situation. Thus the stress response, which is physical arousal, can be elicited by conscious, voluntary action or by subconscious, involuntary (autonomic) activation, which keeps the body in a state of readiness. The constant state of readiness to respond with the fight-or-flight reaction when such a response is unwarranted is called emotional reactivity. If the body remains in this state for long periods, organ systems become fatigued and the result is often organ-system malfunction.

Relaxation training can help reduce emotional reactivity. It promotes voluntary and autonomic control over some central-

**FIGURE 9.4**

Relaxation Training as an Intervention Technique

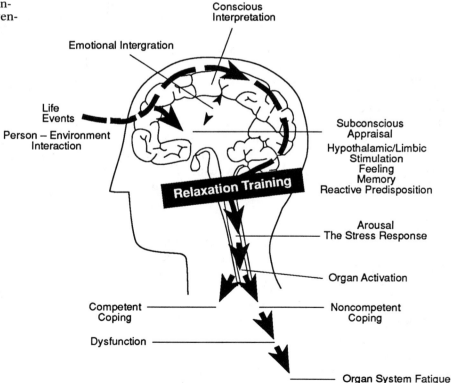

nervous-system activities associated with arousal and promotes a quiet sense of control that eventually influences attitudes, perception, and behavior. Relaxation training fosters interaction with your inner self, and you will learn by actual feeling (visceral learning) that what you are thinking influences your body processes, and that your body processes influence your thoughts. You will come to know your feelings and emotions as part of your thinking experience; your behavior will come more from what is within you, rather than from how you feel you should respond to people and the environment around you.

Stress and tension responses, anxiety, and psychosomatic illnesses are a few behaviors that can reveal the inner workings of the mind and body. These responses become good end-points on which to concentrate stress-reduction efforts. The next section of this chapter will briefly outline relaxation activities designed to quiet your internal environment and reduce the stimulation of the nervous system. These activities decrease sensory stimulation, produce a relaxation response, and then condition that response. The following brief description is presented as an overview to help you understand how the many techniques relate to each other and to specific stressors, and how they might be used to build a holistic stress-management program. Each technique will be discussed in detail in individual chapters throughout the remainder of the book.

### Breathing Exercises

There seems to be a physiological relationship between the centers that control respiration and the centers that control our general nervousness or reactivity. From the ancient yogis to recent researchers, one basic recommendation for calming the body is the use of some kind of breathing technique, specifically *diaphragmatic* breathing. We know that a stressed person breathes differently than a relaxed person. The stressed person will breathe shallowly and rapidly, while the relaxed person will breathe deeply, from the abdomen. In diaphragmatic breathing, you can actually feel the abdomen move in and out as you breathe. Simply sitting down for a few minutes several times a day and controlling your breathing teaches your body to respond in a relaxed manner. If you breathe like a relaxed person, you will be more relaxed, for at least a short period of time. Reducing stress through breathing exercises is covered more fully in Chapter 11.

### Muscle Relaxation

One of the most prevalent stress responses is muscle tension. Excess muscle tension heightens anxiety and is responsible for many psychosomatic illnesses. Most experts in the relaxation field feel that reducing excess muscle tension not only directly reduces total body tension and anxiety, but also indirectly helps eliminate the psychological forerunner of the muscle tension. It is no wonder the muscular system is the one system included in almost every relaxation program; one cannot relax the mind or fully concentrate if the brain is being bombarded by muscle-tension impulses. Whether muscle-tension reduction is considered an end in itself or a means to an end, it is an essential step in stress management. While the word *tension* is synonymous with muscle contraction, in the broad context of stress it usually means excess and inappropriate muscle contraction.

Chronic, long-term tension has been related to numerous disorders, and because the origin of the muscle tension is in the defensive or alerting posture and attitude, these disorders are considered to be psychosomatic. A few of the more common disorders are tension headaches, muscle cramps and spasms (such as writer's cramp), limitation of range of movement and flexibility, susceptibility to muscle injuries (such as tears and sprains), insomnia, a wide variety of gastrointestinal maladies (constipation, diarrhea, colitis), renal system problems, and dysmenorrhea (menstrual cramps). This list seems long, but remember that the muscular system is involved in every body process and in every expression of emotion.

Muscles make up such a large portion of the body's mass that muscle relaxation leads to a significant reduction in total body-tension as well. There are literally hundreds of muscle-relaxation techniques, and almost every relaxation program utilizes some form of neuromuscular relaxation. The objective is to teach the individual to relax the muscles at will by first developing a thinking-feeling awareness of what it feels like to be relaxed.

Neuromuscular relaxation training is a program of systematic exercises that train the muscles and the nervous-system components that control muscle activity. The objective is to reduce the tension in the muscles. All of the techniques have the same primary objective of teaching the individual to relax the muscles on command by first developing an awareness of what it feels like to be tense and then what it feels like to be relaxed. Being able to distinguish between tension and relaxation is the basic skill in learning muscle relaxation.

If you are able to distinguish between tension and relaxation, control over tension will easily follow. As you perfect your ability, you can practice these exercises anywhere, even in short periods of usually "wasted" time, such as while stopped for a red light or while waiting for an appointment. Reducing stress through muscle relaxation is covered more fully in Chapter 12.

### Biofeedback

The simple principle of biofeedback is awareness of body function. This is the first and most important ingredient in changing the behavior that causes the stress reaction. Biofeedback is best understood as an educational tool that provides information about behavior or performance in much the same manner that a congratulatory letter from superiors gives feedback on job performance or the bathroom scale gives information about the success of weight-reduction efforts. If we learn to listen, our body will tell us a lot about its functioning.

A biofeedback instrument magnifies the subtle internal signals so they become more noticeable. It can be used simply as a device that trains or attunes our awareness of body language; for example, thermal measurements of skin temperature can be used to indicate changes in blood flow to a particular region of the body. After only a few training sessions one can usually learn to feel the changes without the instrument. The contraction of skeletal muscles can also be measured in order to detect muscle tension before it reaches the state of producing pain and discomfort. Through training one can then learn to sense even the most minute changes in muscle tension. Likewise, monitoring brain waves can tell us much about states of consciousness and information processing, which can then aid in the voluntary control of consciousness. The possibilities are as numerous as the systems that can be measured.

In another sense, biofeedback is more than a self-monitoring system. It can be used to promote self-exploration, self-awareness, and self-control. Relaxation and tranquility condition the tone of the nervous system to be less reactive, gradually enabling you to begin to change behavior by becoming a more tranquil person. This process disciplines the mind to reduce the constant chatter of imagination and anticipation, allowing for greater problem-centered concentration and often leading to revealing insights and creativity. What starts out as an exercise in relaxation quickly turns into development of self-awareness and self-control. Reducing stress through biofeedback is covered more fully in Chapter 13.

### Visual Imagery

Visual imagery is the use of self-directed mental images of relaxed states. This simple technique centers in conditioned patterns of responses that become associated with particular thoughts. Recall a moment when you allowed your mind to run away and catastrophize a potentially threatening event. You may have been worried about loss of your job, a change in company policy, or perhaps problems with a partner or spouse. You get chills and the hair rises on the back of your neck. This represents a conditioned physiological response to that particular association. The opposite effect can also be generated, producing an equally dramatic but very different physiological response. If you imagine yourself in your favorite relaxation spot, perhaps sitting on a quiet beach with the sun warming your body or fishing your favorite stream, a relaxation response is triggered. The technique of visual imagery simply helps condition relaxation through self-generated recall of relaxed body states and memories of relaxed times in your life. It is a method in which you talk to your body and tell it to relax. It helps if you are able to imagine a scene or a "feeling state" vividly and have already achieved a quiet physical state.

A popular technique used in this form of relaxation capitalizes on the body's ability to follow the commands of the conscious centers of the brain. If you can imagine warmth, the body will tend to reproduce that sensation. Blood flow, responding to the conscious demand, will increase to the desired areas, thereby creating the desired warmth. Such a physiological change would be impossible without a change in the tone of your nervous system, and through such a change relaxation is facilitated and gradually conditioned. Reducing stress through visual imagery is covered more fully in Chapter 14.

### Hatha Yoga

Yoga is a method of physical, mental, and spiritual development based on the philosophies of Lord Krishna. The most popular form in the Western world is *hatha yoga*, which uses positions and exercises to promote physical and mental harmony. Most yoga practice starts with hatha yoga, since it is said to provide the body with the health and endurance needed to learn more advanced forms of yoga. Hatha yoga is practiced for its own rewards, which include strength, flexibility, and reduction of muscle tension; it is also used as a technique to quiet the body in preparation for quiet mental states.

### Physical Exercise

The primary stress response is the fight-or-flight response. This reaction has always helped ensure human survival and continues to do so today. In fact, no amount of relaxation training can diminish the intensity of this innate reflex. Stress is physical, intended to make possible a physical response to a physical threat.

However, any threat, either physical or symbolic, can bring about this response. Once the stimulation of the event penetrates the psychological defenses, the body prepares for action. Increased hormonal secretion, energy supply, and cardiovascular activity signify a state of stress, a state of extreme readiness to act as soon as the voluntary control centers decide what action to take. Usually the threat is not physical, but holds only symbolic significance; our lives are not in danger, only our egos. Physical action is not warranted and must be subdued, but for the body organs it is too late—what took only minutes to start will take hours to undo. The stress products are flowing through the system and will activate various organs until these byproducts are reabsorbed back into storage or gradually used by the body. While this gradual process is taking place, the body organs suffer.

The simple solution is to use the physical stress arousal for its intended purpose—physical movement. The increased energy intended for fight or flight can be used for running, swimming, or bicycling. In this way, one can accelerate the dissipation of the stress products, and if the activity is vigorous enough, it can cause a rebound or overshoot after exercise into a state of deep relaxation (see Figure 9.5).

It is important to note that exercise is a stressor, and competition increases that arousal level. While the stress of the exercise is usually absorbed by the exercise, the stress of competition often sets in motion thoughts and feelings that linger. These thoughts may even become the stimulus for prolonged emotional arousal through the rehash of missed points, social embarrassment, and self-doubt. We often confuse recreation with relaxation—they are not necessarily the same. In fact, for most people they are usually not the same. Ideally, exercise to reduce stress should be devoid of ego involvement. Though strenuous, it should be a time of peace and harmonious interaction of mind and body. In that sense, it may be the most natural of stress-reduction techniques. Reducing stress through physical activity is covered more fully in Chapter 16.

**III. Techniques for Conditioning the Mind and Reducing Arousing Thoughts**

Stress arousal is a psychophysiological response to a psychosocial event. Throughout the day, each new stress situation leaves a residual amount of tension in the body, the accumulation of which cannot all be dissipated. The longer you practice relaxation exercises, the more you dissipate your residual tension and increase your general state of relaxation. Gradually, the relaxed state becomes a stable part of your personality.

Primary therapeutic benefits of this phase of your relaxation

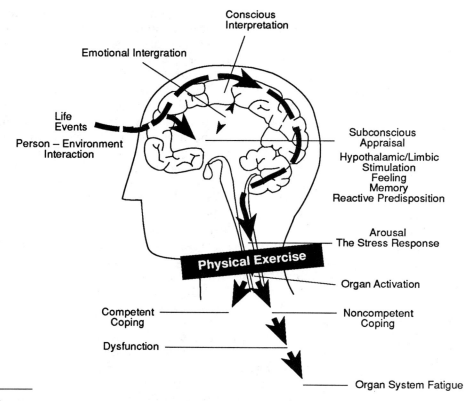

Conscious
Interpretation

Emotional Intergration

Life
Events

Person – Environment
Interaction

Subconscious
Appraisal

Hypothalamic/Limbic
Stimulation
Feeling
Memory
Reactive Predisposition

Arousal
The Stress Response

**Physical Exercise**

Organ Activation

Competent
Coping

Noncompetent
Coping

Dysfunction

Organ System Fatigue

**FIGURE 9.5**

Exercise as an
Intervention
Technique

program include learning to focus your concentration on one thing
at a time (especially on what is happening and what you are feeling
*at the moment*), to quiet internal chatter that often comes from
worrying about the future or feeling guilty about the past, and to
help you separate what is real from what is not real in your life.
When you have learned to stay in the present, to direct your focus
on what is happening right now, and spend less time in needless
worry and fantasy, you become more peaceful.

An important aspect of your stress-management program consists of exercises designed to help you change thoughts and behaviors that continually fuel your stress furnace. Often the ways
in which we process information and relate to others, especially
at work, perpetuate the molehill-to-mountain phenomenon. We are
too ready to allow ourselves to be frustrated, angered, disappointed, or unhappy. We are also too ready to hear and accentuate
the negative instead of the positive. We read into others intentions

that are not really there, and we develop stress-producing patterns of thought.

This phase of the stress-management program will promote self-awareness and suggest ways of reducing such behavior especially as it relates to dealing with the expectations others have for you. These activities are designed to train the mind to reduce arousing thoughts. They reduce stress-arousing memories and anticipations, and instead direct thoughts to produce a peaceful and tranquil state. Representative techniques include many varieties of meditation.

### Meditation

Modern meditative practices represent a mixture of philosophies and techniques descended from ancient yoga and Zen Buddhism. The objectives of meditation are (1) to quiet the body and (2) to quiet the mind. Because of the neurophysiology of the mind (as outlined in Chapter 2), the brain is aroused when the muscles are tense. Continual arousal of the brain makes it impossible to experience a peaceful, tranquil state of mind. This was known centuries ago by those who practiced the Eastern religions and philosophies, and they developed meditation techniques to still the body and the mind. Current meditation techniques attempt to teach us some of the ancient methods of reducing the constant chatter in the mind that nags, frightens, worries, shames, and otherwise keeps us physically tense. As we consciously learn how to reduce mind chatter, we in turn reduce our anxiety and our general stress arousal so that the mind can periodically achieve peace and quiet.

Research has shown that during meditation the activity of most physical systems is reduced. At the same time, the meditator is in complete control of the experience and has control over emotions, body awareness, and memories. Although meditation is a passive state of mind, it is an active process that takes thought, preparation, and practice. Reducing stress through meditation is covered more fully in Chapter 17.

**BUILDING A PROGRAM**

After you have learned some of the relaxation techniques, you then have to refine your use of them so you can relax at will. Once you have developed this ability, you can (1) practice and gradually condition your system to be more tranquil and relaxed, and (2) use it for immediate relief when you feel stressed. The catch in number 2 lies in the ability to recognize stress as it builds, before it pushes you into unproductive emotional states and physical disability.

## The Learning Stage

The following chapters present detailed instructions on a variety of stress-management techniques. Once you have perfected the techniques, you can choose the particular exercise sequence that is most beneficial to you and that meets your immediate needs. As we have said, it is not our intention for you to practice a specific exercise at a specific time for the rest of your life. You will know how, you will know why, and, in the final analysis, you will build your own individual program. However, it is very important that in the learning step you follow the instructions and practice the exercises as suggested. This stage necessitates more structured time involvement, more concentration, and more commitment than will be necessary once you have mastered the techniques.

## Preparation for Exercise

In order for the learning experience to be as effective as possible, you should do whatever you can to create an environment that enhances concentration. Find a quiet environment where you can be alone and not disturbed by the telephone, people, or other interruptions. Some people use ear plugs or play soft, soothing background instrumental music or environmental sounds that are inherently relaxing to them.

If the exercises are being done in a group setting, the room should be large enough so that each participant can stretch out comfortably without feeling crowded. Body position will change with the exercises. Some exercises necessitate lying down, some sitting or standing. Still others can be done in a variety of positions. For those, each individual will have to find his or her own preferred position. For the exercises that involve lying down, a foam mat is helpful for reducing the pressure on body parts.

It is a good idea to place a note on the door to alert potential visitors that quiet is needed. However, it is also advisable to mentally prepare for disturbances that may happen. Expect them, deal with them, and do not allow them to make you angry. Otherwise the emotion of the disturbance will linger long after the physical presence is gone.

Physical factors such as lighting, temperature, and ventilation should be optimal. Clothing should be comfortable. It is best to wear loose, soft clothes that you are not going to worry about wrinkling. If shoes, belt, bra, tie, or collar are too tight, loosen them. The goal is to diminish sensory input to the central nervous system. Most people like to have a clock where it can be seen at a glance to reduce the anxious feelings that arise about the amount of time being spent.

In regard to the time of day that exercises should be performed, there is no best time for everyone. You will have to determine for yourself when and how long. Some programs dictate exactly how much time to spend and when to spend it. That's great if your life is very ordered. But chances are that your life is not that uniform. You are probably active, busy, involved with varying tasks and schedules. To limit your exercise to one specific time of day would ritualize it, and if for some reason you could not exercise at that specific time, you would probably not do it at all that day. Also, there may be times when you just don't feel up to it at that time. If you force yourself too much, you will do it halfheartedly and gain little from the experience. So find a convenient time—if it is the same time every day, fine; if not, that's also fine. The important thing is to engage in the program every day if at all possible.

As to how much time to spend on each session, this again will vary with your schedule. In the learning phase, try to complete an entire series at one time. After that, it would be ideal to complete an entire series, but it is better to work for a few minutes here and there than not at all. You will be surprised how much waiting time during the day can be utilized for exercises, especially the quiet relaxation series. When you are waiting for a meeting or an appointment, a bus, or even one of those seemingly eternal stoplights to change—five minutes here and there can add up quickly—you might just find yourself much less perturbed about being kept waiting if you fill the time with exercises. You can think of it as time for yourself and for your self-improvement.

It must be emphasized that during the exercise and muscle stretching activities your body will move when it is ready. *Do not* go beyond the point of pain or you will tear the tissue and retard your progress. You have spent many years conditioning this state and you cannot reverse it overnight. *Do not* set goals too high too fast. These are powerful exercises with the capability of restoring the natural structure and function to your tissues. Use them as directed until you have reconditioned your body.

**Getting a Direction**

In Chapter 18 we will provide detailed instructions for the step-by-step development of a stress-management program, starting with what you want to accomplish and progressing to the development of the complete program. As you study and practice the techniques presented in Chapters 10–17 you will learn to change your stress response in ways that you never realized. This may change what you expect and, ultimately, what you want to accomplish. However, we think it is important to start with an idea of what you would like to achieve stated in terms of significance in your life. Spend a few minutes now making sure you know what you want, getting a feeling for how motivated you are to get what you want, and how you will know that you have achieved your goal.

To start this process, determine what you want to accomplish. Summarize what you feel are your serious or obvious symptoms of stress. Go back to your stressor profile (at the end of Chapter 8) and examine each of the stressor self-assessments. Identify the stressors to which you are currently vulnerable or may in the future be vulnerable. (Your self-assessment scores will reveal your current status on each stressor, but you will have to estimate your future vulnerability to each of the stressors.) Write in the following space what symptom, situation, or stress response you would like to change.

_____

_____

_____

_____

Write a short, succinct outcome statement, beginning "I want to

_____."

Next, determine how you expect things to be different (one hopes better) in your life once you have achieved your goal. Remember that if your life is not going to change for the better there is not much point in working to obtain the goal, and most people will not put much effort into activities that will not produce positive results. Write a short statement on how you expect things to be better in your life:

_____

_____

_____

The next task is to determine how you will know when you have achieved the desired outcome. What will you accept as proof? If your goal was to be more relaxed, how will you measure the outcome? Write a short list of ways you can prove to yourself that you have achieved your goals.

*These are my proofs:*

_____

_____

_____

Now that you know what you want to accomplish, why you want to accomplish it, and a little about what success might look like, proceed with learning the stress-management techniques presented in Chapters 10–17. When you get to Chapter 18 you will be asked to complete the exercise that you have started here by building your own stress-management program, including the techniques you feel will be most beneficial to you.

CHAPTER TEN

# Techniques
# for Controlling Stress

This chapter describes specific cognitive and behavioral techniques that have been used successfully by clients of ours to construct stress-management programs. The techniques (summarized in Table 10.1) are presented in categories that follow the self-assessment profile categories and are arranged in continuum form—from what are normally the easiest techniques to adopt to the more elaborate techniques demanding deeper change.

**TECHNIQUES FOR CONTROLLING ADAPTIVE STRESS**

Adaptive stress occurs when life situations demand that change occurs. In the Western world, change is seen as "the end" of a period of stability or security of some kind, and is therefore related to fear. Even when change is desired, movement from the old situation in which comfort and security have been established is somewhat stressful. The Eastern concept of change is that it is the only constant and is to be expected, not feared. In our society, in which change occurs quickly, there is little emphasis on the transition between the old and the new. Cultural anthropologist Angeles Arrien reminds us to look at the literature of a culture to find what is most and least important to that culture. She then points out that in the United States there is very little literature on transformation and transition. There are no major rites of passage, no ceremonies that honor the change process. The new is prized, the old is discarded. In this culture there is an expectation that we should make changes quickly and get on to the next item.

Birth and death are excellent examples of the Western "instant change" mentality. After a woman gives birth, she is expected to get right back into her predelivery routine. Likewise, upon the death of a loved one, the bereaved may show their grief perhaps

**TABLE 10.1  Techniques for Controlling Stress**

| CATEGORY | TECHNIQUES |
| --- | --- |
| Adaptive Stress | Establish routines |
| |     Daily routines at work, school, home |
| |     Regular eating and exercise program |
| |     Set sleep patterns |
| |     Rest and relaxation times and places |
| | Avoid change |
| | Plan for change |
| |     Adopt belief that change is constant and to be expected |
| |     Write an action plan for specific changes |
| Frustration | Express your feelings |
| | Goal alternative model |
| | Examine personal beliefs that produce frustration |
| | Learn personal and interpersonal behavior skills |
| Overload | Express your feelings |
| | Negotiate |
| | Time management |
| | Task reduction |
| | Learn to ask for support |
| | Learn to delegate |
| | Expectation history |
| | Examine personal beliefs regarding expectations of self/others |
| Deprivation | Express your feelings |
| | Physical activity plan |
| | Join a social group |
| | Learn to ask for human contact |
| | Examine beliefs that keep you deprived |
| Bioecological | Noise reduction |
| | Keep biorhythm chart to identify highs and lows |
| | Travel-stress reduction (altitude, climate, jet lag) |
| Self-Concept | List resources |
| | Enlist subpersonalities |
| | Compliments |
| | Assertiveness |
| | Interpersonal effectiveness training |
| | Self-talk |
| | Examine beliefs that block positive self-concept |
| Type A | Time management |
| | Concentration |
| | Anger management |
| | Reduce negative self-talk |
| | Goal path model |
| | Examine ego involvement |
| | Practice concentration |
| | Examine beliefs regarding anger, expectations, and perfection |
| Anxious Reactivity | Thought-stopping |
| | Write fear history |
| | Take action |
| | Give away fear |
| | Examine beliefs regarding fear |
| Control | Journal |
| | Calming-down exercise |
| | Reality check |
| | Letting go of judgments |
| | Cognitive restructuring |
| | Examine beliefs regarding control |

through the time of the funeral rites but are then expected to get back to the usual lifestyle.

When changes must occur, three main elements are involved: (1) the present situation, (2) a picture of what the changed situation will be like, and (3) the transitional time between those two situations. What we call change is the transition time that it takes to get from situation A to situation B, as shown in Figure 10.1.

Adaptive stress may occur at various points in Figure 10.1. It may occur at point A, when an individual is asked or expected to change, and that person does not aspire to change. It may also occur at A when an individual is tired of or bored in the present situation, but doesn't know what else to do. It may occur when an individual no longer wants the old situation, aspires to a new situation, but doesn't know how to go about getting there. Then once a new, attainable situation is desired and the individual steps into the transition area, there may be the stress of learning new skills, meeting new people, and so on. Even when the new situation is reached, adaptive stress may occur if the individual doesn't feel comfortable with the change.

Regardless of the point at which one feels adaptive stress, there are techniques that can be used to help resolve or eliminate the problem. The following techniques have been found to be helpful in adaptive-stress situations:

## Establish Routines

If you are happy in your present situation but don't like surprises in your schedule, establish predictable patterns in your life. Write them down. For each routine, give ten minutes or more for transition time from one set of activities to another.

1. Establish daily routines at home, work, school.
2. Establish a regular eating and physical-activity program.
3. Establish set sleep patterns.
4. Establish rest and relaxation times and places. You might establish certain hours of the week as a mental-health getaway. Make sure they are times when you engage in truly relaxing behavior. A vacation during which you travel is usually not free from adaptive stress, so do not count vacations as mental health days unless they are truly relaxing to you.

FIGURE 10.1

Components of Change

**Avoid Change**   If your Life Change Points in self-assessment exercise 1 totaled over 300 and if you are in a position to choose whether or not change is going to occur in your life, avoid change at this time. Some individuals who are going through a great deal of life change choose to stop smoking or go on a diet while their anxiety levels are high. It is usually better to wait until life settles down to engage in new ventures.

**Plan for Change**

### Believe in the Constancy of Change

Adopting the belief that change is one of the constants in life can ready one emotionally and psychologically for change. When change comes, it is expected. Some changes, such as a new boss entering the company or even a new clerk at the grocery store, can be small reminders that change is constant. Other changes, such as an unexpected death, may be much more serious but are also reminders that change constantly occurs.

An exercise for this technique is to say to yourself, "Change is constant," or "I expect things to be constantly changing," whenever you note any kind of change, even a bud turning into a flower or a sunny day being interrupted by storm clouds and rain.

A second exercise is to learn to say what you *prefer* without being *addicted* to the "old" way (Keyes, 1974); for example, "I prefer to have Dr. Jones teach this class, but since she is gone, I'll take it from someone else."

### Write an Action Plan for Specific Changes That You Want

This involves completely thinking through the process shown in Figure 10.1 and then committing to writing a specific plan of action for change. To do this, follow these steps:

1.  Get a good picture of the present situation. Write or even draw it on a piece of paper.
2.  Get a good picture of the situation as you would like it—making sure that it is a picture that you can achieve on your own. We are often confronted with divorced men or women whose ideal picture is of the partner returning and the two of them living happily ever after. Their real need is to paint a picture that they can achieve themselves. Once a realistic picture is clear in your mind, write or draw it on paper.
3.  Prepare a detailed, sequential plan to get from your present situation to your ideal situation.
    a.  Define the ideal situation so that it is clear in your mind.
    b.  List the main subtasks in sequential order—what must be done first, second, and so on.

   c. Under each subtask, identify what resources (both people and materials) will be needed, what skills (new and old) will be necessary, what proof you will insist on in order to know that each subtask is complete, what may block your action at each subtask, and how to get around those blocks.
   d. Identify activities that must be ongoing throughout the transition period (for example, assertiveness training, relaxation training, exercise program)
   e. On one large sheet of paper (or smaller ones taped together), diagram your transition process, using Figure 9.1 as a model. Draw each subtask as a stepping stone.

When the path between situation A and situation B is familiar and active, it becomes less fearful and, thus, less stressful.

**TECHNIQUES TO ALLEVIATE THE STRESS OF FRUSTRATION**

Frustration is a stressor because it is by definition inhibitive. Frustration impedes progress toward a desired goal or blocks desired behavior. The techniques given here present ways that action can be continued, even though you are being thwarted in some part of your life.

**Express Your Frustration**

Until alternatives as satisfying and immediate as the original goal are found, it is helpful to express frustration either by talking with someone else or by writing thoughts down on paper. This helps release the stress buildup and may give insights about the situation.

**Determine Your Real Outcomes**

Using the Outcome Model (Girdano & Dusek, 1988), follow each step from stating what you want to a concrete action plan. The steps are:

**What Do I Want?** While frustration is caused by blocks of progress, many blocks occur because we are really not sure what we want in the first place. If the outcome is not clear, the path is not direct, and we tend to wander off course, letting relatively minor obstacles block our path and cause frustration.

**How Will Things Be Different and Better in My Life When I Get What I Want?** This is the "heart" question. If the path does not have meaning in the first place, it is easy to surrender to frustration. If the outcome is stated in the positive, the human mind will work harder to achieve that outcome. Thinking of one's life in negative terms expands negative energy around the outcome, and the body automatically defends itself against negative events. The ego does not want to face negative inputs, so defenses are built up against the activity. Thus, sometimes the block that frustrates us is of our own creation so that we will not pursue activities that make us feel bad about ourselves.

**What Will I Take as Proof That I Have Been Successful in Reaching My Outcome?**   Sometimes our frustrations and subsequent stress are the result of meeting our real goals, but not knowing it. We have what we wanted, but do not realize it. It is important to set up concrete and countable signposts that will indicate when we are nearing our goal and when we reach it.

**What Are My Useful Resources?**   This will be specific to each project, although after several projects, common resources (especially positive personality traits) will begin to emerge. List all of your internal and external resources. Remember your family, friends, financial ability, and your inner resources that have gotten you to where you are now.

**What Has Kept Me From Reaching This Outcome Before?**   If you have attempted to reach this outcome before or have tried for success in a similar endeavor, what stopped you? Past blocks will almost certainly be blocks in the future unless they are discovered and removed. Spending time analyzing and correcting blocks may be the single most effective frustration-management technique.

**What Am I Willing to Do as a Plan of Action to Get to My Outcome?**   While this is a specific project, you will probably use old successful patterns to help you get to this outcome. If your style works, find a way to adapt it to your new situation. If your old plan does not work, change it by increasing your resources and diminishing your blocks.

Formulate a specific plan, much like that used in the Goal Alternative System presented next.

**Choose Alternatives**

The Goal Alternative System on the following pages is designed to help you cope with frustrational stress by exploring alternatives to goals that have been directly inhibited or stifled.

**Examine Personal Beliefs that May Be Producing Frustration**

The beliefs that we hold regarding our relationship to the rest of the world have been formed very early in life and, therefore, are deeply ingrained. Old, buried beliefs are sometimes difficult to unearth so that we may look at the logic of them in light of our present growth and development. Beliefs formed during childhood are based on the beliefs of significant others and also on the skills and knowledge that the child possesses. The beliefs that worked for a certain period of time may no longer be useful because the individual has new knowledge, skills, and experiences as an adult. The steps that can be used to examine beliefs are given below:

**Question.**   When frustration occurs, say to yourself, "What

### The Goal Alternative System
### Example: Tennis Playing

*Step 1*  What is the desired behavior or goal? *Playing tennis*

*Step 2*  Is this goal immediately obtainable?

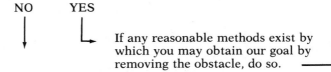

    NO        YES

              └→  STOP! Why are you doing this exercise?

*Step 3*  What is(are) the obstacle(s) that keep(s) you from obtaining this goal?

*Tennis elbow*

*Step 4*  Can this obstacle be removed within a reasonable time period?

    NO        YES

              └→  If any reasonable methods exist by which you may obtain our goal by removing the obstacle, do so.

*Step 5*  Consider your desired goal. Take some time and make a list of the specific rewards or desirable characteristics that make that goal desirable to you. Now go back and give each one of those desirable characteristics a score indicative of how important each one is to you. A score of 1 would be the lowest, 10 the highest. Do this very carefully; it is very important.

| *Rewards* | *Points* |
| --- | --- |
| Being outdoors | 8 |
| Getting exercise | 6 |
| Fast action | 5 |
| Competition | 2 |

*Step 6*  Are there any other reasonable ways to obtain those same rewards listed in step 5?

        YES                         NO
List alternatives,         If you have arrived at this point, it seems
then try them out:         apparent that *all* of those desirable char-

*none*

acteristics listed in step 5 are currently unobtainable. Therefore, instead of feeling sorry for yourself, make a list of alternatives that *are possible* and that have at least some of the same desirable characteristics as the original goal. Select the behavior that results in the highest score possible. This alternative is your best one because it is most similar, based on the points assigned in step 5, to your original behavior.

| *Alternatives* | *Points* |
|---|---|
| *Fishing* | *8* |
| *Golf (outdoor exercise,* | *16* |
| *competition )* | |

## The Goal Alternative System
## Blank Form

*Step 1*   What is the desired behavior or goal? _____

*Step 2*   Is this goal immediately obtainable?

        NO      YES

                  STOP! Why are you doing this exercise?

*Step 3*   What is(are) the obstacle(s) that keep(s) you from obtaining this goal?

_____

_____

*Step 4*   Can this obstacle be removed within a reasonable time period?

        NO      YES

                  If any reasonable methods exist by which you may obtain our goal by removing the obstacle, do so.

*Step 5* Consider your desired goal. Take some time and make a list of the specific rewards or desirable characteristics that make that goal desirable to you. Now go back and give each one of those desirable characteristics a score indicative of how important each one is to you. A score of 1 would be the lowest, 10 the highest. Do this very carefully; it is very important.

| *Rewards* | *Points* |
|-----------|----------|
| _____ | _____ |
| _____ | _____ |
| _____ | _____ |
| _____ | _____ |
| _____ | _____ |

*Step 6* Are there any other reasonable ways to obtain those same rewards listed in step 5?

| YES | NO |
|-----|-----|
| List alternatives, then try them out:<br><br>_____<br><br>_____<br><br>_____<br><br>_____ | If you have arrived at this point, it seems apparent that *all* of those desirable characteristics listed in step 5 are currently unobtainable. Therefore, instead of feeling sorry for yourself, make a list of alternatives that *are possible* and that have at least some of the same desirable characteristics as the original goal. Select the behavior that results in the highest score possible. This alternative is your best one because it is most similar, based on the points assigned in step 5, to your original behavior. |

| *Alternatives* | *Points* |
|----------------|----------|
| _____ | ____ |
| _____ | ____ |
| _____ | ____ |
| _____ | ____ |

would a person have to believe in order to become frustrated in such a situation?"

**Answers.** Examine some possible answers to your questions. The beliefs listed here (Girdano & Dusek, 1988) may provide a starting point.

- I must not change my beliefs, attitudes, or actions because they have gotten me this far.
- I must understand the universe before I can live happily in it.
- I will be seen as an inferior person unless I do well and win the approval of others.
- I cannot exist without sincere and constant love and approval from everyone who is in my life.
- I must be able to do at least one thing with thorough competence.
- Justice, fairness, and equality must prevail or life is too unbearable.
- I must not experience or show negative emotions because they make me perform badly and others don't like them.
- I must control or change people who I consider dangerous.
- I must not question or doubt the beliefs held by authorities. If I do, I should be punished.
- I should get what I want, when I want it, regardless of what others think or do.
- Others must not unjustly criticize me.
- Others should not behave in a stupid or incompetent manner.
- Others will treat me the way I think I should be treated.

**Turning the Belief Around.** After identifying the belief on which the frustration is based, turn the belief around so that it becomes positive. For example: "I cannot purchase the computer I want because my father says it is an inferior machine and I could get a better price on a model that I don't really want. I identify that my frustration stems from my belief that my father knows what is best for me. I turn the belief around to: "I am the only one who knows what is best for me." I can choose to take the advice of others, especially when I honor their expertise, but I must make my own choices."

**Take Action.** Act on the positive belief. Continue to affirm that belief. Write it down on a card and place the card in a conspicuous place in your house or car.

**Learn Personal and Interpersonal Behavioral Skills That Will Help You Carry Out New Beliefs**

Acting on new positive beliefs may call for the learning of new skills such as assertiveness. Telling others that they are no longer expected to control your behaviors may call for preparatory skills that you must be willing to learn. Assertiveness and Interpersonal Effectiveness Training are discussed in detail under the category "Techniques to Enhance a Positive Self-Concept" later in this chapter.

**TECHNIQUES TO ALLEVIATE THE STRESS OF OVERLOAD**

You suffer from overload when faced with excessive demands to the point where your stress response is aroused. Overload is a function of four major factors: (1) time pressure, (2) excessive responsibility or accountability, (3) lack of support, and (4) excessive expectations imposed by yourself or by others. Consider the following techniques for alleviating the stress of overload.

**Express Your Feelings**

Talk with someone or write down your feelings on paper. Do not allow your emotions to get bottled up.

**Negotiate**

If you perceive that your feelings of overload are being brought on by a person, negotiate with that person to reduce the load or the deadline.

**Learn to Manage Time Effectively**

Working under a deadline is the most obvious form of time overload, but much of this stress can be controlled by effective time management. When the task seems too formidable, use the techniques shown in Table 10.2 to set priorities and schedule tasks into a workable, efficient order.

**Divide Tasks into Smaller Parts**

Break a large task down into its smallest workable parts and treat each as a separate task with its own deadlines and requirements. As each task is finished, add it to the others until the entire task is completed.

An example might be a fifty-page report or term paper. Writing

**TABLE 10.2  A Model for Time Management**

Time management involves matching the best combination of time demands with your supply of available time. The following steps provide a means of achieving that goal.

| TIME DEMANDS | TIME SUPPLY |
|---|---|
| 1. List all of the tasks that need to be completed within the given time interval. For example, on Monday consider what things need to be done during the coming week. | 4. Look at your calendar for the week. Identify the blocks of time available *each* day for completing the necessary tasks. |
| 2. Estimate how much time will be needed to complete *each* task. | 5. Match the tasks with the available time blocks in such a way as to make use of available time most constructively. |
| 3. Go back and increase each of the time estimates in step 2 by 10 to 15 percent. This will provide some cushion for error or for unexpected problems. | 6. Many times you will find that there is simply not enough time available to complete all of the tasks. Therefore, you must *prioritize* the tasks. List the tasks in order of their importance so that the most important tasks will be completed. If extra time is available, you may go on to other less important tasks. |

fifty pages may seem to be an incredible task. However, when the paper is reduced to its parts, each part may be only five pages, a much more manageable task.

**Learn to Say What You Want and How You Feel**

- When you feel that someone is imposing more work or responsibility on you than is appropriate at the time, tell him or her that the timing is inappropriate.
- If you do not wish to do a task, say "no."
- Ask for help from others. Sit down and objectively look at your load in relation to those around you. If you get up and make breakfast for everyone before you go to work, cook dinner, straighten the house, and put everybody to bed after you come home from work, and do the laundry on your day off, look at the responsibilities of everyone else in the household. If the responsibilities are out of balance and the expertise of others is sufficient to carry out some of your duties, ask for a family meeting. Discuss the inequities and reassign some of the duties.

**Learn to Delegate**

As in the preceding technique, duties can be shared when you learn to delegate some of the tasks and responsibilities. This is more than asking for what you want, it is giving up some control over how things will be done by completely giving a task to someone else. The connotation of *delegation* is that you are in a position of authority and that others are there for the purpose of helping you complete certain tasks. Be thoughtful when you delegate and take into consideration the workload of others so that you are not the cause of overload for them.

**Do an Expectation History**

Where did your levels of expectation originate? What kind of expectations did you learn from your mother and father? What do (did) your parents and other significant people in your life expect from you? from themselves? from others?

What is a reasonable expectation level? There is an old formula:

$$\text{Happiness} = \text{what you get} \div \text{what you expect}$$

If you get \$100 but you expected \$1000, your quotient is less than 1. If you get \$100 but expected that amount or less, the quotient is 1 or more. When unrealistically high expectations are set, they result in overload stress. When expectations are kept to a minimum and are realistically set, they result in foundational goals rather than system overload.

**Examine Personal Beliefs Regarding Expectations of Self and Others**

Using the discussion on beliefs given in the previous category on frustration, think about your long-held beliefs regarding what you expect from others. What you expect from others is a good reflection of what you expect from yourself. If others cannot please you with their performance, there is a great likelihood that you cannot please yourself with your performance. Some of the negative beliefs that may arise here are:

- Work is not done until it is done perfectly.
- I must always perform at the 90 percent level of effectiveness, creativity, and intellectual excellence or I will be considered a sloppy person.
- Others cannot do the job as well as I can.
- If you want it done right, you have to do it yourself.
- There is no room in the world for a person who performs at less than maximum effort all the time.

When you find that you hold negative beliefs about perfection and expectations, reverse that belief and continue to affirm it until it is the basis for your expectations. Example: "I must perform with perfection or I will not be accepted (loved) by others." This belief might be turned around to: "I will do the best I can within reason. Pleasing myself is more important than pleasing others."

**TECHNIQUES TO ALLEVIATE DEPRIVATIONAL STRESS**

As overload is a stressor because of excessive stimulation, deprivation or boredom is one because of insufficient stimulation. Like all of the stressors discussed here, deprivation is an idiosyncratic and relative phenomenon. In general, deprivation is alleviated by increasing the level of stimulation. The techniques given here present various ways of increasing stimulation and interaction.

**Keep a Journal**

Writing your feelings about loneliness, boredom, or lack of involvement helps alleviate deprivational stress in two ways: (1) It is an active process that may also include creativity, and (2) the expression of negative emotions helps to release them.

**Start a Physical Activity Program**

Become active in a preset or self-originated activity program. Larger cities have YMCAs offering activity courses for small fees. Also available are spas and health clubs, although these are usually more expensive. Every college has a physical education department and campus recreation. Collect catalogs and/or call these establishments to compile a list of possible activities, then choose one or two that you have always wanted to do. Joining activity classes is also a very good way to meet people with interests similar to yours.

If you have the expertise and desire to set up your own activity program, sit down and plan how you will carry it out for the first month. (A plan for starting a physical activity program is presented in Chapter 16). Write your activity plan on a calendar. Also, try to get a friend to join you; motivation is usually enhanced by performing activities with others.

## Join a Social Group

Using the references to institutions (as found in technique 2) that offer physical activities, obtain information from them regarding other activities such as men's or women's support groups, single-parent groups, play-reading groups, and so forth. Your city may have a formal listing of social-support groups available in the community. If you have a special interest but there is no established group, consider starting such a group by placing a notice in your apartment building or dorm, or by placing an advertisement in the local paper.

## Learn to Ask for Human Contact

This technique calls for learning assertiveness skills discussed in the self-concept category later in this chapter. Please read that section.

## Examine Beliefs that Keep You Isolated or Bored

What would a person have to believe to keep themselves unhappily in isolation or boredom?

Possible negative beliefs:

- I do not deserve the company of fun and interesting people.
- I cannot disclose who I am to others or they won't like me.
- People will only hurt me and take advantage of me.
- It takes too much effort to make friends.
- I am perfectly happy being by myself.

As in past discussions of beliefs, the technique here is to not only examine the negative beliefs that keep one in isolation or boredom, but to turn the belief into a positive statement and begin to live by the new belief. Example: "It takes too much effort to find something exciting to do." This belief can be turned around to: "Getting involved in activities I really like to do is becoming easier and easier."

## TECHNIQUES TO ALLEVIATE BIOECOLOGICAL STRESS

Bioecological stress derives from such sources as not being in tune with one's biocycles, change of time zone(s) in a short period of time, noise, cold, heat, humidity, and other environmental sources.

The techniques presented here are specific to the sources discussed in Chapter 6.

**Techniques to
Alleviate Noise**

- Remove yourself from the noisy environment.
- Protect yourself with earplugs while staying in the noisy environment.
- Choose to avoid noisy environments when there is a choice.
- Assert your right to have a quiet environment when others are encroaching on your boundaries.

**Techniques
Involving
Biorhythms**

Chart your biorhythms to identify your highs and lows and then plan activities accordingly whenever possible. This includes daily cycles, monthly cycles (especially females regarding their menstrual cycles), and yearly or seasonal cycles. Forms to chart your cycles are given in Chapter 6.

Plan your air travel and cross-country trips very carefully. Be aware of travel stresses such as the following:

### Change in Elevation

Many skiers or summer vacationers from the "flatlands" arrive at high altitudes and want to perform the same as they do at home. Oxygen is not as available to the system at these higher altitudes, so demands on the cardiovascular and muscular systems must be reduced. Preparing both of these systems before vacation time helps alleviate some of the altitude stress.

The sun is also a factor, especially when rays are being reflected off snow or water. A total sun block or high-sun-protection-factor lotion is a must, especially for winter vacationers who have not exposed their skin to the sun since the previous summer.

Altitude sickness also hampers many mountain visitors. It is especially exacerbated by sudden changes to a higher altitude and by drinking alcohol. Arnica, a remedy made from the arnica Montana plant (which grows on rocky mountainsides), has been used for centuries to alleviate altitude sickness. Arnica in tablet form can often be found in health food stores.

### Jet Lag

Aeromedicine experts estimate that it takes about twenty-four hours to adjust to each one-hour time difference (Reuben, 1987). Jet travel alters more than sleep–wake cycles; it also affects heart rate, blood pressure, respiration, body temperature, urinary output, hormone secretion, and mental functioning because these are all regulated on a twenty-four hour cycle.

To beat jet lag, it helps to manipulate your blood chemistry by providing proteins which affect the brain's biochemistry in the direction of wakefulness and alertness, and by providing carbohydrates which tend to calm the mind and damp out distractions.

According to Reuben, nutrition researchers at MIT suggest this fare for the day of departure:

*Flying west to east:*
   Exercise in the morning
   Breakfast and lunch high in protein
   Dinner and evening snacks high in carbohydrates

*Flying east to west:*
   Carbohydrate breakfast
   Protein lunch and dinner
   Exercise in the afternoon

Plan your arrival for the morning so that you have all day to acclimatize by eating and exercising in the manner given above. Exercise raises the body's temperature, so when you arrive in the east in the morning, vigorous exercise helps you wake up. Vigorous exercise in the afternoon when you arrive in the west helps you stay awake past what would be your bedtime at home. Reuben (1987) points out that eating fatty foods within the first day or two after your arrival counters the effects of a dietary regimen of protein and carbohydrates; while alcohol exacerbates the fatigue of jet lag, so it is best to drink alcohol only in the evening, if at all.

Another way to alleviate the stress caused by jet lag is to schedule a buffer day after you arrive at your destination. Use that day to relax and adjust your internal clock.

### Change in Climate

Just as change in altitude causes stress, so does change in climate (to a hotter, colder, drier, wetter, more humid, or less humid place).

Cold climates demand special clothing. Down-filled or other body-heat-holding outerwear, polypropylene or wool underwear, and wool outerwear are especially suited to cold weather. Dress in layers with wool or some other "wicking" material next to the skin to take the perspiration away from the skin and the material next to the skin. (Winter sports enthusiasts know that cotton kills through hypothermia.) A warm hat, a good pair of gloves or mittens with glove liners, and insulated boots are also necessary for comfort in cold climates. If the weather is bitterly cold (either ambient temperature or because of added wind-chill factor), a scarf and/or face mask may also be helpful in staying safe and comfortable while outside.

Hot and humid climates are especially stressful to those who are not acclimated to them. When traveling in these areas, slow down activity until some acclimation occurs. Because of fluid loss, drink ample liquids, especially good, clear water. Some water-soluble vitamins are lost through sweating, so it is best to maintain adequate intake of the B vitamins and vitamin C. Since potassium and sodium are necessary for water balance in the body, intake of these minerals should also be monitored. A good, balanced diet of fresh fruits and vegetables, calcium-rich foods, whole-grain products, and fish or lean meats normally provides the vitamins and minerals needed for maintaining water balance in the body.

Dry climates also demand that one focus on water balance and care of the skin. However, dry skin does not necessarily mean that low humidity is the culprit. Healthy skin protects itself with natural oils, the production of which is at least in part dependent on the presence of the water-soluble vitamins A, D, E, and K. When the skin cannot lubricate itself, a good natural moisturizer is called for.

## TECHNIQUES TO ENHANCE A POSITIVE SELF-CONCEPT

Everyone can work toward a more positive self-concept. Low self-concept is a result of negative beliefs about one's self, negative self-talk that fuels the old negative beliefs, and the way life experiences are perceived. Until the negative spiral is broken, enhancement of self-concept is not possible. The following techniques present a number of levels of possible change.

### List Your Resources

On paper, write all the resources that you have in your life. You are alive and have attained a certain number of years. What do you have going for you that has helped you get where you are now? In listing resources, remember to include:

1. physical and material resources such as income, clothing, housing, money;
2. social support resources such as family, friends, teachers, and counselors;
3. internal resources such as empathy, tenacity, sense of humor, honesty, you're a good friend to others, and so on

Once you have listed as many items in each category as possible, write each resource on a three-by-five card, placing a new card on the top of the deck each day. On reading the daily resource, repeat several times to yourself or out loud that you possess this quality or resource. Merely reading the words on the card is not enough to enjoy how you feel about yourself and thus enhance your self-concept—you must internalize the resource and accompany it with a positive feeling.

### Enlist Subpersonalities

Having listed internal resources, name them and then use them to help you in stressful situations. This concept was developed in the psychosynthesis movement of the 1960s and 1970s (Vargiu, 1977). For example, a list of internal resources might be:

| caring for others | intelligence | sense of humor |
|---|---|---|
| tenacity | reliability | risk taking |

Give each of the characteristics an alliterative name, such as Connie Caring, Tony Tenacity, Ina Intelligence, Roy Reliable, and so on. Each of these "people" is part of your personality and has been hard at work to help you throughout the years.

When a stressful situation comes up, internally scan your cast of characters and call upon one or more to help you through the situation. Talk to the subpersonality (or write a script between you and the character) and let that part of you donate its expertise to the solution of the situation.

**Affirmations**

Affirmations are statements that you write and repeat affirming that you already have what you envision having. They are written in the first person, present tense. They are positive statements accompanied with positive feeling.

1. Clearly get in mind what you want.
2. See yourself clearly in the situation where you have gained what you want (refer back to step 1). If you cannot see yourself having completely attained your goal, drop back to a point that you can see having accomplished. Work forward from there.
3. Experience the good feeling of having accomplished what you want.
4. Make a meaningful statement regarding the accomplishment of getting what you want.
   "It's easy for me to . . ."
   "I enjoy having . . ."
   "I am becoming more and more . . ."
   These statements should focus on the characteristic or quality you want ("I enjoy being self-confident"), not the ability to get there ("I can become self-confident"). They should be as specific as possible. An affirmation of "I am losing weight easily and quickly" is more specifically stated, "I am easily and quickly reaching my goal of 120 pounds." Putting words such as "easily" and "quickly" into action creates movement from the present situation to the affirmed situation. Words that trigger feelings (for example, joyously, excitedly, lovingly) are also helpful.
5. Write affirmations for all aspects of your life—social, emotional, spiritual, occupational, intellectual, and so on—so that you have a well-rounded life.
6. Say your affirmations at least once a day, but optimally two, three, or more times throughout the day. On rising and before going to sleep are common times committed to affirmations. Other likely times are when waiting for appointments, while driving, or at scheduled times when at work, home, or school.

**Learn to Give and Accept Compliments**

- Practice giving compliments to others and make a study of how they accept them. Do they just say "Thank you," or do they add on a statement of humility? Make your compliments "real" by commenting on something that you really like. Begin with your friends, then expand to others in your work or study space, sales clerks, service people, and so on.
- Begin to accept compliments by giving a smile and a "Thank you." Period. Make no follow-up statement unless it is a positive confirmation of the compliment, for example, "Thank you, I really like it, too."

**Practice Assertiveness**

Verbal assertiveness is saying what you like or dislike about someone or something without using degradation; it is getting what you want, but not at the expense of someone else's self-esteem. Assertiveness is "feel good" communication. Some people confuse assertiveness with aggression. Aggression is demanding, in a bossy and demeaning way, that someone obey your wishes. It is an act of verbal pushing and shoving, with no consideration for the other person's self-esteem. When the other person does not comply or agree, the aggressor insists that he or she is "dumb" or "stupid" or "crazy" for not agreeing. When people respond to a situation aggressively, they often receive counteraggression, alienation, and defensiveness from the other person. Communication is virtually blocked and all who are involved come away from the situation feeling anxious, angry, and misunderstood.

At the opposite end of the scale from aggression is nonassertive or passive behavior (see Figure 10.2). Many have learned in childhood to be passive placaters who do not have the skill to ask for what they want. Their mode of operation is to manipulate. They sit back wishing that someone would notice their needs and fulfill them, or they set up subtle and roundabout ways of getting what they want. Manipulators use guilt to get others to do what they want. They control others with shoulds, oughts, and ifs. Nonassertiveness is highly related to low self-concept.

In becoming more assertive, it is important to know that you have certain inalienable assertive rights, which include:

- saying no and not feel guilty
- changing your mind
- taking your time in planning your answer or action
- asking for instructions or directions
- demanding respect
- doing less than you possibly can
- asking for what you want
- experiencing and expressing your feelings
- feeling good about yourself, no matter what

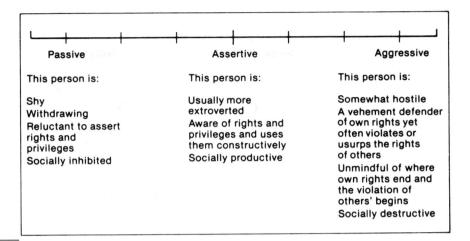

FIGURE 10.2

Assertiveness Scale

Assertiveness training involves operationalizing these rights.

The Assertiveness Ladder (Figure 10.3) is a hierarchy of assertiveness exercises that you might attempt in your daily contacts with other people. The exercises are listed in order, from least to most difficult. Start slowly at the bottom and progress up through the list. You might spend a week or two practicing each one before moving up to the next. If you begin to experience anxiety, drop back to the previous exercise for another week, then try to move up again through the list.

**Exercise 1: Greeting Others.**  Many unassertive people are too shy to greet others or initiate conversations. This exercise consists of initiating at least two exchanges or conversations per day with individuals whom you would not consider close friends. It may be difficult or seem "plastic" at first, but continue trying. You may meet some very interesting people.

**Exercise 2: Complimentary Statements.**  This exercise involves giving others compliments. This is a social behavior that may lead to greater social horizons. Many unassertive people neglect to give compliments by rationalizing "Oh, that's dumb," or "Why would they care what I think?" Giving compliments is polite, and people probably do care what you think, so give it a try.

**Exercise 3: The Use of "I" Statements.**  Many unassertive people are hesitant or afraid to use the word *I*. The reason is that the use of "I" shows ownership, and disagreement with an "I" statement by someone else is often seen by the unassertive person as a rejection of him or her personally. This is not usually the case, though. Don't be afraid to take a position. Let your preferences be known; if you don't, they will never be realized.

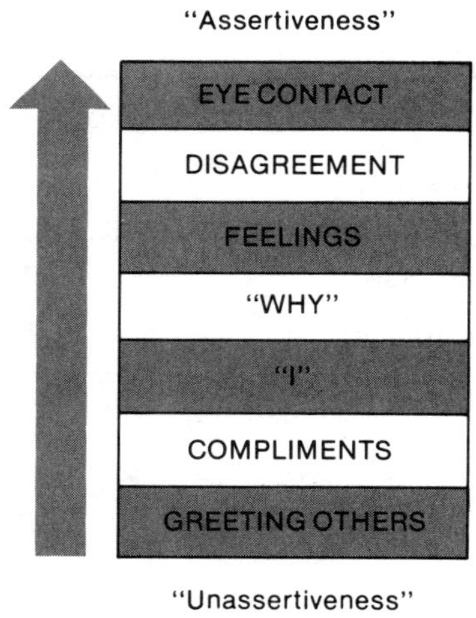

"Assertiveness"

EYE CONTACT

DISAGREEMENT

FEELINGS

"WHY"

"I"

COMPLIMENTS

GREETING OTHERS

"Unassertiveness"

FIGURE 10.3

Assertiveness
Ladder

**Exercise 4: "Why?"** This exercise involves asking "why?" Many unassertive people feel that to ask why represents a challenge—it does not. "Why?" simply asks for additional information. In this exercise, you should ask "why" at least two times a day from people you consider to be "above" you in status, position, or respect—your boss, for example. If you think the word "why" may be too threatening to that person, substitute "What makes you think that?" or "How is that so?" or finally, "Could you help me to understand that better?"

**Exercise 5: Spontaneous Expression of Feelings.** Unassertive people often repress feelings. This exercise consists of having you spontaneously react on a feeling level to someone else's statement or behavior. Repressed feelings are hazardous to your health and well-being; therefore, express them a little at a time. Try to express your emotional reaction at least two times a day. You'll find it gets easier the more you practice. Remember, sometimes it is better to take the risk of hurting someone else's feelings than to keep your feelings bottled up. If that person is your friend, he or she will understand.

**Exercise 6: Disagreement.** This exercise involves disagreeing with someone when you feel that person is wrong. Many people take such disagreement personally, but that is a problem they must work out for themselves. If the other person is secure, he or she will know that disagreement can be a healthy and positive force for new ideas. Give it a try, but be sure not to be arbitrary—if you disagree with someone, make sure you really believe in what you are saying.

**Exercise 7: Eye Contact.**   Maintaining eye contact is often one of the most difficult things for the unassertive person to do. You may find it awkward at first, but continue trying. The best way to attempt maintaining eye contact is to start with short intervals two to three seconds in length. Eventually extend it to four to five seconds, then nine to ten seconds. It is important that you don't stare at people; this is too often interpreted as a challenge. Therefore, use this time interval technique. When you break eye contact, it is important not to look down; maintain your basic eye level. Don't look down!

When you can successfully climb up this Assertiveness Ladder, you will be well on your way to becoming an assertive individual and will have done much to improve your self-concept. Remember that not all assertive behaviors will result in rewards; other people may simply be defensive or aggressive. But don't let their problems hinder you. Feel good about yourself and your new assertive personality.

**Learn Interpersonal Effectiveness Training Techniques**

The final exercise, but perhaps one of the most useful tools you can find for enhancing self-perception, may be referred to as *Interpersonal Effectiveness Training*. Psychologists have used techniques for decades to help their patients improve their self-esteem and overcome dysfunctional passivity and the depression that may result.

Interpersonal Effectiveness Training is best understood within the context of helping people become more interpersonally effective and avoid the problems of passivity and of aggressive behavior (look back at Figure 10.2). As such, Interpersonal Effectiveness Training may also be thought of as a form of assertiveness training, but far broader in scope. It should be used in any interpersonal situation in which you feel yourself pulled toward passive or aggressive behavior. It is *critical* to understand that the goal of such an exercise is *not* merely to "get your way." Rather, the primary goal is to avoid passivity or aggression toward others, both of which lead ultimately to interpersonal dysfunction. However, by avoiding passivity and aggression, you will find that your chances of obtaining what you seek will be enhanced and you will feel better about your own interpersonal effectiveness. Let's examine the process of Interpersonal Effectiveness Training:

### Situation

Any interpersonal situation in which you feel yourself pulled toward interpersonal passivity or interpersonal aggression (refer again to Figure 10.2).

*Steps*

1. Experience the presence of an emotional cue, for example, guilt, anger, loss of self-esteem, or even confusion.

*Analysis*

2. Analyze the situation itself:
   a. Has the other person done anything to violate your interpersonal rights?
   b. Try to see the situation from his or her eyes. If your rights have *not* been violated, don't continue this exercise. Similarly, don't continue if you decide it's really not worth discussion or if you feel it to be unwise from the "interpersonal politics" perspective. Otherwise, if your interpersonal rights *have* been violated, *and* if you feel the issue is worthy of discussion, then continue.

*Action*

3. Describe to the other person what they have done or what has happened that has violated your rights. Simply describe the facts.

4. Continue by telling the other person how the incident has made you *feel*, for example: "I felt . . . cheated, betrayed, stupid, foolish, angry, worthless, sad, etc."

5. Now inform the other person what you would like to see done to correct the situation; that is, so your rights aren't violated. Use the principle of "minimal corrective action." This involves requesting that the situation be corrected but without making anyone else feel or look bad (for example, without punishing anyone). Be careful not to become aggressive here.

6. A final, optional step that you may employ if your wishes aren't met and you feel your rights have still been violated is *escalation*. Escalation simply means that you *inform*, not threaten, the other individual of more action-oriented steps you will pursue if satisfactory action is not taken: for example, you may call someone of higher authority, and so on.

Remember, practice makes perfect, so start slowly at first. Also remember that no matter how interpersonally persuasive you may be, you can't make anyone do anything that he or she doesn't really want to. So, if after step 6 you still haven't gotten satisfaction, be *proud* of yourself; you've done all you could without resorting to passivity or aggression.

Common situations in which this exercise may be useful are:

1. in disputes with clerks while shopping;
2. in disputes with repairmen;
3. with friends or family who have hurt your feelings or violated your rights in some way (it's okay to ask for an apology for step 5);
4. with "pushy" salespeople, and so forth.

**Avoid Negative Self-Talk**

Negative self-talk perpetuates negative feelings about the self and also continues to affirm negative self-beliefs.

1. Monitor yourself for one day and write down all the words and phrases you say to yourself that are negative. You might also enlist the help of others around you—have them identify statements they hear you say about yourself.
2. For each negative phrase you have identified over the period of a day, write a positive follow-up. For example, a negative phrase might be: "You big dummy." Follow it with, ". . . but I like you anyway."
3. After this exercise, each time you hear yourself saying something negative about yourself, add something positive.
4. After mastering step 3, each time you begin to say something negative about yourself substitute a positive statement. Do not even bother to say the negative statement.

**Examine Negative Beliefs**

As discussed in some of the other categories, negative beliefs are the basis for negative feelings and behaviors. What are the core self-concept beliefs on which you operate your life? Some possibilities that may stem from early childhood are:

- I am an unlovable person.
- I do things so poorly that nobody could like me.
- No matter how hard I try, things always turn out badly.
- Nobody likes me so why should I try.
- I am unworthy of the love and attention of others.

When you treat yourself in an unloving way or behave in a way that depreciates yourself, ask "What must a person believe in order to behave in such a self-depreciating way?" Then turn the belief around to a positive statement that you repeat whenever you notice you are being unkind to yourself.

The beliefs that are the basis of your relationship with yourself are also the foundation for your beliefs about other people. This can be used to your advantage by changing your attitudes toward others and becoming more accepting, compassionate, and loving. As you release judgment of others, you may release judgment of yourself. A simple affirmation about others such as "Everyone does the best they can with what they have at any given time" allows you to let others be where they are without having to judge their actions. Such a statement does not mean that the person cannot grow and learn other ways of doing things; it merely says that they are doing the best they can. That affirmation can be extended to the self in stressful times: "I am doing the best I can with what I have right now."

**TECHNIQUES FOR TYPE A BEHAVIOR**

Friedman and Rosenman emphasized that the Type A individual wants to avoid heart disease, not change his or her lifestyle. This fact makes the Type A personality the most difficult personality to work with, because it is the lifestyle and personality that are stressful. When realizing that a lifestyle change is indicated, the Type A who is trying to modify that behavior may quit in frustration. If you are a Type A person, that fact will be the hardest for you to face, but once you realize it, change can successfully occur.

Changing Type A behavior does not mean giving up the desire to achieve or excel. It does mean using behaviors that are more healthfully appropriate.

The following techniques are directed toward the four basic characteristics of the Type A personality: time urgency, anger-hostility, lack of planning, and polyphasic behavior.

**Learn Effective Time Management**

Review the time-management process in Table 10.2.

**Practice Concentration**

Polyphasic thinking and behavior goes on because you allow it to go on. Time may be better spent by concentrating completely on one task, finishing it, and then going on to the next.

1. Read material that makes you concentrate; something with difficult concepts rather than simple ones.
2. When working on one plan and another pops into your mind, say "Stop it" and go back to the original plan.
3. Practice meditation, detailed visualization, progressive muscle relaxation or other relaxation-training techniques in which you must focus on one thing at a time.
4. If a good idea about something else pops up in the middle of another project and you can't "stop it," jot it down and immediately go back to the original project.

**Learn Anger Management[1]**

1. Keep an anger diary for one week. On a three-by-five index card, for each incident jot down what precipitated the anger; how you reacted; how you felt before, during, and after the incident; what you expected from others in the situation; why you think others acted the way they did; your self-talk before, during, and after the incident; and how long the self-talk lasted.
2. Write a list of coping self-talk statements. Under the headings "Before the incident," "When physiologically aroused," "During the encounter," and "After the encounter" write four or five statements you can use to help you stay calm during that time. For example:

[1]Based on Novaco's anger-inoculation techniques, 1975, 1978.

*Before:* I don't need to get angry in this situation.
*Physiological Arousal:* Relax now and stay centered. Breathe . . .
*During:* What is my outcome here? Honey catches more flies than vinegar.
*After:* I did the best I could. That could have been worse. I did a great job.

3. Choose the incident that provoked the least anger and review it in your mind.

4. Use a relaxation technique that works for you (deep breathing, neuromuscular relaxation, and so forth), and while relaxed, go over in your mind the incident you have chosen. As you play through it, insert an appropriate positive coping-statement at the four points outlined above.

   Review the incident using the coping statements.

5. When you can relive this incident with no feelings of anger, choose the next least stressful situation from your diary and repeat the procedure using your positive coping self-statements.

6. When old incidents can be relived without anger, transfer the technique to future potential anger situations in your life.

### Reduce Negative Self-Talk

Reduce negative self-talk using the technique presented in the previous category on self-concept.

### Plan More Adequately

Rushing into tasks without having adequately planned them results in stress that is highly preventable. The remedy is the Goal Path Model given here:

*Step 1:* Define the task:

Reasons for doing the task:

*Step 2:* Can the task be broken down into subtasks?

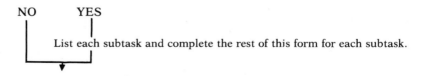

NO          YES

List each subtask and complete the rest of this form for each subtask.

*Step 3:* Evaluation or proofs of success (how will you know when you have succeeded with the task?). List proofs:

*Step 4:* What personnel or help will be needed? List:
↓
What are possible resources for personnel?
↓
Estimate costs and obstacles for getting personnel:
↓
*Step 5:* What materials will be needed? List:
↓
What are possible resources for materials?
↓
Estimate costs and obstacles for getting materials:
↓
*Step 6:* Estimate time required for each task in step 2:
↓
*Step 7:* Hypothesize all possible obstacles or blocks to success:
↓
*Step 8:* For each obstacle, go back and develop at least one contingency plan:
↓
*Step 9:* Evaluate your contingency plan:
↓
*Step 10:* Begin.

**Examine Ego Involvement**

Ego involvement means that the outcome of a behavior or a task will make some reflection on the individual's ego. You know the ego is involved when you ask yourself, "What will someone else think of me if I fail, if I don't do what they want, if the project I'm completing isn't on time?" Ego involvement is often based on rewards from the system or from one specific person, rather than from completing the job for the internal reward of a job well done.

The system rewards Type A behavior, and the Type A personality lives on those rewards. As long as the external rewards are the motivators for action, those who give out the rewards have control over the person seeking the rewards. Changing Type A behavior calls for gradual change to an internal reward system; that is, defining success according to individual outcomes, not outcomes set by outside institutions, family, or friends.

A basic technique here is to ask yourself, "Am I following a path with heart?" If so, the path will be more exciting than stressful. And if it is not a path with heart, remove your ego and view stressful situations with objectivity:

- Am I the only one who can do this?
- Can I be the sole cause of failure at this task?

- Am I verifying others' reactions to me?
- Am I competing rather than cooperating?
- If I were an objective outsider, how would I view this situation?

The Reality Check presented in the category on control later in this chapter and the Goal Path Model discussed in technique 5 of this category may be helpful in reducing ego involvement.

**Examine Beliefs Regarding Anger**

An underlying cause of anger is not getting what we expect, so reducing the incidence of anger involves examining beliefs about expectations. Typical Type A expectations are based on such beliefs as:

- I know how to do it best and quickest.
- If it's not done my way, it's done wrong.
- If you can't do it quickly and excellently, get out of the way.
- If I do everything "by the book," I'll be appropriately rewarded and live happily ever after.
- If I hurry faster, I'll get everything done.

After an anger situation, review your thoughts and behavior. What must you believe in order to think and behave that way? On identifying an irrational or negative belief behind the anger, change it to a positive one such as "Everyone has his own way of doing things that is right for him."

If you cannot identify negative or irrational beliefs, try the empty-chair technique of "being" the other person in a confrontation that you have had (or may have). Sitting in front of an empty chair, pretend that the other person is sitting in it. Say what you have to say to them. Then get up, sit in their chair, and become them. Say what comes immediately to mind in response to your statement to them. Then go back to your chair and become yourself again. Comment on their statement. Do this change of roles until you have an insight into what your beliefs are in this situation. Are they rational? Are your expectations rational?

**TECHNIQUES TO ALLEVIATE ANXIOUS REACTIVITY**

Thought stopping is a technique whereby an individual intentionally breaks the anxious cycle by abruptly leaving the obsessional thoughts. This can be done by two different methods:

**Break the Anxious Cycle Through Thought Stopping**

The more traditional technique of thought stopping involves shouting the word "STOP!" as soon as you become aware of the anxious reliving or catastrophizing. At first the word may be shouted to yourself. If this is not forceful enough, shouting it aloud will successfully destroy the anxious cycle. You may then attend to other less-stressful thoughts.

Another form of thought stopping is to switch abruptly to a pleasing, relaxing image or scene in your "mind's eye" as soon as you become aware of the anxious cycle. The scene should be the same one each time and should be a place, real or imagined, that you find aesthetically pleasing and relaxing. After dwelling on this place for thirty to sixty seconds, slowly reoccupy your mind with real-world demands. If no such relaxing image exists for you, counting backwards from five to one will also work. Simply picture the numbers in your mind as large and bright images. By the time one is reached, the cycle will be broken and you can begin thinking of other thoughts. If the cycle starts again, break it in the same manner. Continue doing so until the cycle remains broken, no matter how many thought-stopping maneuvers are necessary.

**Explore Your Fear History**

Just as the Type A personality is typified by anger, the anxious reactor is typified by fear. To learn more about responding in an anxious manner to stressful situations, write your history of fear. How did you react as a child when frightened? How did your parents react when they were fearful? Was there any one incident from which you seemed to learn the fear reaction?

Choose an anxious situation from your childhood and identify the basis of that anxiety. It may have been a realistic reaction for you as a child, but is it still a realistic response now that you are an adult and have more knowledge and experiential base?

**Take Action**

Fear constricts. The opposite of constriction is expansion or movement. When anxiety strikes, make an immediate plan of action so that you change the old, patterned response to fear. An example of this is the person lying in bed who hears a noise outside the window. An anxious reactor may become terrified and paralyzed in their bed. Making this situation nonstressful calls for getting up immediately, turning on the lights, and looking for the source of the noise. If the source is found to not be harmful, laughter and a pleasant goodnight to the source can end the incident. If the source is not found, an affirmation of "there is nothing here to be afraid of" can end the incident. If the source is found to be harmful, taking action to correct the situation is the only path to follow.

**Give Away Fear**

1. Write a lengthy, scary letter to yourself about your fear. Make it as fearful as possible. Catastrophize. Put it away for a day.

2. Come back the next day and make the letter even worse than it was. Follow the fearful feelings as deeply as you can. Again put it away for a day.

3. Come back the third day with a red pen or pencil and identify the parts of your letter that have no rational basis.

4. After identifying which of your fears may be rational and which parts are not, release all the unrealistic, unfounded fear that you have put into the letter by burning it in a ceremonious manner.

5. Take action regarding the fear that is real.

**Examine Beliefs Regarding Fear**

What are your beliefs about what others can do to you? About your own strength and ability to maintain your security? What is the basis of such beliefs? Change the beliefs to positive statements and begin to affirm that you are always safe and secure. Nothing can harm you.

**TECHNIQUES TO HELP ALLEVIATE THE STRESS OF CONTROL ISSUES**

### Keep a Journal

Whenever you experience the frustration of not being able to control all the things and people around you or you feel that parts of your life are out of control, write your experiences in a journal. Just expressing your feelings about the situation will help alleviate stress.

### Calm Yourself

When your body is experiencing a state of stress arousal, you are likely to interpret the symptoms as a sign that you are losing control. One way you might begin to exert more control over your environment is to first regain control over your body. This exercise is designed to help accomplish that.

### *A Breathing Exercise: Calming Down*

The basic mechanism for stress reduction in this exercise involves deep breathing. The procedure is as follows:

*Step 1.* Assume a comfortable position. Rest your left hand (palm down) on top of your abdomen. More specifically, place it over your navel. Now place your right hand so that it comfortably rests on your left. Your eyes should remain open (see Figure 10.4).

*Step 2.* Imagine a hollow bottle or pouch lying internally beneath the point at which your hands are resting. Begin to inhale. As you inhale, imagine that the air is entering through your nose and descending to fill that internal pouch. Your hands will rise as you fill the pouch with air. As you continue to inhale, imagine the pouch being filled to the top. Your rib cage and upper chest will continue the wavelike rise that was begun at your navel. The total length of your inhalation

FIGURE 10.4

Breathing Exercise

should be 3 seconds for the first week or so, then lengthening to four to five seconds as you progress in skill developments.

*Step 3.* Slowly begin to exhale—to empty the pouch. As you do, repeat to yourself the word *relax.* As you exhale, you will feel your abdomen and chest recede.

Repeat this exercise two times in succession. Then continue to breathe normally for five to ten successive breath cycles, but be sure to emphasize the expiration of each breath as the point of relaxation. Then you may repeat the entire process again—two deep breaths followed by five to ten normal breaths during which you concentrate on releasing any stored tension on the expiration. Should you begin to feel lightheaded or experience any discomfort, stop at that point.

Practice this exercise five to ten times a day. Make it a ritual in the morning, afternoon, and evening, as well as during stressful situations. After a week or two of practice omit step 1. This was for teaching the technique only. Because this form of relaxation is a skill, it is important to practice at least five to ten times a day. At first you may not notice any on-the-spot relaxation. However, after a week or two of regular practice, you will increase your ability to relax immediately. Remember: Consistent practice of these daily exercises will lead to the development of a calmer and more relaxed attitude—a sort of antistress attitude—and when you do have stressful moments, they will be far less severe.

**Check the Reality of the Situation**

With the Reality Check (adapted from Kriegel & Kriegel, 1984), when life seems out of control, the following steps can be taken:

1. Measure in numbers the difficulty of the situation. Get specific if you cannot assess the difficulties in numbers, give them quantitative ratings on a scale of 1 to 10. This causes the mind to think rationally instead of in terms of feelings.
2. Rate your ability to do the job. Have you ever done this job or one like it before? How did you do? What resources do you have that have helped in the past? What new resources have you developed since that time that would help in this situation?
3. Examine the consequences. What is the worst thing that could happen? What is the real likelihood (probability) of that actually happening? Rate this on a scale of 1 to 10.
4. Release the irrational; develop an action plan for the rational.

**Let Go of Judgments**

As in the discussion regarding beliefs about anger and expectations in the category on Type A personality that preceded this one, this technique focuses on acknowledging the right of each person to perform in his or her personal manner without judgment from others.

If you can internalize that you are the only one responsible for your life, you must extend that to others around you. One person cannot make others do that which they do not wish to do. Moreover, one individual does not have the right to use his or her power to manipulate the lives of others.

The simple technique here is to say to yourself whenever you begin to judge others: "They are doing the best they can for themselves at this time."

**Reinterpret Stressors through Cognitive Restructuring**

This refers to changing the meaning of or your interpretation of the environmental stressors around you. Therapists such as Albert Ellis and Aaron Beck argue strongly that the environment is not what causes most people stress, but rather it is their interpretations that actually cause the stress response to become triggered. According to Beck (1976):

| ENVIRONMENTAL STIMULUS | → | COGNITIVE MEANING (INTERPRETATION) | → | EMOTIONS AND STRESS |
|---|---|---|---|---|

The source, then, of dysfunctional emotions and excessive stress is in reality-irrational or maladaptive thoughts (ideation). Cognitive restructuring entails first identifying and then correcting these maladaptive thoughts.

Some of the most common maladaptive, incorrect, or irrational interpretations of environmental events are listed here (based on the work of Ellis and Beck), along with their cognitive solutions/reinterpretations:

*Problem:* The tendency to jump to a specific conclusion without adequate confirmation (overgeneralization).

*Solution:* Search for more evidence that the conclusion is correct. If so, and a problem exists, implement social engineering or problem-solving techniques.

*Problem:* The tendency to blame oneself for problems when there is little or no evidence for such a conclusion.

*Solution:* Search for other possible explanations to explain the problem.

*Problem:* The tendency to see things as "all or none," "good or bad"; that is, the tendency to see only extremes.

*Solution:* Begin to search for the "gray" areas, the in-between states. See that few things are *all* good, or *all* bad.

*Problem:* The tendency to catastrophize about unpleasant events and to "make mountains out of mole hills."

*Solution:* Assess the realistic chances of the catastrophe actually occurring. If chances are high, then begin social engineering or problem-solving strategies. If chances are low, ask yourself: "Couldn't I be using this energy in a better way other than wasting it in worry?"

*Problem:* The tendency to be limited in problem-solving alternatives; that is, an inability to see potential solutions.

*Solution:* Practice exercises in creative, nontraditional problem solving.

These are but a few of the major maladaptive cognitive patterns that often lead to excessive stress. Aaron Beck's book *Cognitive Therapy of Depression* (1979), is an excellent technical guide to such problems, while Albert Ellis and Robert Harper's *A New Guide To Rational Living* (1967) is one of the best nontechnical guides to cognitive restructuring available.

In sum, by controlling your body's response to stressors

through breathing exercises and by controlling your attitudes through exercises such as cognitive restructuring, you will gain far more control over stress, over health, *over life*—and you will find that at the same time you will become far less vulnerable to a dysfunctional need for control.

**Examine Beliefs Regarding the Need to Control Others**

Gawain (1986) points out that the less we trust ourselves, the more we try to control others. As in the other discussions regarding beliefs in this chapter, people with a need to control the people and events around them must look at the irrational or negative belief system that is driving them. Some possibilities may be:

- Everything will fall apart if I do not keep control.
- The only way people will need me is if I am in control.
- No one who is not as bright or talented as I am has the right to be in control.
- If I don't control others, they will try to control me.
- Power is control.

Turn negative or irrational beliefs into positive ones, continue to affirm these positive beliefs by using them as the basis for non-controlling behavior.

## REFERENCES

ARRIEN, A. (1987, August). Cross-cultural healing practices. Seminar presented at the Joy Lake Conference, Reno, NV.

BECK, A. (1976). *Cognitive therapy and the emotional disorders.* New York: International Universities Press.

——— (1979). *Cognitive therapy of depression.* New York: Guilford Press.

ELLIS, A., AND R. HARPER (1967). *A new guide to rational living.* Beverly Hills, CA: Wilshire Book Co.

GAWAIN, S. (1986). *Living in the light.* Mill Valley, CA: Whatever Publishing.

GIRDANO, D., AND D. DUSEK (1988). *Changing health behavior.* Scottsdale, AZ: Gorsuch & Scarisbrick.

KEYES, K., JR. (1974). *Handbook to higher consciousness.* Berkeley, CA: Living Love Center.

KRIEGEL., R., AND M. KRIEGEL (1984). *The C zone: Peak performance under pressure.* New York: Doubleday.

NOVACO, R. W. (1975). *Anger control: The development and evaluation of an experimental treatment.* Lexington, MA: Lexington Books.

———. (1978). Anger and coping with stress: Cognitive behavioral interventions. In J. Foreyt and D. Rathzen (eds.), *Cognitive behavior therapy.* New York: Plenum.

REUBEN, C. (1987). Eating to beat jet lag. *East/West Journal,* May, 58.

VARGIU, J. (1977). Subpersonalities. *Synthesis, 1,* 51–90.

# CHAPTER ELEVEN

# Breathing and Relaxation

**BREATHING CORRECTLY**

Wouldn't you know it! The first thing in life we learned to do, and we learned it wrong. We are referring here to the act of breathing. But, you say, breathing is a natural, automatic body function. How can breathing be right or wrong? You should realize by now that any body process can be altered and, if the practice is prolonged, conditioned. For reasons too numerous and involved to discuss here, most of us have developed and conditioned inefficient and improper breathing techniques. And what could be more important than bringing in fresh air and revitalizing the body tissues? Ancient yoga philosophy states that mind is the master of the senses and breath is the master of the mind, and that breathing is the elixir of life.

Actually, the exchange of air is only one aspect of breathing that is important to the relaxation process. Breathing is an involuntary, automatic function that reflects our general state of stress arousal. But breathing is also voluntary and can be manipulated. If we so desire, we can breathe fast or slow; our inhalations can be deep or shallow; our expirations can be partial or complete; and in some cases, we even "choose" difficult or pathological breathing patterns. By learning to breathe correctly, air is taken in more efficiently, the pulmonary system is strengthened and conditioned, the function of the cardiovascular system is enhanced, greater oxygenation is promoted, the nerves are calmed, and restfulness occurs. The breathing centers in the brain have a facilitating relationship with the arousal centers; therefore, constant, steady, restful breathing promotes relaxation. It is almost impossible to be tense and have slow, relaxed, deep breaths, so control breathing and you control tension. Condition breathing and you condition your system to be more tranquil. The power of deep, steady breathing is instinctual. When you want to control your energy—when lifting a heavy object, for example—you instinctively hold your breath. When you want to center yourself—when pulling the string of a bow or the trigger of a gun, for instance— you instinctively breathe deep and hold. It is your most natural way of centering yourself or concentrating.

Practicing breathing techniques not only facilitates relaxation, it plays a vital role in the prevention of respiratory ailments. Individuals with respiratory disorders like asthma and emphysema can benefit not only from increased oxygenation, but also from learning correct, efficient, and less-stressful breathing patterns. But even for those of us without respiratory-system pathology, breathing is often labored and inefficient. At rest we normally use only one third of our lung capacity. Through breathing exercises, you will be able to vitalize these functions, regulate breathing patterns, build up respiratory reserve, and increase oxygenation capacity.

In correct breathing the floating ribs (lower five pairs) are moved by the intercostal muscles between the ribs and the diaphragm as it lowers toward the abdomen. This movement allows for expansion of the lower lobes of the lungs, creating a vacuum, and the air rushes in. If you keep the abdominal muscles tight during the breathing movement, your diaphragm cannot descend and the lower lobes cannot fill, so a deep breath is possible only by a hyperexpansion of the top lobes, a method that expends much more energy. Many of us have developed the habit of high breathing because it is thought to represent a more "masculine" posture— stomach in, chest out. This is not to say that one should not have strong, taut stomach muscles; on the contrary, contraction-relaxation movements will further strengthen stomach muscles without a chronic shortening developing. It is also important not to neglect exhalation. You must exhale deeply to get the stale, used air out or there is less room for fresh air to enter. Generally, exhalation lasts longer than inhalation. Correct breathing, once mastered, becomes a chronic exercise that expands and contracts the lung tissue, building strength and endurance.

Learning more efficient breathing patterns can be facilitated by the ability to perform and differentiate between the following exercises:

**Upper Costal Breathing**

Use your hands to sense the action of the respiratory movements. Place your hands on the upper third of the chest wall, preferably crossing the hands with the fingertips resting comfortably over the collarbone. You can easily sense the expansion of the upper lobes of the lungs with your fingertips in the open space between the collarbone and the trapezius muscle, which runs behind that bone. Keeping your abdominal wall relaxed, inhale through your nose, expanding the upper ends of your lungs as fully as possible. Hold your breath for three seconds, then let go, exhaling slowly, letting the air gently flow from the mouth. Repeat the exercise five times, resting for five normal breaths between each one. The pause in between is important, as you want to avoid hyperventilation, and allow yourself time to center your thoughts on the activity and reflect on what was sensed or felt.

**Middle Costal Breathing**

Again, let your fingers be your sensors. Place your fingers on the middle third of the chest wall below the nipples (sixth rib). Keeping your abdominal and upper costal area relaxed, inhale through your nose, expanding the mid-chest region as fully as possible. Hold for three seconds and gently exhale through the mouth. Repeat this five times and then relax quietly. Remember to pause between each repetition.

**Diaphragmatic Breathing**

Breathing with the diaphragm is performed by taking a deep inspiration while the belly is pushed down and out by the movement of the diaphragm, thus allowing the lower lobes of the lungs to inflate fully. Your hands are placed on the lower ribs, where they should easily sense the breathing motion. With the upper chest relaxed, inhale deeply. The abdominal wall is pushed up and out. Hold for three seconds and exhale, feeling the abdominal wall descend toward the spine. Repeat this exercise five times. Diaphragmatic breathing stretches the lower lobes of the lungs, thus allowing more fresh air to enter. It also acts to correct shallow breathing habits, allowing increasing depth of inspiration.

**Very Deep Breathing**

Start by exhaling every bit of air from your lungs. Force the air out and feel the space between your belly and spine shrink. When all the air is out, inhale slowly, using the diaphragmatic technique. Picture your lungs as a glass being filled with water—bottom, middle, then top. Hold your breath three seconds and then exhale gently through your nose or mouth. It sounds as though we are asking for an exaggerated, strenuous action, but we are not. Breathe from your diaphragm, naturally and effortlessly. Concentrate on the air traveling through the air passageways. With each expiration feel a sense of increased relaxation. Feel a sense of letting go. Begin to feel the looseness in your body, an uncoiling feeling as you settle down and pull your mind and body together. Repeat this exercise five times, resting between each repetition.

Now that you know how to breathe correctly, go on to the following exercises on breathing. You may want to periodically repeat these learning-to-breathe exercises until you feel that you have them fully mastered. Once you do, just start with these exercises on breathing.

**BREATHING EXERCISES**

**Breathing Down**

During the course of an average day, many of us find ourselves in anxiety-producing situations. Our heart rates increase, our stomachs may become upset, and our thoughts may race uncontrollably. In such moments we tend to make poor decisions or just overreact. It is during such episodes as these that we require fast-acting relief from our stressful reactions, so we can calmly attempt to solve the crisis or problem at hand. The exercise given below has been found effective for quickly calming one down in stressful situations.

The basic mechanism for stress reduction in this exercise involves deep breathing. The procedure is as follows:

*Step 1.* Assume a comfortable position. Rest your left hand (palm down) on top of your abdomen. More specifically, place your left hand over your navel. Now place your right hand so that it comfortably rests on your left. Your eyes should remain open (see Figure 11.1).

*Step 2.* Imagine a hollow bottle, or pouch, lying internally beneath the point at which your hands are resting. Begin to inhale. As you inhale, imagine that the air is entering through your nose and descending to fill that internal pouch. Your hands will rise as you fill the pouch with air. As you continue to inhale, imagine the pouch being filled to the top. Your rib cage and upper chest will continue the wavelike rise that was begun at your navel. The total length of your inhalation should be three seconds for the first week or so, then lengthening to four or five seconds as you progress in skill development. Remember to concentrate on "seeing" the air move as you inhale and exhale.

*Step 3.* Hold your breath. Keep the air inside the pouch. Repeat to yourself the phrase: "My body is calm."

*Step 4.* Slowly begin to exhale—to empty the pouch. As you do, repeat to yourself the phrase: "My body is quiet." As you exhale you will feel your raised abdomen and chest recede.

Repeat this exercise four or five times in succession. Should you begin to feel lightheaded, stop at that point. If lightheadedness remains a problem, consider shortening the length of the inhalation and/or decreasing the total number of repetitions of the four-step exercise.

Practice this exercise ten to fifteen times a day. Make it a ritual in the morning, afternoon, and evening, as well as during stressful

FIGURE 11.1

situations. After a week or two of practice, omit step 1. This was for teaching the technique only. Because this form of relaxation is a skill, it is important to practice at least ten to fifteen times a day. At first you may not notice any immediate relaxation. However, after a week or two of regular practice you *will* increase your ability to relax on the spot. Remember—you must practice *regularly* if you are to master this skill. Regular, consistent practice of these daily exercises will lead to the development of a calmer and more relaxed attitude—a sort of antistress attitude—and when you do have stressful moments, they will be far less severe.

## Controlled Tempo Breathing

This exercise develops powers of concentration, facilitates centering, and helps breath control. You may sit or lie down. Keep your eyes closed. The breathing will be diaphragmatic—quiet, natural, and effortless. Concentrate on your breathing. Become part of it. With one hand, find your pulse in the wrist of the other arm. Count your pulse for one minute. While still counting your pulse, bring part of your attention back to your breathing. Count the number of pulses to make a normal expiration. Do this several times until you have a rhythm. The average will be somewhere between five and ten. As an example, say the number is five. Still monitoring your pulse, breathe in with five beats of your pulse, hold for five, exhale for five, and remain quiet for five. Continue this for three minutes; then sit quietly and prepare for the Breath Counting Exercises. At first you will tend to lose count, but as your powers of concentration increase, you will make it all the way. You can then increase the time spent doing this exercise.

**Breath Counting**    This is another exercise to promote relaxation and increase powers of concentration. You may do this sitting or lying down. As in the Controlled Tempo Breathing exercises, you will use quiet, normal diaphragmatic breathing. Concentrate on your breathing. As you breathe in, think "in." Let the air out and think "out." Think "...in...out...in...out." Now each time you breathe out count the breaths. Count ten consecutive breaths without missing a count. If you happen to miss one, start over. When you get to ten, start at one again. Do this ten times, and then sit quietly. Concentrate, anticipate the breath, block all other thoughts from your mind.

# CHAPTER TWELVE

# Muscle Relaxation

Take a moment and shift your attention from this book to your body. First note your overall position. Are you sitting comfortably? Is your body supported by the chair, or are your back muscles being strained? Are your arms supported, or are you holding the book in the air? Are your fists clenched? Think back to times when you were writing something. Did you ever notice that you were holding the pencil or pen so tightly that it was leaving an indentation in your fingers? Think of another activity, such as driving a car. Have you ever found yourself with a death grip on the steering wheel, producing tension up your arms to your shoulders, neck, back, and even to your head and facial muscles?

These are examples of tension exhibited through the muscles. More specifically, it is excess and needless muscle tension, as it is far more than what is needed to accomplish the task. This excess muscle tension is both a *response* to stress and a *cause* of stress. The often mentioned fight-or-flight syndrome is muscular expression, as are speech, facial expression, and eye movements.

Most movements are readily observable; that is, you can see your fingers move a pencil as you write, but it takes a second look to notice whether there is excess pressure. Excess exertion has nothing to do with the writing movement. It is an outward expression of the anxiety or resentment over what you are writing and/ or it represents the general state of tension constantly with you. It is no mystery that people experienced at observing stress can quickly pick out stressed people by analyzing certain characteristics of their penmanship.

Much of the harmful, stress-producing muscle tension is extremely subtle and almost impossible to detect. If you are thinking defensive thoughts, you start to assume a defensive posture. It is practically impossible to think of an action and not have your muscles prepare for that action. To illustrate this phenomenon, take a pendant on a chain, or tie a key to a string, and hold it out in front of you. Close your eyes and, without moving your hand, imagine the object swinging toward and away from you. After a minute, open your eyes, and chances are it will be moving. Move it side to side, or imagine it circling. Even though your hand did not actually move, the thought was translated to your fingers and tension developed in a rhythmical pattern with enough force to cause the object to move. This shows that we have the ability to anticipate, and this ability is necessary for preparation. Unfortunately, we often spend so much time in unproductive imagined preparation that our bodies adapt by increasing general muscle tension. At several points in this book we mentioned Selye's concept of the disease of adaptation. Muscle tension represents a good example. The individual who is defensive and is constantly imagining actions creates a situation in which the body learns to adapt by maintaining a chronic state of muscle tension.

If such a condition is permitted to exist for an extended period, a wide variety of physical disorders may be produced or exaggerated.

The connection between inordinate muscle tension and disease was made hundreds of years ago, but it was not until the end of the last century that systematic relaxation programs were formulated. The names Schultz, Sweigard, Maja Schade, and Jacobsen became synonymous with relaxation training, as their pioneering work formed the basis of most of the relaxation programs in existence today. There are literally hundreds of techniques now, but all have the same basic objective of teaching the individual to relax the muscles at will by first developing a cognitive awareness of what it feels like to be tense and then what it feels like to be relaxed. If one is able to distinguish between tension and relaxation, control over tension follows almost effortlessly (Jacobsen, 1977).

**NEURO-
MUSCULAR
EXERCISES**

Neuromuscular relaxation trains not only the muscles, but also the nervous system components that control muscle activity. The benefits are, of course, the reduction of tension in the muscles, and as the muscles make up such a large portion of the body's mass, this represents a significant reduction in total body tension. In addition, this training will help you develop a sense of tension awareness. Using the muscles as a biofeedback device, you can develop an inherent autosensory awareness to the point that a little internal alarm goes off when tension starts to rise.

Another benefit is mind control, often mentioned throughout this book. To accomplish any of these techniques one must learn to center on the task or problem and control the mind's tendency to wander aimlessly in daydreams. Neuromuscular relaxation requires concentration, specifically *passive* concentration. As you perfect your ability, you can practice relaxation anywhere, even in short spurts; for example, while stopped for a red light, while waiting for an appointment, or while watching television. Just think of how much time you spend each day just sitting around waiting for things to happen; you might view this "wasted time" as an opportunity to practice relaxation. Two things will happen: first, you will easily get in thirty to sixty minutes of practice a day, and second, you will lose the concept of wasted time—a very important philosophical development necessary for enlightenment (Shapiro & Lehrer, 1980).

**The Learning Phase**

What follows is a detailed set of instructions on how to practice muscular relaxation. The learning phase, of course, necessitates more structured time involvement, more concentration, and more commitment than will be necessary once you master the technique. Once you have perfected it, you will be able to choose the particular exercise sequence that is most beneficial to you and that meets your immediate needs. It is very important, however, that in the learning phase you follow the instructions to the letter.

The exercises presented in this chapter have been used for ten years in our clinical practice and have been proven to be quite effective and easily learned. While they are theoretically based on the concepts of the many relaxation techniques that have preceded them, significant differences exist. We follow a natural patterning to provide a constellation of exercises that we have found more effective and more easily learned than other current relaxation techniques. First you practice the gross muscle actions that you initially developed during the prenatal as well as the neonatal stage. These movements are innate to human locomotion and can be easily identified and controlled. Since these movements provide an exellent basis for cortical learning, you can gain awareness and conscious control over these motor actions. Then you can progress to higher levels of skilled muscle activity. Another important consideration taken into account when these exercises were developed was that they include group muscle action rather than single muscle activity. The brain knows nothing about muscles, only about movements involving many muscles working together. Trying to relax one muscle is difficult and retards learning. Finally, the exercises start from distal muscle groups (feet and legs) and proceed to proximal groups of muscles closer to the head and trunk (Berstein & Given, 1984).

**Preparation**

In order for the learning experience to be as effective as possible, you should do whatever you can to create an environment that enhances concentration. A few minutes spent preparing the environment and the body is a good investment.

First, concentrate on the environment. Do whatever you can to reduce external noise. Find a room away from traffic, with no telephone and with indirect or dim lighting. You may want to use earplugs or earphones, or play soft instrumental music or environmental sounds. As you become more proficient at these exercises, you will not have to take such elaborate precautions, but anything that might enhance initial learning will reduce learning time.

Next, work on preparing your body. A reclined or semireclined position with proper support under the legs is best (see Figure 12.1). Lie down; place your arms at your sides, elbows flexed at about sixty degrees so that the hands and wrists rest on the abdomen. Your hips will naturally flex to about twenty-five degrees, so don't attempt to hold your legs together. Your legs will naturally rotate outward; don't force them straight. In other words, allow the body to assume a position that does not require muscle action to maintain it. If you wish, you may support your neck with a small, soft pillow. If it is difficult for you to maintain a lying position without pain in the lower back due to unusual pull on the lumbar spine, place a pillow under your knees. This helps flatten the back against its support and relieves strain on the lower back. Also, if you have a history of low-back pain, lumbar-disc disease, or any other musculoskeletal disorder or postural condition including round shoulders, overdeveloped muscle mass, or cervical lordosis, you should take individual precautions and adopt the most restful and comfortable position to promote maximum concentration and learning. Any tight clothing, jewelry, belts, and the like should be loosened or removed. In preparing for relaxation, if you experience tingling or numbness in a body area, change your posture to relieve

FIGURE 12.1

Preparatory Position for Relaxation Exercises

the pressure on that area. Above all, if pain or cramps develop during relaxation, rest the muscle until they diminish, then proceed with less intensity.

## Lower Extremities

### *The Ankle*

The first exercise involves the ankle joints (Figure 12.2). No other joints should be involved here. You should be lying in the preparatory position shown in Figure 12.1 and should have proceeded through the breathing exercises. Now pull your feet toward the front of your legs (the movement involved in taking your foot off the gas pedal). The contraction should be felt only in the muscles on the front and outside of the lower leg, not in the calf muscles, which will feel stretched. Your toes should be pulled forward toward your legs as hard as possible, until you feel uncomfortable (short of pain—if pain develops, rest for a moment and proceed less vigorously). Center your thoughts in the muscles experiencing the tension. Try to visualize the tension. Form an image in your mind about this tightness. Hold for a few seconds and let go. Repeat the exercise, this time being sure to synchronize your breathing. Breathe in, pulling the feet up, hold your breath, hold the contraction—then let the air out, relaxing the muscles. Lie quietly for one minute and then repeat.

After you have done this several times and feel comfortable with the activity and the breathing pattern, turn your awareness more toward the relaxation than to the contraction. As you breathe out and relax, allow the muscles to go limp. As you pass over the peak of the contraction, begin to unwind. Try to form a visual image of this relaxed state and hold it in your mind. Repeat this exercise until you have gained confidence in your ability to relax those muscles.

Next, move on to another group of muscles called the plantar-flexor group or calf muscles. They are the exact opposite of the first group. Thus, tightness will be felt in the calf area and the stretching sensation will be felt in the muscle group in the front of the lower leg. Start by taking a deep breath, then push your toes down (as

FIGURE 12.2

Ankle Exercises

in pushing down on the gas pedal) and away from the body as far as possible. Keep the heels down. When you reach the peak of your breath, hold the breath for five seconds, keeping your toes pointed. Now, slowly exhale while allowing the feet to come back to a resting position.

Repeat this exercise three to five times, attempting to synchronize your breathing with the contraction and relaxation phases. As you exhale and let go of the contraction, form a visual image of the tension in the calf muscle flowing out with the air from your lungs. Imagine an unwinding or letting go. Concentrate on the feelings of tension, the feelings of relaxation, and the difference between the two states.

### The Hips and Knees

The best exercise in this group is the extension of the knees and hips, the knees being pushed down into the bed while the legs are kept straight (Figure 12.3). For this exercise, remove the pillow from under your knees if you were using one. The tightness will be felt in front of the thighs and in the buttocks area. You will not be aware of any appreciable stretching force because these muscles are long and serve more than one joint. As always, begin with a deep breath, pushing your hips and knees down into the mat. Hold at the peak of your breath, then exhale and allow the muscles to rest. Again, form an image of the tension; feel the letting go.

Table 12.1 summarizes these lower-extremity exercises. Put

**FIGURE 12.3**

Hip and Knee Exercise

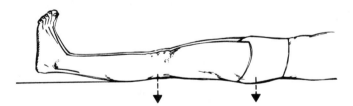

**TABLE 12.1  Summary of Lower-Extremity Exercises**

| | |
|---|---|
| Dorsiflexion of Ankle Joints | Bend up the feet . . . Pull hard . . . Harder! And let go . . . |
| Plantar Flexion of Ankle Joints | Push the feet down as far as you can . . . Push harder! And slacken off the muscles completely . . . |
| Extension of Knee and Hip | Straighten the knees as much as possible . . . Now press the legs down into the mattress . . . Hard . . . Harder! Now relax . . . |

these together in three successive movements. Allow about thirty seconds between each exercise.

**The Trunk**

The first of these two exercises utilizes the extensor muscles of the lower back. This exercise is particularly good for you if you have lower-back discomfort not related to deformity or injury. As a large proportion of our population suffers from tension-related low-back pain, remember the earlier warning: If this or any of these exercises produces pain or spasms, stop the exercise and rest. Then continue with only a moderate amount of contraction, gradually increasing the strength of contraction over several weeks. If pain persists, discontinue this type of relaxation training. In this exercise, you hollow or arch your back, as shown in Figure 12.4. Move your chest slightly toward your chin. The pelvis is fixed on the mat. You will feel the tension in the lower-back area. Synchronize the exercise with your breathing, concentrating on the feelings of tension and relaxation. Repeat five times.

The second exercise is pulling in the abdominal muscles. Keep the legs, pelvis, and shoulders in contact with the mat. Breathe in, contract the stomach muscles, and flatten the lower back against the mat. Hold for five seconds, exhale, and relax.

The trunk exercises are summarized in Table 12.2. Try them both, one after the other with three-second rest intervals between them. At this point, go back and repeat one time each of the exercises you have learned thus far. Concentrate on the feelings of tension and relaxation. The visual imagery is just as important as is the performance of the muscular exercise.

FIGURE 12.4

Trunk Extension

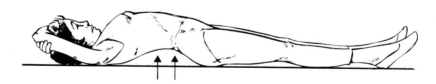

**TABLE 12.2  Summary of Trunk Exercises**

| Extensor Muscles of the Spine | Push the chest forward until you have hollowed the back strongly . . . Lift a little more! And let go . . . |
|---|---|
| Abdominal Muscles | Pull in the abdominal muscles until they are quite flat . . . Pull a bit more . . . And rest . . . |

**The Upper Extremities**

This group of exercises is for the muscles in the upper limbs—around the shoulder, elbow, wrist, and fingers. Remember to start each exercise with deep breathing and follow all the progressive steps (as discussed on page 237).

The first exercise in this group is the extension of the wrist and fingers (Figure 12.5). Exercise both your left and right extremities at the same time. Pull your hands and fingers simultaneously back toward your forearms, keeping your fingers straight. You should feel the tension on the backs of your hands and the backs of your forearms below the elbows. A little pain might be felt near the wrist—this is ligament stretch, don't strain. Hold the tension for five seconds; then relax. Make sure you give yourself a proper rest period so you can focus on the relaxation. Repeat this exercise five times.

The next exercise (Figure 12.6) reverses the previous one. Turn your wrists in (stretching the back of your hand) and clench your

FIGURE 12.5

Wrist and Finger
Extension

FIGURE 12.6

Wrist and Finger
Contraction

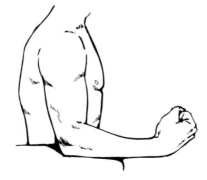

fists very tightly. Hold the tension five seconds; then relax. Repeat five times.

Next, straighten your arms against your sides, keeping your fingers straight (Figure 12.7). Press both arms tightly against your sides. Hold the tension for five seconds; then relax. Repeat this exercise five times.

Finally, do this exercise for your shoulders. Shrug your shoulders up as high as you can—try to touch your shoulders to your ear lobes (Figure 12.8). Hold the tension five seconds; then relax. Repeat five times. This exercise is excellent for stiff necks and shoulders caused by excessive deskwork.

For a summary of upper-extremity exercises see Table 12.3.

**FIGURE 12.7**

Arms Straight against Sides

**FIGURE 12.8**

Shoulder Shrug

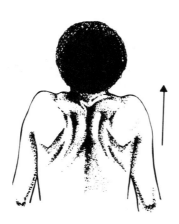

**TABLE 12.3   Summary of Upper-Extremity Exercises**

| | |
|---|---|
| Finger and Wrist Extension | Straighten the fingers and pull back the wrists . . . Pull hard. |
| Flexion of the Fingers and Wrists | Clench your fists and curl your wrists inward. |
| Adduction of Shoulder Joints | Straighten the arms against your sides . . . Press tightly. |
| Shoulder Shrug | Shrug your shoulders high . . . Higher . . . Touch your ears. |

## Head, Neck, and Face

The primary exercise in this group is rotation of the head. The muscles in this region become overworked because we tend to hold a steady partial tension for hours at a time, especially while doing deskwork or driving. If you have chronic neck problems, use extreme care. To do this exercise (shown in Figure 12.9), first close

FIGURE 12.9

Head Rotation

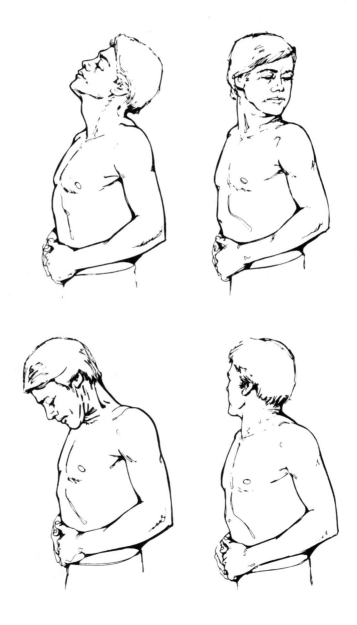

your eyes. Touch your chin to your breastbone. Return, rest for a breath, and move the head backward toward the spine. Return, rest, and then rotate the head so as to look over the right shoulder. Return, rest for a breath, and then look over the left shoulder. Consider these four moves as one exercise and complete them in succession, but do not hurry. Synchronize each movement with your breathing; contract, relax for a few breaths, and continue with the next movement.

Another group of overworked muscles is the facial muscles, especially those involved in talking and chewing. To exercise these, clench your teeth together and draw your facial muscles up tightly (Figure 12.10). Always remember the correct emphasis on breathing. Repeat five times and then relax.

Table 12.4 contains a summary of head, neck, and facial exercises.

## CONCLUSION

The learning phase will take time and concentrated effort, but as learning progresses, it will take less time to complete the exercises. In the beginning, you may tend to fall asleep during practice or

**FIGURE 12.10**

Facial Exercise

**TABLE 12.4  Summary of Head, Neck, and Face Exercises**

| | |
|---|---|
| Rotation | Shut the eyes . . . Now roll the head slowly forward, then slowly back . . . Roll the head to the right, then slowly to the left . . . It's heavy . . . and it's rolling easily—front to back, side to side . . . Now stop, with the face turned forward, and rest . . . |
| Facial Exercise | Clench the teeth together. Now draw up the facial muscles very tightly . . . Tighter! And relax . . . |

feel lethargic afterward. This reaction is due to your mind set if the only time you relax is when you are too tired to do anything else. However, these are precision exercises requiring concentration (albeit passive), and as you become more proficient you will feel rested, relaxed but alert, and full of vigor, strength, and enthusiasm for your daily activities. These exercises are more than relaxation promoting, they are a learning process that provides awareness of states of mind and body in relation to everyday life. Slowly you will begin to notice your posture, how your hand grips objects, your neck position, and facial expression. Being aware of such neuromuscular states is the first step in the change process, and finally you will be well on your way to not only combating tension, but preventing it.

## REFERENCES

BERSTEIN, D. A., AND B. GIVEN (1984). Progressive relaxation: Abbreviated methods. In R. Woolfolk and P. Lehrer (eds.), *Principles and practice of stress management* (pp. 43–68). New York: Guilford Press.

JACOBSEN, E. (1977). The origins and development of progressive relaxation. *Journal of Behavioral Therapy and Experimental Psychiatry, 8.*

SHAPIRO, S., AND P. M. LEHRER (1980). Psychophysiological effects of autogenic training and progressive relaxation. *Biofeedback and Self-Regulation, 5,* 249–55.

# CHAPTER THIRTEEN

# Biofeedback

When you become frightened, anxious, angry, or generally stressed, numerous changes occur in your body—most of them negative. If the stress is moderate to severe, you will have no trouble in recognizing the outward signs. For example, the heart rate speeds up and often you can feel the palpitations in your chest. The palms of the hands become moist with increased sweating, skin may flush or become excessively pale, the pupils of the eyes may change size, your mouth may become very dry, or in some instances salivation may become excessive, muscles may tense to the point of pain or feel so limp that your legs threaten to give way, the stomach "turns over" and you may feel nauseated, breathing rate may increase, and you may have a difficult time swallowing.

Often the stressor is overt—you know what it is or you know you are in a tough situation. More often though, what produces stress is more subtle, not readily apparent. In these situations it is the bodily reactions mentioned above that signal a state of stress and are the triggers for initiation of coping behavior. If you have ever felt any of these symptoms, you have experienced biofeedback; that is, feeding back of biological signals to the source of that activity.

Try a little experiment. Find your pulse and record a resting pulse rate. Take it for several minutes to be sure you have a good sample. Jot down the rate in beats per minute. Now, as you sit quietly, try to imagine a scene or story you find particularly exciting. Really get into it until you can vividly see yourself involved in the situation. After a couple of minutes, stop, take your pulse, and record the beats per minute. Chances are that if you really got yourself into the imagined situation, and if the situation was one you found stressful, you found the second heart rate to be higher than the first.

Try another one! Stand in front of a mirror. Closely observe the pupils of your eyes. Occasionally they will change in size. When they do, try to recall what you were thinking of at that time. Your emotions and thoughts will influence the size of your pupils—a biological signal of the stress response. If you happened to hear a noise or if someone startled you while you were standing in front of the mirror, you probably noticed an increased dilation. To particularly note the effect, have someone clap suddenly and unexpectedly as you look at your pupils in the mirror.

Both the heart-rate and pupil-size exercises are examples of getting feedback from the body. If you could monitor your heart rate continuously, and if the stimulus were steady, just having the information would provide you with the primary ingredient in the biofeedback system—self-knowledge. The fact is that you would get tired of the process, your attention would wax and wane, and you would miss some information. However, through the miracle of technology, an electrical instrument can monitor the heart rate for you. In addition, this handy device can modify the signal to make it more useful. Most important, it can transform the heart-beat signals into light or sound, so that our senses can interpret it easily. Diagramed in Figure 13.1 is an example of a modern bio-feedback system. Such an instrument senses, processes, and gives or feeds back to the individual immediate and continuous electrical signals that represent biological activity, activity the individual would not usually be aware of. Having such information better enables a person to adjust his or her action and augments the learning process.

FIGURE 13.1

Typical Biofeed-back System

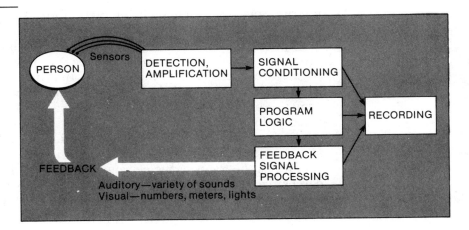

Monitoring biological activity with sophisticated electrical instruments might be thought of by some as a medical device. However, although biofeedback is used in the practice of medicine, it is best described as an *educational tool* that simply provides information about performance—much the same as an examination is used to test a student's progress in the classroom or a bathroom scale is used to give information about body weight.

The body is constantly telling us about its activities. We have learned to key into some feelings, sounds, and outward signs of mind–body function. Stomach contractions are interpreted as hunger, diarrhea and constipation are indicators of gastrointestinal problems, redness and swelling are indicators of possible infection. We have also learned to use physiological parameters like heart rate and blood pressure to assess the body's functioning. When an increase in blood pressure is detected, the individual has some information about the cardiovascular system, and during treatment subsequent blood pressure readings are a constant measure of the success of treatment.

Biofeedback is to some extent a refinement of that feedback system. Instead of diarrhea, which is a rather gross measure of intestinal action, one could measure the minute muscle contraction of various intestinal segments. Thermal measurement of skin can indicate blood flow to a particular region of the body. Measuring contraction of skeletal muscles can detect muscle action before it reaches the stage of producing pain and discomfort.

**INTERACTION WITH THE INTERIOR SELF**

Biofeedback is more than a means of self-monitoring physiological states. It can also be used to promote self-exploration, self-awareness, and self-control. Barbara Brown in *New Mind, New Body* appropriately described biofeedback as an "interaction with the interior self." Through such interaction one learns, by actually feeling (visceral learning), that what he or she is thinking influences body processes, and that body processes or states influence thought processes. Feelings and emotions can be seen more as a part of the cognitive experience. The knowledge of the "inner space" becomes more a part of the total thought and action process. Behavior becomes more internally directed and less habitually conditioned to external forces.

Biofeedback training is itself a conditioning, or perhaps better stated, a reconditioning process. Tranquility neurophysiologically conditions the tonus of the nervous system to be less reactive and desensitizes reactive behavior, and one begins to change behavior by "becoming" a more tranquil person. Research has reported decreases in trait anxiety and Type A behavior, and as a person feels and behaves, he or she eventually becomes (Girdano & Dusek, 1977). The reconditioning or relearning process disciplines the mind to reduce mundane chatter. One experiences (perhaps for the first time) thought clear of imagination and anticipation, allowing greater concentration and often revealing insights and creativity previously subdued by self-doubt. What results is often an increased sense of self: self-concept, self-esteem, and self-realization. Equally important is enhanced discipline (self-discipline) and increased control (self-control).

Thus, what started out as an exercise in relaxation quickly turns into the development of self-awareness and self-control. These qualities are an integral part of a holistic health program as they are central not only to stress-reduction programs, but also to weight-control programs, programs for the aged, fitness programs, cardiovascular rehabilitation, and general health counseling, to mention a few applications.

## HOW BIOFEEDBACK WORKS

The complex electronic instruments and the almost science fiction—like accounts of results obtained using biofeedback give it an aura of mystery and magic. But there is no magic, and the mystery surrounding it pertains only to some as yet unexplained phenomenon regarding the limits of human regulatory capacities. In order to understand the mechanisms of action, we can divide the process into three phases:

1. *Physical or physiological phase:* the release of energy (physical, chemical, thermal, electrical—usually all of these), which can be measured with the appropriate device.
2. *Psychophysiological phase:* mind and body controlling the energy-releasing process—coordination of the voluntary and involuntary nervous systems and the endocrine systems.
3. *Psychological or learning phase:* voluntary control or conditioning process in which biofeedback becomes an essential link.

The body's response to stress is a physical release of energy that produces action and constitutes the function of the organ system. The interaction between cells is one of constant exchange of chemicals (hormones, electrolytes, metabolites, and so on) through the membrane of the cell. These chemicals often carry an electrical charge and sometimes produce physical movement of the cell structure (as in muscles) or movement of cellular secretions (such as in the hormonal, gastrointestinal, and cardiovascular systems). Finally, such movement releases excess energy in the form of heat. Any one of these processes can be measured with the appropriate device, and this constitutes the first phase. The muscles offer a good example. Stimulation of the muscles results in movement of cellular electrolytes that carry an electrical charge. This shift results in a change in the equilibrium of the structural components of the muscle, attracting them toward one another, causing the cells to shorten and the muscle to move. A byproduct of that movement, friction, causes the release of heat. Again, any of these processes can be measured and used as biofeedback. Most biofeedback systems measure the shift of electrolytes and thus measure muscle contraction as an electrical phenomenon.

At the beginning of this section you monitored your heart rate by physical means. The contraction of the muscles in the heart reduces the size of the heart chambers, thrusting blood through the arteries. When the surge of blood passed through the section of artery beneath your finger, that section swelled to such an extent that it could be felt on the surface of the skin. You counted the pulsations and thus became your own biofeedback device. A more efficient system that would accomplish the same purpose would be to monitor the shift of electrically charged chemicals that precede each heart-muscle contraction and to allow the instrument to count them for you. (This is one of a variety of functions of an electrocardiogram.)

A more sophisticated system measures the swelling of the artery in terms of electrical energy. Or, as the blood transfers heat, one could measure the heat shift into an extremity and use that as a measure of cardiovascular function. There are numerous possibilities, but in each case, the instrument becomes your tireless monitor and can transform that energy into a more easily recognizable form. This, then, is the purpose of a biofeedback instrument.

The second or intermediate phase is represented by the psychophysiological control systems: the endocrine and the central nervous systems. The central nervous system is divided into two main components, the voluntary and involuntary. You may wish to refer back to Chapter 2 to refresh your memory. You will recall that the involuntary part of the nervous system is referred to as the autonomic nervous system. This system is a fantastic array of interconnecting nerve cells with which Mother Nature has cleverly endowed us. When a room becomes too warm, peripheral blood vessels located under the skin will dilate to release body heat. It is automatic; we do not have to direct our attention to it and nothing needs to be done on a conscious level. However, if this action is not sufficient and body temperature continues to rise, conscious centers of the brain will be alerted. Association will be made to the environment, memory of past solutions will be triggered, and voluntary action (getting up and turning down the heat) will be instituted.

The autonomic control centers are primarily in the lower centers of the brain, which include the brainstem and interbrain structures of the limbic system, the reticular activating system, the thalamus, and especially the hypothalamus, which monitors body heat very precisely. The hypothalamus also measures blood-sugar level, regulates the gastrointestinal tract, and aids in the control of blood pressure, heart rate, sweat glands, and size of pupils, just to mention a few of its constant tasks. And, most important to this discussion, the homeostatic balance-restoring action it takes need not be pondered by the consciousness centers of the brain.

Theories of psychosomatic illness slowly began to emerge as scientists were confronted with diseases caused or at least exacerbated by overstimulation of the autonomic nervous system, diseases seemingly elicited by conscious perception of environmental and social events. In other words, consciousness was interacting with and influencing the autonomic nervous system. It was then reasoned that if the central processor could influence the autonomic nervous system with fears, worries, and plans, then why couldn't the same process be turned around and have a more tranquil consciousness *reduce* the activity of the autonomic nervous system? Such a feedback system is pictured in Figure 13.2.

The third phase considers the learning mechanisms that operate in biofeedback. In the final analysis there is no one explanation that can fully account for the learning that can develop through the use of biofeedback. Actually, there are several events linked like a chain forming a circle, each adding a measure of control, each influencing the others.

As you can see in Figure 13.1, biofeedback represents a closed-loop system. The control system (the instrument) senses the physiological output from the person (through the sensors, in the illustration) and the person senses the electrical output of the control system (represented by feedback in Figure 13.1). However, it is more than just a stimulus–response situation. The biofeedback instrument is capable of making some decisions about the incoming information and can change the output (feedback) to fit some predetermined criteria. Likewise, an intelligent organism has the ability to recall memory of events related to previous responses and problem-solving attempts and instantly alter the response in relation to the feedback signal. In other words, the individual acts, gets feedback, and acts again, but the subsequent action may be changed from the first if the individual was not satisfied with the results of the previous action.

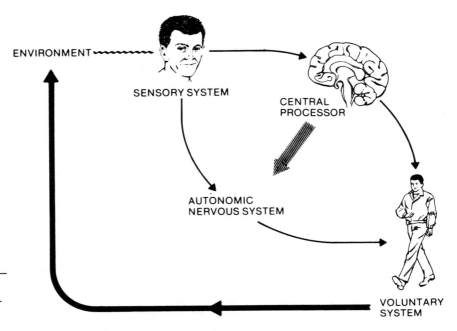

ENVIRONMENT

SENSORY SYSTEM

CENTRAL PROCESSOR

AUTONOMIC NERVOUS SYSTEM

VOLUNTARY SYSTEM

**FIGURE 13.2**

Interaction between Central Processor and Autonomic Nervous System

The output of the biofeedback instrument is electrical activity in the body and represents automatic responses of the brain. The closed loop or circle can be influenced by neural activity occurring in smooth muscle, skin, blood vessels, or any of the levels of the brain previously mentioned.

Let's take a trip around the closed loop and focus in on a few examples of possible mechanisms. One explanation for the action of biofeedback is that it directs attention away from ego-centered, stress-producing consciousness and, in the manner of meditation, induces an altered state of consciousness. Instead of a mantra, the feedback and/or the organ "language" it represents become the focus of attention. In one sense, there is a reduction in the impact of potential environmental stressors, not because the event is altered in any way, but because the focus of attention is guided inward, away from the event. Even without biofeedback the body is a closed-loop system. For example, as in anxious reactivity, cognitive or autonomic arousal can increase muscle tension, which feeds back impulses to the central nervous system, further increasing general arousal, which further stimulates the muscles. Often, awareness of muscle tension causes further muscle tension. Directing attention away from the stressor temporarily reduces arousal output to the viscera, thus reducing muscle tension, which in turn decreases stimulation back to the central nervous system. While this is a temporary situation, two things happen. First, the central nervous system, specifically the limbic and hypothalamic areas, are being conditioned. You will recall from Chapter 2 that this general area of the brain exhibits a tone that to a large extent determines stress reactivity. This tone can be conditioned to be relatively volatile and overreactive, or, by the mechanism just outlined, be conditioned to be more tranquil, increasing one's tolerance to outside stressors.

Second, the cognitive centers now have memory patterns set up for relaxation or at least reduced arousal, and these patterns can be recalled. The biofeedback learning laboratory should create an optimal situation for relaxation. The instrument provides instant feedback, which allows the cognitive mechanism to associate the feedback with the visceral feeling, and then perhaps a mechanism for reproducing that state will develop. The mechanism may be the development of memory patterns for the response, or the development of more efficient neural patterns for production of the response. It is by this same process that control over any visceral activity can be learned. Again, the cognitive can influence or be influenced by the emotional set, and these can in turn affect the autonomic arousal, and so on around the loop. In addition, motor output from the brain can issue specific instructions that are constantly being altered in relation to feedback until the desired outcome is accomplished, be it general relaxation, fine control of one muscle, or the change in blood flow to any one section of the body.

**THE MANY USES OF BIOFEEDBACK**

Illness, especially that thought to have psychosomatic roots, is the malfunction of organ systems. "Treatment" may be generally thought of as the removal of the exacerbating condition, allowing the body to heal itself, or as a process that aids the body in healing itself. Some forms of treatment are surgery, to remove a foreign object of harmful growth; drugs, to destroy bacteria or to augment defense mechanisms; the discontinuance of stressful behavior; or a strengthening of the psychophysiological coping mechanisms.

Considering the previous discussion of mechanisms, it is not difficult to see how biofeedback can aid in the treatment of illness. Even though biofeedback is an educational instrument, its primary use to date has been as a tool to aid in the treatment of conditions as dissimilar as anxiety neuroses and musculoskeletal disorders. Barbara Brown (1977) has indicated that "biofeedback still appears to be the closest thing to a panacea ever discovered" (p. 2), and that "there are more than fifty major medical and psychological problems in which biofeedback has been used with either greater success than conventional treatments or at least with equal benefits" (p. 3). The exciting aspect of biofeedback as treatment is that it is noninvasive and has almost no adverse effects. It works by allowing the body to heal itself—more specifically, by aiding the body to correct imbalances simply by giving information about the imbalance and about the success of the rebalancing action.

We will not attempt to give a complete list of the conditions for which biofeedback has been used; the list would be outdated by the time it appeared in print. Rather, we will briefly discuss the major types of biofeedback; together with knowledge of a particular condition, this discussion should give you the ability to evaluate the potential of using biofeedback in that particular situation.

Any system in the body that emits energy can be used in the biofeedback process. Because of anatomical and physiological considerations, some systems are more difficult to use than others, but by and large, biofeedback technology has advanced to the point where almost anything is possible. The systems that have become most popular for biofeedback are the ones with the most practical application. These include the muscular system, brain waves, and the cardiovascular system. Other forms of feedback that are becoming increasingly more useful are those of the skin and gastrointestinal systems.

## Muscles and Biofeedback

There are two distinctly different applications of biofeedback to the muscular system:

1. Muscle tension and relaxation
2. Neuromuscular rehabilitation

Both utilize the electromyograph (EMG), an instrument that measures the activity of a muscle. More specifically, the EMG measures the electrical energy emitted by the flow of electrically charged particles in and out of a muscle cell just before contraction. The strength of the muscle contraction depends on the quantity of these particles; thus the EMG can give an instantaneous and continuous evaluation of muscle contraction.

Before we go into the application of biofeedback to the muscular system, we should review what we know about the muscle's reaction to stress. A muscle is a mass of millions of cells with the ability to contract, or shorten, thus producing movement. As we learn how to perform activities, patterns of muscle movements are ingrained in our memory and become automatic functions. You do not have to think about how to pick up a pencil, but rather just think of the act and the muscles respond. Other muscle-action patterns are learned as well, such as fighting back, running away, and bracing for anticipated harm, to mention a few. When a threatening situation occurs, each muscle does not have to be commanded to act; one just thinks of the action "run," and the legs move.

This concept is simple enough when the threatening situation is obvious. The muscles contract and the job gets done. However, in our modern, socially controlled world there are few physically threatening situations one must face in the average day. Most threats encountered are symbolic and do not necessitate all-out action of fighting or running. But social forces do cause anger and threaten ego, so subconsciously one prepares for action. This process is referred to as *alerting* or *bracing*. Muscles contract, but not to the extent that movement occurs; thus, one does not get feedback regarding the extent of the muscle activity. What results is an incomplete contraction referred to as *muscle tension*. Muscle tension, then, is a muscle contraction that is inappropriate or in excess; no work is done and it serves no purpose. If the tension is prolonged, the muscles set up a learned pattern of response and chronically assume that state. Chronic, long-term tension has been related to numerous disorders, and because the origin of the muscle tension is in the defensive or alert attitude, these disorders are considered psychosomatic.

Sit back in your chair, close your eyes, and try to focus your thoughts on your muscles. Bend your arm up so that your hand touches your shoulder. The muscle tension is obvious as movement occurs. Next, just think of the same movement. You almost have to hold the arm back as it seems to want to move. Feel the muscles contract ever so slightly. Try the same activity with your forehead. Frown; feel the muscles contract. Then just think of an activity that is unpleasant to you and try to feel the tension that may develop in that area. You are, of course, getting feedback of subtle muscle activity that does not produce movement only because you have not willed the movement.

But just as the gross movement can be controlled, so can the more subtle muscle tension if its existence is known. Unfortunately, most people possess limited ability to sense muscle tension. It is here that the EMG biofeedback instrument can be helpful. If sensing electrodes are placed on the skin over the muscle, subtle contractions can be measured. The signal is specially processed and converted to a light or sound signal, and is fed back to the individual, who can use that information to direct the muscle to relax. In most tension-reduction or general-relaxation programs, muscles of the face and/or neck are used. Tension in these areas generally reflects moods and emotions.

Edmund Jacobsen, one of the eminent experts on muscle tension and relaxation, popularized the concept of mind-muscle interrelationship. He indicated that anxiety and muscle relaxation are incompatible and formulated the idea that one effective way of reducing anxiety was to reduce muscle tension. This concept formed the basis for the most-often used biofeedback program, which uses EMG biofeedback as a technique to develop self-awareness and an awareness of the relationship between emotion and tension. EMG biofeedback has also been used to promote general relaxation, reduce anxiety, treat phobias, and relieve a myriad of other conditions such as tension headache, migraine headache, premenstrual distress, and insomnia commonly associated with muscle tension.

The second major application of EMG biofeedback is in neuromuscular rehabilitation. This process uses the same principle of mind–muscle communication, but here the goal is to make the muscle (which has for any reason lost its function) contract in a coordinated movement pattern. An action command is given, and even if the limb does not move, the EMG will sense even the most minute stimulation of the muscles. Thus, one can keep correcting the thought process until eventually a coordinated movement is possible. One tends to see the restoration of lost function as a modern medical miracle—and indeed it is—but the miracle is in the human potential to relearn activities and behaviors, and to regenerate damaged tissue. Technology has provided a technique of giving information concerning the appropriateness of the action, which facilitates the learning process (Budzynski & Peffer, 1980).

## Brain Waves and Biofeedback

Another popular biofeedback system is the alpha/theta brain-wave instrument, which roughly resembles the EMG. The electroencephalograph (EEG) measures the electrical activity of the brain in a manner similar to the way the EMG measures muscle activity. There are some important differences, though, in that nerve cells, unlike muscle cells, are always acting and do not stop generating electrical activity until death. The nerve-cell membrane potentials (the electric differential between the inside and outside of the cell) are not fixed, but oscillate continuously near the threshold level. Electrical potentials in any part of the nerve cell create an open field of current flow that can be detected at the surface of the scalp. This continuous variation and accompanying impulse discharge produces a spontaneous and often rhythmical flow of current.

The analysis of brain waves is an extremely complex activity, and biofeedback represents but one of the more general applications. The brain wave, like all the other energy waves emitted from the body, has two primary characteristics of interest to biofeedback: the frequency with which the wave occurs and the strength of the signal. The frequency, as we mentioned in Chapter 3, can range from less than 1 cycle per second to 50 cycles per second. As one might expect, with millions of cells simultaneously performing thousands of functions, it is impossible for the entire brain to be producing activity at any one frequency at any given time. Thus, the EEG shows a complex pattern of mixed wave-forms occurring at varying frequencies. However, at any given point there does appear to be a dominant frequency emitted from a specific section of the brain, and the analysis of this dominant frequency has become an important area of study as researchers have begun to associate brain-wave patterns with cognitive functioning, emotion, and states of consciousness (see Figure 13.3).

The slowest wave pattern, the delta wave, is present while the individual is awake but is dominant only during sleep, and its presence is often used as an indication of sleep. Delta signifies a state of consciousness that is not interacting with the external environment. Yet, a few researchers have reported that they have observed delta-dominant brain-wave states accompanied by apparent sleep, but with a measure of consciousness heretofore thought to be impossible. One such report was made by Elmer and Alyce Green, who worked with an Indian yogi, Swami Rama. In experiments where the Swami was demonstrating various levels of control over his consciousness, he produced a state that gave the appearance of sleep; that is, he was lying down, eyes closed, snoring lightly, with delta-dominant brain-wave patterns. Yet, after a twenty-minute period he remembered 90 percent of what

**FIGURE 13.3**

States of Consciousness as Determined by Brain Waves, and Feelings Often Associated with Each State.

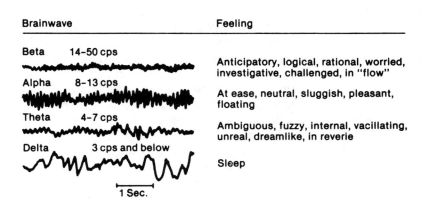

| Brainwave | | Feeling |
|---|---|---|
| Beta | 14–50 cps | Anticipatory, logical, rational, worried, investigative, challenged, in "flow" |
| Alpha | 8–13 cps | At ease, neutral, sluggish, pleasant, floating |
| Theta | 4–7 cps | Ambiguous, fuzzy, internal, vacillating, unreal, dreamlike, in reverie |
| Delta | 3 cps and below | Sleep |

1 Sec.

was said in his laboratory room. The Swami referred to this state as yogic sleep, in which he instructed his mind to rest but to be attentive, not to wander, and not to busy itself warring. Thus, as will be shown with the other brain-wave states as well, what is considered the normal characteristic of a state is not necessarily the exclusive function of that state.

The next wave pattern on the frequency continuum is theta, if theta waves can be called patterns—as these usually occur in sporadic spikes (or peaks in the wave). They constitute less than 10 percent of the daily awake EEG and are most often associated with the hypnagogic state. Try to remember how you feel when you are just starting to fall asleep. While not quite asleep and not quite awake you may have experienced dreamlike hypnagogic imagery that can be visual, auditory, olfactory, tactile, or gustatory. In this state the brain is active but is not actively involved with outside situations, nor are thoughts directed by the will, as in daydreams. The theta state is not necessarily a quiet and relaxed state, as the mind is active. This activity is often associated with creativity. Like the delta state, the theta state is thought to be an internally directed, but not controlled, state of consciousness in which "thinking" in the usual sense does not occur. Rather, "thoughts" are bursts of images not temporally related to external events and not "controlled" by learned inhibitions. Thus, these thoughts are often original and, when they are remembered, represent something new and creative.

It might well follow that the conscious inhibitions or "blocks" that often interfere with creative thoughts often interfere with learning. Thomas Budzynski and colleagues at the University of Colorado Medical Center conducted some interesting research with individuals who were taught to maintain the half-awake–half-asleep theta state. During this time a taped message was played, and the tape would stay on only when the theta wave was dominant in the EEG. Varying tapes of information were presented, and, in general, it was found that individuals who had previously been blocked from assimilating the information or ideas seemed to learn it or accept it during the theta state. The hypersuggestibility is probably a result of the fact that in the theta state there are no learned inhibitions preventing acceptance. There seems to be an uncritical acceptance of the information, which circumvents learned and conditioned blocks.

This type of learning seems to work better with holistic ideas than with factual pieces of information—for example, it is effective in reducing prejudice, guilt, or test anxiety, or in changing certain types of eating behavior or stressful patterns of thinking, rather than in learning specific historical dates. The information must be presented while the individual is in the drowsy, dreamlike, theta state. As this state does not readily communicate with the awake-rational state, most subjects report little learning, but when retested, they just seem to know the information or behave differently. Budzynski (1977) points out that as this information is being directed to the side of the brain (the "nondominant" hemisphere of the brain) that processes ideas rather than factual knowledge, the information learned through this method should be tested using nonverbal recognition techniques. To facilitate learning, the Colorado research team first taught relaxation, then increased the voluntary production of slowed brain waves and coded the information within the rhythm of background music.

Although more research needs to be conducted, it appears that the factual information usually processed by the dominant hemisphere is better learned through traditional methods with the learner in the alert rational mode of consciousness. Westerners have been taught primarily through analytical processes, and as a result our dominant hemisphere learning is highly developed. It is only recently that interest in nondominant learning has increased. Theta or twilight learning appears to be one method of facilitating this neglected mode of learning.

The third slowest brain wave (see Figure 13.3) is called the alpha wave. It is the famous alpha state that is responsible for the rapid growth and popularity of EEG biofeedback. The resurgence in popularity of yoga and meditation, coupled with our reverence for time- and energy-saving machines, has given rise to an alpha fad. Many people were convinced that the mere presence of those magical little 8-to-13-cycles-per-second brain waves was instant mind control. Intuition, accelerated healing, control over pain, higher IQ, improved sleep, even weight loss is attributed to control over alpha.

There is nothing mystical or magical about alpha. It is a slow, synchronized wave, which means that it occurs in rhythmical stepwise fashion indicative of a predictable, nonfluctuating, nonprocessing state. Everyone has alpha waves. When you close your eyes, alpha bursts begin to appear with greater frequency. It is more difficult to remain willfully in alpha for any length of time than to produce it in spurts, but one can be trained to do so.

Subjective reports of the feelings that accompany the alpha state indicate that it is an awake, alert, but calm, restful, and peaceful state, often described as idyllic. It is often difficult to validate such subjective accounts as most people hold preconceived opinions regarding what alpha is supposed to be like. However, most (but certainly not all) authorities in the field agree that alpha waves characterize a state of consciousness free from ongoing ego-involved thought processes. It is this relative absence of sustained thought pattern that is responsible for the more relaxed feeling. We have said that a large part of stress is triggered or augmented by ego-involved arousal thoughts, which are not present during the typical alpha state. Feeding information back to an individual about the general activity of the brain promotes the ability to decrease potentially stress-producing thought patterns.

The fourth and fastest of the major brain-wave patterns is beta. Most of the beta activity occurs below 25 cycles per second. Faster beta is also present but has not been sufficiently studied; however, technological advances in biofeedback instrumentation have increased the likelihood that 40-cycle-per-second beta will be a rich source of study in the near future. Beta is a fast wave of relatively low voltage when compared to alpha. It is not synchronous, which may indicate that it is a diversity of unpredictable thought patterns responding to the outside environment. During beta the brain is usually considered to be working faster and to be involved in more analytical thought than in other states. This does not say anything about the quality of thinking or about right or wrong analysis; it just indicates that the brain is more active. Certainly, not all thinking activity is stressful. One may be in a beta state, thinking, problem-solving, feeling challenged, but not threatened, and not at all stressed. However, while beta does not necessarily mean arousal, arousal almost always occurs during beta. One seldom encounters physiological arousal during alpha.

While it is difficult to describe brain-wave biofeedback without the typical classification of delta, theta, alpha, and beta, it is misleading to think of them as clearly demarcated states. Brain waves represent a continuum of frequency activity that seems to parallel a continuum of mental alertness and activity. Years ago behavioral states were roughly associated with frequency, and generalizations about that behavior have been responsible for the sharp lines that appear to divide the states. More recent research clearly shows that such sharp behavioral lines do not exist. For example, the 6–7–8–9 frequency range is a blend of characteristics of both theta and alpha, and the 12–13–14–15 range blends aspects of alpha and beta.

**The Cardiovascular System and Biofeedback**

It has long been known that the cardiovascular system is very responsive to stress arousal. Ancient scientists observed this relationship, but postulated a purely autonomic reflex action. It is now clear that our thoughts and anticipations can increase the action of the heart in preparation for activity that may or may not ever occur. At the beginning of this chapter, when you monitored your heart rate you observed how what you were thinking influenced the rate of cardiac contraction. Because it is so easy to measure, heart-rate activity represented one of the earliest biofeedback systems. By itself, a faster or slower heartbeat has little significance until one understands that cardiac activity is a balance between the two major divisions of the nervous system, the sympathetic and the parasympathetic. (See Chapter 2.) Thus, in this instance the mechanism that slows the heart is more important than the actual change, as a decrease in heart rate signifies a shift to parasympathetic dominance.

There is some evidence to suggest that a shift in this system represents a total shift in dominance that would act to reduce stress arousal. But even if the shift is only in the cardiovascular system, it feeds back to the central nervous system and further influences arousal via a positive feedback loop. Individuals who suffer anxiety reactions often report palpitations and say that this awareness of cardiac activity further heightens general stress and anxiety. Again, learned control would help reduce this vicious cycle. Finally, heart rate is a good window into the self and is often used to promote self-awareness and control over emotional states.

Another cardiovascular biofeedback system that has proven to be beneficial in clinical situations involves blood pressure, which generally reflects the constrictive and dilative properties of the arteries. This is explained more fully in Chapter 3. Essential hypertension, or high blood pressure of unknown origin, is one of the most prevalent diseases in our society. Even though the exact cause is unknown, we do know that the mechanisms for increased pressure can be influenced by stress arousal. The hypertensive is characterized as an aggressive, sometimes hostile individual who internalizes the anger. The cardiovascular mechanisms serve to prepare the body for the anticipated venting of this anger, which usually does not occur (Pinkerton, Hughes & Wenrich, 1982).

Early studies show that feeding back information about pressure resulted in the learned reduction of blood pressure, which, of course, had tremendous clinical significance. The problem at the present time is the biofeedback instrumentation itself. The standard blood-pressure cuff or sphygmomanometer has been slightly modified to become a feedback device. However, constant inflation of the cuff produces erroneous readings, and the feedback derived from stethoscope sounds leaves much to be desired. A newer method is the pulse-wave velocity technique. In this technique, with each pulse the movement of the artery is transformed into electrical signals that can be measured without a pressure cuff. The time it takes the pulse to reach the extremities is correlated with blood pressure and can provide instant (pulse-by-pulse) feedback on change in pressure.

The most popular cardiovascular-related biofeedback system relates to control over vasoconstriction (constriction of the blood vessels) and vasodilation (dilation of the blood vessels). It was found that information about the activity of the arteries could be gained by simply measuring the temperature of the surface of the skin. The skin is profusely supplied with blood vessels that aid in the conservation and release of body heat. Generalized vasoconstriction is a function of sympathetic tone (remember that most of the blood vessels constrict during stress) and vasodilation is thought to be a change in the tone or an increased dominance by the parasympathetic system. Stressed individuals often exhibit strong sympathetic tone, vasoconstriction, and thus cooler skin temperatures, especially in the extremities.

Based on the pioneering efforts of Elmer and Alyce Green at their Menninger Clinic laboratory, skin-temperature biofeedback has been developed into one of the most versatile and valuable clinical tools. Conditions such as migraine headache, hypertension, and Raynaud's syndrome (a disease in which the blood vessels of the extremities constrict) have been helped with this technique. Skin-temperature feedback involves the most simple of all biofeedback systems: a simple thermistor or diode that changes resistance in response to temperature is attached to a meter or sounding device and the feedback loop is complete. Usually the fingers are used, but other common sites include the forehead, feet, face, back, and abdomen. Multiple-site selection is also employed and averaged to obtain mean temperature, or differential techniques are used to obtain finer control, that is, hand warming or forehead cooling, as was done in the original migraine headache research. Control over skin temperature can be very specific. Several demonstrations have been made in which various individuals have exhibited the ability to increase the temperature of one part of the hand while simultaneously decreasing the temperature elsewhere on the same hand. Control can also be general in that an increase in temperature is thought to reflect a generalized state of relaxation. More importantly, temperature feedback represents a learning exercise for the development of self-awareness and self-control (Stoyva, 1983).

The usual protocol for a skin-temperature exercise incorporates not only biofeedback, but some auto-suggestion or visual imagery techniques as well. The individual must learn to attend passively to the biofeedback while very subtly reflecting on specific thoughts. The mind has memory engrams set up for feeling states, and recalling those states can help the body return physically to a condition in which the peripheral arteries are dilated. An example of such statements is, "I am relaxed, I am quiet.... My arms feel heavy.... My hands feel heavy.... Warmth is flowing through my body.... My hands feel warm.... My hands feel heavy and warm.... I feel relaxed.... My hands are warm."

As previously mentioned, measuring skin temperature does not entail the sophisticated instrumentation necessary in the EEG and EMG system. In fact, several programs have reported satisfactory results simply by taping a baby thermometer to the finger and using that as the feedback device. Granted, the more sophisticated instrument will aid learning tremendously, but this is one system that does not cost great sums of money.

## SUMMARY

This chapter has presented basic information on the most-used biofeedback systems. There are other systems, such as those involving the galvanic skin response, the gastrointestinal system, the respiratory system, and the sex organs, but these are not as popular or as well developed. The references at the end of the chapter list some sources that discuss these systems. We have endeavored to report only the findings generally recognized as factual, but have spiced them with some avant-garde projects by noted researchers. This approach was employed to reduce the sensationalism surrounding biofeedback. The fact is, however, that many of the results reported from both clinical and research programs are sensational. To those who do not understand the interaction between the mind and body or the mechanisms of nervous-system control, biofeedback does seem magical.

Biofeedback can be considered one of the most significant biomedical and educational advances of our times. Although used in the practice of medicine, biofeedback must be considered an educational tool giving information that can aid in the learning of self-control. Often such control can eliminate the cause of or exacerbation of a physical condition that may lead to disease. Biofeedback is not as economically practical as meditation or autosensory neuromuscular relaxation, but it is more efficient and is exact enough for research. As always, the faddist, the instant seekers, and fast-buck promoters are finding ways to misuse and to bilk, but this abuse is far overshadowed by the immense potential that biofeedback promises.

# REFERENCES

BROWN, B. B. (1974). *New mind, new body.* New York: Harper & Row, Pub.

———— (1977). *Stress and the art of biofeedback.* New York: Harper & Row, Pub.

BUDZYNSKI, T. H. (1977). Biofeedback and the twilight states of consciousness. *Psychology Today, 11*(3), 38.

BUDZYNSKI, T. H., AND K. PEFFER (1980). Biofeedback training. In I. L. Kutash and L. B. Schlesinger (eds.), *Handbook on stress and anxiety.* San Francisco: Jossey-Bass.

GIRDANO, D. A., AND D. DUSEK (1977). Performance-based evaluation. *Health Education, 8*(2), 13–16.

GREEN, E., AND A. GREEN (1977). *Beyond biofeedback.* New York: Delacorte Press.

PINKERTON, S., H. HUGHES, AND W. W. WENRICH (1982). *Behavioral medicine: Clinical applications.* New York: John Wiley.

STOYVA, J. (1983). Guidelines for cultivating general relaxation: Biofeedback and autogenic training combined. In J. V. Basmajian (ed.), *Biofeedback: Principles and practice for clinicians.* Baltimore: Williams & Wilkins.

# CHAPTER FOURTEEN

# Autogenics and Visual Imagery

**AUTOGENIC RELAXATION TRAINING: RELAXATION RECALL**

The term *autogenesis* (self-generation) describes almost every form of relaxation exercise; however, the word *autogenic* has become synonymous with a form of relaxation involving self-directed mental images of relaxed states. This simple yet advanced technique centers around conditioned patterns of responses that become associated with particular thoughts. Recall those moments when you allow your mind to run away and conjure up a tragic event. Recall how thinking of yourself or your loved ones dying or being involved in a serious accident gives you chills or raises the hair on the back of your neck. This represents a conditioned physical response to that particular association. The opposite is just as true and produces an equally dramatic physical response. Imagine sitting on a quiet beach with the sun warming your body, and a relaxation response is triggered. Unfortunately, many of us have become more conditioned to negative thoughts than to positive ones; thus the technique of relaxation recall was developed to help condition relaxation.

Relaxation recall is actually a very advanced form of relaxation training; it is learned more rapidly when the individual already possesses some other relaxation skills. For example, we have said many times that it is difficult to concentrate or control the direction of your thoughts if the mind is being bombarded by arousal impulses from the body. The components of relaxation recall—concentration and relaxation—are facilitated by your ability to vividly imagine a scene or feeling state and by the ability to concentrate without arousal. Let's look at one of the techniques included in the exercise plan so you will better understand it when you are asked to perform it. It is known that one of the physical responses that accompanies relaxation is vasodilation, an expansion of the arteries in the skin of the extremities. This produces a warm, heavy sensation as blood flow increases in that area. Generally speaking, relaxed individuals tend to have warmer hands than anxious or stressed individuals. If one can imagine warmth, or on a feeling level can reproduce the heavy sensation, the body has the tendency to "relive" or reproduce that state. A shift in blood flow is impossible without a change in nervous-system tone; thus relaxation is facilitated. After a degree of proficiency has been obtained, we will add a more complex imagination process by utilizing personal visual imagery of a time and place that was particularly relaxing to you. If your "feeling memory" is pretty good and if you have developed some fairly good body control and concentration abilities, the memory of the beautiful times in your life can be one of the keys to controlling stress and tension.

We have said that stress arousal is a psychophysiological response to a particular psychosocial event. Each situation produces an immediate stress response but also leaves a residual amount of tension in the body. Response to subsequent stressors is augmented by the residual left over from previous responses. As the day wears on, response overactivity results from the inability to dissipate residual tension. The physical relaxation produced by relaxation exercises is an immediate reaction, but the more the relaxation state is induced, the more the carryover to times more removed from the exercise time. Gradually you experience a dissipation of residual tension. Thus each new stressful situation will produce a reaction sufficient to deal only with that particular situation without the added-on effect of previous stress arousal. The longer you practice the relaxation exercises, the more your general state of arousal resembles the relaxed state, and the ongoing tensions most detrimental to the body are greatly reduced. After a while, this relaxed state becomes a stable part of your personality. The overactive, rushed individual can become a slowed, cooler-reacting person having the ability to respond with the intensity demanded of each situation as an isolated incident.

Chronically stressed and anxious people do not perceive internal states of arousal and do not associate physical states with emotional arousal. As in a positive feedback system, the physical arousal causes anxious feelings, which further cause physical arousal. Relaxation not only diminishes physical arousal, but promotes stress desensitization by allowing individuals to experience previously stressful situations in a relaxed state, gradually diminishing the stressful experience in their lives and reducing anxiety.

One essential ingredient of mental health—happiness—is the

ability to live each current situation in reality without the effect of adding imaginary consequences of what could or should happen. Perhaps the primary therapeutic benefit of this relaxation program is the development of the ability to concentrate attention on the present, to quiet the imagination, and to distinguish reality from fantasy. You can develop the ability to direct thoughts away from the ego self, the primary source of stress, and direct it to the problem at hand. You can become more problem centered and less ego centered. As you become less stressed, you automatically become more efficient; they go hand in hand.

**Legs Heavy and Warm**

The exercises in this group are quiet concentration activities that can be done either sitting or lying down. The object is to tell yourself to reproduce feelings of heaviness and warmth in the legs. If you are successful, a heavy, warm sensation will occur as blood flow increases in that area. The body will "relive" or reproduce that state and, as we have said, such a shift is impossible without a change in the nervous-system tone. Thus relaxation is facilitated. You must be quiet and undistracted, and you must concentrate.

Start by taking three deep breaths. Repeat the following phrases quietly to yourself: "I am relaxed. I am calm. I am quiet." Go slowly; allow time between each phrase to feel the sensations:

> My right leg is heavy.
> My right leg is heavy and warm.
> My right leg is warm and relaxed.
> I am calm and quite relaxed.
> My left leg is heavy.
> My left leg is heavy and warm.
> My left leg is warm and relaxed.
> I am calm and quite relaxed.
> I am quiet and at peace.
> I am relaxed.

This activity should take about five minutes. When you are done, remain quiet for a few minutes.

**Center of Warmth**

The exercises in this group are quiet concentration activities that may be done in either a sitting or lying down position. You will need quiet, intense concentration on the trunk area of the body. You are going to try to imagine warmth being emitted from the nerve plexus lying behind the stomach and right above the navel. Focus your attention on what you feel is the exact center of your body. The nerves there form a plexus called the *solar plexus*. Softly, slowly, and quietly say to yourself:

> I am relaxed.
> I am calm.
> I am quiet.
> My solar plexus is warm.
> I can feel the heat radiating throughout my entire body.
> My body is warm and relaxed.
> I am quiet and at peace.
> I am relaxed.

This activity should take about five minutes. When you are finished, remain quiet for a few minutes.

## Arms Heavy and Warm

By now you should be familiar with the procedure for this exercise. It will be quiet concentration of heaviness and warmth in the arms and hands. If you had any success with the two previous exercises, you will do very well here. If you had difficulty with those exercises, this one should provide you with a breakthrough. The reasons are that you have better control over hands and arms than over legs and trunk, more nerves innervating fewer muscles, and just more practice in using the upper extremities. You may sit or lie down. Start with a few deep breaths. Center yourself. Close your eyes and concentrate on your hands and arms. Your statements are as follows; repeat them to yourself slowly and quietly:

> I am relaxed.
> I am calm.
> I am quiet.
> My right arm is heavy.
> My right arm is heavy and warm.
> My right arm is warm.
> My right arm is warm and relaxed.
> I am calm and quite relaxed.
> My left arm is heavy.
> My left arm is heavy and warm.
> My left arm is warm.
> My left arm is warm and relaxed.
> I am calm and quite relaxed.
> My body is warm and relaxed.
> I am quiet and at peace.
> I am relaxed.

This activity should take about five minutes. When you are finished, remain quiet for a few minutes.

**Freedom Posturing**

Another form of autogenic or relaxation recall type of relaxation is what we call freedom posturing. This exercise is designed to change thoughts and behaviors that continually fuel the stress response. The basic premise of freedom posturing lies in the interaction between mind and body, in that arousing thoughts produce a tense body and a tense body stimulates central nervous-system arousal; and that the cycle can be broken by changing either the body position or thought process. In addition, this technique seeks to promote self-awareness and reduce the stressful behavior, especially as it relates to dealing with the expectations others have of us.

We will spend less time being uptight if we can recognize who or what is causing us stress, and, most importantly, when we are becoming stressed. You will recall that one of the underlying principles of biofeedback consists of developing self-awareness to the point of being your own early-warning system, sensing stressful arousal before it becomes too severe. Freedom posturing includes exercises to help you develop your autobiofeedback system; that is, to sense your biological state without instruments, by seeing yourself and others during stress.

After learning some of the powerful relaxation techniques, you then have to refine your use of them so as to be able to relax at will. Once you have developed the ability to relax at will, you can: (1) practice and gradually condition your system to be more tranquil and relaxed, and (2) use your ability to relax for immediate relief when you feel stressed. The catch in item 2 lies in our ability to recognize stress as it builds and before it pushes us into unproductive emotional states and physical disability.

If working with another person, just sit back and have him or her read the directions. If you are working by yourself, read the situation, get the idea of what you are being asked to do; then sit back, close your eyes, and work through it. Either way, always close your eyes, because it greatly increases your power of concentration.

**Situation 1.**   Close your eyes, but in your mind's eye see a tense person. It may be someone you know well or just someone you have seen once. What does this person look like when stressed? How is that person sitting? What is he or she doing with his or her legs, arms, face? Concentrate on the person's breathing: Is it fast or slow; deep or shallow; through nose or mouth? What sounds is the person making?

Concentrate on the legs. Are they moving or still; crossed or open? Are the feet flat on the floor? Do they seem to be digging into the floor as if to resist movement; or just the opposite, to provide a firm base from which to spring? Are the legs generally taut, ready for action?

Concentrate on the midsection of the person's body. Is this person hunched over from the shoulders? Bent in the abdomen? Is the back arched? Or is the back being pushed into the chair?

Concentrate on the hands and arms. Are they moving or still? Are the hands clenched into a fist or are they open? Are they pushed down onto the arms of the chair? Are they gripping? Are they crossed in front of the body? Are they tensely straight?

Concentrate on the head, neck, and face. Are the eyes wide open or squinted? Is the head pulled down and are the shoulders up? Is the forehead wrinkled? Are the jaws tightly clenched? Are the neck muscles tightly drawn?

Now assume that position yourself. Tense your muscles as the person you saw in your mind's eye tensed his or her muscles. See yourself in that position. Feel yourself in that position. Where are you? Who are you with? What message (verbal- or nonverbal-implied) is that person giving you? What is he or she expecting from you? Are you feeling pushed to do something you do not want to do? Or are you feeling held back from doing something you want to do? Now leave those thoughts and rest for a moment.

**Situation 2.** Close your eyes and switch your mind's eye to a person you see as being very relaxed. How is this person sitting? Concentrate on this person's arms, hands, breathing, legs, trunk, face. How are they different from those of the tense person? Assume the relaxed position yourself. Where are you? Who are you with? Do you feel free to do what you want to do? In the absence of expectations this is how your body feels. You can help yourself demand your personal freedom by telling your body to position itself in this fashion. Now slowly open your eyes and reorient yourself to the world around you. Feel the energy flowing through your system vitalizing your sense of commitment to your purpose and to yourself. When you feel someone is pushing you or holding you back, assume this freedom posture and be aware of how you are more willing to demand your personal freedom.

**Your Special Place**

Recall a time in your life when you felt very relaxed, peaceful, and tranquil. It may help to close your eyes, relax, and let the images come to you.

Describe the place in the following terms:

1. When was it? _____

2. Who were you with? _____
   *Note:* Even though you might have traveled with another person, do not list anyone else unless that person's image is vividly associated with the relaxation feeling.

3. Where was it? Look around, describe what you see, describe your feelings and sensations:

_____

_____

_____

_____

_____

_____

_____

_____

_____

_____

_____

*Note:* Feelings and sensations are more important than exact topographical descriptions. Here is an example of item 3, somewhat overdone to drive home the point that the location *must* have feeling:

See a lonely stretch of beach with the waves forcefully pounding the rocks and teasing the sand. With each wave the sand feels cool, solid, and resisting, then warm and accepting, caressing my feet. The gentle breeze massages my skin and my hair resembles the grass, bending in response to the wind's gentle persuasion. The sun seductively bathes my skin with warmth, which is then cooled by the breeze. The gulls, precocious and curious, clamor for attention as they proclaim the ecstasy and freedom of flight. My spirit soars with their flight, and as I ride the wind I feel free, open, part of the wind, the sun, the sea, the universe.

Take this a step farther into the realm of fantasy. See yourself gently floating on a raft, drifting deeply into relaxation. Your raft may have the ability not only to float on water, but in the air as well. Feel the wind pick up your raft and gently and safely carry it off the ground as high as you wish it to go, closer to the warmth of the sun. You can fly as high and as far as you wish, looking down on your surroundings, relaxed and calm, as you look at the activities of people and events below. Perhaps you wish to visit a special place and view from your gently floating raft the activities of a special event, knowing that you are above it all, relaxed and calm, gently floating on the wind, leaving all your worries on the ground. Continue your travel for a few minutes and enjoy this special place and experience. As you return from your trip, know that you can return anytime you wish just by closing your eyes, taking a deep breath, and seeing yourself floating on your special raft.

**VISUAL
IMAGERY**

Aristotle wrote, "the soul never thinks without a picture." It is well documented that the pictures in our minds are closely related to physiological arousal and the stress reaction. We now know that what works against us can be turned around to work *for* us—*if* we can control the pictures in our mind. The basic premise is that imagery is an experience and can be regarded in many important aspects as equivalent to an actual experience with a concomitant elevation of stress arousal, the converse being the relaxation response (Klinger, 1980; Kosslyn, 1980; Sheikh, 1983, 1984).

This exercise is only one type in the broad spectrum of visual imagery that is rapidly becoming perhaps the most widely used and researched area in stress management and healing. A guided imagery or fantasy is one in which an individual, by describing an experience, helps another individual form internal visual images. This differs slightly from what we will use here, in that you will be working alone, using a story based on your own experience to elicit internal images that will produce a relaxation response. Construct a guided fantasy illustration to help stimulate your personal imagery that, while based on your personal experience, goes beyond that experience to a relaxation fantasy. Create your own imagined relaxation place and use it in the following exercise:

**PUTTING IT ALL
TOGETHER:
YOUR MINI-
RELAXATION
PLAN**

1. In a quiet room and in a comfortable chair, assume a restful position and a quiet, passive attitude. Take four deep breaths. Make each one deeper than the one before: Hold the first inhalation for four seconds, the second one for five seconds, the third one for six seconds, and the fourth one for seven seconds. Pull the tension from all parts of your body into your lungs and exhale it with each expiration. Feel more relaxed with each breath.

2. Count backward from ten to zero. Breathe naturally, and with each exhalation count one number and feel more and more relaxed as you approach zero. With each count you descend a relaxation stairway and become more deeply relaxed until you are totally relaxed at zero.

3. Now go to that relaxation place outlined in the previous exercise. Stay there for four minutes. Try to vividly, but passively, recall the feelings of that place and time that were very relaxing.

4. Bring your attention back to yourself. Count from zero to ten. Energize your body. Feel the energy, vitality, and health flow through your system. Feel alert and eager to resume your activities. Open your eyes.

## REFERENCES

KLINGER, E. (1980). Therapy and the flow of thought. In J. E. Shorr, G. Sobel, P. Robin, and J. Connella (eds.), *Imagery: Its many dimensions and applications* (pp. 143–52). New York: Plenum.

KOSSLYN, S. (1980). *Image and mind.* Cambridge, Mass.: Harvard University Press, 1980.

SHEIKH, A. A. (ed.). (1984). *Imagination and healing.* Farmingdale, NY: Bagwood Publishing.

—— (ed.). (1983). *Imagery: Current theory, research, and application.* New York: John Wiley.

# CHAPTER FIFTEEN

# Yoga and Stretch-Relaxation

**YOGA**

The word *yoga* is derived from the Sanskrit root meaning "union" or "reunion" and is a method of physical, mental, and spiritual development based on the philosophies of Lord Krishna. Knowledge of these philosophies was passed from enlightened master to student, generation after generation, for thousands of years before the first written record appeared around 200 B.C. in Patanjali's Sutras. Since then, thousands of books have been written describing the many types of yoga, called "paths," which have developed into spiritual schools, in many instances becoming distinctly separate schools in themselves. *Raja yoga*, or *royal yoga*, the path to self-realization and enlightenment, is very similar to the meditative practice described in Chapter 17. The most popular path in the Western world is hatha yoga, which uses positions and exercises to promote physical and mental harmony. Most yoga practice starts with hatha yoga, as it is thought to provide the body with health and endurance needed to learn more advanced forms of yoga. Hatha yoga is practiced for its own rewards, which include strength, flexibility, and reduction of muscle tension, and is used as a technique to quiet the body in preparation for quiet mental states.

**STRETCH–RELAXATION EXERCISES**

The health benefits of the stretch-relaxation techniques have been known for centuries; these exercises form the basis for hatha yoga programs, are an essential part of most calisthenic programs, and represent an innate pattern of movement. Notice your pet dog or cat especially on awakening, but at other times during the day also. It never attempts to get up without first stretching. Humans also naturally go through a series of stretches before arising from sleep or after prolonged sitting. When tightness or tension is sensed, stretching is a natural reflex.

Our modern living patterns are directly responsible for a multitude of health problems, many of which have already been listed in earlier sections of the book. One of the most pervasive is shortened muscles, tendons, and ligaments. Our basic body structure and function have not changed since the days of the caveman, yet our daily activities have changed drastically. Since the body is adaptive, continual sitting during work and leisure will eventually result in shortened muscles, tendons, and ligaments, and eventually result in restricted movements. It is not unusual for adults in their mid-twenties to be so restricted that touching their fingers to their toes while keeping the knees straight is impossible or at least very painful. The spine will condition itself to the state demanded by chronic sitting and lose its natural erect capabilities; the result will be a sitting-type posture while one is standing or walking. This posture naturally produces pain and tension, because body parts are positioned unnaturally. Neck and facial muscles, tendons, and ligaments will pull unnaturally, producing pain in the sensitive tissue around the head, and thus causing headache. It is not at all unusual for the posture and tone of the muscles under the skin to resemble those of the very old. Age lines are not a natural process of aging and are surely not natural in the young or even in those in the middle years.

Chronically shortened muscles do not function properly; excess tension and internal viscosity prohibit normal functioning, and a vicious cycle of the tension reflex develops. Gradually, movements become inefficient and labored; more energy than necessary is required and fatigue causes a chronic tired feeling even after adequate amounts of sleep. It has long been known that a muscle with proper stretch capabilities is stronger, more efficient, and more enduring than one that is chronically shortened. Moreover, such a muscle is more contractible, exhibits less residual tension, and can be relaxed more easily.

Again, one must realize that yoga masters come from a different culture in which both physical structure and physical activity patterns are significantly different than those of Western cultures. Thus, it is difficult for Westerners to completely master all of the positions. Nevertheless, positive results can be derived from yoga, especially if the exercises are chosen for specific outcomes in specific groups of people. For relaxation, we have developed some exercises and postures derived from principles of hatha yoga. These carefully developed exercises have been shown to yield maximal results in the shortest period of time in groups of individuals with no prior experience or special physical conditioning. This program is sequenced to condition natural readiness. *Do not* go beyond your point of pain or you will tear the tissue and retard your progress. You have spent many years conditioning this state and you cannot reverse it overnight. *Do not* set goals too high too fast. These are powerful exercises with the capability of restoring the natural structure and function to your tissue. Use them as directed until you have reconditioned your body.

**Toe Raise;**
**Knee Stretch;**
**Toe Touch**

Even though muscles will contract during these positions, the emphasis is on stretch of muscles and joints. The first exercise is a simple toe raise (Figure 15.1). In a standing position with hands on hips or raised in front of you, balance yourself as high on the tips of your toes as possible. Hold for the count of ten and relax. Repeat this exercise five times and relax.

The second exercise is the knee stretch (Figure 15.2). Sit with your legs folded under you so that your buttocks are resting on your ankles. Your toes should be pointed backward. Place your hands on the floor outside and behind your feet. Straighten your body with head raised high. Hold for a count of ten; relax and repeat five times.

The third exercise, the toe touch (Figure 15.3), stretches the muscles in the back of the leg in three positions. In a standing position with the heels together, toes angled slightly outward and legs straight, bend forward from the waist and place your hands on your knees. Hold for a count of ten and return to standing. If this produced no pain, the second repetition should find you reaching for your ankles. If pain was experienced, repeat the position to your knees. Don't force it; your body will tell you when it is ready to go lower. Hold for a count of ten and return to standing. On the third repetition, place the tips of your fingers on the floor, but assume this position only if no pain was experienced during the last one. Hold for ten and return to standing. The final position, assuming no pain to this point, is to place your palms flat on the floor. Keep your legs straight, bend at the waist, and hold for a count of ten. You will do four repetitions whether you reach the floor or not. Remember, go slowly; your body will tell you when to go on to the next position.

**Back Stretch**
**Forward/**
**Reverse;**
**Standing**
**Trunk Bend**

Here again, the emphasis is on the stretch of the muscle, the recoil, and the sense of relaxation that follows. Concentrate on the "afterfeeling" of extreme relaxation. The stretch relieves the partial contraction and allows the muscle to relax fully.

The first exercise is the back stretch forward (Figure 15.4). As

FIGURE 15.1

Toe Raise

**FIGURE 15.2**

Knee Stretch

**FIGURE 15.3**

Toe Touch

its name implies, you will feel the stretch in different parts of your back as the exercise advances. Lie on the floor. Slowly tensing your stomach muscles, raise your trunk through the sitting position to a point where your head is as close to your knees as possible. Once

**FIGURE 15.4**

Back Stretch
Forward

there, place your hands on your knees, thumb on the inside of your leg, elbow held as high as possible. Hold for ten counts and return to the lying position. Move very slowly. Feel the stomach muscles contract as they raise and lower your upper body. Feel the stretch in the lower back.

On the second repetition, place your hands halfway between your knees and ankles. Try to get your head to your knees; however, go only as far as your flexibility allows. Don't force it—you will get there one day soon. Hold for a count of ten and relax back to the lying position. Feel the stretch and subsequent relaxation in the back slightly higher than in repetition one.

On the third repetition, try for your ankles. Go slowly, feel the stretch a little higher on the back. Try to get your head on your knees. Hold for a count of ten and relax. For the fourth repetition, try to hold your hands on the bottoms of your feet. Draw the trunk toward your legs. Allow your elbows to rest on the floor. Hold for a count of ten and slowly return to the lying position. Relax, feeling the tension release.

For the second exercise, the back stretch reverse (Figure 15.5), you will need to lie down on your stomach. This exercise will stretch the back in the opposite direction. You will feel the muscles in both the back and stomach stretch. Place your hands, palms down on the floor, one on each side of your face. Slowly raise your upper body until you can rest your elbows on the floor. Hold in this position for a count of ten. If this produces no pain, arch your back slowly, moving your head high and back. Hold this position for a count of ten and rest. If this produces no pain, place your palms on the floor and continue to raise your upper body until your arms are straight. Go very slowly, and if you feel pain, return to the last position. Hold for a count of ten and return to the floor and relax. Feel the tension release in the back and stomach. Relax and breathe softly. Repeat the entire sequence five times.

FIGURE 15.5

Back Stretch
Reverse

The third exercise is the standing trunk bend (Figures 15.6 to 15.8). Stand with your feet together, legs straight. The first motion will be a side bend. Stretch your arms over your head. Bend your trunk to the right. Go as far as possible. Try to achieve a right angle to your lower body. Go only as far as you can and when there, hold for a count of ten and return to an erect position. Now repeat to the left. Hold for ten and return. The final move is forward. Bend to a right angle, hold for ten, and return. Move very slowly, feeling the stretch and the contraction. When you have done all three moves, bring your arms down to your side and relax. Sense the feeling of relaxation. Repeat the entire sequence five times.

**Wall Reach; Sky Reach; Shoulder Roll, Back Reach; Shoulder Elevation**

Chances are that you have noticed in yourself or others that after hours of writing or other deskwork the natural tendency is to try to stretch out those cramped fingers, elbows, and shoulders. It is a natural reaction, but most people start too late. First of all, they should have prepared themselves better, and second, they should have stopped more frequently and stretched before cramps developed. That is the purpose of this set of exercises. The emphasis is on the relaxation that follows the recoil of the stretch. Sense it, and sense the difference between that feeling and muscle tension.

The first exercise in this group is the wall reach (Figure 15.9), which is done in the standing position. Stand in front of a wall so that your outstretched arms just reach the wall. Place the palms of your hands against the wall. Now step back about six inches. Extending your arms primarily from the shoulder, reach for the wall. At the same time spread your fingers and extend them backward. When you make contact with the wall, your shoulder, elbow, wrist, and finger joints should be at full extension and stretch. Hold the stretch for a count of five and return. Repeat five times.

**FIGURE 15.6**

Standing Trunk
Bend (first part)

## FIGURE 15.7

Standing Trunk
Bend (second part)

**FIGURE 15.8**

Standing Trunk
Bend (final part)

The next one, the sky reach (Figure 15.10), is very similar except that your arms are outstretched over your head. At full reach pause, then with shoulder movement reach a few inches farther, almost as if you were taking something from a shelf just inches out of your reach or as if you were reaching for the sky. The movement is in the shoulder, so be sure not to rise onto your toes. At maximal extension, hold for a count of five and return to rest. Repeat five times.

While you are standing, do the third exercise, the shoulder roll (Figure 15.11). Clasp your hands behind your back. The object is to roll your shoulders by first dropping them to the lowest possible point, rolling them back, then up as in a shoulder shrug, and then forward before they are lowered once again. Complete five circles and return to rest.

**FIGURE 15.9**

Wall Reach

FIGURE 15.10

Sky Reach

## FIGURE 15.11

Shoulder Roll

**FIGURE 15.12**

Back Reach

The next exercise, the back reach (Figure 15.12), can be done while standing or while sitting, if the back of the chair is not high. Raise your arms above your head and clasp your hands together. Then bend your arms back so that your hands touch the back of your neck. Pause and then stretch so that your hands touch a point farther down your back. Hold the extreme position for a count of five, then rest. Repeat five times.

The last exercise, shoulder elevation (Figure 15.13), is done while either sitting on the floor or standing. Clasp your hands behind your back, allowing them to rest comfortably against your buttocks. Keeping your back straight, raise your arms as high as possible. Hold in the extreme position for a count of five and return to the resting position, but do not unclasp hands. Feel the stretch in shoulders, elbows, and wrists. Feel the relaxation as you return to rest. Repeat five times.

FIGURE 15.13

Shoulder Elevation

# CHAPTER SIXTEEN

# Stress Reduction Through Physical Activity

A number of relaxation techniques have been presented so far in this book, and in the final analysis these techniques share the denominators of ego loss and body awareness. This chapter presents a natural body-emphasis technique that is absolute knowledge to all who love to lose themselves in physical activity—to revert to an original mind–body unity, to rediscover play. Physical activity is a natural way of putting mind and body back together. The movements of dancing, running, skiing, and walking through the woods are natural and necessary for normal growth and development.

Under the influence of the dualistic philosophy, the mind became of great importance to mankind, and the body was left with relative unimportance, except when in ill health. The pendulum started to swing toward the mind when man found that the mind could accomplish more than the body through its use of written and stored information, the basis of technology. The body had been quite perfected by this time and with no great need for bionics, it lived in harmony with mind and nature. It was delicately balanced, with an innate drive to conserve energy—energy gained equaled that expended. (If the movement involved in gaining food expended more energy than the food provided, the person would quickly perish.) Thus, all species survived by becoming efficient, by reading the current and swimming only when necessary. We began to let the mind work while the body conserved its energy, and the mind began to think of ways of extending the body without expending human energy—enter the machine. Through use, the mind grew into the fantastic organ that we still don't fully understand.

To that innate drive of energy conservation man added a

learned one of time efficiency. Reducing the time involved in one activity allows for completion of more activities. The mind is responsible for technological advances, so it is no wonder that development of the mind has taken precedence over development of the body. But as we move away from a mere survival epoch to one of life quality, we have begun to ask the questions: "Save energy for what?" "Save time to do what?" We have also begun to realize that physical inactivity results in degenerative disease and have found it increasingly difficult to cope with the mental overstimulation that accompanies rapid technological growth. Perhaps this is an epoch in which we allow the body to "catch up" with the giant strides of the mind.

The physical nature of man has gone through a resurgence, but instead of casting off technology, we have learned to live with it by replacing physical work with "artificial work" in the form of recreational activity. The difficulty in finding an open tennis court, the packed ski-area parking lots, and the colorful world of runners' warm-up suits all attest to the fact that physical activity is making a strong comeback. In conjunction with its recreational nature, physical activity is regaining recognition for its potential as a relaxation technique, which is in some ways similar to those already discussed, but with several unique characteristics as well.

Relaxation techniques such as meditation, neuromuscular relaxation, or autogenic training are highly preventive in nature; they contribute little to alleviation of tension once the stress response has occurred. A primary contribution of physical activity, on the other hand, is the alleviation of stress-product buildup, with prevention being a secondary aspect. This being the case, we will focus here on three aspects of physical activity: (1) using activity to dissipate or use up the stress products produced by fear, threat to the ego, or by whatever has evoked the hormonal and nervous systems into defensive posture, (2) using exercise preventively to decrease one's reactivity to future stress, and (3) using physical activity on a high-level motivation plane involving a feeling of well-being, tranquility, and transcendence.

## PHYSICAL ACTIVITY AS TREATMENT

Let us look at the treatment role of physical activity in stress management by focusing on a particular problem. Imagine yourself in your work situation being asked to give more time than you can give to do more work than you can possibly accomplish. Then imagine that your personal relations at home begin to be strained because of the overload, the high work expectations on you. Your family wants more of your time. An underlying state of tension is becoming a part of your life, and you begin to doubt your personal effectiveness. Then the crowning blow comes—you are berated in front of your coworkers by your boss and you undergo a massive stress response. Anger, fear, indignation, and rage boil through your body. This is the response we have described many times before—the hormonal and nervous systems ready the body for fight or flight. Now is the time to do one of these, and do it *physically*.

It is important to understand that the stress response endowed in us was intended to end in physical activity. The outpouring of sugar and fats into the blood are meant to feed the muscles and the brain so that they might contend actively with the stressor that has provoked the system. The dilation of pupils occurs to give better visual acuity, to take in apparent threats visually. The increased heart and respiration rates are to pump blood and oxygen to active muscles and stimulated control centers in the brain. This is not a time to sit and feel all of these sensations tearing away at the body's systems and eroding good health. This is the time to *move*, to use up the products, to relieve the body of the destructive forces of stress on a sedentary system. Appropriate activity in this case would be total-body exercise such as swimming; running; dancing; biking; or an active individual, dual, or team sport that lasts at least one hour. (This is assuming you are in adequate physical condition to perform the task.) Such activities will use up the stress products that might otherwise be harmful and that are likely to play a part in a degenerative disease process such as cardiovascular disease or ulcers.

We have mentioned that during the stress response the two adrenal medullar hormones epinephrine and norepinephrine are pumped into the system to ready the body for fight or flight. In laboratory experiments, when norepinephrine is injected into the body, it causes the feeling of underlying anxiety until a social situation triggers a known emotion. For example, if an individual is injected with norepinephrine and is then annoyed by someone, the reported feeling is one of anger; if intimidated by someone or a situation, the feeling reported is one of fear. As norepinephrine is a product of the stress response, it makes the individual highly volatile and vulnerable to adverse emotions if it is not used for its intended purpose—physical activity. The mental and emotional implications here should be apparent. How many times under stress do you "fly off the handle" at very little provocation?

A crystal-clear picture that should be forming is that Mother Nature intended that the stress response be nothing more than preparation for physical activity. Thus, a natural release, which is also increasingly socially acceptable for everyone, is no less than body movement. It is a treatment form that everyone can afford.

This treatment is notably used by two professional coaches. A former Redskin coach would go out and run after football games to wear off the stress products and bring himself down after the game. The other, a basketball coach, has four piles of dirt in his backyard and moves dirt pile A to spot B and so on until his stress level subsides. In American life, we are all coaches of sort—we watch the game being played, we get emotionally involved, and then we sit back and suffer the consequences of not interacting physically. The key factor for all of us is to *recognize* when we're stressed and *act physically* on that response soon after (Mobily, 1982).

## PHYSICAL ACTIVITY IN THE PREVENTION OF DISEASE

The second nature of physical activity is that of prophylaxis— preventive treatment. The value of physical activity in preventing the untoward effects of stress are such that if they could be bottled and sold for people to take a dose a day, the bottle and sales agents would be rich beyond compare, so effective is the product.

Deep within most of us we fear abnormality of the heart; if it beats too fast or too loudly or "skips a beat" we become anxious, because we *are* this muscular organ—when it expires, we are expired! The heart, just like other muscles, is the epitome of *syntropy*—it becomes stronger as we use it appropriately. Exercise is a stressor, so it forces the body to adapt to the stressor. The heart gains in muscular strength during exercise, and that strength carries into the resting state. When it is strong, fewer beats are required to supply the body with blood, so the heart gets more rest and relaxation time (Jerome, 1982).

The respiratory system reacts to exercise in the same syntropic manner, increasing its capacity to take in air and exchange oxygen for carbon dioxide at the capillary level. This respiratory efficiency also carries over into the resting state.

The working muscles, the hormonal system, metabolic reactions, the responsiveness of the central nervous system—all the systems of the body—react in a like manner to physical activity, strengthening one's ability to cope.

The unifying feature here is that (1) during activity the body reacts in an ergotropic manner, that is, all systems are stimulated for action, and (2) that after physical activity, the systems are slowed down in a trophotropic manner, dominated by the parasympathetic nervous system, causing tranquility. About ninety minutes after a good physical bout of exercise there occurs a feeling of deep relaxation. If you are a consistent exerciser, you know that feeling and perhaps are aware of its lasting effects throughout the day. The relaxation that comes after exercise brings with it a certain imperturbability, a lowered resting reactivity to the environment, which helps the regular exerciser to react more appropriately to stimuli. The step is a little lighter, the attitude more positive, and it takes more to get upset.

In using activity as a preventive agent, you should use up stress products daily rather than wait for a psychosocial stressor to trigger the system. This calls for a regular exercise regime. In a preventive exercise program your motivation is of a higher level than the urge to run or hit a ball against a wall when angry or upset. Because of this difference in intensity of purpose, a regular pattern of exercise must somehow be rewarded in its initial stages until it becomes a reward in itself. Exercising with a partner, joining a club, or making certain to engage in an enjoyable activity is helpful for this purpose (Sailer, Schlachter, & Edwards, 1982).

**EXERCISE FOR WELL–BEING, TRANQUILITY, AND TRANSCENDENCE**

The highest purpose of physical exercise is that of well-being: participating because it feels right (and conversely, feels wrong when you don't), because it enhances positive feelings toward yourself that bounce off others as positive energy, because it helps make life complete. The tranquility state, the oneness, the internal calm experienced by those who really become involved in their activity make the prospect of a regular exercise program intriguing.

Exercise is a natural form of expression. We were made to move. And when we do, if social sanctions against it are not too harsh on our psychological acceptance of the activity, we rediscover the original unifying thread of mind and body. It makes us feel naturally healthy, just as we feel we know that we're eating the right foods and dealing with social problems in a self-enhancing manner. But we cannot achieve this feeling unless we enter into activity in a *noncompetitive* way.

**Ego-Void Exercise**

All three aspects of physical activity—treatment, prevention, and especially enhanced well-being—share an important feature: In order to get all the benefits of the exercise, you must choose an activity that is *not ego-involved.* Playing a highly competitive game of golf and wrapping a putter around a tree is not a relaxing activity. Nor is a game of tennis when your ego is on the line. This is one reason why singular activities such as running, biking, or skiing often have greater relaxation rewards than competitive sports in which winning is more important than playing your best.

We are competitive people with a competitive heritage. We compete for money, jobs, space, and glorification of the ego. It may seem odd that our leisure and recreation activities, intended as diversions from competition are themselves competitive. We become conditioned to seek ego enhancement from beating others, and there is no reason to believe we can stop competing just because we are not on the job—the drive to win carries over into all aspects of life. Most of us measure ourselves by comparing ourselves to others. As was mentioned, exercise will burn off much of the stress arousal products, but as Kriegel (1984) points out, competition often creates *more* stress in the form of lingering self-doubt, anger, and embarrassment. Think about your recreational activities. How transcendental are they? Do you lose your sense of time, do the hours seem like minutes? Or do you lose your temper and/or patience with yourself and others? Do you lose your sense of self? Or are you constantly "seeing yourself" and admonishing yourself for bad performance?

Competitive sports are not the only leisure activities that are the culprits here. Performance of singular activities (such as running or skiing) are no guarantee of ego transcendence. "Can I run three miles? Am I running as fast today as yesterday? What if I can't make it the entire distance? I really don't have it any more. Why can't I make a simple parallel turn? Mary can do it, why can't I? I don't think I am skiing any better this year than last year." Some activities are not directly competitive, with a winner and loser in each event, but we can make them competitive by constantly rating our performance against our past performances or against the performances of others (we can even take it upon ourselves to compare our performance with that of a professional athlete!). More importantly, we allow the performance to influence our feelings about ourselves. "It seems as though any reasonably intelligent and halfway coordinated person should be able to learn to ski in a year, so why can't I? What kind of a man can't even run one mile without stopping?" This is the "terrible athlete, therefore terrible person" syndrome.

In two important books on play, Tim Gallwey (Gallwey, 1976; Gallwey & Kriegel, 1977) explained the ego-void state, called *Self II*, as the noncritical, inherent athlete in all of us who can perform without constant self-instruction. It is the part of us that hits that "lucky shot" and is responsible for the better performance that often paradoxically accompanies not really trying. Unfortunately, most of us have enslaved our Self II by our critical, ego-protecting, self-directing Self I. Again, we might look at conditioned response in our society. We have spent so many years of our education in learning and analyzing, with our minds in total control, that we have lost faith and ability to let Self II take over, to get lost in the joy of the movement, to flow with the feeling of the activity, and to correct movements through somatic and visual feedback, not through highly critical cognitive analysis in which we paralyze ourselves by overanalysis.

## High-Risk Activity

Each year more people than ever take to what is called high-risk recreation. They try to exist in the wilderness for days with no food, tents, or weapons; climb high mountains; navigate wild rivers; and do other dangerous activities. Educators have even organized such activities in Outward Bound programs for rehabilitative purposes ("Outward Bound for Inward Change," 1980). The reasons for the upsurge in the popularity of high-risk activities are numerous, but one that stands out is the pleasure and exhilaration the individual receives from success. Many of these situations are "dare not lose" (in the sense that to lose would mean death), so survival is winning. More important, survival is possible only if one totally concentrates on the activity. The innate survival instinct takes over and "demands" total attention. There is no one to clap when you make a good shot or boo when you don't. You don't worry about the appropriateness of your dress, and you cannot allow yourself the luxury of self-indulgence. There are no "what if's."

This was vividly experienced not long ago while we were doing some "light" mountain climbing. (The term "light" is used to avoid giving the false impression that we were climbing Mt. Everest. In "heavy" climbing, you can kill yourself by falling a mile to your death, whereas in light climbing, you fall only half a mile!) Without really intending to do so, we found ourselves in a situation clearly beyond our expectation of danger. Too far up a cliff (of what appeared to be pleasantly climbable boulders) to turn back—climbing down a cliff is more difficult than climbing up it—we went on, vowing to help each other and carefully analyzing each rock, each foothold, each move before making it. The hours passed like minutes; fear was present only in brief fleeting moments when we stopped to rest or thought about the other person falling. While in motion, it was difficult to feel fear, for we didn't really exist, we were "climbing machines" concentrating on the terrain. Although we analyzed our moves, it was in a calculating and businesslike way, with little or no thought to how we looked, what our form was like, nor to the consequences of failure. "Up" was assumed, "down" was not an alternative. The view from the top was more exhilarating than the view from any mountain ten times its majesty that we have easily hiked. We were fatigued, but not tired. We felt alert, alive, and part of that mountain. We had succeeded.

In the following activity self-assessment, if you score below 40 points, you are a very sedentary person and should consider en-

## ACTIVITY SELF–ASSESSMENT

The following self-assessment of your activity level lists activities that are part of the daily routine for many people. In addition, a sample of other activities is given. If you engage in an activity other than that listed, try to approximate that activity with one given here and use the points accorded to it. After completing the exercise, you will have twenty-four hours of activity listed. For each hour or partial hour, multiply the weighted score given for the activity and then total the points. This is your physical-activity score.

After filling out the activity assessment, answer the four questions dealing with your motivational state and physical activity.

*How many hours per day do you spend:*

| | | | | |
|---|---|---|---|---|
| Sleeping | _____ | hours | @ .85 points/hr. | _____ |
| Sitting | | | @ 1.5 points/hr. | _____ |
|   Riding/driving | _____ | hours | | |
|   Study/deskwork | _____ | hours | | |
|   Meals | _____ | hours | | |
|   Watching TV | _____ | hours | | |
|   Reading | _____ | hours | | |
|   Other | _____ | hours | | |
| | _____ | hours | | |
| | _____ | hours | (total sitting x 1.5) | _____ |
| Standing | | | @ 2 points/hr. | _____ |
|   Standing | _____ | hours | | |
|   Dressing | _____ | hours | | |
|   Showering | _____ | hours | | |
|   Other | _____ | hours | | |
| | _____ | hours | | |
| | _____ | hours | (total standing x 2) | _____ |
| Walking | | | | |
|   Slow walk | _____ | hours | @ 3 points/hr. | _____ |
|   Moderate speed | _____ | hours | @ 4 points/hr. | _____ |
|   Very fast walk | _____ | hours | @ 5 points/hr. | _____ |
| Occupational | | | | |
|   Housework, | | | | |
|   Light physical work | _____ | hours | @ 3 points/hr. | _____ |
| Heavy total-body physical exertion | | | | |
|   Rapid calisthenics | _____ | hours | @ 4 points/hr. | _____ |
| Slow run (jog) | _____ | hours | @ 6 points/hr. | _____ |
|   Fast run | _____ | hours | @ 7 points/hr. | _____ |
| Recreational | | | | |
|   racket sports | _____ | hours | @ 8 points/hr. | _____ |
| Competitive sports | _____ | hours | @ 9–10 points/hr. | _____ |
| Stair climbing | _____ | hours | @ 8 points/hr. | _____ |
| *Total hours* | 24 | | *Total Points* | _____ |

| | | | | |
|---|---|---|---|---|
| Do you have an exercise outlet for stress buildup? | Yes _____ | No _____ |
| Do you use it? | Yes _____ | No _____ |
| Do you exercise regularly for its preventive rewards? | Yes _____ | No _____ |
| Have you discovered the transcendental nature of exercise? | Yes _____ | No _____ |

gaging in an activity higher in the point system than the activities you usually engage in. If you score above 55, you are probably enjoying the benefits of physical activity. Everyone who is physically able should have some regular activity worth more than 5 points per hour. To be a "regular exerciser" you should perform that activity five times a week for at least half an hour per session.

Concerning the last four questions on the exercise, if you do not use physical activity to burn off stress products, try it. Choose an activity compatible to you and your lifestyle (Table 16.1 may be of help) and try it out the next time you can't seem to calm down after a confrontation. Do it long enough for it to be physically effective—you'll need to walk longer than you would run to use up similar energy products. If you find you can tolerate this activity, try doing it regularly so you can keep a low stress profile. And if you really learn to love the activity, you will recognize the rewards and want to pass them on to others.

## ADOPTING AN EXERCISE PROGRAM

### Benefits

The benefits of regular exercise are worth the effort it may take to overcome inertia and begin an exercise program. In addition to the stress-management benefits that have been outlined in this chapter there are other parameters that have not yet been mentioned or may help to explain why a fitness program contributes to stress management. These benefits include:

### Stronger Heart and Better "Tuning" of the Heartbeat

The heart is a muscle that increases in size and strength from use. It is the prime mover of blood throughout the body in order for tissues to get oxygen and nutrients. Regular aerobic activity puts overload demands on the myocardial tissue, which responds by becoming stronger. As the heart becomes stronger, it can pump out more blood per beat, resulting in a slower resting heart rate. Aerobic training also changes the timing of the heart so that the heart spends less time in contraction and more time at rest. During the rest portion of the heart cycle, blood flows into the emptied cavities and also through the coronary arteries (the arteries that feed the heart muscle itself). This leaves more time for unrestricted blood flow to the myocardium, which in turn allows better nutrient flow and removal of wastes.

### Increased Muscle Strength and Endurance

Exercise involving the large muscle groups helps develop the size and fluid capacity of the muscles through greater capillarization,

**TABLE 16.1  Activity Chart**

| ACTIVITY | ENERGY USE* | ADVANTAGES | POSSIBLE DISADVANTAGES** |
|---|---|---|---|
| Walking | + + | No cost, no equipment, no special facilities. Everyone can participate. Year-round activity. | Time commitment, must walk fast for conditioning effect. |
| Jogging (less than five miles per hour) | + + + | Promotes weight loss, leg strength, cardiovascular endurance. No special facilities. | May be hard on knees and other joints. Must have physical checkup, proper shoes. |
| Running (more than five miles per hour) | + + + + | Promotes weight loss, cardiovascular conditioning, and well-being. | Must have physical checkup, good shoes. Can be hard on joints. |
| Dancing (vigorous, fast dances) | + + + | Promotes weight control, total-body conditioning, esp. aerobic dancing (doing cardiovascular exercises to music). Year-round activity. | Must be brisk for conditioning. Requires coordination, rhythm for set dance patterns. May be hard on joints. |
| Biking | + + + | Good cardiovascular conditioning, promotes weight control, easier on joints than walking, jogging, running. Energy-saving transportation. | Danger from autos, cost of bike, requires learned skill. |
| Alpine skiing | + + + | Promotes total body conditioning, esp. legs. Enjoyable, apt to promote well-being. | Requires learned skill, expensive equipment. Can be dangerous, esp. if not in condition, from falls, cold weather, and altitude. Seasonal. |
| Cross-country skiing | + + + + | Excellent for cardiovascular conditioning, total-body fitness. Little jar to body joints. Apt to promote well-being. | Requires some learned skill, special equipment. Cold and altitude may be a negative factor. Seasonal. |
| Swimming | + + + | Excellent for cardiovascular conditioning and muscle toning. No jar to joints. | Requires some skill, pool, minimum cost of swimsuit. |
| Racket sport (tennis, squash, racketball) | + + + (+) | Excellent total-body conditioner if fast game is played. Promotes weight loss. | Requires learned skill, special equipment and facilities. Must play at high level for conditioning effect. |
| Golf (walk, carry own clubs) | + + | Enjoyable and relaxing if not self-critical. Some of the same benefits of walking. | Requires learned skill, special equipment. Walking briskly without intermittent stops is a better conditioner. |
| Bowling | + | Relaxing and enjoyable if not self-critical. Better than just sitting. | Almost no conditioning effect. Requires learned skill and special equipment. Not recommended as treatment or preventive relaxation technique. |

**TABLE 16.1  (Continued)**

| ACTIVITY | ENERGY USE* | ADVANTAGES | POSSIBLE DISADVANTAGES** |
|---|---|---|---|
| Calisthenics | + + | Brisk, total-body exercises have conditioning value, esp. muscle toning. No cost, little or no equipment. Year-round activity. | May exacerbate existing muscle problems. Tendency to overdo initially. |
| Weight lifting | + + | Increases strength, improves physique and may improve self-image. Can improve cardiovascular efficiency by lifting lighter weights for greater repetitions or by circuit training. | Requires special equipment. Some risk of muscular injury unless properly trained and prudently utilized. |

*All energy use, of course, depends on the intensity at which one pursues the activity, so only a relative rating system is used here. One "+" denotes least strenuous activity and minimal energy use, while four "+" signs denote highest energy use.
**A possible disadvantage in most of these activities is high-level, ego-involved competition.

increased muscle-fiber mass, and greater efficiency of contraction. Since muscles act as pumps to help blood return to the heart, they develop a positive feedback cycle: They send more blood back to the heart, and the heart pumps out more nutrients and oxygen to the muscles. Without the help of the muscles to send blood back to the heart, the heart takes on the full load of pumping blood throughout the system. This is why it is physiologically correct to cool down slowly rather than just stop after vigorous activity.

### Increased Lung Capacity
Just as in other deep-breathing relaxation exercises, vigorous aerobic activity demands that the lungs expand and the diaphragm drop, which helps squeeze blood from the trunk back to the heart. In addition, intercostal muscles are strengthened and greater oxygenation of the blood occurs.

### Stronger Bones
When the long bones of the body are stressed with exercise, they respond by becoming more dense (thus stronger). This has important implications for those who are vulnerable to osteoporosis.

### Improved Serum-Cholesterol Level and HDL/LDL Ratio
Chronic aerobic exercisers have higher HDL (high-density lipoprotein—as opposed to low-density lipoprotein [LDL]) levels than nonexercisers. HDLs are blood constituents that carry cholesterol

to storage, getting it out of the blood stream so that it is not as likely to be involved in atherosclerotic plaquing of the smooth arterial walls.

### Improved Body Composition

As an individual becomes involved in an aerobic program, the body begins to use up adipose (fat) tissue and develop more muscle tissue. Fat pads diminish, and muscular curves develop and become more apparent. An aerobic exercise program is a must for weight management.

### Increased Range of Motion

As a safety measure, part of every exercise program involves stretching exercises. Without this kind of exercise, the muscles become organized at the semicontracted length and may create muscle cramps, soreness, and chronic pain. The exerciser should be able to enjoy a full range of motion in all muscles. As discussed in Chapter 15, stretching exercises also stimulate the relaxation response.

### Greater Efficiency, Attention, and Economy of Movement

Another safety factor and stress-management benefit of a regular physical activity program is that the body becomes more efficient, cutting down on useless expenditure of energy. It is the difference between the beginning swimmer who thrashes around in the pool, expending great amounts of energy, and the trained swimmer who uses only the necessary energy to get from one end of the pool to the other. Since an activity program contributes to the alleviation of fatigue and anxiety, less meaningless activity is generated in this way.

### Greater Alertness

Aerobic fitness improves nerve transactions throughout the body. All electrochemical transactions become more efficient, resulting in greater overall alertness and awareness.

### Diminished Effects of Aging

Many of the characteristics that we attribute to the aging process are those that characterize the unfit individual. If we were to state the opposing side of each of the nine items just listed, we would get a picture of a debilitating process: inflexibility, low endurance, brittle bones, low respiratory capacity, creeping obesity, less alertness and awareness, and so on. When comparing our senior citizens, those who have been more physically active throughout their lives and continue to engage in vigorous activity appear to be younger and healthier than their nonactive counterparts.

The benefits outlined here, along with the specific stress-management benefits discussed earlier, are compelling evidence that everyone should conduct a personal exercise program. The latter part of this chapter gives a description of how to set up such a program.

**Preprogram Guidelines and Principles**

Before starting an exercise program, consider the five following principles and guidelines to help you understand and enjoy exercise and the physical conditioning you will see and feel in yourself.

### Regularity

The most beneficial exercise is regular exercise. Set up specific days and hours for exercise and stick to them. Most colleges offer regular exercise programs either in physical education classes or in intramural sports. Most cities also have recreation programs that offer a variety of physical activities.

If you are planning your own program, set aside three to five hours a week for vigorous exercise. If you take a formal exercise class, complement it with an independent program on weekends. Three to five one-hour periods of activity per week should provide a good exercise program.

### Variety

A total fitness program includes stretching, muscle-strengthening exercises, and aerobic activity. A mixture of these will keep your fitness program interesting and beneficial.

### The Overload Principle

In order to increase physical strength and endurance, you must push yourself beyond what you can easily do. For example, if you can walk at a brisk pace without being out of breath, you must move faster—at a jog or run—in order to improve your aerobic capacity. If you can easily lift and use a ten-pound dumbbell, a heavier one is necessary to develop your arm muscles beyond their present state. Throughout a fitness program, work with greater resistance until it feels comfortable and then increase the resistance again. When you get to the level of fitness at which you are aiming, level off with a maintenance program (that is, maintain the same strength and endurance level without adding more resistance).

In order for exercise to contribute to a stress-management program it is not necessary to strive for marathon endurance or the strength of an Olympic weight lifter. However, the greatest benefits to all-around health demand that the program increases your fitness level rather than just giving you sporadic exercise.

### Warm Up

Before exercising, it is always necessary to spend from five to ten minutes or more warming up your muscles for better performance and to prevent injury to muscle fibers. Just as you should warm up your car in the winter before racing off, you should warm up your body before demanding contraction of the muscle fibers.

### Cool Down

After vigorous exercise, spend between five and ten minutes cooling down. Walk slowly until your heart rate slows toward normal and stretch the muscles you have just worked.

The following sections discuss each of the three basic kinds of activities that should constitute an activity program: (1) aerobic exercise, (2) flexibility or stretching exercises, and (3) muscular-strength and endurance exercises.

## AN AEROBICS PROGRAM

Most of the benefits of physical fitness come from an aerobics program; that is, activities that are vigorous, rhythmic, and involve the large muscle groups of the body. Cardiorespiratory fitness is effectively enhanced when an individual works at 60 percent of maximum capacity or more, capacity being measured according to heart rate.

## Heart Rate

Your heart rate tells you two important things about aerobic exercise: (1) How vigorous the activity must be for you to benefit from the exercise, and (2) how your system is responding to the exercise program, as reflected by your resting heart rate.

To find out how strenuous your workouts should be, you must have several items of information. One is your *resting heart rate.* Take your pulse for sixty seconds while lying in bed after just waking up. Your pulse is located on the thumb side of your wrist, on the outer side of the tendon that goes down to your hand. It is also located at your temples and other pressure points on your body, including the neck. However, when pressure is applied to the neck to find a pulse rate, the heart responds to the pressure and a true reading may not be taken.

Take your pulse several mornings in a row and average the three mornings. Enter your resting heart rate here:

Date _____   Resting heart rate _____

A second item of information you need to have is your *maximal heart rate*. The formula to determine this is 226 (for females) or 220 (for males) minus your age. Your maximal heart rate tells you how fast your heart can beat under a strenuous workload. The figures for men and women are slightly different because women apparently have a slightly higher maximal capacity (Karvonen, 1959). Enter your maximal heart rate here:

Women: 226 – _____ (age) = _____ (beats per minute)

Men: 220 – _____ (age) = _____ (beats per minute)

When you begin an aerobic or a maintenance program, you must determine your starting abilities. If you are minimally fit (that is, if even minor exertion is exhausting for you), you should begin your aerobic program at 50 to 60 percent of your maximal capacity. As your program gets easier for you, you can increase the load to 60 to 70 percent and higher. If you already engage in vigorous activity, begin your program at 70 to 80 percent maximal. If you are highly trained and very physically fit, you will want to use a range of 80 to 90 percent.

The last item of information that you must have is how to calculate your *training heart rate*. To do this, take 60, 70, 80, and 90 percent of your maximal heart rate. For example, a twenty-year-old male would have a maximal heart rate of 200. Sixty percent of that is 120 beats per minute. Seventy percent of 200 is 140. If this individual is beginning a program at a 60 to 70 percent range of maximal, he should keep his heart rate between 120 to 140 beats per minute during his workout. As he becomes conditioned during his program, he will move up to a 70 to 80 percent range, which then demands that he keep his heart rate between 140 and 160 beats per minute.

When you are doing aerobic exercise, it is important to keep moving slowly as you take your heart rate so that you do not let blood pool in the lower extremities with only the heart beat to pump the blood back up the body. When you move, your legs work as muscle pumps to continually squeeze blood back up to the heart. For this reason, it is recommended that rather than take the pulse for sixty seconds, you take it for six seconds and multiply by ten.

To easily identify whether you are working within your target range, divide the top and bottom figures of the range by ten to identify what a six-second reading should be. In the example above, when working at a 60 to 70 percent range, this man's six-second pulse should be between 12 and 14. When taking a six-second pulse, always count the first pulse as zero in case you just missed a beat. It is better to err on the low side than on the high side.

To determine how intensely you must exercise to get to your training heart rate range, you must experiment. Begin walking at a slow pace for two minutes, then take your six-second pulse. If your heart rate is too slow, pick up the pace and repeat. Repeat this process until you find an intensity that will lift you into your range and keep you there. Take your pulse immediately after you exercise, because your heart rate starts to slow down as soon as you slow down.

It is extremely important that you adhere to your beginning heart-rate range to avoid burnout. Many people who start an exercise program are so highly motivated that they try to get all the benefits in just one day. They exercise too strenuously for too long a time, ending up with aching muscles, joints, and bones, and decide that exercise is not for them.

## Intensity and Duration

An aerobic program will not maximally benefit you unless its intensity is at your training heart rate and its duration is at least fifteen minutes. However, there is an inverse relationship between intensity and duration that makes it possible to gain training effects at lower intensity levels if the duration is longer. This means that even a low-intensity walking program will give you training effects if you walk for a long period of time. Performing an exercise for 3 hours at a heart rate of 110 beats per minute will give you the same training effect as performing one for twenty minutes at a rate of 140 beats per minute (Cooper, 1970).

The American College of Sports Medicine (1986) suggests that you expend a minimum of 300 calories per session in an aerobic exercise program. This might translate into forty to fifty minutes of moderate intensity exercise at 60 to 80 percent of maximal capacity or perhaps twenty to thirty minutes of moderately high-intensity exercise at 80 to 90 percent.

When beginning a program, the duration of exercise should be lower, perhaps as little as five to ten minutes per day (especially if fitness level is very low). Duration should then increase progressively.

## Summary

For developing and maintaining cardiorespiratory fitness, perform large-muscle, rhythmic exercise three to five days a week, fifteen to sixty minutes per workout at 60 to 90 percent of your maximal heart rate.

When you choose an activity, keep your interests, abilities, and objectives in mind. Make sure the activities you choose are compatible with your lifestyle.

Set realistic short- and long-term goals for yourself and keep track of your progress. This helps in motivation and adherence to the program.

Get assistance in starting your program if you need more information, or even for motivation. It may be helpful to work out with others.

Always warm up and cool down.

Aerobic exercises include running, jogging, walking, cycling, rowing, cross-country skiing, aerobic dance, rope skipping, hiking, swimming, bench stepping. Depending on how they are played, many games, such as handball, racquetball, soccer, tennis, and basketball, may be aerobic.

Intermittent activity or activity of low energy output has little effect on increasing cardiovascular fitness.

## A FLEXIBILITY PROGRAM

Stretching exercises are essential to any fitness program. Exercises such as the ones discussed in the previous chapter should be performed for your relaxation program, as well as a part of your aerobic activity. The key to safe, effective stretching is slow, constant pressure. Do not bounce—it may cause harm.

## MUSCULAR– STRENGTH AND ENDURANCE PROGRAMS

Two kinds of programs to develop muscular strength and endurance are available. One is a weightlifting program in which dumbbells, barbells, or machines are used for resistance. These programs are becoming very popular with both men and women and are available in schools, recreation centers, and workout studios. The second program involves using yourself as the resistance. The exercises in this kind of program are often called calisthenics. Whichever program you choose, follow the safety guidelines that apply to the kinds of exercises you will be doing.

The exercises suggested here are the kind that do not necessitate the use of equipment. Although it is not an extensive program, we have included exercises that will strengthen the major muscle groups of the body. From these exercises choose one or more activity for each muscle group. Do the program at least three times per week before or independently of, your aerobic workout. For strength, perform ten repetitions (reps) at a high resistance. For endurance, perform at least twenty-five reps at a lower resistance. After each set of exercises, the muscles involved should feel well worked.

Begin your program by doing one set for each muscle group at a low number of reps. After your muscles become used to the routine, work up to ten reps. When that becomes comfortable, add another set. Work up to three sets. Perhaps the most important principle here is GO SLOWLY. If exercise hurts, you will be less likely to continue it.

**Arms and Shoulders**

No exercise is more appropriate for this body area than the push-up. The following series is graded from easy to difficult. Find the level that fits you and progress from there.

### Wall Push-away

Stand at an arm's length from a wall, place your palms on the wall, and let your body move toward the wall by bending your arms. Now push your body away from the wall, keeping your body straight. If you can do ten reps easily, move your feet farther from the wall and repeat. If that is still too easy, move on to level 2.

### Square-body Knee Push-up

Support yourself on your hands and knees on the floor. Keeping your body bent at the hips, lower yourself to the floor and push yourself back up. If this is too easy, move on to level 3.

### Straight-body Knee Push-up

Support yourself on your hands and knees, keeping your body straight from knees to shoulders. Lower your body and push yourself back up. If you are "giving" in the hips as you come up, go back to level 2.

### Straight-body Push-up from the Toes

Support yourself on your hands and toes, keeping your body straight from shoulders to toes. If you sag or bend in the hips as you push yourself up, go back to level 3.

### Toe Push-up from an Elevated Surface

Get into a straight-body toe push-up position with your toes on an elevated surface such as a step or low ledge. Do your push-ups from that position, keeping your body straight.

**Abdominals**

The straight-leg sit-up is no longer used because of back and leg muscle involvement. To use only the abdominal muscles, the knees are bent, and in some cases elevated. Each of the following exercises demands use of different abdominal muscles, so do ten reps of each.

### Bent-knee, Elevated-feet Curl-up

Lie on your back with your knees bent at a 90 degree angle, feet on a chair seat or other elevated surface. Fold your arms across your chest. Pulling your chin to your chest, curl your upper back off the floor. Be sure to curl up rather than keeping the back rigid.

### Pole Pivots

Put a four-to-five-foot pole (such as a ski pole) on your shoulders, grasping each end of the pole with the hands. With your body facing forward, rotate the upper body ninety degrees to the left and then to the right.

### Knee Lifts

Support yourself on your forearms on parallel bars and lift your knees toward your chest. If you cannot pull both legs up at the same time, bring one knee up at a time (as though running in place). Lift the knees as high as possible.

**Legs and Buttocks**

Most aerobic exercises will strengthen these areas, but running stairs and bench stepping are particularly good for them. Most neighborhoods have a school with a fieldhouse, gym, or stadium complete with tiers of stairs. The main precaution in this exercise is to keep your eyes on the next step. Work your way around the field house or stadium, running up section A, walking across and then down section B as you recover. This gives a good series of reps and recovery phases.

Bench stepping is done by stepping up and down from the floor to a bench or some other elevated surface such as a stair step or the side of a bathtub. Sequence of stepping is left, right, left, right as you step up, up, down, down. The height of the elevated surface and the cadence you set depend on your training heart-rate range and whether you wish to work specifically on strength or endurance—or both. Experiment with different heights and speeds until you find what intensity is best for you. When using this exercise for muscular strength, use a higher bench and do fewer reps (for example, three to five minutes). For muscular and cardiovascular endurance, use a lower step and do more reps (for example, five to fifteen minutes or more).

**Back**

Upper- or lower-body lifts are good back strengtheners. The easier kind is to lie face down on the floor, hands behind your head, and lift your legs and hips off the floor. Go slowly, do not jerk up into the position. Do the same with the upper body. When you start your program, have someone hold your upper back or hips as you lift the other extremity.

For a more strenuous workout, lie face down on an elevated surface with either the upper or lower body hanging over the edge.

Have someone hold down the part not being moved, and lift the other part to a horizontal position.

**Groin and Pelvis**

Lie on your back, knees bent, feet on the floor, arms at the sides. Lift your hips so that your body forms a straight line from shoulders to knees. Hold, relax back down to the floor, and repeat.

Another way to strengthen the muscles in this area is to do the belly-dance movement. Standing with feet a shoulder width apart, bend the knees, slightly dropping the buttocks in a direct line down over the knees. Using only your pelvis, tilt it forward, sticking your buttocks out in back. Return to center and then tilt the pelvis back by pulling the buttocks under you. Again using just the pelvic area, tilt one hip up to the side, return to center, and then tilt the other hip up to the side. Because of the slight knee bend, you will feel this in the thighs, too.

**Ankles and Feet**

Stand on your toes on a thick book, letting your heels rest on the floor. Lift yourself onto your toes slowly, going clear up into a tiptoe position. Return your heels to the floor and repeat.

A less-strenuous exercise is to lie on your back on the floor, resting your feet about twelve inches up on the wall. Slowly push off the wall with the ball of the foot, one foot at a time. Go slowly and really push the wall away.

**SUMMARY**

One does not have to be a stock-market analyst to realize that one of the fastest-growing industries in the world is recreation. True, we have more leisure time and we need to fill a void, but beyond that, people are beginning to recognize that it is very difficult to remain healthy while performing only sedentary tasks. So while some are driven to physical activity to counter boredom, others are trying to prevent degenerative diseases, and still others are driven to activity because the activity itself is "right" and reinforcing. To many, physical activity is the only transcending experience they have ever had, so they seek to reproduce the feeling and search for more active leisure-time pursuits.

Unfortunately, modern men and women (at least in the industrialized world) are obsessed with recreation and pursue it with the same diligence and competition with which they pursue work. In fact, for many the only difference between work and recreation is that one may be done behind a desk and the other is done on a golf course. Everything else is the same. Critical analysis is present, as is competition and ego defense, so the participant is often left with self-doubt and extended worry over performance and its reflection on personality and character.

In order for you to use a physical activity as a relaxation technique, it must be void of competition and ego involvement. Otherwise it is a mere diversion of your time.

## REFERENCES

*American College of Sports Medicine guidelines for exercise testing and prescription* (3rd ed.) (1986). Philadelphia: Lea and Febiger.

COOPER, K. (1970). *The new aerobics.* New York: Evans.

GALLWEY, T. (1976). *Inner tennis.* New York: Random House.

GALLWEY, T., AND B. KRIEGEL (1977). *Inner skiing.* New York: Random House.

JEROME, J. (1982). Getting it all back. *American Health*, March/April, 62–68.

KARVONEN, M. J. (1959). Effects of vigorous exercise on the heart. In F. F. Rosenbaum and E. L. Balknap (eds.), *Work and the heart* (pp. 44–53). New York: Paul B. Hoeber.

KRIEGEL, R. (1984). Getting back to the C zone. In D. Dusek and B. Karshmer (eds.), *Freedom seminars* (pp. 44–53). Denver: Corporation for Professional Education.

MOBILY, K. (1982). Using physical activity and recreation to cope with stress and anxiety: A review. *American Corrective Therapy Journal*, May/June, 60–68.

Outward bound for inward change. (1980). *Management Review.* May, 4–5.

SAILER, H. R., J. SCHLACTER, AND M. R. EDWARDS (1982). Stress: Causes, consequences, and coping strategies. *Personnel, 59.*

# CHAPTER SEVENTEEN

# Meditation

One of the main stress-intervention points in a holistic program of stress management is that of conditioning the mind to reduce internal arousal. Meditation is the time-honored technique for going within and moving beyond thoughts and habit patterns to a quiet centeredness.

Meditation teaches us to let go of the past, let go of the future, and just "be." Our childhood enculturation conditions us to be "human doings": we are rewarded for doing things to please others. Rarely do Westerners learn to tap into that deep essence of personal being. It is as though we are hyperactive children reacting to all stimuli coming in, not having the neurophysiological capability to damp out the unimportant messages. Like the hyperactive child, the undisciplined mind jumps from worries about yesterday to fears of tomorrow, from desires to demands to planning, judging, comparing. Meditation disciplines the mind to tune out the tensions and pressures from others and from ourselves. It tunes us in to our own centeredness, the very basis of our physical, mental, emotional, and spiritual health.

One of the main benefits of meditation is increasing one's resistance to negativity, thereby reducing one's reactivity to former stressors. Practiced meditators learn to eliminate the surface chatter of the mind, the constant thinking, planning, remembering, and fantasizing that occupy the mind every waking second and keep the ego firmly implanted in consciousness. As ego chatter diminishes, so do ego defenses. Anxiety is reduced, and thus arousal is reduced as both the body and mind achieve the quiet and peace natural to an ego- or self-transcendent state of consciousness.

The art of meditation is the ability to maintain a state of passive concentration in which alertness and control are maintained, but in such a way as not to be tension-producing. The meditator is in complete control of the experience.

In the meditative state, one is aware of subtle thoughts, energy, and creative intelligence. It is an intended process that takes thought, preparation, and practice. The meditator is thus left with feelings of creativity and accomplishment and a generally positive feeling about the activity. Because there is a marked reduction in the activity of most bodily systems governed by the autonomic nervous system, the meditator usually feels a heaviness or numbness in the extremities and an extreme sense of relaxation and calm. Electroencephalographic (EEG) studies of experienced students of transcendental meditation (TM) show that brain waves are slowed during meditation, suggesting that the meditative state and a low-brain-wave state are synonymous. In alpha and theta states the brain shows greater right-hemisphere activity, whereas the beta state shows greater activity in the left hemisphere. It has been generally established that tranquil states are most often related to slowed-brain-wave states. Thus researchers and clinicians use EEG biofeedback to train individuals to produce and maintain brain-wave states at will to achieve peacefulness in their daily lives.

It is important to note that meditation is not a religion (although it is an integral part of some religions, such as Zen Buddhism), and it is not prayer. Praying is beseeching or asking for desires to be met; meditation is listening to one's inner voice. In this way meditation helps put us in touch with our own inner teacher and find our own answers, rather than depending on someone or something else to do our bidding.

## TYPES OF MEDITATION

According to the teachings of Buddha, the source of our problems is our extreme attachment to our senses, thoughts, and imagination. Peace can be attained only when we free ourselves from these attachments, directing our awareness inward, transcending the incessant bombardment of the consciousness so as to experience a quiet body, a subtle mind, and a unified spirit.

These teachings generally state the simple goals of meditation, which have motivated millions of seekers for hundreds of years. Although the goals are simple, the fundamentals of meditation are often misunderstood, for meditation itself is difficult to define. Meditation is not a physiological state, nor is it a specific psychological state. It is not a philosophy, it is not a religion, it is not a technique, and it is not a state of mind—but it *is* a combination of all of these. Meditation is so basic that it has transcended time, culture, races, religions, and ideologies. It is so simple that millions have used it, yet so advanced that it represents the highest order of human activity—the living condition that most closely approximates the divine state of universal oneness.

Meditation can best be understood as a state of mind, of consciousness, or of spirit. But it is most often defined in terms of an act or a technique. There are numerous techniques of meditation embodied in different philosophies and religions; although meditation is intended to be a central component in one complete style of living, a few of its techniques have been successfully extrapolated by Western culture for the purposes of relaxation and tension reduction.

The philosophical goals of meditation cannot be achieved without training. The great number of meditation groups or "sects" that have arisen throughout the world are the result of differences in techniques and ways of mastering techniques rather than of different philosophies. The most popular meditative techniques in Western society are based on the specific concentration and contemplation practices of ancient yoga and Zen Buddhism.

Yoga, a Sanskrit word meaning "reunion," is an elaboration of philosophies and teachings that Lord Krishna left his disciples; they have been transmitted from generation to generation by enlightened masters. Several yoga paths have developed into spiritual schools, and in many instances these paths have become separate disciplines in themselves. Bhakti yoga, the path of devotion to God, uses devotional chanting and worship. Jnana yoga, the path of knowledge, teaches wisdom and understanding. Some others are karma yoga, the path of action and selfless services; hatha yoga, the path of health which uses exercise as a means to physical and mental harmony; and raja yoga, or royal yoga, the path of self-realization and enlightenment. According to Palanjali's Sutras, the most authoritative source of yoga philosophy, all other forms of yoga are just preparation for meditation and realization of the raja pathway, through which the divine potential of the soul can be revealed. Although yoga practices are used by various religious groups, yoga is not a religion, and thus is free of dogmatism and orthodoxism. Yoga teaches methods of concentration and contemplation to control the mind, subdue the (primitive) consciousness, and bring the physical body under control of the will. It releases the innermost consciousness to release the true forms of the self.

Zen, as originally conceived, was not a philosophy; it had no doctrine and was anti-intellectual. Having no doctrine, it was not a religion and did not deny or affirm the existence of God, a soul, or a spirit. Specific doctrines, rituals, and intellectual inquiries associated with it were merely attempts by various sects to discipline and guide the seeker. Zen seeks to open the mind itself, to make it its own master free of unnatural encumbrances. In this sense, Zen is chaotic, undisciplined, and unteachable. So, to accomplish the goals of Zen, various disciplines have grown with various teachers, each of whom thought of a better method to teach the undisciplined mind to reach this freedom. Meditation is at the core of all the techniques.

**Concentration**
Common to all forms of meditation are concentration and the closely related techniques of contemplation and mental repetition.

*Concentration* here implies attention to one subject, and thus control of the mind's usual habit of flipping from one subject to another. Control of the mind through selective attention reduces ego consciousness, and nondirected attention heightens awareness and, in some disciplines, is thought to release energy. Concentrating on physiological processes or internal sensations as the mystical "third eye" or getting into the rhythm of breathing is used in several disciplines. One type of yoga, Kundalini yoga, theorizes potential energy coiled up in the nervous system, which you can awaken by relaxing and thinking you can magnetize your entire body until you feel light and heat flowing through your body and a great ocean of consciousness flowing around you. Visual imagery is used in Hindu and Buddhist practices; the mind's eye concentrates on the thousand-petal lotus. A more popular Zen Buddhist practice is to concentrate on breathing by counting breaths while working to eliminate all other thoughts and feelings. When ten breaths are counted without losing the count, the mind is more ready to contemplate *mu*. (Mu is an example of a mantra [see the following paragraph].)

Another vehicle for concentrative meditation is the verbal or mental repetition of a word or sound called a *mantra*, meaning "hymn" or "calming sound." A mantra can be a single word, such as *mu* or *om*; a phrase from holy scripture; a name for a god, such as Hare Rama or Hare Krishna; or specially selected words thought to be calming because of their resonance qualities, as is the practice in popular transcendental meditation (TM). TM is a classical Hindu mantra technique based on the teaching of the Hindu teacher Sankaracharya and made popular by Maharishi Mahesh Yogi through the ambitious worldwide organization called the Students International Meditation Society.

Maharishi Mahesh Yogi, born Mahest Prasod Varma in 1918, received a degree in physics at Allahabad University in 1942, but before he began the normal, prearranged (destined) lifestyle, he met and became a disciple of a religious leader, Swami Brahmanada Saraswati, and spent the next thirteen years studying with him. After this period of intense study and meditation, he was given the task of finding a form of effective meditation simple enough that everyone in the world could learn it.

After spending two years in a Himalayan cave, he began traveling throughout India addressing small gatherings of people on the technique of meditation he had found. Realizing it would take twenty years of this type of practice to reach the rest of the world and not being averse to the use of mass communication and advertising, he launched a worldwide campaign to bring TM to everyone. Realizing that things happen faster in the West and that Americans were open to new ideas, he concentrated his efforts there.

TM is not a religion or a philosophy and does not demand any particular lifestyle of its practitioners. This fact is particularly responsible for its wide acceptance in the West. TM is a technique of expanding conscious awareness and producing a state of restful alertness, indicative of the fourth state of consciousness, self-transcendence. Unlike the contemplative techniques, TM is not an intellectual analysis but rather a direct experience of going beyond surface thought to reach the quiet, subtle awareness that is the desired outcome of most meditative techniques. The technique of TM is a simple mantra said to be somehow matched to each meditator. The mantras themselves are not unique to TM, but come from Sanskrit texts still in use today. Examples of Sanskrit mantras are *Shyam*, which is the name of Lord Krishna, and *Aing*, a sacred sound of the Divine Mother.

The secrecy of the mantra, a much-criticized practice of TM, is an attempt to discourage those other than regular TM instructors from teaching the technique. However, TM readily advertises that it is a simple, natural technique that takes only twenty minutes to learn, as it is the most fundamental aspect of the self.

The Maharishi claims that TM is neither a contemplative nor a concentrative technique because the mantra is passively allowed to repeat itself in the mind. Especially in the initial phases, however, the mantra is actively concentrated on. But as with other concentrative techniques, the vehicle may soon disappear, leaving the attention without focus and with an awareness of nothing, also referred to as *pure consciousness*. The Maharishi theorizes that thinking the mantra has a vibratory effect on the nervous system, dissolving stress and freeing the mind to pursue its naturally subtle state of consciousness.

**Contemplation**

Contemplation—*zazen* or *dhyana* in Sanskrit—is one of the three basic branches of Buddhism. It is closely related to concentration, the primary difference being that the object of contemplation (usually an external object, or *mandala* ) has symbolism, and it is the significance rather than the object that becomes the focus. The Zen Buddhist *koan,* a question puzzle or riddle such as "What is the sound of one hand clapping?" has no answer. Rather, it is an artificial instrument to force an open mind and develop in students the Zen consciousness. In most meditative techniques, *dhyana* (sitting quietly, cross-legged in contemplation) is an end in itself. However, in pure Zen, *dhyana* or *zazen* is practiced as a means of solving the *koan* and is not an end in itself.

The same is true for Christian meditation that uses objects such as the crucifix, a picture or statue of a religious figure, or spiritual passages and prayers as a focus for contemplation as a means to consciousness of Christ. One of the more complete systems of Christian or religious meditation has been outlined by the Association for Research and Enlightenment, made up of the followers of the "Sleeping Prophet," Edgar Cayce. Cayce was adamant in his belief that contemplation should be only a means and not an end, and he quoted Jesus's warning in the Parable of the Displaced Demon, in which the evil spirits that were cast out of an empty mind quickly returned with other devils, leaving the man worse off than before. To Cayce, meditation was attuning the mental and physical body to its spiritual source, seeking to know the relationship to the Maker. There is no emptying in the mind-void sense, only emptying of that which hinders the creative forces from rising along the natural channels or centers. The seven spiritual centers, or *chakras,* are recognized as the endocrine glands, which provide energy for psychic and religious experiences. Cayce additionally defined meditation as a prayer from within the inner self, and distinguished between prayer and meditation: prayer was external attunement, a pleading, a petition to the Holy Spirit; meditation was an internal attunement, a seeking to know our relationship with God, an inpouring from the Holy Spirit. Cayce's form of meditation uses the Lord's Prayer as a focus for contemplation.

The contemplation techniques of Christian meditation are similar to those of other types in that they are employed to transcend ego consciousness. The primary difference is in the focus of the contemplation. Whatever the technique, though, the desired outcome is control of consciousness and direction of mind.

**MEDITATION AND THE REDUCTION OF STRESS AROUSAL**

The primary purpose of meditation—peace, enlightenment, and spiritual growth—cannot be obtained as long as the mind is in turmoil and the body is aroused. Thus, most meditative techniques have seemingly elaborate preparatory procedures designed to induce physical relaxation, and meditation itself quiets the mind. Relaxation, an indirect product of meditation, can be therapeutic in the treatment or prevention of psychosomatic disorders.

Even though meditation is thousands of years old and the physiological feats of yoga masters are legend, the "scientific" study of the psychophysiological processes of meditation is still in its infancy. Meditation only recently became scientific when Wallace (1970) published the results of a study showing that the body significantly decreases its consumption of oxygen during meditation, thus producing a hypometabolic state (a slowing down of the body processes). The skin shows increased resistance to the passage of an electrical current, which indicates decreased arousal of the autonomic nervous system. Wallace also found a decrease in the lactate/ion concentration, another measure of decreased metabolism; a decrease in heart rate and cardiac output (quantity of blood pumped by the heart per minute), indicating a reduction in the workload of the heart; a decrease in respiration rate; and an increase in the amount of time the brain emits slowed brain waves, indicating a more restful state. This restful state physiologically resembled sleep in many ways, but in totality it was significantly different from sleep. The meditator was found to be in a restful state, but was awake and alert, and exhibited increased reaction time, improved coordination, and improved efficiency of perception and auditory ability.

Later research both supported and refuted, at least in degree, Wallace's early findings. This only points out the difficulty of such research, which is due mainly to subject variability and differences in meditation techniques. For example, variations in length of the meditative session and experience of the meditator are extremely important. Obviously, the more one meditates the greater should be the ability to change psychophysiological states. EEG records of Zen masters show a predominance of alpha and theta brain waves during meditation, which become more marked with years of practice; beginning meditators, on the other hand, show only slight changes in brain-wave patterns.

Another difficulty in research is the difference in the meditative state itself. As mentioned, meditation is not a unitary phenomenon, but a series of states including quiet sitting, passive concentration, mental deautomatization or desynchronization, a neutral or mind-void stage, and, especially in accomplished meditators, a brain-directed stage. Measurements taken during each of these phases could yield different results. More recent research has found decreased oxygen utilization in meditators, but a decrease not nearly as dramatic as the one observed by Wallace, whose subjects' metabolism rates seem to have been somewhat above normal when they started (Pagano et al., 1977). This indicates that the significance of the results may be related to subjects' starting point and illustrates that immediate benefits are related to the initial arousal of the individual. Even though hundreds of studies have been conducted and thousands of words written, we are just now starting to understand the physiological state of meditation.

As we have seen, stress arousal is a psychophysiological response to a particular psychosocial or environmental situation. Each situation produces an immediate stress response but may also leave a residual amount of tension in the body. Response to subsequent stressors is augmented by this leftover tension. As the day wears on, response overactivity results from the inability to dissipate residual tension. The physiological relaxation experienced by the meditator is a short-term phenomenon, but the more the relaxation state is induced, the more carryover there is to the nonmeditative state. Meditation helps dissolve tension by quieting the mind's tendency toward "afterthoughts," which prolong the stress response and at least temporarily reduce the physical arousal of the organs. Thus each new stressful situation will produce a reaction sufficient to deal with that particular situation without the added effect of previous stress arousal. The longer one meditates, the more his or her general state of arousal resembles the meditative state, and the ongoing tensions most detrimental to the body are greatly reduced. The accomplished meditator develops the ability to direct thoughts away from the ego self, the primary source of stress. The meditator experiences temporary transcenence, but just as the physiological state gradually becomes a stable trait, so can an individual learn to live a life of increased ego transcendence (Lehrer, Woolfolk, Rooney, McCann & Carrington, 1983; Woolfolk, Lehrer, McCann & Rooney, 1982).

**HOW TO MEDITATE**

1. Quiet your external environment. Turn your telephone ringer off, play some soft classical or other soothing instrumental music (use earphones if you need to), and so on.

2. Sit with your spine straight and your hands folded in your lap. Take some deep breaths and relax your muscles.

3. Before you open yourself to meditation, extend a protecting envelope of energy around yourself. Some visualize a white-light energy field eight feet in diameter about themselves.

4. Spend ten minutes in a concentration exercise (see the following

section) to clear the mind, quiet the active left hemisphere of the brain, and direct your energy.

5. Open your palms and spend ten minutes in "neutral," a period of not controlling or focusing your thoughts. Flow with whatever you may feel; stay calm with relaxed interest. Touch whatever comes to you and let it go.

6. Once more, close your hands and focus again on a protective envelope of energy about you so that you may remain open to your positive energy yet be protected from others' negative energy.

7. Wiggle around and let the energy flow throughout your body.

8. Get up and get on with your other activities.

Some of the following suggestions may be helpful in filling out the preceding outline. It is easier to form the habit of meditating if it is written into your daily schedule. In the early stages it may be best to meditate at the same time each day. It is better not to meditate on a full stomach or when you are very sleepy, but if these are the only times you have to meditate, it is better to use them than to pass up the practice.

It is better to sit in a comfortable armchair or in a cross-legged position than to recline. This keeps the spine straight and helps ensure that you do not fall asleep. If you prefer to recline, bend your arm at the elbow with your hand straight up in the air. If you fall asleep, your forearm will fall and awaken you.

During the concentration exercise you may wish to repeat a word, idea, or phrase that depicts for you peace, beauty, or a spiritual ideal. *Om*, a Sanskrit word meaning "one" or "I am one, we are one," is the universal mantra. More than just spoken, it is softly chanted aloud on each exhalation ("aaaaaaooooooommmmm") at your individual pitch and tonality. Group meditation using *om* as the collective mantra is a very soothing experience. Or you may wish to use a visual focus rather than sound during the concentration exercise. A candle flame, a picture that produces serenity for you, or a mandala may be a good eyes-open focus. Whatever visual you use, be sure it doesn't offer your left hemisphere food for thought, or it will be busy analyzing, planning, and evaluating. A mandala (a simple geometric pattern) is used for meditation because the left hemisphere quickly tires of the simple pattern while the rest of your mind continues to focus on it. The circle with a dot in the center, the equilateral triangle with the tip at the top, and the square have been used for centuries as meditation aids. Some meditators use visual imagery (eyes closed) as their focus of concentration.

During the free-fall period when you are open to whatever comes into your mind, you may feel dizzy or nauseous because of the energy flow that you are enhancing. Holding the index finger to the thumb may help control some of that energy flow.

**CONCENTRATION
EXERCISES**

The following activities may help motivate you to begin a meditation routine or keep your interest in meditation alive.

**Chakra
Breathing**

According to yoga theory, there are a number of energy centers in the spine, and these centers correspond with endocrine glands. The first chakra (see Figure 17.1) is at the base of the spine, in the coccyx, or tailbone, and has the connotation of security. It is generally assigned the color red. Up the spine at the level of the ovaries is the second chakra, which connotes sensuality and sexuality and is given the color orange. The third chakra is at the *hara,* or power center, at the center of the body near the navel; its associated color is yellow. Next is the heart chakra, connoting love; the color is green. The fifth chakra is at the throat, connoting expression; the color is blue. The sixth chakra is at the "third eye," or the middle of the forehead, and has the connotation of intuitive, intellectual, and psychic powers; the color is indigo. The highest chakra, at the anterior fontanel on the top of the head (a baby's "soft spot") is the spiritual chakra; the color is violet. The assignment of colors to the seven chakras follows the arrangement of colors in a rainbow.

In this concentration exercise, focus on each of the chakras,

**FIGURE 17.1**

The Seven Chakras
(Energy Centers)

beginning at the coccyx, as you breathe through them. Imagine that you are pulling in energy through the first chakra, activating that energy center. You may imagine that it is a wheel you spin, a glass ball that you are clearing, or any other imagery that helps you feel the energy of that center clearing. Take as many breaths at that level as needed. Then breathe through the first chakra, taking the energy up to the second chakra, clearing it out. Again take as many breaths as you need to clear it. As you breathe out, let the energy flow out of the first chakra, as though you were continually clearing the pathway up and down the spine between the two chakras. Follow this procedure up the spine to the third, fourth, fifth, sixth, and finally the seventh chakra. Concentrate on the clearing process as you breathe energy in and out of each energy center.

After completing this exercise, go into your ten-minute neutral period of meditation.

## Sound, Sight, Feeling

Begin with the number three, four, or five (depending on how active your outside environment is; for this example we will use five). Close your eyes and listen for five different sounds in your environment. Then, with eyes closed or open, visually focus on five different things. If your eyes are closed, you may see colors, designs, or visions of people, places, or things. You may open and close your eyes; you are not locked into one mode. Then tune into five different feelings. They may be emotional feelings, or kinesthetic feelings such as the sensation of your hands resting on your lap. That is round number one.

In the second round, focus on *four* sounds, sights, and feelings that are *different from* the ones you heard, saw, and felt before.

In the next round, focus on *three* sounds, sights, and feelings that are *different from* the ones you heard, saw, and felt in the two rounds before this.

In the next round, focus on *two* sounds, sights, and feelings that are *different from* the ones you heard, saw, and felt in the three previous rounds.

In the final round, focus on *one* sound, one sight, and one feeling, all of which are *different from* the ones you experienced before.

If your environment is very quiet, you may wish to begin at 4 or 3 and work down.

## Sky Watching

This exercise may be done in daytime or at night. Experience both. Sit or lie on your back and stare at the sky, with or without its clouds, stars, satellites, planets, and so on, and breathe in its energy from the edges of the universe. It is not uncommon for meditators to relive wonderful childhood sky-watching experiences.

**Native American Reverse Counting**

This exercise begins as you stand facing the east (early morning is an ideal time). Beginning at sixty, count backward to the beat of your heart or to your breathing, until you reach twenty-eight. At that time call in energy from the universe with open arms, moving the energy into your heart with your open palms. Do this several times. Then generate energy by passing the not-completed circle of middle finger to thumb (see Figure 17.2) of the right hand through the open part of the not-completed circle of middle finger to thumb of the left hand. You may feel a pull of energy as circles pass in and out. Then affirm to the universe all that you are. Affirmations are stated in the present tense. (For tips on making affirmations, see the section in Chapter 10 on techniques for enhancing a positive self-concept.) After making your affirmations continue counting backward from twenty-seven to zero. When you reach zero visualize that your negativity has been washed away for the day and locked out. Then count back up to six to seal in your positive energy.

**Breathing**

A number of breathing techniques can be used for concentration activities. The simplest is to count each exhalation while performing yogic (diaphragmatic or very deep) breathing as explained in Chapter 11. Count up to twenty and back down to zero. It doesn't matter if you lose count, merely start over again, concentrating only on the breath, not on your ability to count the breaths.

**THE FOUR MEDITATION POSITIONS**

According to Angeles Arrien, professor of cultural anthropology and counseling at the California Institute of Integral Studies and JFK University, there are four basic meditation positions, which are to be used for their particular meanings. She uses the Native

FIGURE 17.2

Thumb–Middle Finger Circles for Energy Generation

American medicine wheel to depict and explain them. These four meditation positions and meanings are as follows.

**Standing Meditation**

This is the warrior position, and is to be used when we need to get in touch with our power so that we may confront that which challenges us. The challenge may be an exam, the need to be true to ourselves, a sports competition, or any other daily challenge.

Facing north, the place of our inner warrior, stand with your feet a shoulder width apart, knees slightly bent, hands resting lightly on the thighs. Keep your eyes open and focus up at about forty-five degrees. Focus on a fixed point and concentrate on generating power within yourself to meet your challenge.

**Moving Meditation**

This is creative meditation and holds the eastern point on the medicine wheel, the place of illumination. This type of meditation is useful when you seek insight into new ways of doing things. It speaks to your inner creative person.

This meditation position is one of movement—walking, running, hiking, cross-country skiing, even riding in a car. Before using moving meditation, fill your mind with facts you wish to put together in a new way. An author beginning a new chapter of a novel might review the characters, the situation, the overall plot, pertinent research, and so on, before going out for a walk in the woods. The meditation exercise is to clear the mind and be present within the environment, enjoying the path, the beauty of the day, and whatever presents itself, just touching it and letting it go.

Another way to work with your material is to talk out loud to it as you move. Let whatever words come up be spoken without premeditation. Many moving-meditation practitioners have surprising results with this method.

**Lying Meditation**

This meditation calls up the healer within, and so is used when physical, mental, emotional, or spiritual healing of self or others is appropriate.

Lying on your back, feet toward the south (the direction on the medicine wheel that connotes emotions and matters of the heart), place your left hand over your heart and your right hand over the left. Arrien calls this position *cradling*. During meditation, focus on healing that part or person that needs healing.

**Sitting Meditation**

This meditation is for calling up the inner teacher. It is the method outlined in the section "How to Meditate," and is used when you need wise and objective counsel.

**THE NEED FOR PRACTICE**

Meditation is a skill you must practice if you are to enjoy its benefits. Meditation is not difficult to learn. However, many people are hindered by lack of confidence in their ability to meet their expectation of what meditation is and can do for them. Meditation is not so simple that mere ritual will overcome the hyperactivity of a mind planning, scheming, thinking about, and reacting to the distractions to which we are all subjected. One cannot go full steam one minute and be tranquil the next. Preparation for quietness is an essential step.

Meditation must be practiced, but one cannot labor at it. You cannot force yourself into transcendence. The key phrase in learning meditation is "let go."

Some may be tempted to withdraw from life through meditation. The purpose of meditation is to enhance the experience of life, not to be a vehicle for withdrawing from life. Meditative tranquility trains the mind to allow active participation in an active life without unnecessary stress. Meditation is not a substitute for living.

## REFERENCES

ARRIEN, A. (1987, August). Cross-cultural healing practices. Seminar presented at the Joy Lake Conference, Reno, NV.

LEHRER, P. M., R. WOOLFOLK, A. ROONEY, B. McCANN and P. CARRINGTON (1983). Progressive relaxation and meditation: A study of psychophysiological and therapeutic differences between the two techniques. *Behavior Research and Therapy, 21,* pp. 651–62.

PAGANO, R., et al. (1977). Oxygen consumption, H, EMG, and EEG during progressive muscle relaxation (PMR) and transcendental meditation (TM). Report to the Eighth Annual Meeting of the Biofeedback Society of America, Orlando, FL.

WALLACE, R. K. (1970). Physiological effects of transcendental meditation. *Science, 167,* 1751–54.

WOOLFOLK, R. L., R. LEHRER, B. McCANN, and A. ROONEY (1982). The effects of progressive relaxation and meditation on cognitive and somatic manifestations of daily stress. *Behavior Research and Therapy, 20,* pp. 461–68.

# CHAPTER EIGHTEEN

# Your Personal
# Stress-Management Plan

To this point we have discussed what stress is and what can be done to avoid excessive stress and burnout. However, knowing educational theory alone is usually insufficient to initiate a lasting behavior change. Most people require a plan of attack. This portion of the text is designed to help in the development of an individualized plan for personal stress management. In an overwhelming majority of cases, people experience stress because they have a stressful lifestyle and have learned through years of conditioning to react in a stressful manner. With regard to health and illness, a stressed person is one who exhibits physical arousal in response to social-emotional conditions. This exaggerated arousal is usually unnecessary to deal effectively with the situation. A vicious cycle develops until minor happenings are met with major arousals, and the individual never really relaxes.

The stressed person experiences what can be termed psychophysiological arousal since both psychological and physiological systems are activated. This arousal may be caused by long-standing physical conditions such as migraine headaches, gastrointestinal disturbances, muscle tension, and so forth. Symptoms of stress may also be psychological, with such conditions as confusion, forgetfulness, depression, and anxiety. Usually various physiological and psychological manifestations occur together, but the precise way that individuals manifest the stress reaction varies greatly. Since the stress reactions are so complex and varied, it follows that no two individuals will react in exactly the same manner to a similar stressor. The type of stimulus that causes the stress response in individuals is highly variable; what causes one person excessive stress may cause less stress or even no stress for another individual.

This is because stress is a reaction based on the individual's *perception* of the circumstances or situation. It is safe to say that no two individuals perceive any given stimulus in exactly the same manner.

By understanding the concepts and nature of stress, it becomes evident that the management of stress is best achieved by an intervention plan that is "custom-made" for the individual. You will recall from an earlier section of this volume that we suggested personal stress management be holistic, meaning:

1. individualized
2. practically designed to suit your preferences
3. multidimensional
4. flexible

**DEVELOPING THE PLAN**

Summarize what you feel are your serious or obvious symptoms of stress. Give them serious thought. Try this visualization exercise.

**Step 1. What Do You Want to Accomplish?**

### Exercise 1: Goals

Find a comfortable sitting position. Kick off your shoes, lean back, and relax. Sit quietly. Tell yourself that you are going to use the next five minutes to focus on yourself and to relax. Gently close your eyes. As you inhale, feel the air filling and expanding your chest, into your stomach area, and down into your abdomen. When your lungs feel full, hold the breath for five seconds, then begin to slowly exhale, controlling the air as your abdomen begins to contract. Push all of the air out of your body at the end of your exhalation. Repeat three times.

After practicing the full breathing part of the exercise, shift your attention to your body. Scan your face, shoulders, upper back, lower back, abdomen, legs, knees, and ankles. Ask yourself, "How do I experience the stress in my life?" "Which sections of my body are affected when I am stressed?" "What happens to those body parts?" Scan your body, becoming more and more aware of your body as you go inside of yourself to gather this information. Remember this information for further use. Focus on your breathing again, and when you are ready, open your eyes. Slowly stretch your hands, feet, arms, and legs as you become active again.

The above exercise is an opportunity to get in touch with yourself and to discover the ways in which you internalize stress. Use the space below to write what you felt during this first body-scanning exercise.

*Exercise 1: Report*

_____

_____

_____

_____

To further your insights about how stress affects you and to begin developing that awareness, complete Exercise 2. Your responses to this exercise may indicate which systems in your body are likely to be subjected to stress arousal and become weakened. This exercise lists some of the potential signs of arousal in three major categories. Check the symptoms you usually experience and then describe (on the lines provided) additional symptoms you may also experience.

### Exercise 2: Signs and Symptoms

(check if usually experienced)

*Musculoskeletal Signs*

_____ stiffness in neck

_____ fingers and hands tremble or shake

_____ twitch in muscles (specific muscle: _____)

_____ difficulty standing still or sitting quietly

_____ stuttering or stammering speech

_____ frequent headaches (location on head: _____)

_____ muscles feel tense (specific muscles: _____)

_____ voice quivers

_____ nervous mannerisms; for example, biting nails, pulling hair, tapping feet, etc.

_____ other

*Visceral Signs*

_____ heart pounding

_____ light headed or faint

_____ cold chills

_____ cold hands

_____ cold feet

_____ dry mouth

_____ profuse sweating (location: _____)

_____ upset stomach

_____ sinking feeling in stomach

_____ frequent digestive disturbance

_____ moist or sweaty palms

_____ flushed or hot face

_____ other

*Mood and Disposition*

_____ preoccupied

_____ frequent insomnia

_____ feeling uneasy or uncomfortable

_____ nervous or shaky

_____ feel confused

_____ forgetful

_____ feel insecure

_____ overexcited

_____ feel angry

_____ irritated

_____ worried

_____ anxious

_____ exhausted

_____ other

### Exercise 3: Stress and Stressors

For this exercise you will want to close your eyes to let this visualization help you picture your stress and stressors. Think about each question, then open your eyes and write your thoughts in the space provided.

1. Close your eyes, but in your mind picture a tense person. Scan your picture of this stressed person. What does the person look like when he or she is stressed? What is the person doing with his or her legs . . . arms . . . face? How is this person sitting or standing? Also picture the people and activities surrounding this individual in the stressful situation.

2. How are you like the image of the stressed person? How are you different?

3. Can you recall a stressful environment or situation in your life? How is this environment like your image and how is it different?

Generally, what are the major ongoing stressors in your life? To better understand these stressors and to add to your picture of your stress reaction, do the following exercise:

1. Go back to your stressor profile (at the end of Chapter 8) and examine each of the stressor self-assessments.
2. Identify the stressors to which you feel vulnerable. Your self-assessment scores will reveal your current degree of stress for each stressor.
3. List your top three stressors in descending order.

My most significant stressors are:

a. (score:_____)

b. (score:_____)

c. (score:_____)

Pick one of these three to work on first and write it here:

_____

Write a short statement on why you have chosen this stressor over the other possibilities.

_____

_____

Have you ever taken steps to reduce this stressor before?
☐ Yes ☐ No

If yes, what were the results _____

If not, why not? _____

Write a brief but specific outcome statement:

I want to _____

Rate on a scale of 1 to 10 how ready you are to alleviate this stressor.
1 . . . . . . . 10
Low              High

Rate your ability to do it now.
1 . . . . . . . 10
Low              High

If you did not give yourself at least an 8 on both scales, your chances of success will be decreased. In that case you may wish to reconsider your other major stressors and focus on your second choice.

### Step 2. How Will Things Be Different or Better in Your Life?

This question is often overlooked in stress-management programs. It is the motivation question. Everyone is committed to some degree, and everyone undertaking a stress-management program would like to be more in control, but only the very committed will finish the program and change the behaviors necessary to be successful. The committed will be able to visualize the new behavior and clearly see how life will be different or better than it was with the old behavior. To strengthen that picture in your mind try the following visualization exercise.

#### Outcome Visualization

Outcome visualization is used for programming or imprinting a new thought about behavior or belief about oneself. The technique involves seeing, hearing, and feeling yourself doing the new behavior. By mentally practicing the desired new behavior, a potentially stressful situation that would have previously triggered the old behavior instead triggers the new behavior because it has been rehearsed in the mind. Try this now.

#### Exercise 4: Visualization

Close your eyes and visualize yourself having accomplished the new behavior. Visualize yourself without the stressor, or as a more relaxed person in the old stressful situation.

If you have difficulty in this exercise, if may mean that you are ambivalent about giving up the stressful behavior because, on some level, that behavior has served a very useful purpose, possibly for many years. Sometimes individuals cling to stressful behaviors due to some conscious or subconscious gain or benefit. Most stress behaviors are done for a positive reason, whether that purpose is consciously known or not. When an individual experiences difficulty in or ambiguity about giving up an old behavior, it is time to explore what is causing this reluctance.

The phenomenon of continuing a negative behavior because it fulfills some need is called *secondary gain* and the exact nature of the secondary gain is often not realized on a conscious level. For example, some commonly observed secondary gains accompanying excess stress are:

1.  Maintaining control of life—many people fear becoming lazy and feel that keeping their "nose to the grindstone" protects them.
2.  A strong need to please others and gain recognition often pushes people to take on more than they can handle.
3.  Control of others through manipulation or to give oneself permission to rest or quit—this occurs when people overwork themselves to the point of fatigue, illness, or accident.

### Step 3. How Do You Know When You Have Achieved an Outcome? What Will You Accept as Proof?

As with step 2, this critical phase of the program is often forgotten or omitted. It is easy to accept vague statements such as "I will feel better," or "I will look better," or "I will have more energy." However, you must have definite, measurable proofs. How will you know that you feel better, look better, or have more energy? What will you accept as proof for these outcomes? The important word in this step is *measurable*. If your outcome is being more relaxed, how will you measure that outcome?

If you are having difficulty setting behavioral proofs, think of how you would observe this behavior in someone else. For example, how would you know a person was energetic; what behavior would be proof or evidence of that to you? You might make a list of the behaviors and apply them to your situation. If you are still experiencing difficulty, choose a personal friend or someone in the movies or on TV who exhibits the behavior you desire. What would you accept as proof or evidence that the other person has the behavior? Can you make a similar observation in your life? If the answer is yes, it can be accepted as proof, and the process continues.

One of our participants, who was working on a stress-management program with an outcome of self-confidence, had difficulty with step 3 until he identified the movie character *Cool Hand Luke* as the model for his behavior. Cool Hand Luke not only provided him with a model for his targeted behavior, but the name also became a reminder or "anchor" of a self-confident resource state.

Write a short list of ways you can prove to yourself that you have achieved your stated outcome.

*These are proofs:* _____

_____

_____

## Step 4. What Are Your Useful Resources?

This is an enjoyable part of the program because it helps build self-esteem by recalling resources and successes. When you feel confident about your ability to succeed in obtaining your outcomes, almost nothing will hold you back. Resources are both internal (personal characteristics) and external (environmental, social, economic). Examples of internal resources are integrity, tenacity, will power, energy, a sense of humor, self-love, and other self-concept issues. External resources may be the money to buy a good set of running shoes, the availability of certain facilities, or a devoted partner who will give support during the program. Resources may be general (as the suggestions given above) or they may be specific to a situation (such as the *Cool Hand Luke* example given above). Both are very useful, but the best resources are the ones that use a specific skill that has been programmed in a certain situation.

### Finding a Resource State

The intent of finding a resource state is to give you access to positive feeling states within yourself. The process itself builds self-esteem, promotes good feelings about the person at the time, and can be "anchored" into the mind and body for retrieval of these positive feelings at later times.

### Exercise 5: Resources

**Techniques.** Scan through your experiences and choose a time when you felt very fulfilled, confident, joyful, peaceful—a state that felt very good to you. There have probably been many, many experiences in the past that would be appropriate, but choose one specific time and experience.

The resource-state exercise gives the very best results when you can take yourself back to relive a specific experience. Generalities do not work as well because they are not as powerful as a singularly wonderful experience or feeling state. When finding a resource state, you should be able to go back and actually "be there" again. You can smell the flowers and look down and recreate what color of shoes you had on; can hear again what you were saying to yourself, and can command the very same feeling you felt at the time of the original experience because you are *in* the original experience again. Get back into the original experience, create a detailed picture, "hear" all the sounds in the experience, recreate the feeling you had at the time. You might want to select a colorful name that will have special meaning and help you recall the feeling. Some of the effective names people have chosen have been *Strawberry Blond, Cool Hand Luke, Smart Lady, Eagle Wings,* and *Hot Shot.* Others have come up with words such as *confident* or *strong,* which describe their resource state; or words like *rock* or *soaring,* which depict location or action at the time. The colorful and specific names elicit greater response than the generic names, perhaps because words like *strong* or *confident* or *rock* can conjure up many other meanings for many people.

### Exercise 6: Coping Skills

_____ 1. Give yourself 10 points if you feel that you have a supportive family.

_____ 2. Give yourself 10 points if you actively pursue a hobby.

_____ 3. Give yourself 10 points if you belong to some social or activity group that meets at least once a month (other than your family).

_____ 4. Give yourself 15 points if you are within five pounds of your "ideal" bodyweight, considering your height and bone structure.

_____ 5. Give yourself 15 points if you practice some form of deep relaxation at least three times a week. Deep-relaxation exercises include meditation, imagery, yoga, etc.

_____ 6. Give yourself 5 points for each time you exercise 30 minutes or longer during the course of an average week.

_____ 7. Give yourself 5 points for each nutritionally balanced and wholesome meal you consume during the course of an average day.

_____ 8. Give yourself 5 points for each time you do something that you really enjoy, "just for yourself," during the course of an average week.

_____ 9. Give yourself 10 points if you have some place in your home that you can go in order to relax and/or be by yourself.

_____ 10. Give yourself 10 points if you practice time-management techniques in your daily life.

_____  11. Subtract 10 points for each pack of cigarettes you smoke during the course of an average day.

_____  12. Subtract 5 points for each evening during the course of an average week that you take any form of medication or chemical substance (including alcohol) to help you sleep.

_____  13. Subtract 10 points for each day during the course of an average week that you consume any form of medication or chemical substance (including alcohol) to reduce your anxiety or just calm you down.

_____  14. Subtract 5 points for each evening during the course of an average week that you bring work home; work that was meant to be done at your place of employment.

_____      Total Score

This exercise was developed by George Everly for the U.S. Department of Health, Education, and Welfare in conjunction with the National Health Fair.

If you have not calculated your total score, do so now. A "perfect" score would be 115 points. If you scored in the 50 to 60 range, you probably have an adequate collection of coping strategies for most common sources of stress. However, you should keep in mind that the higher your score, the greater your ability to cope with stress in an effective and healthful manner. Also pay particular attention to the adaptive-versus-maladaptive coping dichotomy. Items 1–10 are all adaptive health-promoting coping tools, but items 11–14 are all maladaptive, health-eroding ways of coping with stress. How did you do? Ideally, you would limit your coping strategies only to adaptive techniques.

How do you cope with stress? What techniques do you employ to give yourself a sense of mastery (or self-efficacy) over the environment and how do you handle the stress it can elicit? Exercise 6 was designed to help you see how you cope with the stress in your life.

Cohen and Lazarus defined coping as "efforts, both action-oriented and intrapsychic, to manage . . . environmental and internal demands, and conflicts among them, which tax or exceed a person's resources. Coping can occur prior to a stressful confrontation, in which case it is called anticipatory coping, as well as in reaction to a present or past confrontation."

As was discussed in Chapter 5, coping behavior can be dichotomized to add greater clarity to the concept. Coping behavior may be considered adaptive or maladaptive. Adaptive coping tactics are tactics that can be successfully employed to reduce stress and promote long-term health.

1. Look at your coping assessment. Items 1–10 help you manage stress and avoid burnout when practiced on a consistent basis. Items 11–14 may help you cope with stress in the short run, but they can erode your health in the long run.

2. List your three most commonly practiced coping tactics.

My most commonly used coping techniques are:

a. _____

b. _____

c. _____

(Are they adaptive, as in items 1–10? Or are they maladaptive, as in items 11–14?)

Write one or two statements describing a personal resource that will help you achieve your goal. Write them in the form of affirmative statements, as if you already have the resource, because you do. Example: "I am organized and I always obtain my goals."

Affirmation 1. _____

_____

Affirmation 2. _____

_____

Everyone possesses the skills for achievement of outcomes— they usually have not associated their positive resources with the problem situations or have blocked their use for some reason. The following is an outline of the procedure used for maximizing the use of resources in obtaining outcomes:

1. List your resources.
2. If each resource is valid, you will feel good about it and be excited to use it.
3. Decide what you will accept as proof that you have use of the resource. Look for measurable behaviors.
4. You should be able to create a resource state. Going to your resource state should make you feel better.
5. Think of specific ways to recall and use each resource in getting your desired outcome.

6. If the resource is one of high energy, but you remain "down," either the resource is not a positive, well-anchored one or you are choosing to be "down." When you choose to remain in the problem state, it is time to suspect a secondary gain(s), which, as mentioned, is a hidden benefit of being "down."

7. You should be seeking support in your environment for the use and reinforcement of stated resources.

## Step 5. What Are Your Blocks to Success?

Within each individual who has ambiguous feelings about behavior change, there is a part that would like to achieve the outcome, but there is another part that is afraid to try or to succeed. Feelings and actions that prevent a person from achieving his or her outcomes are called blocks to success. Blocks may be exaggerated parts of the stress problem itself, for example, excessive anxiety; lack of skills such as assertiveness; personality characteristics such as excessive anger; or secondary gains, including fear of failure or fear of success.

### Fear of Failure

If a person with stressful behavior fails to adopt the new outcome behavior or fails to change the problem behavior, conditions are no better or no worse. The negative behavior has simply been kept a while longer (which would have happened if they had not attempted the program in the first place). Many people see this as no harm done. Others see that some harm has been done because failure at an attempted program diminishes self-esteem and self-efficacy. Individuals who "fail" at a program are likely to think less of themselves, and more importantly, the program is associated with negative feelings. It will take more motivation to try again. An individual may say to himself or herself, "I tried that once and it didn't work, so why bother." Many people would rather not try than risk failure, so they simply do not go beyond finding out what the problem is, or they rationalize the situation away. If the activities in step 2 did not result in a clear picture of how life will be better, you will need to work on activities to increase the probability of program success.

### Fear of Success

Fear of success is the reason most people fail to change health behaviors. Health behaviors are developed to fulfill a need; they all have a positive intention behind them. Unfortunately sometimes the behavior turns out to be unhealthy. Nevertheless, it did something positive or it would have spontaneously extinguished itself. When a certain behavior is eliminated (for example, a stressful lifestyle), the need for that behavior (recognition or sympathy from others for being a hard worker) will go unfulfilled unless a substitute behavior is adopted to fulfill the old need, or the old need is eliminated. Fear of success occurs when a person finds that the thought of being without that behavior or lifestyle is often too much to face, so he or she "fails" to change. If you are not making progress at the expected rate, or if you are not practicing relaxation techniques or completing homework assignments, chances are that you are not ready to give up the old behavior.

**Step 6. Devise a Plan of Action**

### Exercise 7: Techniques and Times

Review Chapters 9–17. As you do, your task will be to identify two or three of the stress-management techniques discussed there that you are not currently using. As you review the numerous options, remember to consider your personal preferences, and be practical.

Write down some techniques or action plans that would help you accomplish your outcomes.

_____

_____

_____

_____

Set a timetable for achieving this goal.

1. Break the total time into smaller intervals (for example, one month into four weeks.)
2. Make a calendar of specific day-to-day activities and place it where you can see it. An example is provided. Specific exercises and techniques are abbreviated. A blank calendar is also provided to get you started. A large month-by-month appointment calendar is preferable for your ongoing program.

For each week write outcome and resource statements. This week's outcomes:

_____

_____

_____

This week's resource statements: _____

_____

_____

_____

Establish a program of activities. Get help from a health professional if needed. Design a practical plan in order to implement the new stress-management techniques you've just selected. In the space that follows, describe how you will integrate these new techniques into your daily and/or weekly habits. Use the contract method that follows. Many participants have found it an effective method for organizing their activities and for helping with their motivation. For example:

*Technique 1*

_____ *Yoga* _____

How it will be used:

*Every morning before breakfast when*
*I feel excessive tightness in muscles.*

Stress-Management Activities Contract

*On this day* _____  _____  _____
              (month)     (day)      (year)

I have decided to begin to use the following new stress-management techniques:

*Technique 1* _____

    How it will be used: _____

_____

*Technique 2* _____

    How it will be used: _____

_____

*Technique 3* _____

    How it will be used: _____

_____

_____  _____
(signed)     (date)

_____
(witnessed)

Remember, stay flexible, reevaluate your plan in two to four weeks; and if you need to change this personal plan, do so.

## Step 7. Devise a Revised Plan

*Technique 1* _____

    How it will be used: _____

_____

_____

*Technique 2* _____

    How it will be used: _____

_____

_____

*Technique 3* _____

    How it will be used: _____

_____

_____

Use the tools shown on the following pages:

**Practice Reminder Calendar**

# APRIL

| SUNDAY | MONDAY | TUESDAY | WEDNESDAY | THURSDAY | FRIDAY | SATURDAY |
|---|---|---|---|---|---|---|
| | | 31 | 1 | 2 Breathing Ex. / Breathing Ex. / Breathing Ex. / D.D.___ | 3 Breathing Ex. / Breathing Ex. / Breathing Ex. / D.D.___ | 4 Breathing Ex. / Breathing Ex. / Breathing Ex. / D.D.___ |
| 5 Breathing Ex. / D.D.___ | 6 Breathing Ex. / D.D.___ | 7 Breathing Ex. / D.D.___ | 8 Breathing Res. Statm. / D.D.___ | 9 Breathing Res. Statm. / D.D.___ | 10 ROW 1+ Res. Statm. / D.D.___ | 11 ROW 1&2+ Res. Statm. / D.D.___ |
| 12 NEW Res. Statm. / AM Row 1 / PM ROW 2+ Res. Statm. / D.D.___ | 13 AM ROW 2+ Res. Statm. / PM ROW 1+ Res. Statm. / D.D.___ | 14 AM Breathing Ex. Res. Statm. / PM ROW 1 / D.D.___ | 15 AM Breathing Ex. / PM ROW 2 / D.D.___ | 16 AM Breathing+ROW 1+Res Statm. / PM Breathing+ROW 2+Res Statm. / D.D.___ | 17 AM Breathing+ROW 1+Res Statm. / PM Breathing+ROW 2+Res Statm. / D.D.___ | 18 AM your choice / PM Your choice / D.D.___ |
| 19 NEW Res. Statm. / ROW 1, 2+ Res. Statm. / D.D.___ | 20 Your choice / D.D.___ | 21 ROW 1+Res. Statm. 2+Res. Statm. / D.D.___ | 22 AM 3 A,B,C / PH 3 A,B,C,D+ Res. Statm. / D.D.___ | 23 AM 3 A,B,C,D+ Res. Statm. / D.D.___ | 24 AM 3 A,B,C,D+ Res. Statm. / PM Your Choice / D.D.___ | 25 AM 3 A,B,C,D+ Res. Statm. / PM Your choice / D.D.___ |
| 26 AM 3 A,B,C,D+ Res. Statm. / PM 3 A,B,C,D / D.D.___ | 27 AM 3 A,B,C,D / PM Breathing+ Res. Statm. / D.D.___ | 28 AM 3 A,B,C,D / D.D.___ | 29 AM B4 or C4 or D4 / PM Relaxation Recall+Res. Statm. / D.D.___ | 30 AM Relaxation Recall+Res. Statm. / D.D.___ | E3 You are on your own | PEACE |

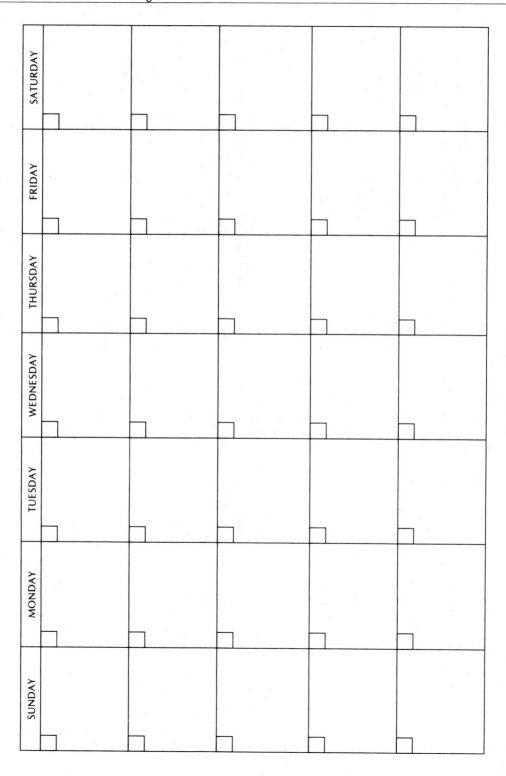

DAILY DIARY

| STRESS How felt in the body | STRESSOR Cause or situation | Underlying content or root cause | Your Action | Potential ways of Alleviating STRESS or STRESSOR |
|---|---|---|---|---|
| | | | | |
| | | | | |
| | | | | |

Choose two different times of the day, and fill in the following information on how you feel. Try to do this at the same times each day.

| Dull | 1 2 3 4 5 6 7 | Alert |
|------|---------------|-------|
| Sluggish | 1 2 3 4 5 6 7 | Energetic |
| Sad | 1 2 3 4 5 6 7 | Happy |
| Doubtful | 1 2 3 4 5 6 7 | Self-assured |
| Anxious | 1 2 3 4 5 6 7 | Tranquil |
| Withdrawn | 1 2 3 4 5 6 7 | Outgoing |
| Depressed | 1 2 3 4 5 6 7 | Exhilarated |
| Hungry | 1 2 3 4 5 6 7 | Sated |
| Weather poor | 1 2 3 4 5 6 7 | Weather good |
| Concentration: Poor | 1 2 3 4 5 6 7 | Concentration: Good |
| Stress high | 1 2 3 4 5 6 7 | Stress low |
| No exercise | 1 2 3 4 5 6 7 | Good exercise |
| Poor quality of sleep | 1 2 3 4 5 6 7 | Good quality of sleep |
| Overall quality of day: Poor | 1 2 3 4 5 6 7 | Overall quality of day: Good |

*Complete the practice report form:*

*Practice Feedback Report Form*

Date _____       What time of day did you practice? _____

Where is your quiet place to practice?

How did you calm and ready yourself for exercises?

Practice Report

| Date | Exercise | Effects | Difficulty<br>Easy, Moderate, Hard | Comments |
|------|----------|---------|-----------------------------------|----------|
|      |          |         |                                   |          |

*Evaluate results:*

**A SAMPLE PRACTICE PLAN**

A total plan is more than just a promise to use certain techniques. It includes keeping a list of carefully selected techniques, records of the times used, feedback on your progress, and evaluation of success. Here is a sample plan.

  A. Techniques
    **1.** Breathing and centering
    **2.** Resource statements
    **3.** Technique 1: Goal Path Model or other cognitive activity
    **4.** Technique 2: Muscle relaxation
    **5.** Technique 3: Meditation
  B. Practice Plan
    **1.** Practice each daily sequence two times a day.
    **2.** Ponder or repeat to yourself the resource statements you have made.
  C. Record Keeping
    **1.** Record times and make some notes about your experience with the practice.
    **2.** Complete daily diary monitor for progress.

Most athletic coaches agree that good practice leads to good performance on game day. The same philosophy applies to stress management. Good practice of relaxation techniques will lead to good application of the skills when needed. Take time to fill out the practice feedback sheets. If your practice is not going well, do something about it now!

## REFERENCE

COHEN, F., and R. LAZARUS (1979). Coping with the stresses of illness. In G. Stone, F. Cohen, and N. Adler (eds.), *Health psychology* (pp. 217–54). San Francisco: Jossey-Bass.

# Index